Dedicated to Joseph A. Cobb

BEHAVIOR CHANGE

Methodology, Concepts, and Practice

The Fourth Banff International Conference on Behavior Modification

edited and introduced by

Leo A. Hamerlynck
Lee C. Handy
Eric J. Mash
University of Calgary

Research Press
2612 North Mattis Avenue
Champaign, Illinois 61820

Copies of this book may be ordered from the publisher at the address given on the title page.
ISBN 0-87822-089-5

CONTENTS

PREFACE

This is the fourth volume of the series of publications resulting from the Banff International Conferences on Behavior Modification. Since the first conference in 1969, the conferences have been held in early spring in Banff, Alberta, Canada. The conferences are designed to facilitate the exchange of ideas and data among behavioral scientists and professionals. Guest faculty are invited to lead discussions of specific areas within behavior modification. Informal discussions are scheduled as well as formal meetings. This balance of schedule along with restricted registration and outstanding discussion leaders has produced a stimulating and reinforcing environment.

Distances, schedules, and the restricted audiences preclude wide attendance at the conferences. Consequently, this series of publications has equal status with the conference proper. Past Conference topics and faculty were:

1969: I. Ideal Mental Health Services*

Nathan Azrin
Ogden Lindsley
Gerald Patterson
Todd Risley
Richard B. Stuart

1970: II. Services and Programs for Exceptional Children and Youth*

Loren and Margaret Acker
Wesley C. Becker
Nancy Buckley
Donald Cameron
L. Richard Crozier
David R. Evans
Leo A. Hamerlynck
Ogden Lindsley
Patrick McGinley
Nancy J. Reynolds
James A. Sherman
Richard B. Stuart
Walter Zwirner

1971: III. Implementing Behavioral Programs for Schools and Clinics*

Joe A. Cobb
Rodney Copeland
R. Vance Hall
Ogden Lindsley
Hugh McKenzie
Garry L. Martin
Jack L. Michael
Gerald R. Patterson
Ernest G. Poser
Roberta S. Ray
Richard B. Stuart
Carl E. Thoresen

The papers which follow represent the responses of the authors, and in part their "centers," to a request to prepare papers directed at Critical Issues in Research and Practice. Three centers were selected for invitation representing groups of scientist/practitioners leading the field of behavior modification. These were State University of New York at Stony Brook; University of Kansas, Lawrence; and University of Oregon, Eugene. Chairmen for the groups were, respectively, Gerald Davison, Montrose Wolf, and Gerald Patterson. Their only specification was to produce papers directed at issues facing their respective groups. Richard Stuart was invited as a discussant and contributed a paper for inclusion in the Conceptual Issues section.

The support and guidance in the planning and conduct of the conferences by the University of Calgary's Division of Continuing Education has been vital. Specific praise is due for the performance of Randy Meeks and Donna Fraser. Equal praise is due to the staff at the Banff Centre headed by Dr. David Leighton. The physical environment and staff of the meeting rooms, residence hall, and dining hall were strong factors in the success of the 1972 conference.

We thank the other members of the editorial board who also served on the planning committee: Dr. Park Davidson, Psychology and Dr. Frank Clark, Social Work.

Finally, thanks to our teachers and colleagues who started it all and our families and students who maintain us.

L. A. H.
L. C. H.
E. J. M.

* The publications from 1969 and 1970 are currently out of print. With the 1971 proceedings Research Press became the publisher, and *Implementing Behavioral Programs for Schools and Clinics* is the first of the series contracted.

INTRODUCTION

L. A. Hamerlynck

> The new principles and methods of analysis which are emerging from the study of reinforcement may prove to be among the most productive social instruments of the twentieth century. (Skinner, 1958, pp. 94-99).

This hopeful prediction by B. F. Skinner set the tone and level of aspiration for the small but productive minority of psychologists, educators, social workers, and psychiatrists dedicated to the development and practice of the "social instruments" collectively called behavior modification (Bijou, 1970). The growth of behavior modification has been phenomenal, especially when it is recalled that the initial efforts were usually made in hostile professional and scientific environments (Krantz, 1971). Overt hostility is still very evident and in fact could easily have been an issue for discussion in this book. Not all behavior modifiers are able to refuse to respond to our critics in the way Dr. Skinner ignored Noam Chomsky (Skinner, 1972). However, the strategy of ignoring distractions and building adaptive behavioral repertoires may prove to have validity in the academic and scientific environments just as it has proven powerful in clinics, classrooms, and homes. In any event, behavior modification has assumed considerable importance in scientific conferences as evidenced by a quick review of programs, notes, papers, symposia, and lectures (even total conferences such as the Banff series), while specialized publishers such as Research Press prosper. In other words, the "Whoopee Stage" (Patterson, 1969) which involved the reestablishment of the Law of Effect has passed, and the 1970's are proving to be a period of development, refinement, and close examination of assumptions and procedures.

Implementing Behavioral Programs for Schools and Clinics (Clark, et al., 1972) was directed at the questions of training behavior modification specialists for the initiation of change and the maintenance of desired outcomes. These were the major problems in the transition from demonstration programs to the establishment of behavior modification technology into the general social and helping profession systems. This continues as a critical issue and is apparent in several papers of the present volume (Reid and Hendriks, Walker and Hops, Patterson). But, other issues have emerged, specifically those of methodology, conceptual questions, and (the continuing) new applications. There is a strong interaction between these issues related to their common denominators of complexity of environments and behaviors. The topics discussed in this book derive from this complex interaction in terms of data forms, data collection and analysis, ethical concerns, and the need to explore concepts of stimulus control, multiple schedules, heterogeneous chains, and adaptive behavior typology to account for complex social interactions and develop procedures for analyzing them.

B. F. Skinner set beautiful behavioral objectives. The high rate of success for early work applied to human problems provided the reinforcement to build the "social instrument" predicted by Skinner in 1958 for aiding the human condition. But it is a long step from the automated data collection of the laboratory to the *in vivo* observation of antecedent events, behavior, and consequences in a classroom, home, or in the community. "The personal observation of behavior on such a scale is unthinkable," was what Skinner (1958) said in reference to his work with Ferster leading to *Schedules of Reinforcement*. The section entitled Methodological Problems and Developments reflects the problems facing behavior modifiers in terms of their strong reliance upon direct observation. Behavior modification has developed past the point where the level of sophistication set by the problem behaviors permitted simple counts of "head bangs," "out-of-seat," or "nags." As soon as problems were posed like stealing, aggressive behavior, school failure, marital discord, frigidity, obesity, etc., the methodological base of the science and the technology became critical.

Conceptual Issues arise in quick response to extension of efforts to study complex behaviors and environments. Such issues are typified by the necessity of re-examining some activity, assumption, or goal which in the past appeared self-evident or was unimportant. Ethics and counter-control are obvious issues of the current developments in behavior modification. I suspect that the day negative reinforcement as a treatment vector was proposed, i.e., aversion therapy, is when ethical questions became salient. When behavior modifiers were first developing the technology, it was seldom that reference was made to aversive controls, except to indicate that such procedures contained high side costs. For example,

> Besides the fact that punishment usually works for only a short time, it also gets both the child and the parent upset. Punishment is simply not an effective

way to train a child. One purpose of this book is to show a way of teaching your child that works better than _______. (Instructional frame from Patterson and Gullion, 1968, p. 10)

But aversive controls will work and are a part of behavior modification.

With the extension of efforts of study and treatment to complex behaviors and controlling environments, it has become evident that the study and manipulation of the consequences of the targeted behaviors are both incomplete, if not improbable. Consequently, Patterson and his colleagues (Reid and Hendriks, Hops and Cobb) present their efforts of including stimulus control and chaining in their work with aggression and stealing. The requirement of analyzing a basic behavioral repertoire as the entering behavior for classroom instruction is discussed by Hops and Cobb. Finally, this section illustrates the critical factor of training and the accounting for motivational levels in attempting to study and ameliorate deviant behaviors in the home and classroom.

The third section includes papers which illustrate New Applications of behavior modification research and practice. While simultaneously examining the data base, questions of design and analysis, and various ethical factors, these papers vividly demonstrate that behavior modification is now at the stage of development where the benefits of behavioral psychology are evident for ourselves, family, and hometowns—not just the institutionalized and obviously handicapped. I hope that our science can solve the issues posed here so that demonstration becomes reality.

References

Bijou, S. W., What psychology has to offer education—now, *Journal of Applied Behavior Analysis*, 1970, *3*, 65-71.

Clark, F. W., Evans, D. R., and Hamerlynck, L. A. *Implementing Behavioral Programs for Schools and Clinics.* Champaign, Ill.: Research Press, 1972.

Krantz, David L. The separate worlds of operant and non-operant psychology. *The Journal of Applied Behavior Analysis,* 1971, *4*, 61-70.

Patterson, G. R., Paper presented at the First Banff International Conference on Behavior Modification, 1969.

Patterson, G. R. and Gullion, M. E. *Living With Children*. Champaign, Ill.: Research Press, 1968.

Skinner, B. F. A startling vision of the past. *Saturday Review of Literature,* July 15, 1972, Vol. *LV*, No. 25.

Skinner, B. F. Reinforcement today, *American Psychologist,* 1958, *13*, 94-99.

CONTRIBUTORS

Orin D. Bolstad
University of Oregon, Eugene

Joseph A. Cobb
University of Oregon, Eugene

Gerald C. Davison
State University of New York at Stony Brook

Dean L. Fixsen
University of Kansas, Lawrence

A. F. C. J. Hendriks
Oregon Research Institute, Eugene

Hyman Hops
University of Oregon, Eugene

Stephen M. Johnson
University of Oregon, Eugene

Richard R. Jones
Oregon Research Institute, Eugene

Ronald Kent
State University of New York at Stony Brook

W. Charles Lobitz
University of Oregon, Eugene

Joseph LoPiccolo
University of Oregon, Eugene

K. Daniel O'Leary
State University of New York at Stony Brook

G. R. Patterson
Oregon Research Institute and University of Oregon, Eugene

Elery L. Phillips
University of Kansas, Lawrence

John B. Reid
Oregon Research Institute, Eugene

Karl Skindrud
Oregon Research Institute, Eugene

Richard B. Stuart
University of Michigan, Ann Arbor

Hill M. Walker
University of Oregon, Eugene

Robert L. Weiss
University of Oregon, Eugene

Montrose M. Wolf
University of Kansas, Lawrence

ONE

Section One: Methodological Problems and Developments

ONE

Introduction

Eric J. Mash

It is somewhat unusual for a treatise about an essentially applied endeavor—behavior modification— to start out with a section on methodology. The sequential precedence given to method in this volume represents both a natural and a rational selective process. The natural selection process can best be described with some historical background.

In initially formulating the Banff Conference—1972, the fruition of which is represented by this book, a number of outstanding centers for behavior modification research and practice were invited to present papers dealing with what they saw to be the "critical issues" for behavior modification as it moved into the Seventies. On an a priori basis it was not known what the identified issues would be. As it turned out, however, a recurrent theme throughout the papers presented at the conference was that of method. This theme was represented as a general concern for the quality of data—and more specifically with issues of *experimental design, data collection,* and *data analysis.*

In terms of rational selection, behavior modification is probably more closely tied to scientific-laboratory procedures and method than any other therapeutic-educational approach. With learning theory as its base, as represented by the work of Pavlov, Watson, Skinner, etc., a methodological orientation is deeply embedded within historical antecedents. In addition to rational selection on an historical basis, the fact that the papers on theory and practice presented in later sections may be directly attributable to methodological advances also provides a logical basis for placing methodology first. For example, the theoretical and practical work presented by the group from Oregon (particularly Patterson) may in a number of instances be related to their development of one of the most sophisticated systems for the collection and analysis of naturalistic observation data that has ever been available. Wolf and his colleagues at Kansas have always relied heavily upon advances in data collection technology in developing innovative delivery systems for institutional, school, and home environments. The same regard for methodology may also be ascribed to the Stony Brook workers, Davison and O'Leary.

The first paper in this section, by Johnson and Bolstad, is a most ambitious effort. When ambition is accompanied by excellence, the rewards are great, and this paper is a veritable fountainhead of information and ideas. The authors begin with a reiteration of the importance of sound data for behavior modification, and progressively deal with the increasingly complex issues of observer agreement and accuracy (in terms of both calculation of these measures and generalizability), observer effect, observer bias, reliability, and validity. A noteworthy feature of this paper is that questions about data are raised with the authors' own data as a framework for discussion. Many treatments of methodology may be accused of being devoid of data—not so in this paper.

Johnson and Bolstad's paper (as well as those of O'Leary and Kent and Skindrud) are, in part, concerned with questions having to do with the use of human observers as data collection instruments in naturalistic settings. Included here are whether observers bias (Skindrud), distort (O'Leary and Kent), or in other ways provide data which is either not reliable or generalizable. There is some irony in the fact that naturalistic observation data as a base for developing theories as well as implementing intervention programs is currently being challenged. When intervention strategies were confined exclusively to once-a-week visits to clinics or school psychologists' offices, outcires of "You don't know what it's really like" resounded. "You should see him at home" or "You should see him in class" became the word of the day. So practitioners went to see him at home and at school, and lo and behold there were new outcries. Where the observer was visible, the new outcries took the form of, "You should see him when you're not here." Could it be that people were really saying, "You should see him like *I* see him." If this is the case, then what place has verbal report?

The paper by O'Leary and Kent has a dual emphasis. The first deals with the types of experimental designs which are likely to provide behavior modifiers with the greatest gains. Extensive discussion of difficulties involved with the use of the reversal design (ABA) as a control procedure is followed by suggestions for alternative or supplementary designs to deal with different questions. There is a concern for behavior modification research within a social context, with accountability to the society in which we function. To deal with the questions critical for decision making within a social system, behavior modification must demonstrate its effectiveness with particular populations over particular periods of time, *relative* to alternative approaches or to no treatment at all.

After extensive recommendations for future research directions, O'Leary and Kent discuss the assessment of observer reliability. As with Johnson and Bolstad's paper, issues of observer accuracy are discussed in relation to the authors' own data and experiences. A major conclusion of this paper is that, with respect to observer reliability, what you see is *not* very often what you get! The discrepancy between observers' data when they are monitored (checked) as opposed to their data when they believe themselves to be unmonitored is rather dramatic. In addition, observers may drift away from category definitions as originally specified by the researcher, such that they may agree with one another but not with the investigator.

Skindrud's paper attempts to identify possible biasing of data, by observers, as a function of their receiving information about the families which they are observing. Specifically, does knowing that a family has been identified as "deviant" or that they are in treatment, influence the manner in which the observers see that family? A possible, and seemingly unlikely, conclusion to be drawn from Skindrud's paper is that "blind" observers see best; that is, the less the observers know about a situation, the less likely they are to introduce bias into the situation.

The last paper by Jones is especially timely. Preceded by recommendations for a new emphasis in experimental design, new procedures for data collection, and the collection of new types of data, Jones cautions us against the possible effects that these developments will have on our statistical analysis. He makes the point that the assumptions underlying analyses for more traditional measuring instruments may not apply to serially dependent behavioral frequency and rate measures. Further, the ways we develop for summarizing these measures may require new types of data analysis procedures.

In summary, the collection of papers in this section represents a comprehensive and stimulating presentation of some of the critical questions about behavior modification research methodology. The papers reaffirm behavior modification's close cognation to science, and provide a solid foundation for examining the theoretical notions and practical applications which follow in later sections.

Methodological Issues in Naturalistic Observation: Some Problems and Solutions for Field Research[1]

1

Stephen M. Johnson and Orin D. Bolstad

> Encapsulated schools of thought have occurred in all sciences at some stage in their development. They appear most frequently during periods where the fundamental assumptions of the science are in question. Manifesto papers, acrimonious controversy, mutual rejection, and isolation of other schools' strategies are hallmarks of such episodes (Krantz, 1971, p. 61).

History may well reveal that the greatest contribution of behavior modification to the treatment of human problems came with its emphasis on the collection of behavioral data in natural settings. The growth of the field will surely continue to produce greater refinement and proliferation of specific behavior change procedures, but the critical standard for assessing their utility will very likely remain the same. We will always want to know how a given procedure affects the subject's relevant behavior in his "real" world.

If a behaviorist wants to convince someone of the correctness of his approach to treating human problems, he is generally much less likely to rely on logic, authority, or personal testimonials to persuade than are proponents of other schools of psychotherapeutic thought. Rather, it is most likely that he will show his behavioral data with the intimation that this data speaks eloquently for itself. Because he is aware of the research on the low level of generalizability of behavior across settings (e.g., see Mischel, 1968), he is likely to be more confident of this data as it becomes more naturalistic in character, i.e., as it reflects naturally occurring behavior in the subject's usual habitat. As a perusal of the behavior modification literature will indicate, these data are often extremely persuasive. Yet, the apparent success of behavior modification and the enthusiasm that this success breeds may cause all of us to take an uncritical approach in evaluating the *quality* of that data on which the claims of success are based. A critical review of the naturalistic data in behavior modification research will reveal that most of it is gathered under circumstances in which a host of confounding influences can operate to yield invalid results. The observers employed are usually aware of the nature, purpose, and expected results of the observation. The observed are also usually aware of being watched, and often they also know the purpose and expected outcome of the observation. The procedures for gathering and computing data on observer agreement or accuracy are inappropriate or irrelevant to the purposes of the investigation. There is almost never an indication of the reliability of the dependent variable under study, and rarely is there any systematic data on the convergent validity of the dependent measure(s). Thus, by the standards employed in some other areas of psychological research, it can be charged that much behavior modification research data is subject to observer bias, observee reactivity, fakability, demand characteristics, response sets, and decay in instrumentation. In addition, the accuracy, reliability, and validity of the data used is often unknown or inadequately established.

But the purpose of this paper is not to catalogue our mistakes or to argue for the rejection of all but the purest data. If that were the case, we would probably have to conclude with that depressing note which makes so many treatises on methodology so discouraging. Although dressed in more technical language, this purist view often expresses itself as: "You can't get there from here." We can get there, but it is not quite as simple as perhaps we were first led to believe. The first step in getting there is to define and describe those factors which most often jeopardize the validity of naturalistic behavioral data. To this end, we will review a host of investigations from many laboratories which demonstrate these methodological problems. The second step is more constructive in nature: to suggest, implement, and test the effectiveness of various solutions to these dilemmas of methodology. Because behavioral data has become the primary basis of our approach to diagnosing and treating human problems, the endeavor to improve methodology is perhaps the most critical task for strengthening our contribution to the science of human behavior.

We will argue that the same kinds of methodological considerations which are relevant in other areas of psychology are equally pertinent for behavioral research. At least with respect to the requirements of sound methodology, the period of isolation of behavioral psychology from other areas of the discipline should quickly come to an end.

Throughout this paper, we will rely heavily on the experience of our own research group in meeting, or at least attenuating, these problems. We take this approach to illustrate the problems and their possible solutions more precisely and concretely. Most of our solutions are far from perfect or final, but it is our hope that a report based on real experience and data may be more meaningful than hypothetical solutions which remain untested. Thus, before beginning on the outline of methodological problems and their respective solutions, it will be necessary for the reader to have a general understanding of the purposes and procedures of our research. This research involves the observation of both "normal" and "deviant" children and families in the home setting. The observation system employed is a modified form of the code devised by Patterson, et al. (1969). This revised system utilizes 35 distinct behavior categories to record all the behaviors of the target child and all behaviors of other family members as they interact with this child. The system is designed for rapid sequential recording of the child's behavior, the responses of family members, the child's ensuing response, tec. Observations are typically done for 45 minutes per evening during the pre-dinner hour for five consecutive week nights. The observations are made under certain restrictive conditions: (a) all family members must be present in two adjoining rooms, (b) no interactions with the observer are permitted, (c) the television set may not be on, and (d) no visitors or extended telephone calls are permitted. Obviously, this represents a modified naturalistic situation.

On the average, these procedures yield the recording of between 1,800 and 1,900 responses and an approximately equal number of responses of other family agents over the total period of 3 hours and 45 minutes. The data is collected in connection with a number of interrelated projects. These include normative research investigations of the "normal" child (e.g., Johnson, et al., in press); research involving a behavioral analysis of the child and his family (e.g., Wahl, et al., in press; Karpowitz, 1972; Johansson, et al., 1971); outcome research on the effects of behavior modification intervention in families (Eyberg, 1972); comparisons of "normal" and "deviant" child populations (Lobitz and Johnson, 1972); and studies of methodological problems (Johnson and Lobitz, 1972; Adkins and Johnson, 1972; Martin, 1971). These latter studies will be reviewed in detail in this paper. More recently, we have begun to investigate the generality of children's behavior across school and home settings, and to document the level of generalization of the effects of behavior modification in one setting to behavior in other settings (Walker, et al., 1972). Research is also in progress to relate naturalistic behavioral data to parental attitudes and behavioral data obtained in more artificial laboratory settings. With all of these objectives in mind, it is most critical that the behavioral data collected is as valid as possible, and it is to this end that we explore the complex problems of methodology presented here.

Observer Agreement and Accuracy I: Problems of Calculation and Inference

The most widely recognized requirement of research involving behavioral observations is the establishment of the accuracy of the observers. This is typically done by some form of calculation of agreement between two or more observers in the field. Occasionally, observers are tested for accuracy by comparing their coding of video or audio tape with some previously established criterion coding of the recorded behavior. For convenience, we will refer to the former procedure as calculation of observer agreement and the latter as calculation of observer accuracy. In general, both of these procedures have been labeled observer *reliability*. We will eschew this terminology because it tends to confuse the simple requirement for observer agreement or accuracy with the concept of the reliability of a test as understood in traditional test theory. As we shall outline in section three, it is quite possible to have perfect observer agreement or accuracy on a given behavioral score with absolutely no reliability or consistency of measurement in the traditional sense. Generally, the classic reliability requirement involves a demand for consistency in the measurement instrument over time (e.g., test-retest reliability) or over-sampled item sets responded to at roughly the same time (e.g., split-half reliability). An example may help clarify this point. If two computers score the same MMPI protocol identically, there is perfect "observer agreement" but this in no way means that the MMPI is a reliable test which yields consistent scores.[2] Although the question of reliability as traditionally understood has been largely ignored in behavioral research, we will argue in section three that it is a critical methodological requirement which should be clearly distinguished from observer agreement and accuracy.

There is no one established way to assess observer agreement or accuracy, and that is as it should be, because the index must be tailored to suit the purposes of each individual investigation.

Three basic decisions must be made in calculating observer agreement. The first decision involves the stipulation of the unit score on which the index of agreement should be assessed. In other words, what is the dependent variable for which an index of accuracy is required as measured by agreement with other observers or with a criterion? An example from our own research may help clarify this point. We obtain a "total deviant behavior score" for each of the children we observe. This score is based on the sum output of 15 behaviors judged to be deviant in nature. An outline of the rationale and validity of this score will be given in a later section. Suffice it to say, whenever two observers watch the same child for a given period, they each arrive at their own deviant behavior score. These scores may then be compared for agreement on overall frequency of deviant behavior. It is obvious that the same deviant behaviors need not be observed to get high indexes of agreement on the total number of deviant behaviors observed. Yet, for many of our purposes, this is not important, since we merely want an index of the overall output of deviant behavior over a given period. The same procedure is, of course, applicable to one behavior only, chains of behavior, etc. The point is that the researcher must decide what unit is of interest to him for his purposes and then compare agreement data on that variable. In complex coding systems like the one used in our laboratory, it has been customary to get an overall percent agreement figure which reflects the average level of agreement within small time blocks (e.g., six to ten seconds) over all codes. In general, we would argue that this kind of observer agreement data is relatively meaningless. It has limited meaning because it is based on a combination of codes, some of which are observed with high consensus and some which are not. Furthermore, the figure tends to overweigh those high-rate behaviors which are usually observed with greater accuracy and underweigh those low frequency behaviors which are usually observed with less accuracy. Patterson (personal communication) has reported that the observer agreement on a code correlates .49 with its frequency of use. Since it is often the low base-rate behaviors which are of most interest to researchers, an overall index of observer agreement probably overestimates the actual agreement on those variables of most concern.

The second question to be faced involves the time span within which common coding is to be counted as an agreement. For most purposes of our current research, score agreement over the entire 225 minutes of observation is adequate. Thus, when we compute the total deviant behavior score over this period, we do not know that each observer sees the same deviant behavior at the same time. But, good agreement on the overall score tells us that we have a consensually validated estimate of the child's overall deviancy. For some research purposes, this broad time span for agreement would be totally inadequate. For conditional probability analysis of one behavior (cf. Patterson and Cobb, 1971), for example, one needs to know that two observers saw the same behavior at the same time and, depending on the question, that each observer also saw the same set or chain of antecedents and/or consequences. This latter criterion is extremely stringent, particularly with complex codes where low-rate behaviors are involved, but these criteria are necessary for an appropriate estimate of accuracy.

Once one has decided on the score to be analyzed and the temporal rules for obtaining this score, one must then face the problem of what to do with the scores to give a numerical index of agreement. The two most common methods of analysis are percent agreement and some form of correlational analysis over the two sets of values. Both methods may, of course, be used for calculation of observer agreement either within one subject or across a group of subjects. Once again, neither method is always appropriate for every problem, and each has its advantages and disadvantages. The most common way of calculating observer agreement involves the following simple formula:

$$\frac{\text{number of agreements}}{\text{number of agreements + disagreements}}$$

What is defined as an agreement or disagreement has already been solved if one has decided on the "score" to be calibrated and the time span involved.

Use of this formula implies, however, that one must be able to discriminate the occurrence of both agreements and disagreements. This can only be accomplished precisely when the time span is relatively short (e.g., 1-15 seconds) so that one can be reasonably sure that two observers agreed or disagreed on the same coding unit. It has been common practice for investigators to compare recorded occurrences of behavior units over much longer time periods and obtain a percent agreement figure between two observers which reflects the following:

$$\frac{\text{smaller number of observed occurrences}}{\text{larger number of observed occurrences}}$$

The present authors would view this as an inappropriate procedure because there is no necessary "agreement" implied by the resulting percent. If one observer sees 10 occurrences of a behavior over a 30-minute period and the other sees 12, there is no assurance that they were ever in agreement. The behavior could have occurred 22 or more times, and there could be absolutely no agreement on specific events. The two observers did not necessarily agree 84% of the time. Data of this kind can be more appropriately analyzed by correlational methods if such analysis is consistent with the way in which the data are employed for the question under study. Although the same basic problem mentioned above can, of course, occur, the correlational method is viewed as more appropriate because: (a) the correlation is computed over an *array* of subjects or observation time segments, and (b) the correlation reflects the level of agreement on the total obtained score and it *does not imply any agreement on specific events.*

Whenever using the appropriate method of calculating percent observer agreement, i.e., the first formula given above, the investigator should be particularly cognizant of the base-rate problem. That is, the obtained percent agreement figure should be compared with the amount of agreement that could be obtained by chance. An example will clarify this point. Suppose two coders are coding on a binary behavior coding system (e.g., appropriate vs. inappropriate behavior). Further suppose that the observers have to characterize the subject's behavior as either appropriate or inappropriate every five seconds. Now, let us suppose, as is usually the case, that most of the subject's behavior is appropriate. If the subject's behavior were appropriate 90% of the time, two observers coding randomly at these base rates (i.e., .90–.10) will obtain 82% agreement by chance alone. Chance agreement is computed by squaring the base rate of each code category and summing these values.[3] In this simple case, the mathematics would be as follows: $.90^2 + .10^2 = .82$. The same procedure may, of course, be used with multi-code systems.

The above .90–.10 problem may be reconceptualized as one in which the occurrence or nonoccurrence of inappropriate behavior is coded every five seconds. If, for purposes of computing observer agreement, we look at only those blocks in which at least one of two observers coded the occurrence of inappropriate behavior, the chance level agreement is drastically reduced. The probability that two observers would code occurrence in the same block by chance is only $.10^2$ or one percent. It would not be theoretically inappropriate to count agreement on nonoccurrence but, in the present example and in most cases, this procedure is associated with relatively high levels of chance agreement.

Whenever percent agreement data is reported, the base-rate chance agreement should also be reported and the difference noted. Statistical tests of that difference can, of course, be computed. As long as the base-rate data is reported, the percent agreement figure would always seem to be appropriate. For obvious reasons, however, it becomes less satisfactory as the chance agreement figure approaches 1.0.

The other common method of computing agreement data is by means of a correlation between two sets of observations. The values may be scores from a group of subjects or scores from *n* observation segments on one subject. This method is particularly useful when one is faced with the problem of high chance agreement or where the requirement of simple similarity in ordering subjects on the dependent variable is sufficient for the research. As we shall illustrate, correlation is also particularly useful in cases where one has a limited sample of observer agreement data relative to the total amount of observation data.

In general, correlations have been used with data scores based on relatively large time samples. In other words, they tend to be used for summary scores on individuals over periods of ten minutes to 24 hours. There is no reason why correlation methodology could not be applied to data from smaller time segments, e.g., five seconds, but this has rarely been done. So, studies using correlation methods have generally been those in which one cannot be sure that the same behaviors are being jointly observed at the same time.

In using correlation methods for estimating agreement, one should be aware of two phenomena. First, it is possible to obtain high coefficients of correlation when one observer consistently overestimates behavioral rates relative to the other observer. This difference can be rather large, but if it is consistently in one direction, the correlation can be quite high. For some purposes this problem would be of little consequence, but for other purposes it could be of considerable importance. The data can be examined visually, or in other more systematic ways, to see to what extent this is the case. This problem can be virtually eliminated if one uses many observers and arranges for all of them to calibrate each other for agreement data. Under these circumstances, one will obtain a collection of regular observer figures and a list of mixed calibrator figures for correlation. This procedure should generally correct for systematic individual differences and make a consistent pattern extremely unlikely. The second problem to be cognizant of in using correlations is that higher values become more probable as the range on the dependent variable becomes greater. This fact may lead to high indexes of agreement when observers are really quite discrepant with respect to the number of occurrences of a given behavior they are observing. To illustrate, let us suppose we are observing rates of crying and whining behavior in preschool children over a five-hour period. Some particularly "good" children may display these behaviors very little and, given a true occurrence score of 7, two observers may obtain scores of 5 and 10 on this behavior class. Other children display these behaviors with moderate to very high frequency. For a child with high frequency, our two observers may give us scores of 75 and 125 respectively. If these examples were repeated throughout the distribution of scores, and if there were little overlap, a high correlation would be obtained. This would be even more true, of course, if one observer consistently overestimated the rates observed by the other. Yet, even this possibility does not necessarily jeopardize the utility of the method. It must merely be recognized, examined, and its implication for the question under study evaluated. In our own research we want to catalogue the deviancy rates of normal children, compare them with deviant children, and observe changes in deviancy rates as a result of behavior modification training with parents. For these purposes, general agreement on levels of deviant responding is sufficient.

In our research on the normal child, we have had 47 families of the total 77 families observed for the regular five-day period by an assigned observer. On one of these days an additional observer was sent to the family for the purpose of checking observer agreement. The correlation between the deviant behavior scores of the two observers was .80. But, in a purely statistical sence, this figure is an underestimate of what the agreement correlation would be for the full five days of observation. Since we are using a statistic based on five times as much data, we want to know the expected observer agreement correlation for this extended period. Adding time to an observation period is analogous to adding items to a test. The problem we are faced with here is very similar to that dealt with by traditional test theorists who have sought, for example, to estimate the reliability of an entire test based on the reliability of some portion of the test. In our case, we want to know the expected correlation for the statistic based on five days when we have the correlation based on one day. The well-known

Spearman-Brown formula (Guilford, 1954) may be applied to this end (as in Patterson, et al., in press; Patterson and Reid, 1970; Reid, 1967).[4]

$$r_{nn} = \frac{nr_{tt}}{1 + (n\text{-}1)r_{tt}}$$

where r_{tt} = reliability of the test of unit length
n = length of total test.

With the Spearman-Brown correction, the expected observer agreement correlation for the deviant behavior score is .95. This same procedure has also been applied to other statistics of particular interest in this research including: (a) the proportion of the parent's generally "negative" responses (corrected agreement = .97), (b) the proportion of the parent's generally positive responses (corrected agreement = .98), (c) the median agreement coefficient of the 29 behavior codes observed for five or more children (corrected agreement = .91), (d) the median corrected agreement of the 11 out of 15 deviant behavior codes used (r = .91), (e) the number of parental commands given (corrected agreement = .99), and (f) the compliance ratio (i.e., compliances/compliances plus noncompliances) of the child (corrected agreement = .92). As our research is completed, we will be presenting observer agreement data using different statistics, computed in different ways, and evaluated by different criteria.

The primary point of this section is to indicate that there are many ways of calculating observer agreement data and there is no one "right way to do it." The methods differ on three basic dimensions: (a) the nature and breadth of the dependent variable unit, (b) the time span covered, and (c) the method of computing the index. Each investigator must make his own decisions on each of these three points in line with the purposes of his investigation. But, the investigator should be guided by one central prescription—*the agreement data should be computed on the score used as the dependent variable.* It makes no sense to report overall average agreement data (except perhaps as a bow to tradition) when the dependent variable is "deviant behavior rate." In addition, it makes little sense to make the agreement criteria relative to time span more stringent than necessary. If the dependent variable is overall rate of deviant behavior for a five-day period, then this is the statistic for which agreement should be computed. It is not necessary for this limited purpose that both observers see the same deviant behavior in the same brief time block.

Before closing this section on the computation of observer agreement, we should address the somewhat unanswerable question of the minimum criteria for the acceptability of observer agreement data. In other words, how much agreement is sufficient for moving on to consider the results of a particular study? When using percent observer agreement, it would seem reasonable, at the very minimum, to show that the percent agreement is greater than that which could be expected by chance alone. When dealing with correlation data, one should at least show the obtained correlation to be statistically significant. These criteria are, of course, extremely minimal and certainly far below those commonly used in traditional testing and measurement to establish reliability (e.g., see Guilford, 1954). Yet, these criteria do provide a reasonable lowest level standard, and there are some good reasons why we should not be overly conservative on this point. In the first place, complex codes, which may provide us with some of our most interesting findings, are very difficult to use with complete accuracy. On the basis of our experience, and that of G. R. Patterson (personal communication), we consider an overall percent agreement of 80% to 85% as traditionally computed as a realistic upper limit for the kind of complex code we are using.

Furthermore, to the extent that less than perfect agreement represents only unsystematic error in the dependent variable, it cannot be considered a confounding variable accounting for *positive* results. *Any positive finding which emerges in spite of a good deal of "noise" or error variance is probably a relatively strong effect.*

Low observer agreement does, however, have important implications for negative results. This gets us back to the fundamental principle that one can never prove the null nypothesis. The more error in the measurement instrument, the greater the chance for failing to discover important phenomena. Thus, just as with traditional test reliability, the lower the observer accuracy, the less confidence one can have in any negative findings from the research.

Observer Agreement and Accuracy II: Generalizability of Observer Agreement Data

All of the preceding discussion on the calculation of observer agreement relies on the assumption that the obtained estimates of agreement are generalizable to the remainder of the observers' data collection. In most naturalistic behavioral research, however, this assumption cannot go unchallenged, and this brings us to our next, and largely soluble, methodological problem. To illustrate this problem, let us take the not untypical case of an investigator who trains his observers on a behavioral code until they meet the criterion of two consecutive observation sessions at 80% agreement or better. After completing this training, the investigator embarks on his research with no further assessment of observer agreement. There are three basic problems with this methodology which make the generalizability of this agreement data extremely questionable. These are: (a) the nonrandomness of the selected data points, (b) the unrepresentativeness of the selected data points in terms of the time of the assessment, and (c) the potential for the observer's reactivity to being checked or watched. The first two problems may be rather easily solved in all naturalistic research, but the third problem represents quite a challenge to some forms of naturalistic observation. Let us explore these problems in more detail.

The nonrandomness of selecting the last two "successful" observation sessions in a series for establishing a true estimate of agreement should be very obvious. It is not unlikely that, had the investigator obtained several additional agreement sessions, he would find the average agreement figure to be lower than 80%. It is quite possible that our observers had, by chance, two consecutive "good days" which are highly unrepresentative of the days to come. One can almost visualize our hypothetical investigator, after the first day of highly accurate observation, saying to his observers, "That was really a good one; all we need is one more good session and we can begin the study." But now we are getting into problems two and three.

The second problem of unrepresentativeness in terms of time has previously been discussed by Campbell and Stanley (1966) and labeled *instrument decay*. That is, estimates of observer accuracy obtained one week may not be representative of observer accuracy the next week. The longer the research lasts, the greater is the potential problem of instrument decay. In the case of human observers, the decay may result from processes of forgetting, new learning, fatigue, etc. Thus, because of *instrument decay*, our investigator's estimate of 80% agreement is probably an exaggeration of the true agreement during the study itself. The problem of instrument decay is also often compounded by the fact that during observer training there is usually a great deal of intense and concentrated work with the code, coupled with extensive training and feedback concerning observer accuracy. This intensity of experience and feedback is usually not maintained throughout the course of the research, and, as a result, the two time periods are characterized by very different sets of experiences for the observers.

The third problem of generlizability of this agreement data involves the simple fact that people often do a better, or at least a different, job when they are aware of being watched as opposed to when they are not. Campbell and Stanley (1966) have labeled this problem *reactive effects of testing.* It is likely that, when observers are being "tested" for accuracy, they will have heightened motivation for accuracy and heightened vigilance for critical behaviors or for the coding peculiarities of their calibrator. This point has been brought home dramatically to us on more than one occasion by the tears of an observer after earning a particularly low agreement rating. Thus, because of the reactivity problem, estimates of observer agreement obtained with the awareness of the observer are likely to overestimate the true agreement level which would be obtained if the observer were not aware of such calibration.

Fortunately, all of the preceding logical arguments have been investigated in some recent research largely contributed by John Reid of the Oregon Research Institute. His first published study on this problem (Reid, 1970) was, from the observer's point of view, almost identical to the hypothetical example just discussed. In this study, observers were trained for a maximum of eight days on complex behavioral coding of video tape material in a laboratory setting. They were trained until they obtained 70% agreement on two consecutive days for 15 minutes of observation per day. In each training session, feedback was given to the observers concerning their accuracy, but in the immediately following assessment session no such feedback was given. After training was completed, the observers were led to believe that they would be the only ones seeing the subsequent tapes because criterion protocols had not been previously constructed and the tapes would have to be erased immediately after coding so that they might be reused. Observers were urged, therefore, to be very careful in their subsequent coding. On each of four consecutive days after reaching criterion, the observers were asked to complete 30 minutes of observation on similar stimulus materials. The first 5 minutes of each session served as a practice period in which the experimenter gave feedback to the observer when necessary. Although the observers were not aware of it, criterion protocols had been prepared on these video tape materials, thus providing a covert assessment of observer accuracy. Throughout the study, observer agreement was computed by comparing the data entry with the standard protocol. Both errors of commission and omission were counted. This is the type of overall and generally stringent accuracy criteria which we earlier recommended against for most research purposes. In any event, all observers reached the 70% agreement criterion at or before eight days of training, and the average agreement during the two criterion days was 75.50%. The average agreement during the following four days, however, was only 51.25%, representing a drop of nearly 25 percentage points. Now it is obvious that, in this first study, all three confounding problems were present—(a) unrepresentativeness of the criterion days, (b) instrument decay due to passage of time, etc., and (c) reactivity to being tested. This is the procedure, however, which is representative of many investigations in the field. Reid's study certainly demonstrates the potentially powerful impact of these confounding influences. Because of the relatively short time span involved in this study, it is likely that most of this effect is attributable to the reactivity problem.

A more recent study by Taplin and Reid (in preparation) sheds greater light on the contribution of each of these confounding influences. Although differing in details from the earlier investigation, the basic procedures and concepts were the same. After training to a criterion of 70% agreement, the observers were assigned to one of three groups: (a) no-check group—the procedures in this group essentially replicated those of the former study such that the observers were unaware of agreement assessment beyond the criterion period; (b) spot-check group—in this group, observers were told that their accuracy would be checked from time to time during the experimental phase, but that they would be aware of when these checks would be made. This group controls for the problems of unrepresentativeness of criterion day performance as well as instrument decay, but does not control for reactivity to testing; (c) random-check group—in this group, the observers were told that their accuracy would be checked randomly in 20% of the sessions but that they would not be aware of when these checks occurred. This procedure not only controls for the first two problems, but also controls for the reactivity problem by making it *constant*. In other words, it is likely that the knowledge of a "potential" assessment of accuracy will increase the observer's motivation and vigilance. Yet, this is not a confounding influence since any random assessment of accuracy in the series will not be *unrepresentative* of the other points in the series. Thus, whenever practically possible, this strategy of random assessment without observer awareness or assessment on every observation occasion is most consistent with rigorous research requirements. The results of the Taplin and Reid study are presented in Figure 1 and

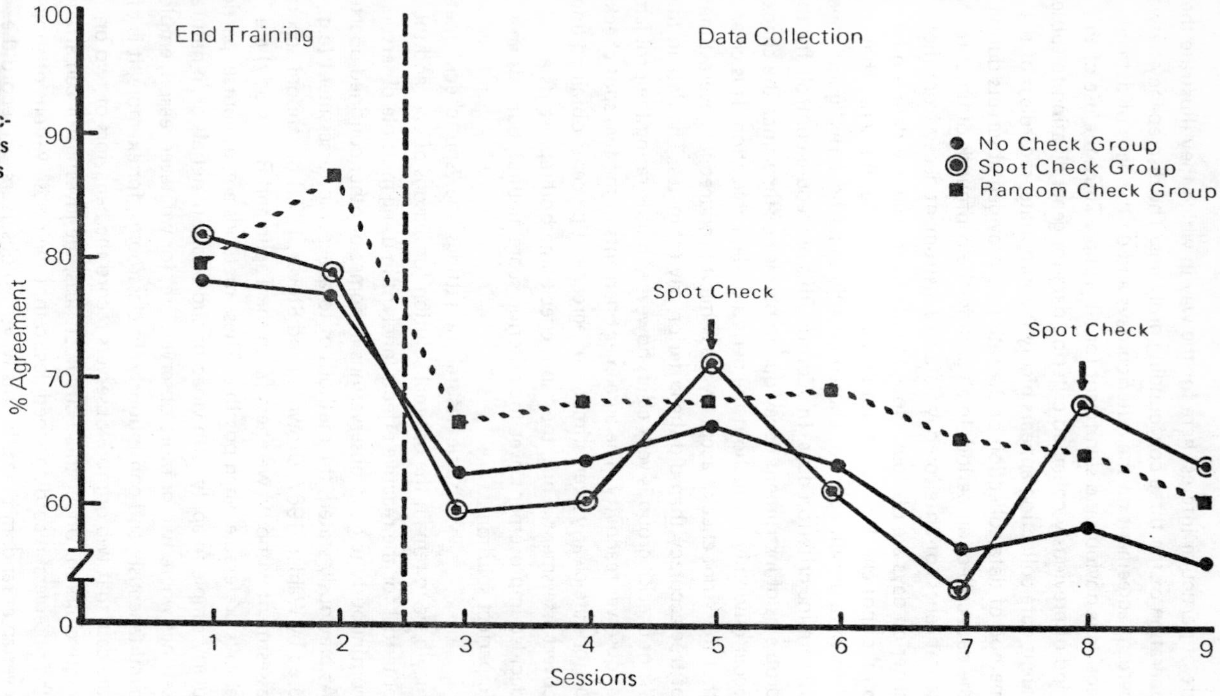

Figure 1

Mean agreement with criterion for three instructional groups over sessions (Taplin and Reid, in preparation)

are of particular interest here for the way in which they illustrate the operation of the three confounding problems. The discrepancy between percent agreement on the criterion days and on the days of data collection is obvious and significant for all groups. Thus, the use of this kind of previously collected criterion data for generalization to subsequent data collection appears highly inappropriate, regardless of the method of data collection or the rationale provided observers during the data collection period. In all groups, the confounds of unrepresentativeness of criterion day data and instrument decay from the criterion days are obvious. Now, the observer accuracy data produced on the spot check days are not unrepresentative, in the sense that these days were presumably not chosen initially as particularly "good" ones, as were the criterion days. In addition, this procedure controls for the problems of instrument decay due to passage of time since the checks occur randomly throughout the period of data collection. It is clear that the "spot check" accuracy assessment produced less overestimation of true accuracy than did the criterion day estimates. The data in this "spot check" group is very clear, however, in illustrating the problem of observer reactivity. The agreement percents in the two spot check periods are clearly overestimates of agreement percents obtained under covert assessment. Thus, the "spot check" method represents a decided improvement over the criterion score method, but it is an imperfect solution.

In some naturalistic settings, the "spot check" method may have to remain the optimal solution for reasons of cost and the potential for the reactive effects inherent in using multiple observers continuously (e.g., in observations in homes or other confined quarters). As previously stated, the methods of total accuracy assessment (e.g., as used by Wahler, 1967; Browning and Stover, 1971) or random accuracy assessment without awareness (as in the Taplin and Reid study) are always preferable when possible. These methods are, of course, particularly simple to apply with video or audio tape materials or in natural settings where two or more observers are, for whatever reason, employed simultaneously and continuously. In classrooms, for example, it is often the case that two or more observers record the behaviors of two or more children. Under these circumstances, the investigator can arrange the observers' recording schedules so that their observations of subjects overlap at random times. In this way, two observers can record the behavior of the same subject at the same time without either having knowledge of the ongoing calibration for agreement occurring at that *specific* time. This procedure would replicate the "random-check group" of Taplin and Reid (in preparation) in a field setting. It would probably be difficult, if not impossible, to keep the fact of random calibration a secret from the observers for any extended period, but, as stated earlier, this is no real problem because the randomly collected data without *specific* awareness is representative of accuracy at other times. The Taplin and Reid data would suggest that the motivational effects of informing observers of the random checks slightly increases the level and stability of their accuracy scores. (Compare the three groups' accuracy levels and stability in the data collection period in Figure 1.)

In more recent research, Reid and his colleagues have directed their efforts to finding ways of eliminating the instrument decay or "observer drift" observed in all previous studies regardless of the method of monitoring. In several long-term research projects, including our own (e.g., Johnson, et al., in press), the one directed by G. R. Patterson, et al., in press), and the one reported by Browning and Stover (1971), continuous training, discussion of the coding system, and accuracy feedback are provided for the observers. It is possible that this kind of training and feedback could eliminate, or at least attenuate, observers' accuracy drift as well as the problem of the unrepresentativeness of "spot check" accuracy assessments. To test this hypothesis, DeMaster and Reid (in preparation) designed a study in which three levels of feedback and training during data collection were compared on a sample of 28 observers. The observers were divided into 14 pairs and all subsequent procedures were carried out in the context of these fixed pairs. The three experimental groups were as follows: Group I—Total Feedback—In this group observers (a) discussed their observation performance together while reviewing their coding of the previous day's video tape, (b) discussed their previous day's observation with the experimenter in terms of their agreement with the criterion-coded protocol, and (c) received a daily report of their accuracy with respect to the criterion protocol; Group II—Pair Agreement Feedback—In this group, observers were given the opportunity to discuss their performance, as in (a) above, and were given a daily report on the extent to which each observer's coding protocol agreed with the protocol of the other observer. Subjects in this group were deprived of a discussion or report of their level of agreement with the criterion protocols; Group III—No Feedback—Subjects in this group were deprived of the kinds of feedback given in the previous two conditions and were instructed not to discuss their work among themselves to eliminate a possible "bias of the data." This group was similar in concept to the random-check group in the Taplin and Reid (in preparation) study in that they were told, as were all other subjects, that their accuracy would be checked at random intervals in the data collection period. The dependent variables were: (a) the agreement scores between pairs of observers and (b) the "accuracy" scores reflected by the percent agreement with the criterion protocols.

The results showed that the intra-pair observer agreement scores were significantly higher than were scores reflecting agreement with the criterion. These results tend to corroborate the hypothesis forwarded by Baer, et al. (1968) and Bijou, et al. (1968) that high intra-pair agreement does not necessarily reflect proper use of the coding system. We shall call this problem "consensual observer drift." It is very important to note, however, that the design of this study, which placed observers in fixed and unchanging pairs, would tend to maximize this effect. In the field studies referred to above, observers typically met in larger groups for training and feedback, and observers rotated in calibrating each other's observations. Under these circumstances, the effects of consensual drift would logically be expected to be less potent. Indeed, further data from the DeMaster and Reid (in preparation) study lends support to this argument. On those video tape materials where more than one pair of observers had coded the sequence, the investigators compared the fixed pair agreement with the agreement between observers in other pairs. In all cases, the members of a fixed pair agreed more with one another than they did with the observers in the other pairs. Thus, this idiosyncratic drift of fixed pairs may be greater than drift experienced under currently employed field research procedures. Yet, a recent study by Romanczyk, et al. (1971) showed that during assessment of overt agreement, observers would change their coding behavior to more closely approximate the differential coding styles of their calibrators. Thus, it is possible for observers to produce one kind of consensual drift with some calibrators and an opposite consensual drift with others to yield artifically high observer agreement data. The manipulations in the Romanczyk, et al. study were quite powerful, however, and one can question the generalizability of these artificially induced conditions to real field studies. Nevertheless, this study does demonstrate the potential for powerful and *differential* consensual drift.

In spite of these considerations, one must realize that it is impossible in an ongoing field observation to have a "pure" criterion protocol, since one cannot arbitrarily designate one observer's protocol as the "true" criterion and the other as the imperfect approximate. But, one can attenuate this problem considerably by having frequent training sessions with observers on pre-coded video tape material or on pre-coded behavioral scripts which may be acted out live by paid subjects. The importance of this recommendation is underlined by DeMaster and Reid's (in preparation) second important finding. Analysis of the data indicated a significant main effect for feedback conditions, with the total feedback group doing best, followed by the intra-pair feedback group and the no feedback group, respectively.

It may be of interest to review briefly how our own project stacks up with regard to these considerations and to suggest ways in which it and similar projects might be improved. Initial observer training in our laboratory consists of the following program: (a) reading and study of the observation manual, (b) completion of programmed instruction materials involving pre-coded interactions, (c) participation in daily intensive training sessions which include discussion of the system and coding of pre-coded scripts acted out live by paid but nonprofessional actors, and (d) field training with a more experienced observer followed immediately by agreement checks. Currently, when an observer obtains five sessions with an average overall percent agreement of 70% or better, she may begin regular observation without constant monitoring. All observers continue to participate in continuous training and are subject to continuous checking with feedback. This is accomplished in two ways. First, each observer is subject to one spot-check calibration for each family she observes. This calibration may occur on any one of the regular five days of observation. Both observers calculate their percent agreement in the traditional way immediately after the session and discuss their disagreements at this time. If they cannot resolve their disagreement on a particular or idiosyncratic problem, they immediately call the observer trainer, who serves as sort of an imperfect criterion coder. From time to time, idiosyncratic problems arise which cannot be resolved by the coding manual alone. Decisions on how to code these special cases are made by the group and the trainer and are entered in a "decision log" which is periodically studied by all observers. These special circumstances are unfortunate and provide an opportunity for consensual drift, but are part of the reality with which we must deal. The "decision log" helps attenuate the drift problem on these decisions, and most of these problems tend to be idiosyncratic to one or two families. The second aspect of continual training involves a *minimum* of one 90-minute training session per week for all observers involving discussion and live coding experience. We have been negligent in not retaining our pre-coded scripts over time and re-coding these from month-to-month and year-to-year. On the basis of our review of Reid's excellent work, we have now begun to correct this error by retaining these scripts and subjecting them to re-coding periodically to check the problem of consensual observer drift. As will be obvious, we use the imperfect method of "spot check" calibration for observer agreement, but Reid's data is encouraging in that it indicates that the kind of intensive and continual training outlined here may attenuate the problems associated with this method. Furthermore, our observers are convinced that calibration scores obtained on a single day of observation are probably lower than would be obtained over two or more days of observation. The reason for this belief is that the calibrator would logically have more difficulty in adapting to each new home environment and identifying the subjects of observation on the first day in the home than on subsequent days. Unfortunately, we have no hard data to prove this hypothesis, but we have begun to do more than one day of calibration on families in order to test it.

The problem of consensual drift is also attenuated in this project by the practice of having each observer calibrate all other observers. We recently began to employ only one calibrator for reasons of convenience and cost, but the recent literature has persuaded us to return, at least partially, to multiple calibration among all observers.

As stated earlier, the problems associated with reactivity to testing for observer agreement could largely be solved by procedures which involved coding of audio or video tapes. This is true because one could arrange calibration on a random basis without observer awareness. Because procedures of this kind could also solve or attenuate problems of observer bias and subject reactivity, we are beginning to consider such procedures more seriously for future research and are now involved in pilot work on the feasibility of them. Short of this, we must be content with the "spot check" method as outlined and attempt to attenuate the problems associated with this method by use of extensive training and feedback as suggested by DeMaster and Reid (in preparation).

Reliability of Naturalistic Behavioral Data

One must look long and hard through the behavior modification literature to find reliability data on naturalistic behavior rate scores. In classical test theory, the concept of reliability involves the consistency with which a test measures a given attribute or yields a consistent score on a given dimension. Theoretically, a test of intelligence, for example, is reliable if it consistently yields highly similar scores for the same individual relative to other individuals in the sample. There are several approaches to measuring reliability, including split-half measures, equivalent forms, test-retest methods, etc. Each method has a somewhat different meaning, but the basic objective of each is an estimate of the consistency of measurement.

It is difficult to tell whether behaviorists have simply neglected, or deliberately rejected, the reliability requirement for their own research. The concept of reliability comes out of classical test theory and is obviously allied to trait concepts of personality. Behaviorists may feel that the concept is irrelevant to their purposes. After all, we know that there is often very little proven consistency in human behavior over time and stimulus situations (e.g., see Mischel, 1968), so why should we require a consistency in our measurement instruments that is not present in real life? Behaviorists may feel that reliability is an outmoded concept and belongs exclusively to the era of trait psychology. If this is, in fact, the reason for the neglect of the reliability issue in behavioral research, it represents a serious conceptual error and a clear misapplication of the meaning of the data on the lack of behavioral consistency so eloquently summarized by Mischel (1968). It is true, of course, that behaviorists employ more restricted definitions of the topography of the relevant response dimensions (e.g., hitting vs. aggression) and that they often include more restrictive stimulus events in defining these dimensions (e.g., child noncompliance to mother's commands vs. child negativism). Yet, the fact remains that we are still dealing with *scores* that reflect behavioral dimensions. If the word "trait" is offensive, then another label will do as well. Furthermore, the scores are obtained for the same purpose that trait scores are obtained—to correlate with some other variable. Generally, behavior modifiers "correlate" these scores with the presence or absence of some treatment procedure, but certainly the data are not limited to this one objective. In our own research, for example, we are currently comparing children's deviant behavior rates in their homes with their deviancy in the school classroom (Walker, et al., 1972) and comparing the deviancy rates of "normal" children with those observed in referred or "deviant" children (Lobitz and Johnson, 1972). The most elementary knowledge of the concept of reliability tells us that some minimal level of behavior score *reliability* is necessary before we can ever hope to obtain any significant relationship between our behavioral score and any external variable. Thus, the requirement of score reliability is just as important in research employing behavioral assessment as it is in more traditional forms of psychological assessment, but with only a few exceptions (e.g., Cobb, 1969; Harris, 1969; Olson, 1930-31; Patterson, et al., in press) behaviorists have ignored this important issue.

As a consequence of the reasoning presented above, we have been particularly cognizant of the reliability of the scores used in our research. We were quite encouraged to find, for example, that the odd-even, split-half reliability of our "total deviant behavior score" in a sample of 33 "normal" children was .72. This reliability was computed by correlating the total deviant behavior score obtained on the first and third days and first half of the fifth day with the same score obtained from the remainder of the period. After applying the Spearman-Brown correction formula, we found that the reliability of this score for the entire five-day observation period was .83. This relatively high level of reliability indicates that this score should, at least in a statistical sense, be quite sensitive to manipulation or to true relationships with other external variables such as social class or educational level of the parents. Other behavioral scores which are important in our research include: (a) the proportion of generally negative responses of the parents (corrected reliability = .90), (b) the proportion of generally positive responses of parents (corrected reliability = .87), (c) the median reliability of the 35 individual codes (r = .69), (d) the corrected median reliability of the deviant codes = .66, (3) the number of parental commands during the observation (corrected reliability = .85), and (f) the compliance ratio (i.e., compliances/compliances + noncompliances) of the child (corrected reliability = .49). The reliability of the compliance ratio is not as high as we might have wished, but it may still be sufficiently high to be sensitive enough for powerful manipulations. We have been less fortunate in obtaining good reliability scores on some other statistics important to our research efforts. For example, the compliance ratios to specific agents, i.e., to mothers or fathers, have yielded rather low reliabilities. The reasons for this are twofold. First, ratio scores are always less reliable than are their component raw scores because they combine the error variance of both components.. Second, and of more general importance, these scores are based on relatively few occurrences. On the average, for example, fathers give only 36 commands over the five-day period. These occurrences must then be divided for the compliances and noncompliances and further split in half for the odd-even reliability estimate. By the time this erosion takes place, there are few data points on which to base reliability estimates. This problem is even more profound when we use one day of compliance ratio data to compute *observer agreement* on this statistic, since, on the average, fathers give only 7.2 commands per day. Thus, when we are dealing with behavioral events of fairly low base rate, observer agreement correlations and reliability coefficients may often not be "fairly" computed because there is simply not enough data. In classical test theory terminology, there may often not be enough "items" on the behavioral test to permit an *accurate* estimation of the reliability of the score. What should we do with cases of this kind? A methodological purist might argue that we should throw out such data and use only scores with proven high reliability and observer agreement. We would argue that this course would be a particularly unfortunate solution for several reasons. First, low base-rate behaviors are often those of special importance in clinical work. Second, if low reliability reflects nothing more than random, unsystematic error in the measurement instrument, it cannot jeopardize or provide a confounding influence on *positive* results (i.e., it cannot contribute to the commission of Type I errors). But, either low reliability or low observer agreement does have profound implications for the meaning of *negative* results (i.e., the commission of Type II errors). Fortunately, the effects of many behavior modification procedures are so dramatic that they will emerge significant in spite of relatively low reliability or observer accuracy.

In one of the other few examples of reliability data in the behavior modification literature, Cobb (1969) found that the average odd-even reliability of relevant behavioral codes used in the school setting was only .72. Yet, he found that the rates of certain coded behaviors showed strong relationships to achievement in arithmetic. Thus, relatively low reliability or observer agreement jeopardizes only slightly the meaning of *positive* results, but leaves *negative* results with little meaning. There is, however, one very critical qualifying point to this argument. It is that the error expressed in low reliability or observer accuracy *must* be random, unsystematic, and unbiased. With this consideration in mind, we now proceed to what are perhaps the most important methodological issues in naturalistic research—observer bias and observer reactivity to the observation process.

The Problem of Observer Bias in Naturalistic Observation

Shortly after the turn of the century, O. Pfungst became intrigued with a mysteriously clever horse named Hans. By tapping his foot, "Clever Hans" was able to add, subtract, multiply and divide and to spell, read, and solve problems of musical harmony (Pfungst, 1911). Hans' owner, a Mr. von Osten, was a German mathematics teacher who, unlike the vaudeville trainers of show animals, did not profit from the horse's peculiar talents. He insisted that he did not cue the animal and, as proof, he permitted others to question Hans without his being present. Pfungst remained incredulous and began a program of systematic study to unravel the mystery of Hans' talents.

Pfungst soon discovered that, if the horse could not see the questioner, it could not answer even the simplest of questions. Neither would Hans respond if the questioner himself did not know the answer. Pfungst next observed that a forward inclination of the questioner's head was sufficient to start the horse tapping, and raising the head was sufficient to terminate the tapping. This was true even for very slight motions of the head, as well as the lowering and raising of the eyebrows and the dilation and contraction of the questioner's nostrils.

Pfungst reasoned and demonstrated that Hans' questioners, even the skeptical ones, expected the horse to give correct responses. Unwittingly, their expectations were reflected in their head movements and glances to and from the horse's hooves. When the correct number of hoof taps was reached, the questioners almost always looked up, thereby signaling Hans to stop (Rosenthal, 1966).

Some fifty years later, Robert Rosenthal began to investigate the importance of the expectations of experimenters in psychological research. In his now classical article, Rosenthal (1963) presented evidence suggesting that the experimenter's knowledge of the hypothesis could serve as an unintended source of variance in experimental results. In a prototypical study, Rosenthal and Fode (1963) had naive rats randomly assigned to two groups of undergraduate experimenters in a maze-learning task. One group of experimenters was told that they were working with maze-bright animals, and the other group was told that their rats were maze-dull. The group of experimenters which was led to believe that their rats were maze-bright reported faster learning times for their subjects than the group which was told their animals were maze-dull. An extension of this finding to the classroom was offered by Rosenthal and Jacobson (1966). Teachers were led to believe that certain, randomly selected students in their classrooms were "late bloomers" with unrealized academic potential. Pre- and post-testing in the fall and spring suggested that children in the experimental group (late bloomers) had a greater increase in IQ than did the controls.

The purpose of this section is to examine the problem of experimenter-observer bias in naturalistic observational procedures. The amount of literature dealing directly with observer bias in naturalistic observation is sparse (Kass and O'Leary, 1970; Skindrud, 1972; Kent, 1972). However, Rosenthal has written an extensive review of experimenter bias in behavioral and social psychological research (Rosenthal, 1966). In spite of failures to replicate many of Rosenthal's findings (Barber and Silver, 1968; Clairborn, 1969) and extensive criticisms of Rosenthal's methodology (Snow, 1969; Thorndike, 1969; Barber and Silver, 1968), the massive body of literature compiled and summarized by Rosenthal (1966) remains the best available resource for conceptualizing the phenomenon of observer bias and for isolating possible sources of bias relevant to naturalistic observation. A brief review of this literature follows with a focus on integrating implications from the literature with naturalistic observational procedures. In addition, we will give consideration to the few experiments which have directly investigated observer bias in naturalistic observation and further consider some proposals for experiments yet to be conducted. Finally, suggestions for minimizing observer bias will be outlined, and data on this problem from our laboratory will be presented.

Conceptualization of Observer Bias

Rosenthal (1966) has defined experimenter bias "as the extent to which experimenter effect or error is asymmetrically distributed about the 'correct' or 'true' value." Observer errors or effects are generally assumed to be randomly distributed around a "true" or "criterion" value. Observer bias, on the other hand, tends to be unidirectional and thereby confounding.

Sources of Observer Bias

An important distinction should be drawn between observer error and observer effect on subjects. Invalid results may be contributed solely by systematic or "biased" errors in recording by observers. Or, invalid findings may be obtained as a result of the effect that the observer has on his subjects (Rosenthal, 1966). First we will consider recording error as a source of observer bias.

Kennedy and Uphoff (1939) illustrate the problem of recording errors in an experiment in extrasensory perception. The observers' task was simply to record the investigator's guesses as to the kind of symbol being "transmitted" by the observer. Since the investigator's guesses for the observers had been programmed, it was possible to count the number of recording errors. In all, 126 recording errors out of 11,125 guesses were accumulated among 28 observers. The analysis of errors revealed that believers in telepathy made 71.5 percent more errors increasing telepathy scores than did nonbelievers. Disbelievers made 100 percent more errors decreasing the telepathy scores than did their counterparts. Sheffield and Kaufman (1952) found similar biases in recording errors among believers and nonbelievers in psychokinesis in tallying the results of the fall of dice. Computational errors in summing recorded rates have also been documented by Rosenthal in an experiment on the perception of people (Rosenthal, et al., 1964).

It is doubtful that these recording and computational errors were intentional. However, as Rosenthal (1966, pp. 31-32) notes, data fabrication or intentional cheating is not absent in psychological research, especially where undergraduate student experimenters are employed as data collectors. Rosenthal points out that these students "have usually not identified to a great extent with the scientific values of their instructors." Students may fear that a poor grade will be the result of an accurately observed and recorded event which is incompatible with the expected event. Of two experiments by Rosenthal designed to examine intentional erring by students in a laboratory course in animal learning, one revealed a clear instance of data fabrication (Rosenthal and Lawson, 1964), and the other showed no evidence of intentional erring but did show some deviations from the prescribed procedure (Rosenthal and Fode, 1963). Another study employing student experimenters by Azrin, et al. (1961) replicated Verplanck's (1955) verbal conditioning experiment. However, an informal post-experimental check revealed that data had been fabricated by the student experimenters. Later, the authors employed advanced graduate students as experimenters and found that Verplanck's results were not replicated.

The implications for naturalistic observation are obvious. Observer error, whether it be unintentional or intentional, incurred during recording or during computation, must be guarded against by accuracy checks and by carefully concealing the experimenter's hypotheses. Although checks of observer agreement do not rule out the possibility of bias among the observers whose data is compared, at least suspicion is aroused where agreement figures are low and disagreements are consistent. Ideally, observers should not be made responsible for the tallying of their own data. Computations should be made by a non-observer who is removed from knowledge of the observations. Observers should be selected on the basis of their identification with scientific integrity, and admonitions against possible biasing effects should be repeated during the course of the experiment. Finally, observers should be encouraged to disclose to the experimenter both the nature and sources of any information they receive that might be relevant to the objectivity of their observations. A questionnaire, filled out after observation sessions, can facilitate this disclosure.

The other source of observer bias discussed by Rosenthal (1966) is the effect of the observer's expectancy on the subject. If an observer has an hypothesis about a subject's behavior, he may be able to communicate his expectations and thereby influence the behavior.

Expectancy effects have previously been alluded to in Rosenthal's study with animal laboratory experimenters (Rosenthal and Fode, 1963) and teachers in the classroom (Rosenthal and Jacobson, 1966). Rosenthal's first major study in expectancy effects is instructive in its simplicity. Rosenthal and Fode (1963) had ten experimenters obtain ratings from 206 subjects on the photo person-perception task. All ten experimenters received identical instructions except that five experimenters were informed that their subjects would probably average a +5 success rating on the ten neutral photos while the other five experimenters were led to expect a -5 failure average. The results revealed that the group given the +5 expectation obtained an average of +.40, whereas the -5 expectation group yielded a score of -.08. These differences were highly significant, and subsequent replications have supported these findings (Fode, 1960; Fode, 1965).

The implications of these findings for naturalistic observational procedures are most discomforting. If, as in the Rosenthal laboratory studies, observers in the natural setting can communicate their expectancies to their subjects such that the subjects' behaviors fall in line with those expectations, a serious threat to internal validity is posed. Assuming that humans are no less sensitive to subtle cues than Mr. von Osten's horse, it seems reasonable to infer that observer expectancy effects are operative in the natural setting. Consider the not atypical case of an observer who records selected deviant behaviors of a child in a classroom before, during, and after treatment. Seldom is it not obvious to the observer when treatment begins and ends. Assuming that an observer might infer the expectations of the experimenter in such a setting, how might he communicate these expectations to his subjects? One way of influencing the targeted child would be by nonverbal, expressive cues. Expressions of amusement by the observer during baseline might inflate deviant behaviors. During intervention, expressions of disapproval or caution by the observer might reduce the subject's deviant rate. These biasing effects might be systematic and confounding.

Although few studies have systematically assessed the effects of observer bias in the natural setting, many field investigators have taken note of the expectancy phenomenon and have included procedures to minimize its effect. One such technique is to mask changes in experimental conditions (e.g., Thomas, et al., 1968). Another is to keep observers unaware of assignment of subjects to various treatment or control conditions (e.g., O'Conner, 1969). The addition of new observers in the last phase of a study who are naive to previous manipulations is another approach (e.g., Bolstad and Johnson, in press).

Three studies in the nautral setting shed further light on expectancy effects with naturalistic observational procedures. Rapp (1966) had eight pairs of untrained observers describe a child in a nursery school for a period of one minute. One member of each observer pair was subtly informed that the child under observation was feeling "under par" today and the other that the child was "above par." In fact, all eight children showed no such behaviors. Seven of the eight pairs of observers evidenced significant discrepancies between partners in their description of the children in the direction of their respective expectations. Both recording errors and expectancy effects on the subject's behavior may have contributed to this demonstration of observer bias.

A second study by Azrin, et al. (1961) employed untrained undergraduate observers who were asked to count opinion statements of adults when the adults spoke to them. The observations of those who had been exposed to an operant interpretation of the verbal conditioning phenomenon under study were the exact opposite of those given a psychodynamic interpretation. Again, both the expectancy effects of the observer on the subject and recording errors may have accounted for the observer bias. Post-experimental inquiries by an accomplice student revealed that recording errors were the main factor. The accomplice learned that 12 of the 19 undergraduates questioned intentionally fabricated their data to meet their expectations.

A third study by Scott, et al. (1967) allows a comparison between the simultaneous observations of hypothesis-informed (Scott herself) and uninformed observers. The observers coded behavior into positive and negative acts from an audio tape recording of the targeted child and his peers. The informed observer's data differed significantly from the others' in the direction of the experimenters' hypothesis.

These three studies strongly suggest that data collected by relatively untrained observers are influenced by observer expectations. Do these findings generalize to the observations of professional observers who are highly trained in the use of sophisticated multivariate behavior codes? As indicated earlier, the amount of available research which directly pertains to this question is limited and somewhat equivocal.

Kass and O'Leary (1970) conducted the first systematic attempt to manipulate observer expectations in a simulated field-experimental situation. Three groups of female undergraduates observed identical video taped recordings of two disruptive children in a simulated classroom. The observers were trained in nine category codes of disruptive behavior. Group I was then given the expectation that soft reprimands from the teacher would increase the rate of disruptive behavior. Group II was told that soft reprimands would decrease disruptive behavior. And, Group III was given no expectation at all about the effects of soft reprimands. Each group was given rationales for each specific expectation. The effects of these expectations were assessed by having the observers record four days of baseline and five days of treatment data. The interaction between the mean rate of disruptive behavior in the three conditions and the two treatment conditions was significant at the .005 level, indicating the presence of observer bias. Kent (1972) has suggested that these reported effects of expectation bias were confounded with observer drift in the accuracy of recording. When different groups of raters, who are interreliable within groups, fail to frequently compute agreement between groups, they may "drift" apart in their application of the behavioral code. However, it should be noted that when this drift, comprised of recording errors, is aligned asymmetrically in the direction of the expectation, then the drift is, by definition, observer bias.

Skindrud (1972) attempted to replicate the findings of Kass and O'Leary (1970). Observers were divided into three groups, and each group was given a different expectation about video taped family interactions. The first group was given the expectation that when the father was absent there would be more child deviant behaviors than when the father was present. A second group was given the opposite expectation. Appropriate rationales were provided for each of these two groups. A control group was added with no expectations provided regarding the father's presence or absence. All observers were checked at the end of training on the rates of deviant behaviors they recorded and subsequently matched on this variable when assigned to conditions. Throughout the study, observer agreement data was collected randomly. During training, reliability was checked daily, and the average observer agreement prior to the beginning of the manipulation was 64%. The results of the study gave no evidence for observer bias. There were no significant differences between groups and no significant interaction effects. There was little drift in the accuracy with which the code was used. Sequential reliabilities were computed for the increase, decrease, and control groups with average observer agreements of 58.5%, 57.6%, and 58.4%, respectively. These accuracy figures were computed by comparisons with previously coded criterion protocols. The relatively small and consistent decline in accuracy is consistent with the failure to find bias.

A similar unsuccessful attempt to replicate the results of Kass and O'Leary (1970) was reported by Kent (1972). Kent found that knowledge of predicted results was not sufficient to produce an observer bias effect. However, when the experimenter reacted positively to data which was consistent with the given predictions and negatively to inconsistent data, a significant observer bias effect was obtained.

The literature dealing with observer bias in naturalistic observation is both sparse and contradictory. Furthermore, the few studies available have focused exclusively on only one source of observer bias, namely, either recording errors or errors of apprehension. Thus far, no one has systematically investigated the effects of the observer's expectancies on the subjects' behavior. In the three studies reported above, all observations were made from video taped recordings. There were no opportunities for the observers to communicate their expectancies to their subjects. Yet, in most studies employing naturalistic observational procedures, observers do have that opportunity.

An important study which needs to be conducted is one which examines the observer's expectancy effects on the subject. First, it would be interesting to determine if observers could nonverbally communicate their expectancies to subjects such that the subject's behavior changes in the direction of the expectancy. The next step, of course, would be to replicate this same design without specifically asking observers to attempt to influence subjects, but merely to give them an expectation.

Perhaps the most important test of observer bias effects will be the one which combines recording errors and effects of observer expectancy on subjects in the naturalistic setting. One can question the generalizability of highly controlled laboratory studies to live observations and to research projects in which the observers are more invested in the outcome of the research. The generalizability of studies which employ only taped versions of a subject's behavior is further limited by excluding the possible effects of an observer's expectancy on his subject's behavior.

Another variable which seems crucial to observer bias in the naturalistic setting is the observer's responsiveness to admonitions to remain scientific, objective, and impartial in the collection of data. Rosenthal (1966) stresses the importance of the experimenter-observer's identification with science and objectivity. He cites evidence suggesting that graduate students obtain less biased data than undergraduates and interprets this difference as a function of identification with science. Perhaps observers who are repeatedly reminded to be impartial might be less susceptible to the influence of biasing information than observers not given these admonitions.

A dimension which seems important in considering observer bias is the specificity of the code. In most of the Rosenthal literature, the dependent variable is scaled between such global poles as success and failure. Intuitively, it seems logical that the more ambiguous the dependent measure, the greater the possibility for bias. A multivariate coding system, with well-defined behavioral codes might be expected to restrict interpretive bias. This is an empirical question worthy of examination.

Another variable which might greatly affect observer bias is observer agreement. The greater the observer agreement, the less likely is observer bias, even among observers with the same expectancy.

Until more information is available on observer bias effects in naturalistic observation, it seems very critical to do everything possible to minimize the potential for these effects. Whenever possible, observers should not have access to information that may give rise to confounding consequences and should be encouraged to reveal the nature and source of any information they do receive. In our research, we are currently observing both families in clinical treatment and "normal" or nontreated families. Knowledge of a family's status might seriously affect the observer's data. Also, knowledge about treatment stages (baseline, mid-treatment, post-treatment, and follow-up) might affect the observers' data. After each observation, it is our policy to have observers fill out a questionnaire concerning the nature and source of any biasing information. Thus far, of 75 observations of referred families, observers have considered themselves informed only 36% of the time. And, in all of these cases, their information was correct. This information usually comes from a member of the family being observed (56%). Other sources of information include information leaks from the therapists (12%), the Child Study Center Clinic generally (16%), and other sources (16%). Of the observers considering themselves informed as to the clinic vs. "normal" status of the families, 29% also considered themselves informed as to treatment stage, but only two-thirds of these observers were correct in their discrimination. In only 20% of the cases did the observer actually know the status of the case (i.e., clinic vs. "normal") and the treatment stage (baseline vs. after baseline). Of the observers considering themselves completely uninformed of the families' status, their guessing rate (clinical or "normal") barely exceeded chance at 51%. Their guesses as to the four stages of treatment were 36% correct and 80% correct on the discrimination between baseline and after baseline.

Of the "normal" families seen, observers have considered themselves informed as to family status only 17% of the time. However, in only 45% of these cases were the observers actually correct in making the discrimination. In the uninformed observations, however, observers were able to guess the family's status correctly 75% of the time.

Not only are these questionnaires beneficial in gauging the amount of potentially biasing information that observers discover, but they are helpful in two other ways as well. First, by revealing sources of information leakage, steps can be made to eliminate these sources. Second, questionnaires, given after each family is observed, serve as a regular reminder for the importance of unbiased, objective recording of behavior.

It is difficult to make any firm conclusions about the presence or absence of observer bias in naturalistic observation. Clearly, more research is needed on this question. However, it should also be clear that the potentially confounding influence of observer bias cannot be ignored and that steps can and should be taken to minimize its possible effect.

The Issue of Reactivity in Naturalistic Observation

In the previous section, we have considered the effects of an observer's bias in naturalistic observation. In this section, we will discuss the effect of the observer's presence on the subjects being observed. Whereas observer bias can potentially invalidate comparisons by creating confounding influences, the reactive effects to being observed primarily constitute a threat to the generalizability of the findings. That is, subjects' observer behavior in the natural setting may not generalize to their unobserved behavior. Webb, et al. (1966) have defined reactivity in terms of measurement procedures which influence and thereby change the behavior of the subject. Weick (1968) has also referred to reactivity as "interference" or the intrusiveness of the observer himself upon the behavior being observed. Clearly, situations which are highly reactive in terms of "observer effects" are not likely to be generalizable to situations in which such effects are absent.

Reactive effects have been studied with two basic paradigms: (a) by the study of behavioral stability over time and (b) by comparison of the effects of various levels of obtrusiveness in the observation procedure. In employing the first method, investigators have typically examined behavioral data for change over time in the median level and variance of the dependent variable. In general, it has been assumed that change reflects initial reactivity and progressive adaptation to being observed. This interpretation is particularly persuasive if there is an obvious stability in the data after some initial period of change or high variability. While this is a viable way of checking for reactivity effects, it is a highly indirect method and relies on assumptions concerning the causes of observed change. It is obvious that other processes could account for such change. Furthermore, a lack of change certainly does not indicate a lack of reactive effects. The second method, comparing obtrusive levels of observation, appears less inferential than the first method. The problem with this method is that it only provides a picture of relative degrees of reactivity between obtrusiveness levels; it does not provide a measure of the degree of reactivity relative to the true, unobserved behavior. However, this problem can be remedied if one of the observational treatments in the comparison is totally unobtrusive or concealed.

To what extent does reactivity occur in naturalistic observation? The literature addressing this question is commonly reported in reviews to be contradictory (Wiggins, in press; Weick, 1968; Patterson and Harris, 1968). Several studies have been cited as providing evidence that reactive effects may be quite minimal. Others have been cited which suggest that reactive effects are quite pronounced. The purpose of this review is to: (a) reconsider the contradictions in the literature on reactivity, (b) "tease out" those factors which seem to account for reactivity, and (c) propose further investigations which would isolate the factors.

In a number of reviews on reactivity, several studies have been consistently cited which support the position that reactivity does not consistute a major threat to generalizability. One such study is the timely investigation of a Midwest community by Barker and Wright (1955). In this admirable study, careful naturalistic observations were made of children under ten years of age and their daily interactions with peers and parents. The authors assumed that reactive effects were short-lived and that the adults and other members of the families quickly habituated to the presence of the observers. In addition, it was reported that, with the younger subjects in the sample, reactive effects were slight. However, these findings should be interpreted with much caution. What is easily lost sight of in the summaries of this work is that the observers in this study were free to interact with the subjects in a friendly but nondirective manner. In fact, the basis for the authors' conclusion that reactive effects were not pronounced was the finding that "only" 20% of the children's behavioral interactions were with the observer. Allowing the observer to interact with the subject must certainly have increased the intrusiveness of the observer and provided the opportunity for the observer to influence the subject's behavior. The authors' other conclusion that reactivity, as measured by frequency of interactions, positively correlated with age is also suspect in that children below the age of five were not always informed that they were being observed, whereas children above this age were.

Another study commonly cited in support of the minimal reactivity position is that of Bales (1950). In this controlled laboratory investigation, the behavior of a discussion group was not found to be changed by three levels of observer conspicuousness. This finding, however, may be limited to the laboratory setting.

Two additional studies, frequently mentioned as supportive of the minimal reactivity argument, made use of radio transmitter recording in the naturalistic environment. Soskin and John (1963) had a married couple wear a transmitter the entire time they were on a two-week vacation. Purcell and Brady (1965) outfitted adolescents in a treatment center with a similar recording device for one hour a day. When the protocols in both studies were examined for the frequency of comments about being observed or listened to, it was found that such references declined to a zero level either during the first or second day of recording. This is not to say, of course, that these subjects were not still aware of, and affected by, the recording device; the results only indicate that the subjects talked about the device less after the first day.

A recent investigation by Martin, et al. (1971) can also be interpreted as providing evidence for low levels of reactivity to observation. This study involved 100 elementary school children, ages five to seven. Equal numbers of male and female subjects were assigned to five observation conditions following exposure to an aggressive model: (a) observer absent, (b) female adult observer present, (c) male adult observer present, (d) female peer observer present, and (e) male peer observer present. During the free-play session, the subjects' aggressive behavior was recorded by observers behind a one-way mirror. No significant differences in aggressive behaviors were obtained between the observer-present and observer-absent conditions. The absence of differences between these two levels of obtrusiveness in observation suggests little or no reactivity to the presence of an observer. Within the observer-present condition, however, it was found that peer observers significantly facilitated imitative aggressive responding in both boys and girls compared to adult observers. Also, there was more imitative aggression when the observer was the same sex as the subject. The girls, but not the boys, showed significant increases in aggressive output over time when the observer was present but not when the observer was absent. This latter finding suggests that girls manifest initial reactivity to the presence of an observer but later habituate to the observer's presence. It is interesting that both paradigms for measuring reactivity were used in this investigation and that each method supports different conclusions about the degree of reactivity. In considering the generalizability of these findings to naturalistic observation procedures, it should be noted that observers in this study were instructed to not pay attention to the subjects and were either seated facing away from the subjects (adult observers) or given a coloring task to complete (peer observers). With naturalistic observation procedures, on the other hand, observers typically pay very close attention to their subjects.

For the most part, those studies which have been purported to give evidence for minimal levels of reactivity to observation have been based on data of questionable meaning and/or restricted to highly specific circumstances (e.g., Bales, 1950; Martin, et al., 1971).

Many other studies have been cited as demonstrating considerable reactive effects of observation in naturalistic settings. One such study is that of Polansky, et al. (1949). These investigators observed delinquent children in a study of group emotional contagion phenomenon. The children were informed that the observers were studying their reactions to various aspects of the summer camp program. The authors report that during the first week of observations, the children essentially ignored the presence of the coders. But, during the second week, many "blow-ups" occurred which were directed against the coders, especially by the older children. The authors speculate that the aggressiveness of the children can be explained, in part, as resistance to being observed. They also concede, however, that this resistance hypothesis was confounded by "the second week syndrome," which they describe as an increasing anti-adult aggressiveness that typically evolves after the children have adjusted to the camp, peaking in the second week. It is unclear as to what to conclude from this study about reactivity. Was reactivity most prevalent when children were aggressive toward the observers in the second week? Or, was reactivity most intrusive during the first week when the delinquent children were "suppressing" aggression prior to habituating to the unfamiliar environment? And, more importantly, how much of this pattern of cooperation in the first week and anti-adult aggressiveness in the second would have occurred in the absence of observers? This question is left unanswered by the Polansky, et al. study.

A more sophisticated study illustrating considerable reactive effects is that of Roberts and Renzaglia (1965). In this study, eight therapists saw two "clients" (students solicited from an introductory psychology course) for three sessions. The three conditions were: (a) with a tape recorder in the room, (b) microphone only, and (c) with a concealed microphone and a concealed recorder. While no differences were found as to the number of minutes that subjects talked in each condition, it was found that the clients made more favorable self-references when they knew they were being recorded (conditions a and b) and more unfavorable self-references when they did not realize they were being recorded (condition c). While the generalizability of this study is limited by the small number of subjects and the structured situation employed, it does provide evidence for reactivity effects.

The Bechtel (1967) study has also been presented in reviews as a study demonstrating considerable reactive effects. Bechtel studied the movements of people in an art museum with an automated recording device, called an hodometer. In one condition, subjects were requested to go through the art exhibit in one room and rank the prints according to preference. Subjects of another group were given the same instructions and also were informed that they were being observed. For the first group, subjects were found to leave the room with an average latency of 313 seconds, covering an average area of 76 square feet. The second group left after 220 seconds and covered only 58 square feet. Bechtel concludes that being observed constituted an aversive situation which led to escaping the room faster. No statistics were provided to determine whether or not the reported averages were significantly different, nor were the number of subjects in each condition reported. Unfortunately, this kind of study does not provide any information about the habituation effects, since subjects were allowed to leave the setting.

A more recent investigation by White (1972) employed concealed observation in a situation which more closely approximates naturalistic observations in the home. The study took place in a large laboratory room which contained the essential features of a family living room. This setting also allowed for concaled, overhead observation. Mothers were instructed that an observer would be alternating 30-minute observation periods of her and her children with another mother-child combination in an adjacent living room environment. In point of fact, no other mother-child combination existed, nor did an adjacent living room environment. But, the deception allowed for a comparison of observer-present vs. observer-absent behavior via the concealed observation window. The dependent variable, as in the Bechtel study, was represented by activity level measured in terms of the distance covered in the room by the family members. Preliminary data analyses have revealed that the experimental manipulation—introducing an observer into the room—markedly reduced the activity level of the families. This difference represents reactivity relative to true, unobserved behavior, given the limitations of the laboratory setting.

Few studies have systematically investigated observer reactivity in the natural setting of a family's home. Littman, et al. (1957) provide evidence for reactive effects due to the presence of an observer. They found that for some families a six-hour adaptation period in their own homes was sufficient for habituation to the presence of an observer. However, for one of four families, stability of data was not realized even after six hours of adaptation.

A study by Patterson and Harris (1968) has also been cited as evidence for considerable reactive effects to observation in a naturalistic environment. This study is the only one available which was designed specifically to manipulate and measure observer effects in the homes of the families observed. In this study, data obtained from mothers on their own families were compared with the data on the same families collected by an outside observer. There were three conditions, with five families per condition: (a) the mothers collected the first five ten-minute sessions of observational data and an outside observer collected the second five sessions of data on the child and father only (M-0), (b) the observer collected all ten sessions as a test for habituation effects (0-0), and (c) the mothers collected all ten sessions as a control for habituation effects (M-M). The dependent variables were the rate of total behaviors and the rate of deviant behaviors. A problem in the research design of this study should be noted. The mother was present in the family as a participant in condition b and the second half of condition a, but was not a participant when she was an observer in condition c and the first half of condition a. These comparisons are confounded by mother presence and absence. In spite of this confound, which would probably bias in favor of showing group differences, no main effects for groups were found in analysis of variance for either the rate of total interactions or deviant behaviors. Thus, on the initially selected dependent variables, no reactive effects were apparent.

Patterson and Harris also divided their groups into high- and low-rate interactors on the basis of the first five sessions. On the frequency of total interactions measure, high-rate interactors in the first five sessions showed significant reductions in rate during the last five sessions. The authors describe this decline as a "structuring effect" in that the subjects appeared to program some activity together in the first five sessions. Conversely, the low-rate interactors in the first five sessions showed slight increases in rates during the last five sessions. The authors describe this transition as an habituation effect in that subjects initially involved themselves in solitary activities or attempted to escape the observational situation but later adjusted to it and interacted more. In general, there were no changes in deviant behavior from the first set of five observations to the last set of five. The only significant finding was that subjects who displayed low rates of deviant behavior in the first five sessions (under the M-0 condition) increased their rate in the last five sessions. However, it is possible that the mothers were recording less deviant behaviors and more positive behaviors in the first five sessions than were the observers in the second five sessions, thus contributing differentially to main trials effects. An observational study by Rosenthal (1966) supports such a thesis. He found that parents tended to code more positive changes in their children than were actually present. And, Peine (1970) found that parents were less observant of their children's deviant behaviors than were nonparent observers.

Patterson and Harris conclude that "generalization about 'observer effects' should probably be limited to special classes of behavior" (p. 16). A more recent study by Patterson and Cobb (1971) analyzed the stability of each of the 29 behavior codes used in their coding system. If it is assumed that individuals adapt to the presence of an observer over time, then a repeated measures analysis of variance should reveal differences in the mean level of various behaviors. Patterson and Cobb analyzed data for 31 children from problem and nonproblem families over seven baseline sessions. None of the changes in mean level for the codes produced a significant effect over time. The investigators conclude that the observation data were fairly stable for most code categories. It is possible, of course, that had observations continued over a longer period of time, significant changes in mean level for some behaviors would have been discovered. Given that families were rarely observed on consecutive days by the same observer, it is possible that different observers could have resensitized the families each day, thereby extending the period required for adaptation.

In summary, there are a few well-designed studies which have discovered reactive effects (e.g., Roberts and Renzaglia, 1965; Bechtel, 1967; White, 1972), but there are several others where the meaning of the results is unclear. There can be little doubt that the entire question has been inadequately researched. Any general conclusions about the extent of reactivity in naturalistic observation would seem premature at this time.

As White (1972) points out, the finding of reactive effects seems to depend on many factors, including the setting (e.g., home, school, laboratory), the length of observation, and the constraints placed on subjects by the conditions of observation (e.g., no television during observations, remaining within two adjacent rooms, etc.). Furthermore, it should be realized that reactivity may or may not be discovered depending upon what paradigm of measurement is used (e.g., Patterson and Harris, 1968; Martin, et al., 1971) and what variables are analyzed as dependent variables (e.g., Roberts and Renzaglia, 1965; White, 1972). Unless these factors are controlled for in comparing experiments on reactivity, both contradictions and consistencies as to the relative presence or absence of reactivity may falsely appear.

Assuming that reactivity to being observed in naturalistic settings does occur, even if only to some minimal degree, the critical task is to localize the sources of interference so that they can be dealt with more directly. Four such sources will be discussed and experiments will be proposed to measure the extent of their instrusiveness.

Factor 1: Conspicuousness of the Observer

The literature points to the level of conspicuousness or intrusiveness of the observer as an important factor contributing to reactivity. Presumably, the more novel and conspicuous the agent of observation, the more distracting are the effects upon the individuals being observed. It would also follow that longer habituation periods would be required for more distracting observational agents in order to achieve stability of data.

Bernal, et al. (1971) compared two observation procedures which would presumably vary on obtrusiveness. These investigators compared data collected by an observer with that collected by means of an audio tape recorder which was switched on by an automatic timing device. The family members involved in this study were aware of the presence of the recorder but were unaware of the exact time of its operation. The primary purpose of this study was to explore the feasibility of the audio tape method and to explore the relationship of data collected by the two methods rather than to study reactivity *per se*. The results indicated that, *during the same time interval*, there was a high relationship between the mother's command rate as coded by the observer and from the tape (r = .86) but that the observer coded more commands. Similar results were obtained when the observer's data was compared with data based on coding of the audio tapes from *different time intervals*. The question arises as to how much of the discrepancy in the latter case was due to differences in levels of reactivity and how much was due to differences associated with the source of coding. The authors point out, for example, that the observer could code gestural commands while the coder using the tape could not. Since the discrepancies at the same time and at different times were of the same general order of magnitude, it is likely that most of the observed differences across time were due to the material on which coding was based rather than to differences in subject reactivity. To study the impact of reactivity effects separately, one might design such a study so that the same stimulus materials would be used for coding.

We are currently completing a study on reactivity which employs this strategy to compare reactivity associated with an observer present in the home carrying a tape recorder vs. the tape recorder alone. This study involves six days of observation for 45 minutes per day with single-child families. The two conditions are alternated so that the observer is present one evening and not present the next. The observer is actually a "bogus" observer. All behavioral coding is done on the basis of the tapes. It is our suspicion that reactivity to the tape recorder will be short-lived and minimal compared to the reactivity associated with the observer present.

If these hypotheses are substantiated in this and other research, alternatives to having an observer present in the home should be explored. One solution to be seriously considered would be extended use of portable video or audio tape recording equipment. These recording devices could remain in the homes over an extended observation period to facilitate habituation effects. In addition, the devices could be preprogrammed to turn on and off at different times during the day so that the observed would not know when they are in operation (as in Bernal, et al., 1971). This solution, which would, of course, require full knowledge and consent of the parties involved, appears to be a promising one for attenuating reactivity effects as well as solving problems of observer bias.

Factor 2: Individual Differences of the Subjects

Some people might be expected to manifest more reactivity to the presence of an observer than others. A "personality" variable such as guardedness might be correlated with degree of reactivity. For example, scores on the K scale of the MMPI (or other comparable tests) might be related to the effects of being observed in a natural setting.

The literature also suggests that age is correlated with reactivity. Several authors (Barker and Wright, 1955; Polansky, et al., 1949) have suggested that younger children are less self-conscious and thereby less subject to reactive effects than older children. The Martin, et al. (1971) study also suggests that sex might be an important factor accounting for different levels of reactivity. Experiments are needed which compare these individual difference variables in the natural setting with naturalistic observation procedures.

Factor 3: Personal Attributes of the Observer

Evidence from semi-structured interviews suggests that reactive effects may also be contributed by the unique attributes of the observer. Different attributes of the observer may elicit different roles on the part of the subject, depending upon what might be appropriate given the observer's attribute. Rosenthal (1966) reports several such attributes that have been demonstrated to yield differential effects, including the age of the observer, sex, race, socio-economic class, and the observer's professional status (i.e., undergraduate observer vs. Ph.D. therapist). Martin, et al. (1971) also discovered that both the factors of age and sex of the observer had differential effects on the subjects being observed. Varying any of these dimensions parametrically would be relatively simple in investigating this problem in the natural setting.

Factor 4: Rationale for Observation

Another factor that may be important in accounting for reactivity is the amount of rationale given subjects for being observed. Whereas the Bales (1950) study found no differential reactivity of three levels of observer conspicuousness in a group-discussion setting, Smith (1957) found that nonparticipant observers aroused hostility and uncertainty among participating group members. Weick (1968) suggests that the discrepency in the results of these studies may be a function of different amounts of rationale for the presence of an observer. We hypothesize that a thorough rationale for being observed might be expected to reduce guardedness, anxiety, etc., and thereby reduce the reactivity.

Observer reactivity is a problem that cannot be easily dismissed for naturalistic observation. There is sufficient evidence to suggest that observer reactivity can seriously limit the generalizability of naturalistic observation data. Clearly, factors accounting for reactivity need to be investigated and solutions derived to minimize the effects of the observer on the observed.In the next section, we will describe how reactivity, in addition to posing a problem for generalizability, can also interact with and confound the dependent variable.

Observee Bias: Demand Characteristics, Response Sets, and Fakability

Reactivity to observation will always be a problem for naturalistic research, but it would be a relatively manageable one if we could assume it to be a relatively constant, noninteractive effect. That is, if we knew that the presence of an observer *reliably* reduced activity level or deviant behavior by 30%, for example, the problem would not be too damaging to research investigations involving groups of subjects. But what if the observee's reactivity to being observed interacts with the dependent variable under study?

Let us take the example of a treatment study on deviant children in which observations are taken prior to and after treatment. Prior to treatment, the appropriate thing for involved parents or teachers to do is to make their referred child appear to be deviant in order to justify treatment. The appropriate response at the end of treatment, on the other hand, is to make the child appear improved in order to justify the termination, please the therapist, etc. These are the demand characteristics of the situation. In this case, the reactivity to being observed is not constant or unidirectional, but interacts with and confounds the dependent variable. It is possible that any improvement we see in the children's behavior is simply the result of differential reactivity as a consequence of the demand characteristics of the situation. Now, let us suppose we employ a waiting list control group and collect observational data twice before beginning treatment and at the same interval as used for the treated group. This procedure provides an excellent pretest—post-test control for our treated group. But what of the demand characteristics of this procedure? On the first assessment, the involved parents or teachers will probably behave in the same general way as their counterparts in the treated group, but by the second observation they may be more desperate for help and even more concerned to present their child as highly deviant. Thus, simply as a result of the demand characteristics involved, we might expect our treatment group to show improvement while the control groups would show some deterioration.

We also may wish to compare our referred children with children who are presumably "normal" or at least not referred for psychological treatment. Once again, however, we might anticipate that parents recruited for "normative" research on "typical" families would be more inclined than our parents of referred children to present their wards as nondeviant or good. In other words, a response set of social desirability could be operative with this sample, making them less directly comparable to the referred sample.

These arguments would, of course, be even more persuasive if we were dealing with the observed behavior of the adults themselves. The foregoing observations on children assume, however, that the involved adults are capable of influencing children to appear relatively "deviant" or "normal" if they wish to do so (i.e., that observational data on children is potentially fakable by adult manipulation).

A study by Johnson and Lobitz (1972) directed at testing this assumption has just been completed. Twelve sets of parents with four- or five-year-old children were instructed to do everything in their power to make their children look "bad" or "deviant" on three days of a six-day home observation and to make their children look "good" or "nondeviant" on the remaining three days. Parents alternated from "good" to "bad" days in a counterbalanced design.

Four predictions were made regarding the behavior of both children and parents. During the "fake bad" periods, it was anticipated that, relative to the "fake good" periods, there would be: (a) more deviant child behaviors, (b) a lower ratio of compliance to parental commands, (c) more "negative" responses on the part of parents, and (d) more parental commands.

Predictions a, c, and d were confirmed at or beyond the .01 level of confidence. Only the child's compliance ratio failed to be responsive to the manipulation. It will be recalled from the section on reliability that this statistic is by far the least reliable and thus the least sensitive (statistically) to manipulation. These results, which demonstrate the fakability of naturalistic behavioral data, indicate that this kind of data may *potentially* be confounded by demand characteristics and/or response sets.

We are aware of only one other study involving naturalistic observation which helps demonstrate this problem (Horton, et al., 1972). This study involved one teacher who was under the instruction of a "master" teacher for the purpose of raising her classroom approval behavior. She was observed, without her knowledge, by students in the class. The results clearly showed that her approval behavior was at a much higher rate when she was being observed by the "master" teacher than when she was not being observed. Generalization from overtly observed periods to periods of covert observation was very minimal indeed. More generalization was found when the "master" teacher's presence in the classroom was put on a more random schedule. This study is not completely analogous to most naturalistic research because, in this case, the observer and trainer were the same person, and the study is limited in generalizability because of the N = 1 design. Yet, in most cases the observed are aware that the collected observational data will be seen by the therapist, teacher, or researcher, and if the problem exists for one subject, it is a potential problem for all subjects. *Observee* bias is really a special case of subject reactivity to observation. Thus, the potential solutions outlined in the previous section apply here as well. In general, we suspect that observation procedures which are relatively unobtrusive and which allow for relatively long periods of adaptation will yield less reactivity and *observee* bias.

Validity of Naturalistic Behavioral Data

Just as behaviorists have ignored the requirement of classical reliability in their data, they have also neglected to give any systematic attention to the concept of validity. Most research investigations in the behavior modification literature which have employed observational methods have relied on behavior sampling in only one narrowly circumscribed situation with no evidence that the observed behavior was representative of the subject's action in other stimulus situations. In addition, behaviorists have largely failed to show that the obtained scores on behavioral dimensions bear any relationship to scores obtained on the same dimensions by different measurement procedures. This fact calls into serious question the *validity* of any of this research where the purpose has been to generalize beyond the peculiar circumstances of the narrowly defined assessment situation. Of course, the methodological problems we have presented thus far all pose threats to the validity of the behavioral scores obtained. But, we would argue that even if all these problems could somehow be magically solved, the requirement for some form of convergent *validity* would still be essential. As with reliability, there are many different methods of validation, but as Campbell and Fiske (1959) point out:

> Validation is typically convergent; a confirmation by independent measurement procedures. Independence

> of methods is a common denominator among the major types of validity (excepting content validity) insofar as they are to be distinguished from reliability. . . . Reliability is the agreement between two efforts to measure the same trait through maximally similar methods. Validity is represented in the agreement between two attempts to measure the same trait through maximally different methods.

Thus, convergent validity is established when two dissimilar methods of measuring the same variable yield similar or correlated results. Predictive validity is established when the measure of a behavioral dimension correlates with a criterion established by a dissimilar measurement instrument.

With only a few exceptions, behaviorists have restricted themselves to face or content validity. And, of course, it must be admitted that the face validity of narrowly defined behavioral variables is often quite persuasive. This is particularly true in cases where the behavioral dimension under study has *very* narrow breadth or "band width." After all, a behaviorist might argue, what can be a more valid measure of the rate of a child's hitting in the classroom than a straightforward, accurate count of that hitting. While this argument is persuasive, two counter arguments must be considered. First, because of all of the methodological problems we have presented thus far, one can never be certain that the observed rates during a limited observation period are completely valid or generalizable even to very similar stimulus situations. While many of the problems we have outlined can be solved and others attenuated, it is unlikely that all of them will ever be completely eliminated. Second, is it not still of consequence to know whether our estimates of behavior rate have any relationship to other important and logically related external variables? Is it not important, for example, to know whether or not the teacher and classmates of an observed high-rate hitter perceive this child as a hitter? It does seem important to us, particularly for practical clinical purposes, since we know that people's perceptions of other persons' behavior often have more to do with the way they treat those persons than with the actual behavior. The need for establishing some form of convergent validation becomes even more profound as the behavioral dimensions we deal with increase in band width. As we begin to talk about such broad categories as appropriate vs. inappropriate behavior (e.g., Gelfand, et al., 1967), deviant vs. nondeviant behaviors in children (e.g., Patterson, et al., 1969; Johnson, et al., in press), or friendly vs. unfriendly behaviors (e.g., Raush, 1965), we are labeling broader behavioral dimensions. At this level we are dealing with constructs, whether we like to admit it or not, and the importance of establishing the validity of these constructs becomes crucial. In most cases, these broad behavior categories have been made up of a collection of more discrete behavior categories and, in general, the investigators involved have simply divided behaviors into appropriate-inappropriate or deviant-nondeviant on a purely a priori basis. While the categorizations often make a good deal of sense, i.e., have face validity, this hardly seems a completely satisfactory procedure for the development of a science of behavior.

We have had to face this problem in our own research, where we have sought to combine the observed rates of certain coded behaviors and come up with scores reflecting certain behavioral dimensions. The most central dimension in this research has been the "total deviant behavior score" to which we have repeatedly referred in this chapter. Let us outline here the procedures we have used to explore the validity of this score. Although we had a fairly good idea of which child behaviors would be viewed as "deviant" or "bad" in this culture, we attempted to enhance the consensual face validity of this score by asking parents of the "normal" children we observed to rate the relative deviancy of each of the codes we use in our research. Thus, in our sample of 33 families of four- and five-year-old children, we asked each parent to read a simplified version of our coding manual and characterize each behavior on a three-point scale from "clearly deviant" to "clearly nondeviant and pleasing." We established an arbitrary cut-off score and characterized any behavior above this cut-off as deviant. This resulted in a list of 15 deviant behaviors out of a total of 35 codes. The second step in validating this score and our implicit deviant-nondeviant dimension was presented in a study by Adkins and Johnson (1972). We had already divided our 35 codes into positive, negative, and neutral consequences. This categorization was done on a purely a priori basis with some help from the data provided by Patterson and Cobb (1971) on the function of some of these codes for eliciting and maintaning children's behavior. We reasoned that behaviors which parents viewed as more deviant would receive relatively more negative consequences than would behaviors viewed as less deviant. To test this hypothesis we simply rank ordered each behavior, first by the mean parental verbal report score obtained and second by the mean proportion of negative consequences the behavior received from family members. The results of this procedure are presented in Table 1. Not all 35 behaviors are included in this analysis, and the complex reasons for this outcome can more parsimoniously be explained in a footnote.[5] In any case, the Spearman Rank Order Cor-

Table 1 Coded Behaviors as Ranked by Two Methods: Parental Ratings and Negative Social Consequences*

Behavior Rank by Parental Rating	Behavior Rank by Proportion of Negative Consequences	Mean Parent Rating for Behavior	Proportion of Negative Consequences to Behavior
1 Whine	13	1.056	.125
2 Physical Negative	2	1.074	.527
4 Destructive	8	1.204	.352
4 Tease	5	1.204	.382
4 Smart Talk	4	1.204	.390
6 Aversive Command	3	1.208	.428
7 Noncompliance	12	1.278	.175
8 High Rate	16	1.307	.064
9 Ignore	11	1.370	.205
10 Yell	10	1.537	.215
11 Demand Attention	15	1.611	.083
12 Negativism	6	1.685	.375
13 Command Negative	1	1.833	.569
14 Disapproval	9	1.870	.235
15 Cry	14	1.962	.097
16 Indulgence	22	2.093	.027
17 Command Prime	27.5	2.132	.000
18 Receive	18	2.222	.052
19 Talk	23	2.278	.020
20 Command	7	2.296	.355
21 Attention	25	2.556	.013
22 Touch	20	2.648	.043
23 Independent Activity	26	2.704	.005
24 Physical Positive	21	2.741	.034
25 Comply	17	2.759	.053
26 Laugh	19	2.778	.044
27 Nonverbal Interaction	24	2.833	.012
28 Approval	27.5	2.926	.000

*Spearman rank-order correlation between columns 1 and 2 = .73 ($p < .01$).

relation between the two methods of characterizing behaviors on the deviant-nondeviant dimension was .73. This was an encouraging finding, but we noticed that the most dramatic exceptions to a more perfect agreement between the two methods involved the reasonable command codes (Command Positive and Command Negative). These codes are used when the child reasonably asks someone to do something (positive command) or not to do something (negative command). Naturally, most parents felt that these innocuous responses were nondeviant. But, behaviorally, people do not always do what they are asked to by a four- or five-year-old child, and since noncompliance was coded as a negative consequence, it seemed that this artifact of our characterization might have artifically lowered the correlation coefficient. By eliminating these two command categories from the calculation, the correlation coefficient was raised to .81.

The third piece of evidence for the validity of the deviant behavior score comes from the Johnson and Lobitz (1972) study already reviewed in the previous section. In this study, parents were asked to make their children look "good" or "nondeviant" for half of the observations and "bad" or "deviant" on the other half. They were *not* told how to accomplish this, nor were they told what behaviors were considered "bad" or "deviant." The fact that the deviant behavior score was consistently and significantly higher on the "bad" days lends further evidence for the construct validity of the score.

While evidence for the convergent or predictive validity of behavioral data is difficult to find in the literature, there are some encouraging exceptions to this general lack of data. Patterson and Reid (1971), for example, found an average correlation of .63 (p .05) between parents' observations of their children's low-rate referral symptoms on a given day and the trained observer's tally of targeted deviant behaviors on that day. Several studies have found significant realtionships between academic achievement and behavioral *ratings* of children in the classroom (Meyers, et al., 1968; D'Heurle, et al., 1959; Hughes, 1968). The data base of these studies is somewhat different from that currently employed by most behaviorists because they involve *ratings* by observers on relatively broad dimensions, as opposed to behavior rate counts. For example, dimensions used in these studies included "coping strength," defined as ability to attend to reading tests while being subjected to delayed auditory feedback (Hughes, 1968), or "persistence," defined as ". . . uses time constructively and to good purpose; stays with work until finished" (D'Heurle, et al., 1959). Nevertheless, these studies demonstrate the potential for behavioral observation data to provide evidence of predictive validity. Two other studies (Cobb, 1969; Lahaderne, 1968) have yielded similar predictive validity findings based on behavioral rate data. Lahaderne (1968) found that attending behavior, as observed over a two-month period, provided correlations ranging from .39 to .51 with various standard tests of achievement. Even with intelligence level controlled, significant correlations between attending behavior and achievement were found. Cobb (1969) obtained similar results in correlating various behavior rate scores with arithmetic achievement, but found no significant relationship between the behavior scores and achievement in spelling and reading. These predictive validity studies are very important to the development of the field as they suggest that manipulation of behavioral variables may well result in productive changes in academic achievement.

In our own laboratory, we are exploring the convergent validity of naturalistic behavioral data by relating it to measures on similar dimensions in the laboratory which include: (a) parent and child interaction behavior in standard stimulus situations similar to those employed by Wahler (1967) and Johnson and Brown (1969), (b) parent behavior in response to standard stimulus audio tapes similar in design to those used by Rothbart and Maccoby (1966) and parent behavior in standardized tasks similar to those used by Berberich (1970), and (c) parent attitude and behavior rating measures on their children. Unfortunately, at this writing, most of this data has not been completely analyzed, but an overall report of this research will be forthcoming. A recent dissertation by Martin (1971), however, was devoted to studying the relationships between parent behavior in the home and parent behavior in analogue situations. By and large, the results of this research indicated no systematic relationships between the two measures. The same general findings for parents' responses to deviant and nondeviant behavior were replicated in the naturalistic and the analogue data, but correlations relating individual parental behavior in one setting with that in the other were generally nonsignificant. We do not know, of course, which, if either, of the measures represents "truth," but this study underlines the importance of seriously questioning the assumptions usually made in any analogue or modified naturalistic research. As Martin (1971) points out, these negative results are very representative of findings in other investigations where naturalistic behavior data has been compared to data collected in more artificial analogue conditions (e.g., see Fawl, 1963; Gump and Kounin, 1960; Chapanis, 1967).

Before closing this section on validity, we would like to briefly take note of the efforts of Cronbach and his associates to reconceptualize the issues of observer agreement, reliability, and validity as parts of the broader concepts of generalizability. A full elaboration of generalizability theory goes far beyond the purposes of this chapter, and the interested reader is referred to several primary and secondary sources for a more complete presentation of this model (e.g., Cronbach, et al., 1963; Rajaratnam, et al., 1965; Gleser, et al., 1965; Wiggins, in press). According to this view of generalizability, the concerns of observer agreement, reliability, and validity all boil down to a concern for the extent to which an obtained score is generalizable to the "universe" to which the researcher wishes the score to apply. Once an investigator is able to specify this "universe," he should be able to specify and test the relevant sources of possible threat to generalizability. In a typical naturalistic observational study, for example, we would usually at least want to know the generalizability of data across (a) observers, (b) occasions in the same setting, and (c) settings. Through the generalizability model, each of these sources of variance could be explored in a factorial design and their contribution analyzed within an analysis of variance model. This model is particularly appealing because it provides for simultaneous assessment of the extent of various sources of "error" which could limit generalizability. In spite of the advantages of this factorial model, there are few precedents for its use. This is probably more the result of practical problems rather than a resistance to this intellectually appealing and theoretically sound model. Even if one were to restrict oneself to the three sources of variance outlined above, the resulting study would, for most useful purposes, be a formidable project, indeed. Projects of this kind appear to us, however, to be well worth doing, and we can probably expect to see more investigations which employ this generalizability model.

It should be pointed out that the generalizability study just outlined does not really speak to the traditional validity requirement as succinctly defined by Campbell and Fiske (1959): "Validity is represented in the agreement between two attempts to measure the same trait through maximally different methods." As stated earlier, to fulfill this requirement, one must provide evidence of some form of convergent validity by the use of methods other than direct behavioral observation. The generalizability model can, theoretically, handle any factor of this type under the heading of methods or "conditions," but the analysis of variance model employed requires a factorial design. Thus, it would seem extremely difficult and sometimes impossible to integrate factorially other methods of testing or rating in a design which encompassed the three variables outlined above: observers, occasions, and settings. As a result of these considerations, we question the extent to which *one* generalizability study, at least in this area of research, can fulfill all the requirements of observer agreement, validity, and reliability which we view as so important. Rather, it is likely that multiple analyses will still be necessary to sufficiently establish all of the methodological requirements we have outlined for naturalistic observational data. These multiple analyses may, of course, involve analyses of variance in a generalizability model or correlational analyses as traditionally employed.

Krantz (1971) points out that the basic controversy over group vs. individual subject designs has contributed largely to the development of the mutual isolation of operant and nonoperant psychology. Since the measurement of reliability and convergent validity is typically based on correlations across a group of subjects, the operant psychologist may feel that these are alien concepts which have no relevance for his research. We would dispute this view on the following logical grounds. Reliability involves the requirement for consistency in measurement and without some minimal level of such consistency, there can be no demonstration of functional relationships between the dependent variable and the independent variable. Efforts are currently underway to discover statistical procedures for establishing reliability estimates for the single case (e.g., see Jones, 1972). Any operant study which involves repeating manipulative procedures on more than one subject can be used for reliability assessment by traditional methods. Once such reliability is established, either for the individual case or for a group, we can be much more confident in the data and its meaning. Validity involves the requirement of convergence among different methods in measuring the same behavioral dimension. Where the validity of a measurement procedure has been previously established for a group, we can use it with more confidence in each individual case. Where it has not, it is still possible to explore for convergence in a single case. We can simply see, for example, if the child who shows high rates of aggressive behavior is perceived as aggressive by significant others. This procedure may be done with some precision if normative data is available on the measures used in the single case. Thus, with normative data available one can explore the position of the single case on the distribution of each measurement instrument. One could see, for example, if the child who is perceived to be among the top five percent in aggressiveness actually shows aggressive behavior at a rate higher than 95% of his peers. The requirements of reliability and validity are logically sound ones which transcend experimental method and means of calculation.

These methodological issues, like all others presented in this chapter, are highly relevant for behavioral research, even though they may at first seem alien to it as the products of rival schools of thought. It has been our argument that the requirements of sound methodology transcend "schools" and that the time has come for us to attend to any variables which threaten the quality, generalizability, or meaningfulness of our data. Behavioral data is the most central commonality and critical contribution of all behavior modification research. The behaviorists' contribution to the science of human behavior and to solutions of human problems will largely rest on the quality of this data.

Footnotes

1. The preparation of this manuscript and the research reported therein was supported by research grant MH 19633-01 from the National Institute of Mental Health. The writers would like to thank their many colleagues who contributed critical reviews of this manuscript: Robyn Dawes, Lewis Goldberg, Richard Jones, Gerald Patterson, John Reid, Carl Skindrud, and Geoffrey White.

2. The authors would like to credit Lee Sechrest for first suggesting this illustrative example.

3. The authors would like to credit Donald Hartman for clarifying this as the appropriate procedure for establishing the level of agreement to be expected by chance.

4. For additional justification of the use of this statistical procedure for problems of this kind, see Wiggins (in press).

5. Several behaviors which are used in the coding system are not included in the present analysis. The behaviors Humiliate and Dependency could not be included because they did not occur in the behavioral sample. Repeated noncompliance and temper tantrums were not used on the verbal report scale because they are subsumed in other categories (i.e., tantrums are defined as simultaneous occurrences of three or more of the following—Physical Negative, Destructiveness, Crying, Yelling, etc.). Nonresponding of the child was excluded *post hoc* because it was clear that parents were responding to this item as ignor-

ing rather than mere nonresponse to ongoing activity (i.e., it was a poorly written item).

References

Adkins, D. A. and Johnson, S. M. An empirical approach to identifying deviant behavior in children. Paper presented at the Western Psychological Association Convention, Portland, Oregon, April 1972.

Azrin, N. H., Holz, W., Ulrich, R., and Goldiamond, I. The control of the content of conversation through reinforcement. *Journal of the Experimental Analysis of Behavior*, 1961, *4*, 25-30.

Baer, D. M., Wolf, M. M., and Risley, T. R. Some current dimensions of applied behavior analysis. *Journal of Applied Behavior Analysis*, 1968, *1*, 91-97.

Bales, D. F. *Interaction process analysis*. Cambridge: Addison-Wesley, 1950.

Barber, T. X. and Silver, M. J. Fact, fiction, and the experimental bias effect. *Psychological Bulletin Monograph*, 1968, *70*, No. 6, Part II, 1-29.

Barker, R. G. and Wright, H. F. *Midwest and its children: The psychological ecology of an American town.* New York: Row, Peterson, 1955.

Bechtel, R. B. The study of man: Human movement and architecture. *Transaction*, 1967, *4*, 53-56.

Berberich, J. Adult child interactions: I. Correctness of a "child" as a positive reinforcer for the behavior of adults. Unpublished manuscript, University of Washington, 1970.

Bernal, M. E., Gibson, D. M., William, D. E., and Pesses, D. I. A device for recording automatic audio tape recording. *Journal of Applied Behavior Analysis*, 1971, *4*, 151-156.

Bijou, S. W., Peterson, R. F., and Ault, M. H. A method to integrate descriptive and experimental field studies at the level of data and empirical concepts. *Journal of Applied Behavioral Analysis,* 1968, *1*, 175-191.

Bolstad, O. D. and Johnson, S. M. Self-regulation in the modification of disruptive classroom behavior. *Journal of Applied Behavior Analysis*, in press.

Browning, R. M. and Stover, D. O. *Behavior modification in child treatment: An experimental and clinical approach*. Chicago: Aldine-Atherton, Inc., 1971.

Campbell, D. T. and Fiske, D. Convergent and discriminant validation by the multi-trait, multi-method matrix. *Psychological Bulletin*, 1959, 56, 81-105.

Campbell, D. T. and Stanley, J. C. *Experimental and quasi-experimental designs for research.* Chicago: Rand McNally, 1966.

Chapanis, A. The relevance of laboratory studies to preschool situations. *Ergonomics*, 1967, *10*, 557-577.

Clairborn, W. L. Expectancy effects in the classroom: A failure to replicate. *Journal of Educational Psychology*, 1969, *60*, 377-383.

Cobb, J. A. The relationship of observable classroom behaviors to achievement of fourth grade pupils. Unpublished doctoral dissertation, University of Oregon, Eugene, 1969.

Cronbach, L. J., Rajaratnam, N., and Gleser, G. C. Theory of generalizability: Liberalization of reliability theory. *British Journal of Statistical Psychology,* 1963, *16*, 137-163.

DeMaster, B. and Reid, J. B. Effects of feedback procedures in maintaining observer reliability. Oregon Research Institute, Eugene, in preparation.

D'Heurle, A., Mellinger, J. C., and Haggard, E. A. Personality, intellectual, and achievement patterns in gifted children. *Psychological Monographs: General and Applied,* 1959, *73,* 13, Whole No. 483.

Eyberg, S. An outcome study of child-family intervention: The effects of contingency contracting and order of treated problems. Unpublished doctoral dissertation, University of Oregon, Eugene, 1972.

Fawl, C. Disturbances experienced by children in their natural habitats. In R. G. Barker (Ed.), *The stream of behavior.* New York: Appleton-Century-Crofts, 1963. Pp. 99-126.

Fode, K. L. The effect of non-visual and non-verbal interaction on experimenter bias. Unpublished master's thesis, University of North Dakota, 1960.

Fode, K. L. The effect of experimenters' and subjects' anxiety and social desirability on experimenter outcome bias. Unpublished doctoral dissertation, University of North Dakota, 1965.

Gelfand, D. M., Gelfand, S., and Dobson, W. R. Unprogrammed reinforcement of patients' behavior in a mental hospital. *Behavior Research and Therapy*, 1967, *5*, 201-207.

Gleser, G. C., Cronbach, L. J., and Rajaratnam, N. Generalizability of scores influenced by multiple sources of variance. *Psychometrika*, 1965, *30*, 395-418.

Guilford, J. P. *Psychometric methods.* New York: McGraw-Hill, 1954.

Gump, R. and Kounin, J. Issues raised by ecological and "classic" research efforts. *Merrill-Palmer Quarterly*, 1960, *6*, 145-152.

Harris, A. Observer effect on family interaction. Unpublished doctoral dissertation, University of Oregon, Eugene, 1969.

Hathaway, S. R. Some considerations relative to nondirective counseling as therapy. *Journal of Clinical Psychology*, 1948, *4*, 226-321.

Horton, G. O., Larson, J. L., and Maser, A. L. The generalized reduction of student teacher disapproval behavior. Unpublished manuscript, University of Oregon, Eugene, 1972.

Hughes, L. D. A study of the relationship of coping strength to self-control, school achievement, and general anxiety level in sixth grade pupils. *Dissertation Abstracts,* 1968, *28* (A) (10), 4001.

Johansson, S., Johnson, S. M., Martin, S., and Wahl, G. Compliance and noncompliance in young children: A behavioral analysis. Unpublished manuscript, University of Oregon, Eugene, 1971.

Johnson, S. M. and Brown, R. Producing behavior change in parents of disturbed children. *Journal of Child Psychology and Psychiatry*, 1969, *10*, 107-121.

Johnson, S. M. and Lobitz, G. Demand characteristics in naturalistic observation. Unpublished manuscript, University of Oregon, Eugene, 1972.

Johnson, S. M., Wahl, G., Martin, S., and Johansson, S. How deviant is the normal child: A behavioral analysis of the preschool child and his family. *Advances in Behavior Therapy,* in press.

Jones, R. R. Intraindividual stability of behavioral observations: Implications for evaluating behavior modification treatment programs. Paper presented at the meeting of the Western Psychological Association, Portland, Oregon, April 1972.

Karpowitz, D. Stimulus control in family interaction sequences as observed in the naturalistic setting of the home. Unpublished doctoral dissertation, University of Oregon, Eugene, 1972.

Kass, R. E. and O'Leary, K. D. The effects of observer bias in field-experimental settings. Paper presented at a symposium entitled "Behavior Analysis in Education," University of Kansas, Lawrence, April 1970.

Kennedy, J. L. and Uphoff, H. F. Experiments on the nature of extra-sensory perception: III. The recording error criticism of extra-change scores. *Journal of Parapsychology*, 1939, *3*, 226-245.

Kent, R. The human observer: An imperfect cumulative recorder. Paper presented at the Fourth Banff Conference on Behavior Modification, Banff, Alberta, Canada, March 1972.

Krantz, D. L. The separate worlds of operant and nonoperant psychology. *Journal of Applied Behavior Analysis*, 1971, *4*, 61-70.

Lahaderne, H. M. Attitudinal and intellectual correlates of attention: A study of four sixth-grade classrooms. *Journal of Educational Psychology*, 1968, *59*, 320-324.

Littman, R., Pierce-Jones, J., and Stern, T. Child-parent activities in the natural setting of the home: Results of a methodological pilot study. Unpublished manuscript, University of Oregon, Eugene, 1957.

Lobitz, G. and Johnson, S. M. Normal versus deviant—Fact or fantasy? Paper presented at the Western Psychological Association Convention, Portland, Oregon, April 1972.

Martin, M. F., Gelfand, D. M., and Hartmann, D. P. Effects of adult and peer observers on boys' and girls' responses to an aggressive model. *Child Development*, 1971, *42*, 1271-1275.

Martin, S. The comparability of behavioral data in laboratory and natural settings. Unpublished doctoral dissertation, University of Oregon, Eugene, 1971.

Meyers, C. E., Attwell, A. A., and Orpet, R. E. Prediction of fifth grade achievement from kindergarten test and rating data. *Educational and Psychological Measurement*, 1968, *28*, 457-463.

Mischel, W. *Personality and assessment.* New York: Wiley, 1968.

O'Conner, R. D. Modification of social withdrawal through symbolic modeling. *Journal of Applied Behavior Analysis,* 1969, *2*, 15-22.

Olson, W. The incidence of nervous habits in children. *Journal of Abnormal and Social Psychology*, 1930-31, *35*, 75-92.

Patterson, G. R. and Cobb, J. A. A dyadic analysis of "aggressive" behaviors. In J. P. Hill (Ed.), *Proceedings of the Fifth Annual Minnesota Symposia on Child Psychology,* Vol. V. Minneapolis: University of Minnesota, 1971.

Patterson, G. R. and Cobb, J. A. Stimulus control for classes of noxious behaviors. Paper presented at the University of Iowa, May 1971, Symposium, "The control of aggression: Implications from basic research." J. F. Knutson (Ed.). Aldine-Atherton, Inc., 1972, in press.

Patterson, G. R., Cobb, J. A., and Ray, R. S. A social engineering technology for retraining the families of aggressive boys. In H. E. Adams and L. Unikel (Eds.), *Issues and trends in behavior therapy*. Springfield, Ill.: Charles C. Thomas, in press.

Patterson, G. R. and Harris, A. Some methodological considerations for observation procedures. Paper presented at the meeting of the American Psychological Association, San Francisco, September 1968.

Patterson, G. R., Ray, R. S., and Shaw, D. A. Direct intervention in families of deviant children. *Oregon Research Bulletin*, 1969, *8*.

Patterson, G. R., Ray, R. S., Shaw, D. A., and Cobb, J. A. Manual for coding family interactions. Document No. 01234, sixth revision, 1969. Available from ASIS National Auxiliary Publications

Service, c/o CCM Information Service, Inc., 909 Third Ave., New York, N. Y. 10022.

Patterson, G. R. and Reid, J. B. Reciprocity and coercion: Two facets of social systems. In C. Neuringer and J. Michael (Eds.), *Behavior modification in clinical psychology*. New York: Appleton-Century-Crofts, 1970.

Patterson, G. R. and Reid, J. B. Family intervention in the homes of aggressive boys: A replication. Paper presented at the American Psychological Association Convention, Washington, D. C., 1971.

Peine, H. A. Behavioral recording by parents and its resultant consequences. Unpublished master's thesis, University of Utah, 1970.

Pfungst, O. *Clever Hans: A contribution to experimental, animal, and human psychology* (Translated by C. L. Rahn). New York: Holt, 1911.

Polansky, N., Freeman, W., Horowitz, M., Irwin, L., Papanis, N., Rappaport, D., and Whaley, F. Problems of interpersonal relations in research on groups. *Human Relations*, 1949, *2*, 281-291.

Purcell, K. and Brady, K. Adaptation to the invasion of privacy: Monitoring behavior with a miniature radio transmitter. *Merrill-Palmer Quarterly*, 1965, *12*, 242-254.

Rajaratnam, N., Cronbach, L. J., and Gleser, G. C. Generalizability of stratified-parallel tests. *Psychometrika*, 1965, *30*, 39-56.

Rapp, D. W. Detection of observer bias in the written record. Cited in R. Rosenthal, *Experimenter effects in behavioral research.* New York: Appleton-Century-Crofts, 1966.

Rausch, H. L. Interaction sequences. *Journal of Personality and Social Therapy*, 1965, *2*, 487-499.

Reid, J. B. Reciprocity in family interaction. Unpublished doctoral dissertation, University of Oregon, Eugene, 1967.

Reid, J. B. Reliability assessment of observation data: A possible methodological problem. *Child Development*, 1970, *41*, 1143-1150.

Roberts, R. R. and Renzaglia, G. A. The influence of tape recording on counseling. *Journal of Counseling Psychology*, 1965, *12*, 10-16.

Romanczyk, R. G., Kent, R. W., Diament, C., and O'Leary, K. D. Measuring the reliability of observational data: A reactive process. Paper presented at the Second Annual Symposium on Behavioral Analysis, Lawrence, Kansas, May 1971.

Rosenthal, R. On the social psychology of the psychological experiment: The experimenter's hypothesis as unintended determinant of experimental results. *American Scientist*, 1963, *51*, 268-283.

Rosenthal, R. *Experimenter effects in behavioral research.* New York: Appleton-Century-Crofts, 1966.

Rosenthal, R. and Fode, K. L. The effect of experimenter bias on the performance of the albino rat. *Behavior Science,* 1963, *8*, 183-189.

Rosenthal, R., Friedman, C. J., Johnson, C. A., Fode, K. L., Schill, T. R., White, C. R., and Vikan, L. L. Variables affecting experimenter bias in a group situation. *Genetic Psychology Monographs*, 1964, *70*, 271-296.

Rosenthal, R. and Jacobsen, L. Teacher's expectancies: Determinants of pupils IQ gains. *Psychological Reports,* 1966, *19*, 115-118.

Rosenthal, R. and Lawson, R. A longitudinal study of the effects of experimenter bias on the operant learning of laboratory rats. *Journal of Psychiatric Research*, 1964, *2*, 61-72.

Rosenthal, R., Persinger, G. W., Vikan-Kline, L. E., and Mulry, R. C. The role of the research assistant in the mediation of experimenter bias. *Journal of Personality*, 1963, *31*, 313-335.

Rothbart, M. and Maccoby, E. Parents' differential reaction to sons and daughters. *Journal of Personality and Social Psychology*, 1966, *4*, 237-243.

Scott, P., Burton, R. V., and Yarrow, M. Social reinforcement under natural conditions. *Child Development*, 1967, *38*, 53-63.

Sheffield, F. D., Kaufman, R. S., and Rhine, J. B. A PK experiment at Yale starts a controversy. *Journal of American Social and Psychical Research*, 1952, *46*, 111-117.

Skindrud, K. An evaluation of observer bias in experimental-field studies of social interaction. Unpublished doctoral dissertation, University of Oregon, Eugene, 1972.

Smith, E. E. Effects of threat induced by ambiguous role expectations on defensiveness and productivity in small groups. *Dissertation Abstracts*, 1957, *17*, 3104-3105.

Snow, E. E. Unfinished pygmalion. *Contemporary Psychology*, 1969, *14*, 197-199.

Soskin, W. F. and John, V. P. The study of spontaneous talk. In R. G. Barker (Ed.), *The stream of behavior*. New York: Appleton-Century-Crofts, 1963. Pp. 228-281.

Taplin, P. S. and Reid, J. B. Effects of instructional set and experimental influence on observer reliability. Oregon Research Institute, Eugene, in preparation.

Thomas, D. R., Becker, W. C., and Armstrong, M. Production and elimination of disruptive classroom behavior by systematically varying teacher's behavior. *Journal of Applied Behavior Analysis,* 1968, *1*, 35-45.

Thorndike, R. L. Pygmalion in the classroom: A review. *Teacher College Record*, 1969, *70*, 805-807.

Verplanck, N. S. The control and the content in conversation: Reinforcement of statements of opinion. *Journal of Abnormal and Social Psychology*, 1955, *51*, 668-676.

Wahl, G., Johnson, S. M., Martin, S., and Johansson, S. An operant analysis of child-family interaction. *Behavior Therapy*, in press.

Wahler, R. G. Child-child interactions in free field settings: Some experimental analyses. *Journal of Experimental Child Psychology*, 1967, *5*, 278-293.

Walker, H. M., Johnson, S. M., and Hops, H. Generalization and maintenance of classroom treatment effects. Unpublished manuscript, University of Oregon, Eugene, 1972.

Webb, E. J., Campbell, D. T., Schwartz, R. D., and Sechrest, L. *Unobtrusive measures: A survey of non-reactive research in the social sciences.* Chicago: Rand McNally, 1966.

Weick, K. E. Systematic observational methods. In G. Lindsey and E. Aronson (Eds.), *The handbook of social psychology*, 1968, *2*, 357-451.

White, G. D. Effects of observer presence on mother and child behavior. Unpublished doctoral dissertation, University of Oregon, September 1972.

Wiggins, J. S. *Personality and prediction: Principles of personality assessment.* Reading, Mass.: Addison-Wesley, in press.

Behavior Modification for Social Action: Research Tactics and Problems[1,2]

2

K. Daniel O'Leary and Ronald Kent

Reversibility: The Strength or Weakness of Behavior Modification

During the decade of the Sixties clear reversals of experimental effects in behavior modification were reinforced by the academic and scientific community as evidence of the clarity of our experimental effects. For example, one could start a token reinforcement program and see an increase in appropriate classroom or ward behavior and upon withdrawal of the token program see a decrease in appropriate behavior. Similarly, one could increase positive forms of teacher attention and then upon a decrease in teacher attention to appropriate classroom behavior, the appropriate classroom behavior would decrease. In both instances reversals of effects could be brought about by a change in experimental manipulation. As clear reversals were obtained by behavior modifiers, the fervor of the behavioral approach grew more and more intense, and investigators patted one another on the back singing the praises of behavior modification. Until recently much of the work in behavior modification, particularly within an operant framework, has relied heavily, if not almost exclusively, on reversal or single subject designs. For example, a perusal of journals like *Journal of Applied Behavior Analysis* or *Behavior Research and Therapy* will document that the preponderance of research in the area of classroom management has involved reversal designs. The strength of reversal and single subject designs has been expounded elsewhere on a number of occasions, and Sidman's (1960) arguments in particular have been heeded by many investigators in applied behavior analysis. Following Sidman's advice, behavior modifiers have focused on control of variables for a single subject rather than producing differences between groups. Certainly, the effectiveness of procedures such as token reinforcement programs and contingent teacher attention has been convincingly demonstrated with reversal designs (O'Leary and O'Leary, 1972).

Investigators who do not share the conceptual framework of the behavior modification approach, however, may view with disdain the clear reversibility evidenced in many studies. Instead they may comment disparagingly as follows:

> "You are producing transient changes in behavior."
>
> "You have limited behavior change which fails to generalize across time and situations."
>
> "You are not getting to the heart (root) of the problem; had you, clearly you would not have had such a reversal effect."

In fact, commitment to single subject and particularly reversal designs may well be forcing investigators to look at behavior change procedures which are limited in scope and of short-lived effectiveness. For example, if one is using a reversal design he cannot build programs and demonstrate effects which are long-lived for if the effects are long-lived, he clearly would not obtain a reversal. Most importantly, ABAB or reversal designs pursued singularly may well prompt colleagues who do not share our conceptual framework to say, "I told you so. You are focusing on variables of minor social consequence." Five to seven years ago it was somewhat startling to show that regressed crawling or operant crying could be instated, eliminated, and reinstated with social attention because of the implications such manipulations had for a host of interventions. Similarly it was rather dramatic to show how sharply disruptive behavior could be reduced in a classroom. However, today we need to demonstrate that our procedures have effects which are long lasting and which can be implemented practically. The import of the factors which have been so clearly isolated in reversal and single subject studies used in the past decade should not be lessened. Rather, at this point in the evolution of behavior modification research, the need to turn to alternative designs for different questions than those addressed in the past is strong. More specifically, for a number of problems there is a need to utilize group designs with various control groups in which treatment or aspects of a treatment being implemented are specified.

In the past, some behavior modifiers have responded to questions about the longevity of treatment programs with the following answer: "The question is meaningless. If you believe in behavioral principles, the program will have a lasting effect only as long as the people in the environment to which my subject returns reinforce the behavior which I taught." For some this answer sufficed—but it should not have. It should not have for such an answer renders efforts for long-term social change unimpressive and impractical.

We should be able to teach clients to use their verbal behavior (the things they say to themselves) to control their social behavior, e.g., to control their avoidance behaviors, to control their aggression, to control their nervous mannerisms. It seems that even if a client's spouse or friends were not reprogrammed, positive changes in a client would prompt positive reactions in others that would maintain his behavior. In fact, there does appear to be some replicable evidence that by utilizing a client's verbal skills, one can produce both long- and short-term changes in clients (Paul, 1966). In general, however, demonstrations that verbal skills can control significant social behavior are limited with adults and completely nonexistent with children. Because of this there is continued interest in the need for some reprogramming of the client's environment.

Given a behavioral framework with an emphasis on overt social skill and some manipulation of environment, the question concerning generalization could be, "Are you programming your clients well enough so that the natural environment, with *some* consultation from you, maintains the appropriate behavior of your client?" Stated differently, can you, with minimal reprogramming of the client's family, friends, or by using a half-way house, do better than treatment X, Y, or Z or a control group which receives no treatment? Behavioral scientists must certainly continue to be interested in clear demonstrations of experimental effects as evidenced using single subject designs, but politicians, hospital administrators, and mental hygiene officials are not likely to be strongly convinced by clear reversible effects seen in several classrooms, several wards, or several homes. Rather, in the long run they will be interested in remission rates, recidivism rates, and reincarceration figures. They will wish to know with what percentage of teachers and parents do manipulations work. Of additional interest is the relative cost of behavioral treatment compared to other treatments. Finally, they will wish to know how well these treatment effects are maintained by the agents of change (teachers, attendents, and parents) when consultants withdraw from the scene. These questions suggest the need for control groups and the need to initiate large scale research projects, both of which will be admittedly difficult to execute but of potential major social consequence.

Baer (1971) addressed the issue of need for control groups in a slightly different fashion. He stated that critics of behavior modification "should not have stopped arguing that the behaviors we remediated were only symptoms and not the basic reality of the problem." In brief, he argues that in one sense we can answer whether we have addressed the basic reality of the problem if we have achieved a "cure."

> That is, if you can make massive changes in behaviors of considerable social importance, there is then an objective real-world 'cure' to be measured. That cure can be measured in the behavior of the society which either continues to see the client as uncured, or else accepts him as appropriate. In the first case, society will continue to refer him for treatment; in the second case, it will not. (Baer, 1971, p. 363)

Whether the subject in Baer's example is cured or not in the sense that he is happy and productive is debatable. Remission rate is an extremely fallible criterion of success. However, at least by one criterion—the absence of being referred for treatment—the client appears cured. To establish whether or not utilization of behavioral principles can cure clients or educate children better than either no treatment or alternative modes of treatment, control groups are needed. As Baer put it in discussing the need for group designs,

> . . . the face logic of behavioral analysis (recently demonstrated in single subject designs) is not enough to establish its correctness. Now that it is on the brink of handling massive behavior modification problems with large numbers of children, it can test, rather than assert, the goodness of that logic. (p. 366)

For example, although generally powerful treatment effects are often seen using token reinforcement procedures, it is only within the past two years that data have accumulated which even begin to seriously address the problem of long-term effects of such programs in classrooms. A study of Walker and Buckley (in press) is probably the best in this regard. However, even in this study the children were observed for only a two-month follow-up period in which variants of the original token program were implemented to help maintain behavior during follow-up. That is, social and/or token reinforcement were continued systematically, and with these variants of the token program, subjects showed higher rates of appropriate behavior in follow-up than did controls. However, there was no significant change in academic behavior that could be attributed to the treatment. Since variants of the token program used during follow-up were not attempted before the major token program, it is not known if the major token program was critical to the change obtained in follow-up. Finally, a two-month follow-up is a rather short period to assess long-term effects. This follow-up data from the token classroom showed almost *full* maintenance of appropriate behavior for two months, yet according to teacher report, several children eight months later again exhibited relatively high rates of disruptive behavior.

These comments are not meant to detract from the importance of Walker and Buckley's work. Rather they emphasize that there are no clear-cut data indicating that token programs for "problem" children have long lasting effects. If significant changes in the behavior of large groups of children, teachers, and schools are to be made, these questions of long-range effectiveness must be answered. In the long run, the public controls the reinforcers. If behavioral procedures work, they must be evaluated relative to others to obtain reinforcers provided by society.

In addition to addressing questions of comparative and long-range effectiveness of programs, there is a need to address questions of generalizability across various program implementers, e.g., parents, teachers, or attendents. Many of the published studies to date have been "research-clinical" studies where it appears that *the effects obtained may be proportional to the immediate reinforcers available to the change agents and/or the investigator.* For example, many studies, particularly of the reversal or multiple baseline variety, employ credit to teachers, consultation money to the change agent, credit for in-service days, payment for change or maintenance in behavior, praise from the experimenter*, promise of authorship to the change agent, or promise of trips to meetings. Or the study may be an M.A. or Ph.D. thesis where commitment to get change is maximal. Such powerful incentives may help to demonstrate clear functional relations among variables; but where such incentives are absent the research findings may not always be obtained. For example, we know of failures of token systems, yet few are published. Also, teachers may react very differently to procedures such as contingent praise, time out, and daily report cards.

An example from a Stony Brook research project involving token reinforcement demonstrates the variability of teacher response to an incentive program. The effectiveness of a captain vs. teacher administered token system in which two teachers, each with

---

* Cossiart, et al. (in press), in an interesting study related to this issue, have shown that the change in the children's behavior in the classroom was related to the feedback and social reinforcement from the experimenter.

two classes, used both systems were compared. That is, either the teacher or an elected child-captain actually decided who should receive the tokens and in turn distributed them to the children. While the token programs were successful in all four classes, in one teacher's room both the teacher and the captain administered token programs were more effective in reducing disruptive behavior than in the other teacher's classes. Thus, there was an interaction with the treatment procedure and the teacher who implemented the program.

In addition to the need for producing effects with group designs in order that there be maximal social impact, group designs may be appropriate for a number of other reasons. A reversal may be inappropriate because of ethical reasons (e.g., with head banging). Further, it may be impossible to return to exactly the same base condition after an experimental program has been effected. As mentioned elsewhere (O'Leary and Drabman, 1971), even where reversals are carefully monitored (and most are not) the reversal may be quite different from the earlier condition.. Some factors such as rules may be impossible to reverse. For example, research involving rules is not very convincing where a teacher institutes classroom rules and then simply stops using them or modifies the rules drastically such that a child is reinforced for greatly different or even deviant behavior. In addition, testing the separate and combined effectiveness of rules paired with token reinforcement cannot be done unequivocally using a single subject design because of order or sequence effects (Kazdin, in press).

The need for addressing questions using various experimental strategies is particularly made apparent when one realizes that different effects may be observed depending upon the type of experimental design used. For example, Grice and Hunter (1964) and Willis (1969) have shown that different experimental strategies—within- vs. between-group designs—have led to different results in that type of design has interacted with reinforcement schedule. The following example provides an instance where a reversal or withdrawal of an experimental procedure might be particularly reactive in that the subject would be influenced across time in a deleterious way with a withdrawal or reversal of experimental procedure. If one repeatedly withdrew and reinstated a punishment procedure such as time-out from reinforcement, the effectiveness of the time-out might gradually decrease across time. On the other hand, had the time-out procedure been used in a group design for an equivalent amount of days that time-out was used in the individual subject design, the effect of time-out might be greatest in the group design.

Producing generalization also forces us to look carefully to group designs. In studies of generalization of effects using single subject designs (reversal or multiple baseline designs), one must assume or demonstrate that there is no change in the behavior observed during the control or base phase of a multiple baseline design. While in short-term studies with children no such change may occur, we have found in studies during the past two years that disruptive behavior decreased in the no token phase as well as the token phase of the day. In addition there is evidence that certain problem behaviors such as lack of concentration, fighting, and demanding adult attention tend to diminish with age (Shectman, 1971). Others, including Miller (1972) and Quay (1972), have also found a decrease in deviant behaviors across ages.

A related problem is that there is often a correlation among dependent measures as evidenced by the correlations among various measures of classroom disruptiveness (Werry and Quay, 1969). If one is addressing the problem of producing response generalization in a multiple baseline design, one must be able to demonstrate effects above and beyond the change resulting from the natural correlation between the target measures of interest. For example, if changing attentive behaviors also changes out-of-seat behaviors, this may simply be a demonstration that changing one behavior will perforce (because of the natural correlation between such variables) change the other behavior. That is, the observed change in the untreated behavior may not be due primarily to generalization of the treatment effect. Generalization of the treatment effect can be shown most clearly only if the two behaviors do *not* tend to show natural correlative changes.

Fortunately some behavioral researchers have or are now using control groups of various kinds. Probably one of the most important areas where behavior modification procedures will have a national impact is in the area of education of Head Start and Follow-Through children. In this case the use of comparison groups was prompted by the federal government's desire to evaluate various methods of teaching young children. Eighteen to twenty university based models to teach young children are now being compared ranging from the affective and cognitive approaches to the behavioral approaches represented by Bushells' Behavior Analysis Model and the Engelmann-Becker model. Preliminary data from thousands of children indicate the superiority of the two behavioral approaches over all others in bringing about academic change. While it is true that precise research demonstrating relationships among various teacher and child beahviors will not emanate from such research, this large-scale comparative research will have major social and political clout.

One of the potentially most important studies from a large-scale treatment vantage point is that of Gordon Paul at the University of Illinois. Paul is working in a state mental hospital with adult schizophrenic patients comparing the effectiveness of token reinforcement programs and social milieu programs. In the latter programs, reasons for behavior are discussed with the patient by group members, the responsibility of an individual's behavior toward the group is emphasized, and staff expectancies for normal behavior are made clear. Subjects were randomly assigned to treatments where the same staff implemented both the token reinforcement and milieu treatment, and both expeimental treatments were compared with an "untreated" state hospital control group. Specification of cost analyses and staff training are hallmarks of this study now nearing completion. Such group studies are obviously difficult to implement and involve a high risk in that significant effects across a several-year period may not occur. On the other hand, such research is of the variety now critically needed in the behavior modification area. If one or both of the treatments are more effective (token reinforcement or milieu treatment) than the control group both while the patient is in the hospital and when he returns home, this study should have strong social consequences for various hospital programs.

Patterson and his colleagues have compared their methods of dealing with aggressive boys with certain types of control groups. Wolf is now beginning research with random assignment of pre-delinquent boys to Achievement Place (See Chapter 10) and to other treatment facilities. In addition, we are starting a study where behavior modification procedures used by therapists working as consultants to parents and teachers will be evaluated in terms of the effectiveness in changing academic and social behavior of young school children. This work will compare the effectiveness of Ph.D. level consultants with control groups receiving no systematic treatment, and with Ph.D. level consultants working conjointly with behaviorally trained teachers who consult with the classroom teachers of the problem children.

At this juncture in the evolution of behavior modification we strongly need comparative research in order to have large scale social impact. While many are convinced of the value of behavior modification techniques, there are others who are equally sincere in their belief that if extensions of their treatment procedures were applied many social ills would be solved.

In summary, the single subject design, while having served behavior modifiers well in the past, will now be a weakness rather than a strength if used to the exclusion of other designs. Initially, it was the goal of behavior modifiers to carefully demonstrate functional relationships among variables using single subject designs (Bijou, 1965), but at this point research is needed which will provide data enabling us to compare our treatment effects with carefully specified control groups and thereby convince people with a *broad* diversity of views that our procedures are both practical and effective.

It is quite likely that research involving comparisons of various treatments or of treatments and controls will involve smaller differences than have been reported in many studies to date. Similarly, as behavioral scientists become more interested in small but important differences that may be influencing treatment outcomes, they will need to be more attuned to methodological problems inherent in field-experimental research, for both group and single subject designs. Over the past two years we have been examining methodological problems which, if ignored, may lead one to make completely erroneous conclusions from the data. Experimenters using group designs in field-experimental settings where small but significant differences have been found may have produced differences which are the result of methodological problems alone. In particular, the observer who has long been used as if he were a cumulative recorder must be viewed as a source of systematic variability which may greatly confound certain data.

The Human Observer: A Faulty Cumulative Recorder

One important aspect of any behavior modification study utilizing observational recordings of behavior is the assessment of reliability among observers. A majority of investigations in the area of child behavior modification employ observational data in assessing the effects of experimental interventions. The reliability of these measures is routinely estimated by comparing periodically, during the study, the simultaneous recordings of two or more observers viewing the same behavior. Measures of agreement thus calculated are presented to demonstrate a consistency in the recording of observed behavior between observers and across time. High reliability suggests that data from two or three observers does not reflect idiosyncratic judgments and that alternate observers, appropriately trained, would produce similar data. Thus a study may be executed utilizing a small number of highly trained observers rather than a large and random sample of all potential observers.

We have recently been accumulating evidence that procedures *routinely* employed in estimating the reliability of observational data may produce spuriously high levels of agreement. All of our research has been based on a nine category observational code for measuring disruptive behavior of children in a classroom setting (O'Leary, et al., 1971). The nine categories are: out of chair, modified out of chair, playing, vocalization, noise, orienting, touching others' property, aggression, and time off task (not attending to assigned work). This code, which has been employed in a number of studies, defines in highly specific terms, for each category, the behaviors to be included and excluded. A detailed observational manual including definitions of the nine categories is provided. Reliabilities reported reflect the number of agreements between two observers in recording the occurrence of a particular category of behavior during a particular twenty-second interval, divided by the number of agreements plus disagreements in recording each occurrence. Trained observers are expected to obtain reliabilities of .70 or better employing this code and this method of computation of level of agreement. Other computational procedures common to the behavior modification literature which produce numerically higher estimates of reliability include: dividing the number of agreements on occurrence *and* nonoccurrence by the number of agreements plus disagreements on occurrence and nonoccurrence (Cooper, et al., 1970), dividing the smaller frequency of occurrence obtained by one observer by the larger frequency obtained by a second observer (Schwarz and Hawkins, 1970), and using the phi coefficient (Winkler, 1970).

It is generally assumed that the process of reliability assessment is nonreactive—that obtained reliabilities reflect the consistency of observational data generated at times when reliability is not being measured. As a consequence of this assumption, neither the fact that reliability is being assessed nor the identity of the assessor with whom an observer's recordings will be compared are routinely concealed. Reid (1970) reported that observers obtained median reliabilities of .75 when they were aware that reliability was being assessed. Reliabilities dropped to a median of .51 when they were told that their reliability would not be assessed further. Romanczyk, et al. (in press) hypothesized that assessed reliability of observers is inflated not only by the knowledge that an assessment is taking place but also by knowledge of the particular assessor with whom their recording is to be compared. This would be the case, for example, if observers adjusted their rating criteria to more closely match the idiosyncratic interpretation of the behavioral code by any particular assessor.

Romanczyk, et al. assessed the reliability of each of five trained observers with each of two assessors under two different conditions. During *overt assessment* observers were told either that Assessor I was performing the reliability assessment or that Assessor II was performing the assessment. During *covert assessment* observers were not told that a reliability assessment was being performed. In fact, during both conditions the two assessors recorded simultaneously with the particular observer whose reliability was being measured. This permitted computation, during the overt assessment condition, of reliability coefficients with the identified and with the unidentified assessor.

One purpose of this study was to determine if observers would match idiosyncracies of different assessors in application of the behavioral code. For this reason, four of the nine categories of the behavioral rating code were modified to produce stable but differential observational criteria. As a result of these modifications the code employed by Assessor I produced a higher frequency than the code employed by Assessor II on two categories: vocalization and noise. In employing the modified code, Assessor I would record even the softest vocalizations and also any "mouthings" the child might make as vocalizations while Assessor II would record only the louder vocalizations and ignore such behaviors as humming, whispering, and sighing. Further, the behavioral code was modified so that Assessor II would record a greater frequency than Assessor I on two other behaviors: playing and orienting. It was required that these differential observational criteria be sufficiently well-defined so that the assessors would be consistently reliable with each other at a moderate level and, particularly, that the level of reliability between assessors would not vary across experimental conditions. In short, an artificial difference was created between the ratings of Assessor I and Assessor II.

For two-and-one-half weeks prior to the experimental conditions, each assessor employed his respective version of the modified code and, at regular intervals, computed reliability with each observer a median of four times (range two-four). At these times, the assessor and the observer jointly determined the number of agreements and disagreements and calculated the reliability coefficient. These four reliability computations provided the only opportunity for observers to note the unique observational criteria being employed by the two assessors. At *no* time, however, did either reliability assessor make any statement that overtly constrasted his rating criteria with that of the other assessor.

During the experimental conditions, both assessors measured the reliability of particular observers simultaneously for both the overt and covert assessment conditions. In the overt condition, the assessors alternated as the identified and unidentified assessor. Data were collected over a three-week period on eight separate days, and the results are based on a total of 191 separate 12½-minute observation periods, as recorded by the five observers and the two reliability assessors. An analysis of variance of reliability between the two assessors revealed no significant differences across the experimental conditions.

Mean reliabilities of the observers with the identified and unidentified assessors on modified categories during the overt assessment condition are presented in Figure 1. Across the eight days of the study, reliabilities on all nine categories averaged .77 with the identified assessor and .53 with the unidentified assessor. It is clear from these data that when differences exist among assessors in their application of an observational code, observers are able to match those differences.

The mean reliabilities of observers on modified categories with an identified assessor during overt assessment conditions and with the two unidentified assessors during covert assessment conditions are presented in Figure 2. As can be seen, reliability drops from an average across the eight days of the study of .77 with known assessor and overt assessment to an average of .33 with covert assessment. In addition, these investigators compared the frequency of disruptive behavior recorded under conditions of overt and covert reliability assessment. These data, presented in Figure 3, indicate that observers recorded only 80 percent as much disruptive behavior when their reliability was not being assessed.

The clear implication of these data is that an overt reliability assessment, performed at regular intervals throughout a study, may not reflect the consistency of data generated on a day-to-day basis and that studies reporting reliabilities from .70 to .80 may be generating data which is actually reliable at levels from .30 to .40. Further consideration of these data will be made after examination of two additional sources of error in reliability estimation which seem best categorized as "cheating."

In executing a field-experimental evaluation of behavior modification procedures, it is often the case that observers go to the experimental setting on a regular basis unaccompanied by the experimenter. Under these conditions, the observers are periodically asked to

Figure 1

Average Reliability of Observers with Known and Unknown Assessors During Overt Assessment Condition

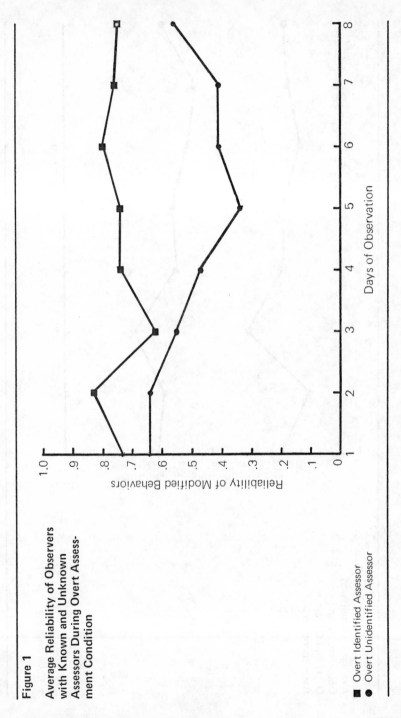

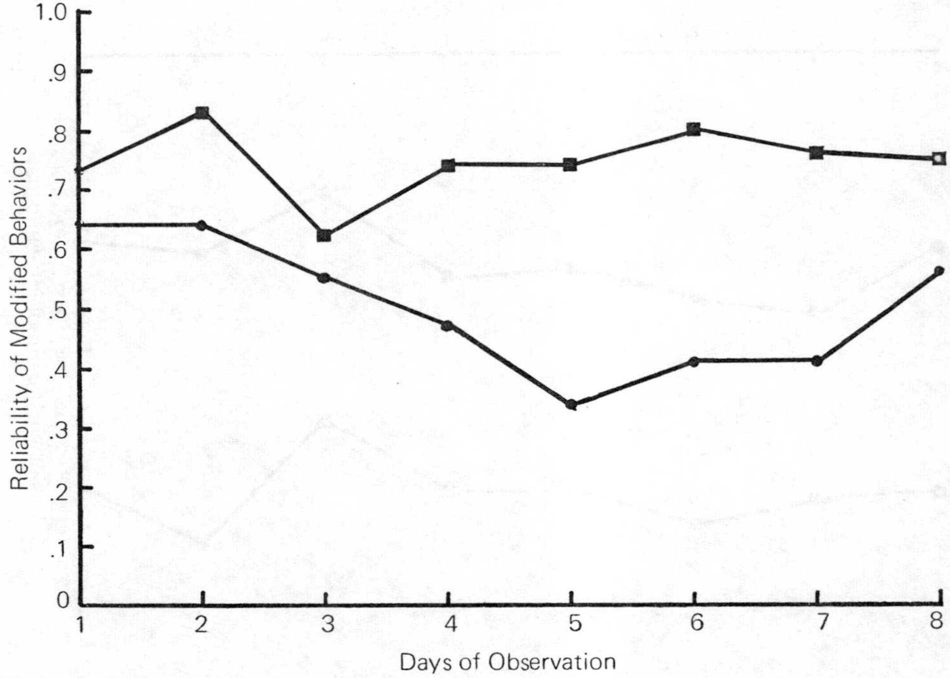

Figure 2

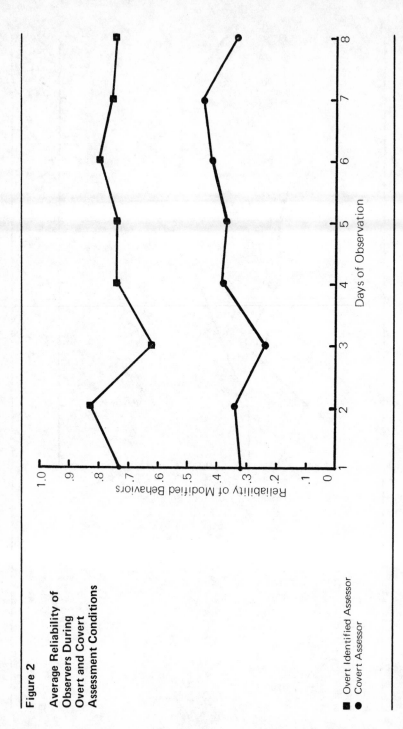

Average Reliability of Observers During Overt and Covert Assessment Conditions

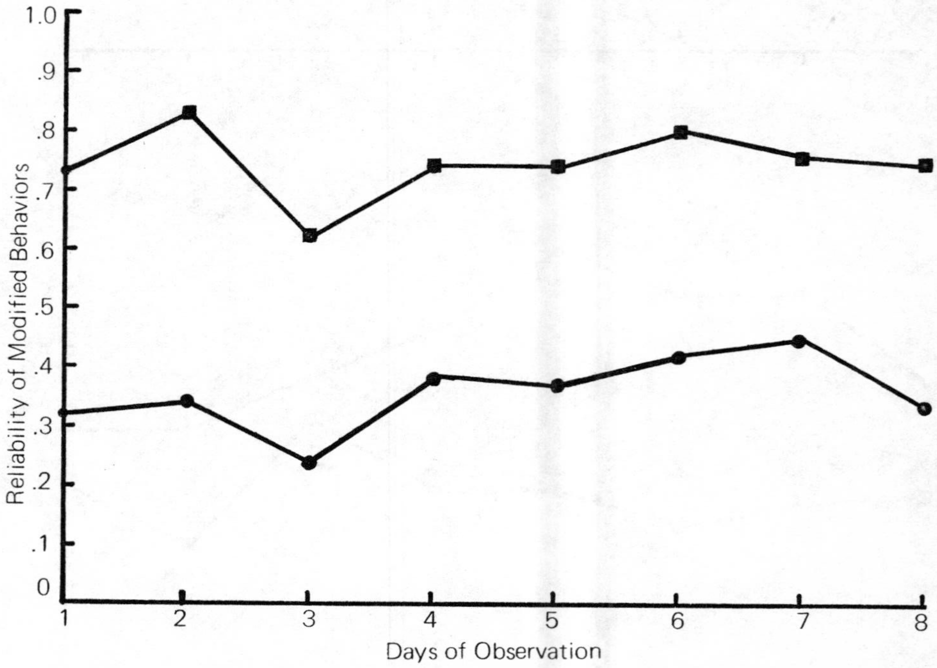

■ Overt Identified Assessor
● Covert Assessor

Figure 3

Average Frequency of Disruptive Behavior Recorded During Overt and Covert Assessment Conditions

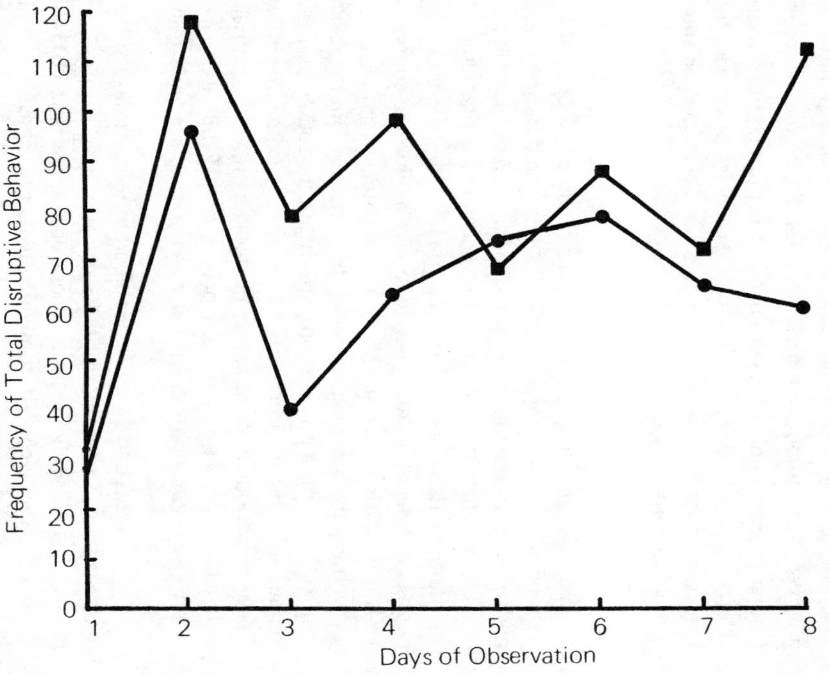

■ Overt Identified Assessor
● Covert Assessor

observe the same behavior simultaneously and to compute a reliability coefficient. Implicit in this request is the desire of the experimenter to obtain accurate and high measures of agreement. There exists with this arrangement the possibility that observers might, rather than disappoint their employer, cheat to obtain high reliabilities. This could be accomplished either by communicating with one another during the process of behavioral recording, by modifying their recordings to increase the level of agreement, or by producing computational errors which spuriously inflate the reliability coefficient.

In preparation for a recent study in our laboratory, three groups of four observers were trained to apply the behavioral code to video tape recordings of children in a classroom. During the initial training period, all recording and reliability computation was accomplished with an experimenter in the room, thereby lessening the possibility of communication among observers and modification of recordings during reliability computation. In fact, it was emphasized that any observer caught cheating would receive an F in the course in child behavior modification research. During the final stages of training we arranged for the experimenter to be called from the room during entire 12½-minute observation periods and the subsequent reliability computation. Figure 4 presents a comparison of the reliabilities obtained during periods that the experimenter was present and absent. This graph demonstrates a systematic tendency for reliabilities, averaged across the twelve observers, to be higher when observers were left unsupervised.

A second study in our laboratory illustrates a different kind of cheating. Two groups of five pairs of observers were trained in application of the behavioral code and computation of reliability. These observers recorded from video tapes the behavior of children in a classroom setting and, after one of every four observation periods, calculated reliability with their partners. The five pairs of observers who would view a particular video tape simultaneously were supervised by two experimenters who stressed that communication and modifying recordings were strictly forbidden. However, it was not until after the study that we checked their calculations of reliability for mathematical errors. Figure 5 presents a comparison of the reliability of recordings as computed by the observers and as computed by the experimenter. These data demonstrate a consistent tendency toward errors in computation which spuriously inflated the level of agreement.

The data presented here seem consistent with the emphasis in many laboratories on reliable recordings. Observers will, it seems, at times of reliability assessment, record more accurately, attempt

Figure 4 **Average Reliability of Observers When Experimenter Was Present vs. Absent**

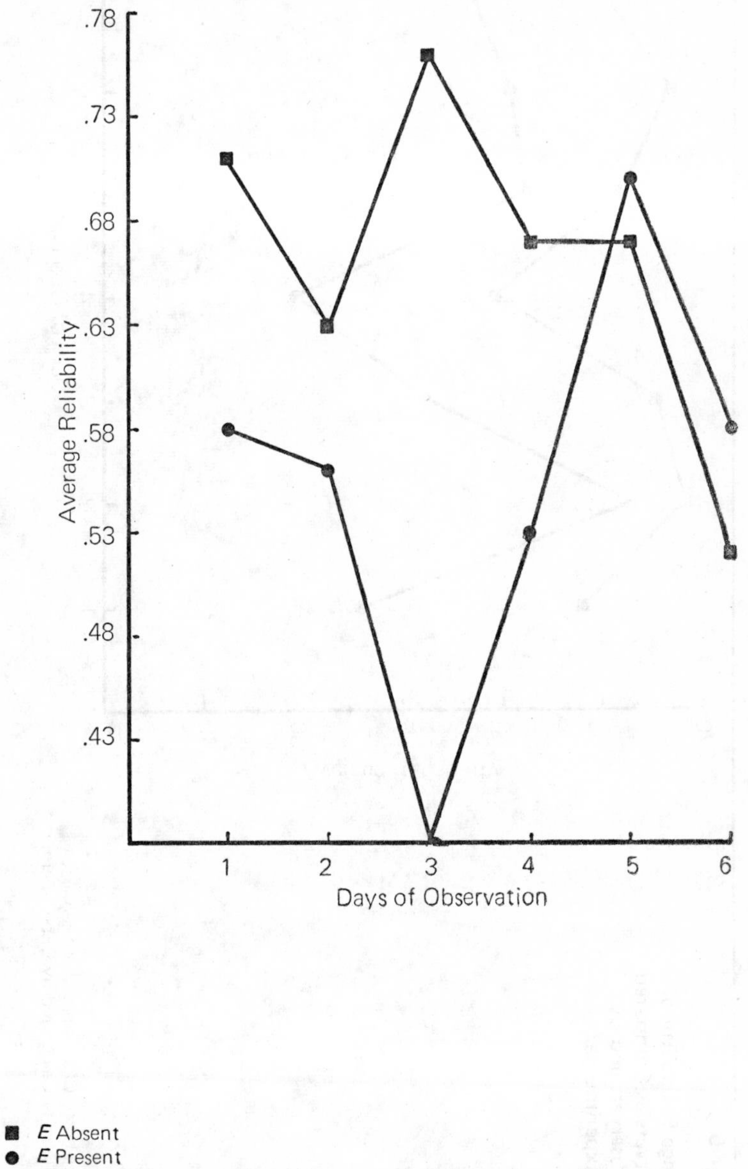

Figure 5

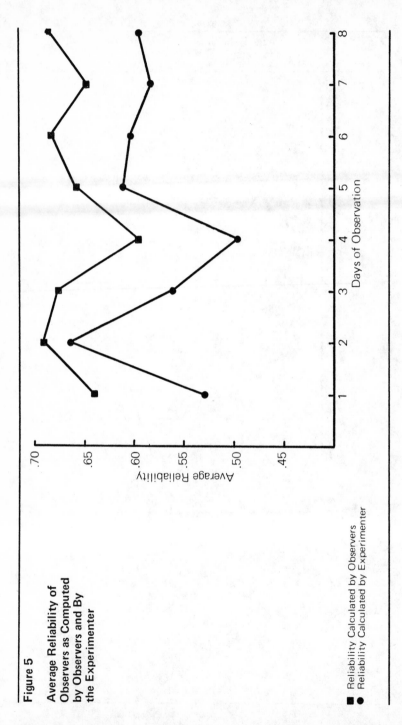

Average Reliability of Observers as Computed by Observers and By the Experimenter

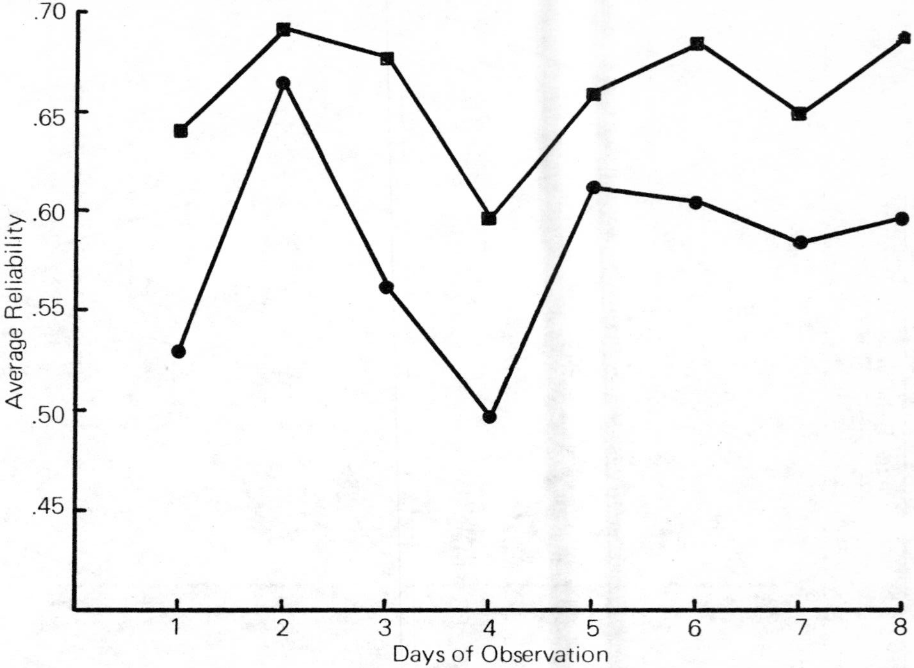

■ Reliability Calculated by Observers
● Reliability Calculated by Experimenter

to match the assessor, communicate with the assessor and/or modify their recordings to correspond with those of the assessor, and produce errors in computation which inflate the reliability coefficient. It seems that occasional overt reliability assessments may fail to reflect the characteristics of observational data when assessment is not being performed.

These data suggest several procedural modifications which would produce more accurate estimates of reliability. Assessment of level of agreement must not be known to the observer. One way to accomplish this would be to monitor observers continually via an experimenter who is present throughout the study and covertly checks reliability. Alternately, this checking could be accomplished via a closed circuit television camera. Under these circumstances, the recordings of observers could be evaluated at any time, without their knowledge. A second, more practical arrangement would involve two or three observers who would be working together in a particular setting. Each member of this group would be given a schedule specifying the person to be observed during a particular time interval, and these schedules would arrange for occasional simultaneous observation of the same behavior by two observers. When recordings were returned, the experimenter could determine the level of agreement of these simultaneous observations. The potential difficulty with this less costly arrangement is that observers, if motivated to do so, could easily determine from one another which observation intervals would allow reliability assessment and respond as they would to an overt reliability assessment.

Accurate reliability assessment provides a critical indication of the generality of observational measures. Higher reliability increases the likelihood that recordings are not idiosyncratic to the particular observers employed. Further, high reliability may serve as one indication to the experimenter of the amount of measurement error in his data and, thus, of the amount of data necessary to provide a sensitive evaluation of treatment effects. However, even high reliability allows the possibility of significant differences between the frequencies recorded by two different observers. This could be the case, for example, if one of two observers were employing a slightly expanded definition of a particular behavior. In the context of high agreement, one observer would record frequencies of behavior which were slightly but consistently higher than those of the second observer. This circumstance could be particularly problematic if the two observers were assigned to record data from different experimental conditions, or if one recorded treatment effects and the other follow-up data. This arrangement could systematically distort experimental data by confounding observer effects with treatment effects.

High levels of agreement among observers do not eliminate the possibility of biases in recording shared by observers. For example, if all observers anticipated a decrease in level of disruptive behavior during a particular experimental condition and, in fact, recorded only the most blatant disruptions during that condition, it is possible that high levels of agreement could be maintained in the context of severely distorted data.

Finally, high reliability bears no relation to the validity of a particular measure. It seems that reliability can be purchased at the expense of the substantive meaning of a particular measurement. For example, we have attempted to increase the reliability of our measure of aggression by eliminating intent and contextual cues from the definition. Higher reliabilities were obtained, but it did not seem that with the new definition we were measuring what we conceptualize as "aggression." The best strategy in developing reliable and meaningful measures of behavior may involve focusing on reliable but simplified indices which are strongly related to the occurrence of more complex categories of behavior. As an example of this strategy, Montrose Wolf and his colleagues have employed a measure of height of a subject's eyes while sitting as an index of "posture" in an interview situation. With the use of a closed circuit television monitor, this can be measured with extremely high reliability and seems, conceptually, strongly related to good posture.

To this point, we have been discussing reliability among observers within a group. Such observers would generally work together in a particular setting and compute reliability with one another. Recently, investigators in the area of child behavior modification have begun to utilize between-group experimental designs involving different treatment procedures in different settings. Under these circumstances, a particular group of observers is often assigned to a particular classroom or school and continues throughout the course of the study to gather data from that setting. This arrangement often makes it impractical to directly evaluate the reliability of observers in one group with observers in another group. It seems important to ask: Are observers who are reliable with other members of their group likely to be reliable with observers in other groups?

In preparation for a large-scale study, we recently attempted to train 40 observers to reliably apply our code of disruptive behavior to video tapes of children in a classroom setting. These observers were trained in three groups of 13 or 14 members each. Subsequent to each observation period of five or ten minutes, the experimenter would randomly pair observers, and they would compute reliability and discuss differences in recording with the experimenter. This procedure eliminated the possibility of any observer adjusting his recordings to match those of another observer with whom he would compute reliability. After 15 such one-and-one-half hour sessions, reliability among the observers seemed to have asymptoted at an average of .55 to .60. Although this was not yet sufficient agreement to begin data collection, for training purposes we divided the observers into the eight groups of five observers who would ultimately be exposed to different experimental conditions. After three additional training sessions, during which observers observed, computed reliability, and discussed disagreement only with members of their group, intra-group reliability rose to an average of .70. However, this arrangement introduced the possibility that different groups had developed systematically different observational criteria. If this occurred, the differential criteria would be confounded with the differential experimental conditions. As a test of this possibility, we retained four of these groups and obtained from them recordings of the behavior of two children on each of eight 12½-minute video tapes over a four-day period. During these four days, members of each group computed reliability with one another after one observation period each day. In analyzing these data we found significant differences in the ratings of the four groups on seven of the nine categories of disruptive behavior. The two categories which were unaffected, touching others' property and aggression, were sufficiently low in frequency of occurrence that no significant differences could be expected. Figures 6 and 7 present the data for two of the categories of behavior most dramatically affected. In producing these figures, we selected the two groups accounting for the greatest differences in recording on each category. It seems clear that the magnitude of differences is sufficient to distort treatment effects, had these groups been assigned to view different treatment conditions. Further, the instability of differences eliminates the possibility of developing "individual equations" to adjust the ratings of each group of observers to comparability.

It seems that the process of computing reliability and discussing differences in recording modifies an observer's interpretation of the behavioral code to more closely match those observers with whom he is working. When observers are divided into different groups, different modifications of the code may emerge. It should be emphasized that these modifications seem to have an essentially random effect on frequencies generated and must be differentiated from possible system-

Figure 6 **Drift in Frequency of Vocalization Recorded By Two Groups of Observers**

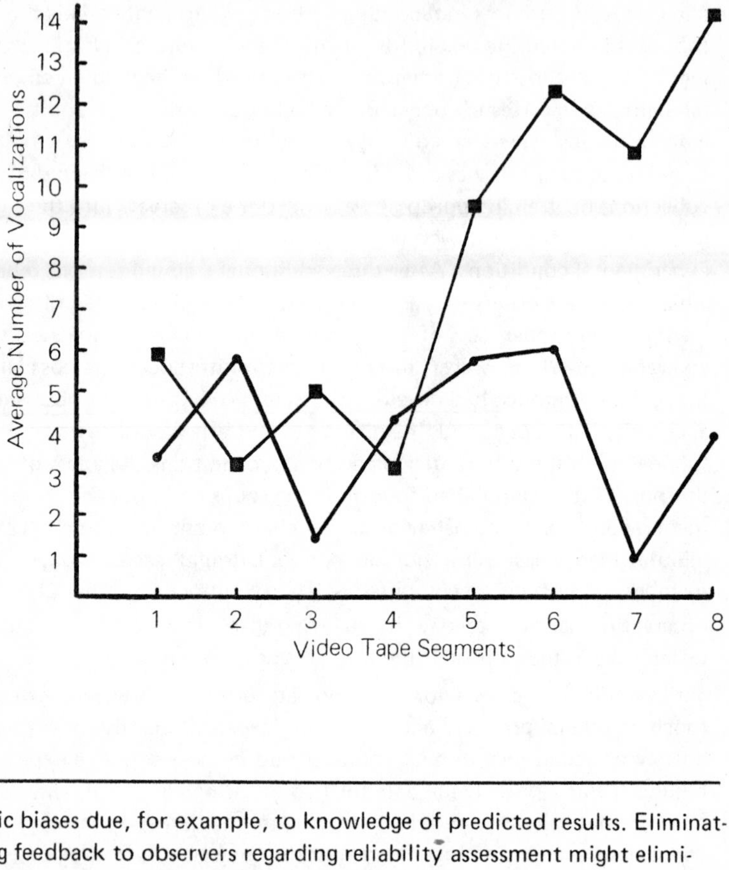

atic biases due, for example, to knowledge of predicted results. Eliminating feedback to observers regarding reliability assessment might eliminate this problem. More likely, however, each observer would develop unique modifications of the behavioral code.

These data suggest that it is unwise to confound individual observers or groups of observers with different experimental conditions. However, even in single group, within-subject designs, there exists the possibility that observers may "drift" in their application of a behavioral code, yielding data recorded during one experimental condition incomparable to data recorded during a subsequent condition. Montrose Wolf (personal communication, 1972) has suggested a procedure of training a new group of observers several weeks after the initiation of a study and assessing their comparability to observers who have been collecting data in the field-experimental setting. When no dif-

Figure 7

Drift in Frequency of Noise Recorded By Two Groups of Observers

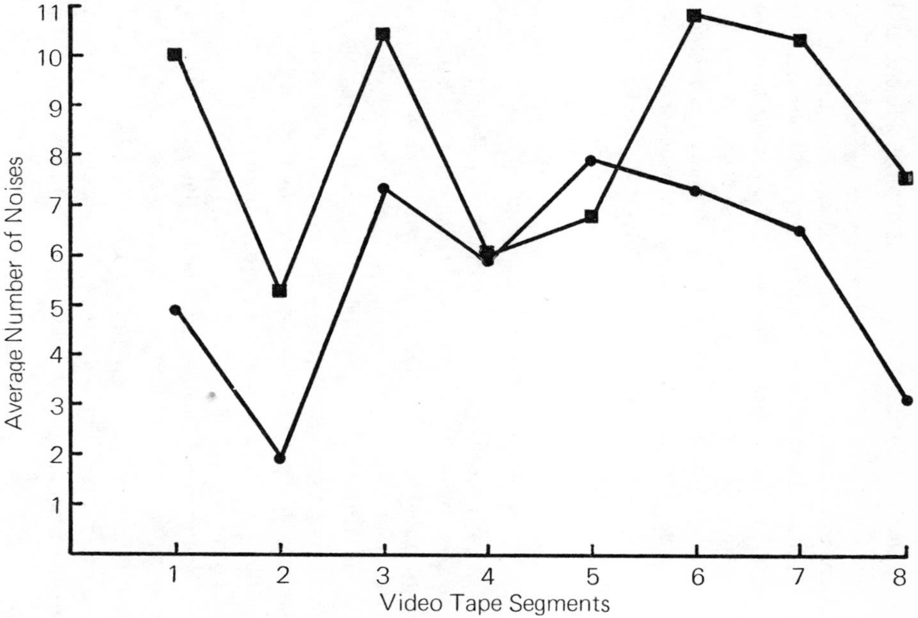

ferences are found between the two groups of observers, it is clear that drift has not occurred. However, in the absence of such information, it seems prudent to take one of several steps to avoid confounding observer drift with differential treatment interventions. In between-subject designs, one could employ a single group of observers to record data from all treatment groups. Alternately, several groups of observers could be rotated periodically from one treatment group to another. Clearly neither of these procedures guarantees that the recordings from a particular experimental condition will represent comparable applications of the behavioral code at any two points in time. This procedure does assure, however, that the data from each treatment group will be equally affected by any modifications in the behavioral code which do occur.

In within-subject designs, the critical comparisons involve one experimental condition instituted at one time and another condition instituted subsequently. Assuming that observer drift is a random phenomenon, one might employ a number of independent observer groups across all experimental conditions. For example, if experimental conditions each lasted a week or longer, different groups of observers could be employed on each day of the week. Drift among groups would thus add to the variation of data from each condition but would not distort comparisons of one condition to another. An alternate procedure would involve video taping the behavior of interest during all experimental conditions and showing these recordings to observers in random order. When this is impractical, observation of video tapes of a sample of behavior from each experimental condition would provide a measure of the veridicality of behavioral recording obtained *in vivo* across time.

In view of the difficulties associated with observational recording, one might well consider abandoning measurement of behavior requiring a judgment. In fact, Winnett and Winkler (in press) have suggested the more critical importance of product measure, particularly in a classroom setting. As there seems to exist only a moderate correlation between social behavior and academic product in the classroom, we routinely obtain both types of measurements. However, even in the case of product measures, data regarding social behavior often provide a measure of the degree to which important stimulus factors have remained constant across experimental conditions. For example, when measuring the number of products correct before and during a token program, it is critical to measure the degree to which the teacher instructs, as well as prompts and reinforces problem completion during baseline and treatment conditions. In the absence of such data, it is impossible to conclude that the reward contingency is the critical factor in producing change.

Use of product measures does not eliminate judgment factors which seem so problematic in observational recording of behavior. It seems likely that evaluations of handwriting or short answers in the classroom may also suffer from lack of consistent judgment. In other settings of interest to child behavior modifiers, such as the home or the playground, product measures are simply not available. In fact, it seems there is an entire realm of social behaviors, such as cooperation among children, creativity, and following instructions, which are of direct interest and for which there are no tangible products.

We must remain interested in such home measures as those obtained by Patterson and his colleagues, and in classroom measures such as those obtained by a host of investigators. We must conclude that measures of social behavior will continue as a dependent variable of major importance, not only for clinical psychologists but also in the areas of social and developmental psychology. It is necessary to develop our measurement and research technology sufficiently to allow us to interpret such measures unambiguously.

We have encountered and investigated a variety of sources of distortion in reliability and frequency measures of disruptive behavior. We are now able to design studies around these problems and, further, to seek developments in training of observers and in the categories of behavior which will lessen the import of these biases. However, our investigations have only considered the particular set of behavioral measures we employ. These difficulties may exist to a greater or lesser extent with other behavioral measures.

The moral of this paper should be clear. Behavioral recordings, like all other measurements, must be studied for potential biases. In the absence of such information, observers should be regarded as an experimental factor which must not be confounded with experimental conditions. Utilization of behavioral measurement in conjunction with carefully selected experimental designs can provide convincing demonstrations of treatment effectiveness which will prevent behavioral intervention from becoming a fad of the Sixties and insure its role as a means of social action for the Seventies.

Footnotes

1. The authors are indebted to Susan G. O'Leary and Joyce N. Sprafkin for their comments on an earlier version of this manuscript.

2. Our research was supported in part by Research Grants OEG-2-710017 and OEG-0-71-2872-607 from the Office of Education and in part from National Science Foundation Grant GU-3590.

References

Baer, D. M. Behavior modification: You shouldn't. In E. A. Ramp and B. L. Hopkins. (Eds.), *A new direction for education: Behavior analysis*. Lawrence: University of Kansas Follow-Through Center, 1971.

Bijou, S. W. Experimental studies of child behavior, normal and deviant. In L. Krasner and L. P. Ullmann (Eds.), *Research in behavior modification*. New York: Holt, Rinehart and Winston, 1965.

Cooper, M. L., Thomson, C. L., and Baer, D. M. Modification of extreme social isolation by contingent social reinforcement. *Journal of Applied Behavior Analysis*, 1970, *3*, 153-157.

Cossiart, A., Hall, R. V., and Hopkins, B. L. The effects of experimenter's instructions, feedback and social reinforcement on teacher praise and student attending behavior. *Journal of Applied Behavior Analysis*, in press.

Grice, G. R. and Hunter, J. J. Stimulus intensity effects depend upon type of experimental design. *Psychological Review*, 1964, *71*, 247-256.

Kazdin, A. E. The token economy: An evaluative review. *Journal of Applied Behavior Analysis*, in press.

Miller, L. C. School behavior check list. *Journal of Consulting and Clinical Psychology*, 1972, *38*, 134-144.

O'Leary, K. D. and Drabman, R. Token reinforcement programs in the classroom: A review. *Psychological Bulletin,* 1971, *75*, 379-398.

O'Leary, K. D. and O'Leary, S. G. *Classroom management: The Successful use of behavior modification.* New York: Pergamon Press, 1972.

O'Leary, K. D., Romanczyk, R. G., Kass, R. E., Dietz, A., and Santogrossi, D. Procedures for classroom observation of teachers and children. Unpublished manuscript, 1971.

Paul, G. L. *Insight versus desensitization in psychotherapy: An experiment in anxiety reduction.* Stanford: Stanford University Press, 1966.

Quay, H. C. Patterns of aggression, withdrawal and immaturity. In H. C. Quay and J. S. Werry, *Psychopathological disorders of children.* New York: Wiley, 1972.

Reid, J. B. Reliability assessment of observation data: A possible methodological problem. *Child Development*, 1970, *41*, 1143-1150.

Romanczyk, R. G., Kent, R. N., Diament, C., and O'Leary, K. D. Measuring the reliability of observational data: A reactive process. *Journal of Applied Behavior Analysis,* in press.

Shectman, A. Age patterns in children's psychiatric symptoms. *Child Development*, 1971, *41*, 683-693.

Sidman, M. *Tactics of scientific research.* New York: Basic Books, 1960.

Schwarz, M. L. and Hawkins, R. P. Application of delayed reinforcement procedures to the behavior of an elementary school child. *Journal of Applied Behavior Analysis*, 1970, *3*, 85-96.

Walker, H. M. and Buckley, N. Reprogramming generalization and maintenance of treatment effects across time and settings. *Journal of Applied Behavior Analysis*, in press.

Werry, J. S. and Quay, H. C. Observing the classroom behavior of elementary school children. *Exceptional Children*, 1969, *35*, 461-470.

Willis, R. D. Shock intensity, partial reinforcement, and experimental design effects in the acquisition of conditioned suppression. Unpublished doctoral dissertation, University of Illinois, 1969.

Winkler, R. C. Management of chronic psychiatric patients by a token reinforcement system. *Journal of Applied Behavior Analysis*, 1970, *3*, 47-55.

Winnett, R. A. and Winkler, R. C. Current behavior modification in the classroom: Be still, be quiet, be docile. *Journal of Applied Behavior Analysis*, in press.

Wolf, M. Personal communication, 1972.

Field Evaluation of Observer Bias Under Overt and Covert Monitoring[1]

3

Karl Skindrud[2]

A subtle and persistent problem in behavioral research is that of observer bias. Pawlicki (1970), in his review of behavior therapy research with children, cites observer bias as the most pervasive of five common methodological problems. Rosenthal (1966) reports evidence that the observer's recordings (Kennedy and Uphoff, 1939; Scheffield, et al., 1952; Rosenthal, et al., 1964), interpretations (Rapp, 1965; Smith and Hyman, 1950), data fabrication (Azrin, et al., 1961; Rosenthal and Lawson, 1964), and even the behavior of the person being observed (Rosenthal and Fode, 1963; Masling, 1965) are likely to be influenced by the observer's expectations. While the effects of other methodological problems such as observer agreement and accuracy and subject reactivity (Johnson and Bolstad, 1973) appear to be constant or vary randomly with treatment conditions, observer bias interacts with treatment conditions, confounding the results (Rosenthal, 1966).

Laboratory Studies of Observer Bias

Investigations by Rapp (1965), Scott, et al. (1967), and Azrin, et al. (1961) illustrate the influence of observer expectations on reported observations. The Azrin, et al. (1961) study employed untrained undergraduate observers who were to track one behavior in adults with whom they were conversing. The observations of those who had been exposed to an operant interpretation of the phenomenon under study were mirror images of those reported by observers who had been given a psychodynamic interpretation.

Rapp (1965) had eight pairs of observers describe the behavior of a given nursery school child for one minute. One member of each pair had been led to believe that the child under observation was feeling "under par" and the other that the child was "above par." Seven of the eight pairs of observers wrote descriptions that differed significantly as a function of these instructions.

Scott, et al. (1967) compared the observations of "uninformed observers" with simultaneous observations on the same subject by an "informed observer" (the experimenter herself). Agreement was high among the uninformed observers, and the informed observer's data differed significantly from theirs in the direction of support for the experimenter's hypotheses

The above studies suggest that data collected by relatively untrained or unmonitored observers are influenced by observer expectations. However, are the observations of professionally trained observers employing multivariate behavioral coding systems also susceptible to expectancy effects? Several studies have dealt with this question. Kass and O'Leary (1970) had informed, uninformed, and misinformed observers code video taped interactions of deviant behavior before and after intervention. The mean rate of deviant behavior over the nine code categories recorded differed significantly ($p < .005$) between the three observation conditions. However, the authors report a confound between the bias groups and assessment of inter-observer reliability which made the results of this study suspect (O'Leary and Kent, 1972). An unconfounded partial replication revealed that "the behavioral ratings produced by these observers were totally unbiased" (Kent, 1972). An independent and unconfounded cross-validation of the Kass and O'Leary study by Skindrud (1972) on a different population of observers and with a family rather than a classroom interaction code produced no evidence of observer bias.

All of the studies on multivariate code systems cited above were conducted under controlled conditions with video taped interaction. As a result, the generalizability of these findings to *in vivo* observation conditions in the field may be limited for a number of reasons. First, direct observations of social interaction in the field are often conducted under conditions where changes are expected *and observed*. No actual changes in the rates of deviant behavior occurred in most of the above studies. Second, the collecting of observation data from video taped social interaction may not approximate the collection of observations in the field (observer agreement and accuracy can be more stringently monitored with video tape, observers cannot see or hear as well with video tape, etc.). Third, in all of these studies, the behavior of the experimenter was controlled so that he only manipulated observer expectancies but did not differentially reinforce observers for reporting rates of deviant behavior supporting the experimenter's hypotheses. During field evaluations of behavior therapy, do observers unintentionally exaggerate treatment effects because such results generally make therapists and experimenters happy? Skindrud (1972) and Kent (1972), in independent pilot investigations attempting to bias observers through the presentation of both instructional sets *and selective reinforcement of confirming data*, report significant trends in the direction of bias. Fourth, the use of video tape prevents observers from influencing the behavior of the subjects they are observing. Several investigators (Rosenthal and Fode, 1963; Masling, 1965) have shown this to be an important source of confounding expectancy effects.

Assessment of Observer Bias in Field Experiments

The argument can be made that most of the above-cited studies remove so many sources of possible observer bias or so stringently monitor the behavior of the observer that generalization from video tape to field observation studies is questionable. If a major purpose of investigation is to determine the extent to which the observational data of experimental-field studies may be influenced by observer bias, the evaluation of such bias should be carried out as an integral part of any major experimental-field study. The two studies reported below, although preliminary, represent an evaluation of one alternative for the assessment and control of observer bias under field conditions used by the Social Learning Project (Patterson, 1970) at the Oregon Research Institute. Specifically, the observations obtained in homes by observers informed as to the normal vs. deviant status of families being observed, the research hypotheses being investigated, and the treatment status of the families being observed, were compared with those obtained on the same families by an uninformed observer.

The observations of the uninformed observer were compared with those of the informed observers under two conditions: (1) where observations were made simultaneously of identical family interaction, and (2) where observations were made on adjoining days of the same family but of different social interaction. Research by Reid (1970), Romanczyk, et al. (1971), and O'Leary and Kent (1972) has shown that observations obtained by overt monitoring (such as the simultaneous observations) and by covert monitoring (as in the adjoining observations) differ in both levels of reliability and frequencies of deviant behavior reported. The two types of monitoring clearly represent different observation conditions with which observer bias may interact, and therefore may require separate field evaluations.

The hypotheses tested in the two studies reported herein are:

I. Observers informed as to the normal vs. deviant status of families being observed will record neither more nor less deviant behavior in *normal families* than an uninformed observer. The expectations of informed and uninformed observers are assumed equivalent in this condition.

II. Observers informed that the observed family is *in treatment* to reduce deviant behavior and that the treatment methods are generally effective will record significantly less deviant behavior than an uninformed observer.

III. Observers informed as to the normal vs. deviant status of families being observed will record significantly more deviant behavior in *deviant families during a pre-treatment condition* than an uninformed observer.

Method

Sample. The observers in both studies were recruited from the community by means of advertisement in the local newspaper. Seven of the applicants were hired as observers for the Social Learning Project. They had scored above a WAIS Vocabulary IQ of 120 and above the 75th percentile on the Employee Aptitude Survey Verbal and Numerical Reasoning Tests and the Minnesota Clerical Tests. All were females, with a mean age of 43 years. Most of them were married, had raised their children, and were seeking part-time employment. Five of the women were kept informed of all aspects of the field study for which they were collecting data and will be referred to as the "informed observers." Two of the women were kept uninformed of the field study and will be known as the "uninformed observers" or "calibrating observers." The Social Learning Project hired and trained one new observer each nine months to serve as "calibrator" for the rest of the observer staff. Her responsibility was to provide a measure of the reliability and objectivity of the informed observers. The policy of using the most recently trained observer as "calibrator" was based on the assumptions that (1) she would be the easiest to keep uninformed about the field study and (2) she would, after training, be most closely tied to the standard code definitions in the coding manual (Patterson, et al., 1969). As Romanczyk, et al. (1971) and O'Leary and Kent (1972) suggest, experience as an observer does not necessarily increase observer accuracy.

The fact that this field evaluation of observer bias took place within the context of the ongoing research of the Social Learning Project limited the sample size and design of the evaluation. Data collection for both studies covered a period of 18 months and involved data from all of the informed observers. However, while it was possible to use data from both uninformed observers for the study of adjoining observations, the data from only one of the calibrators was available for use in the study of simultaneous observations.

Observer training and agreement. A complete description of the observation procedures can be found in Patterson and Cobb (1971). They describe the coding system as follows:

> The coding system was developed gradually during the period of 1966 (J. Reid, 1967) through the present as a function of extensive observations in forty or fifty homes of both deviant and non-deviant children. It is designed to test some specific hypotheses based upon social learning principles and is therefore *not* an omnibus system. Currently it consists of thirty categories which describe various behavioral events: Approval, Attention, Command, Command Negative, Comply, Cry, Disapproval, Dependency, Destructiveness, High rate (hyperactive), Humiliate, Ignore, Indulge, Laugh, Noncomply, Negativism, Normative, No Response, Play, Physical Negative, Physical Positive, Proximity, Receive, Self-Stimulation, Talk, Tease, Touch, Whine, Work, and Yell (p. 100).

Training to a criterion of 80% inter-observer agreement took about one month for each observer. The trainees first studied the coding manual (Patterson, et al., 1969) and then received experience coding video tapes of family interaction made in the homes of active children. The trainees were constantly checked against a "fine-grained" criterion coding of the interaction determined by the observer trainer and given feedback on their accuracy. Following this, the trainees accompanied experienced observers into the homes of families and coded "live" family interaction. Inter-observer agreement was computed to provide the trainee with feedback on accuracy.

The observers were trained to focus on one family member as a subject, code his behavior, and then code the responses of other family members to him. The observer recorded the subject's next behavior and responses to that, and so on. The observers recorded all of the interactions between the subject and other family members occurring between 30-second "beeps" provided by a signalling device on their clipboards. The average rate of interaction is five per 30 seconds, or about 100 behaviors every five minutes.

Agreements between observers were counted when there was agreement on both the behavior and the agent as well as on the timing and sequencing of the behavioral events. Reliability consisted of the total number of agreements divided by agreements plus disagreements, expressed as percent. Mean percent agreement between the informed and calibrating observer on the simultaneous observations made in the homes was 82%. It was not possible to determine the reliabilities of the adjoining observations, as they were not obtained in pairs. However, the research by Reid (1970) and Romanczyk, et al. (1971) cited above, reporting a drop of at least 25 percentage points when reliability was not overtly monitored, suggests that the reliability of the adjoining observations may have been considerably less than the 82% obtained for simultaneous observations.

Home observations. The observations were made in the homes of either normal families or deviant families referred to the Social Learning Project for treatment because of aggressive, out-of-control, pre-delinquent behavior by at least one boy in the family. Fourteen normal and 15 deviant families were observed in the two studies reported.

Three sets of observations were obtained: (1) those taken on normal families in the baseline phase; (2) those taken on deviant families in baseline; and (3) those taken on deviant families in the intervention phase of the Social Learning Project's treatment program.

Independent variable. The five observers in the informed group were made aware of the normal vs. deviant and baseline vs. treatment (intervention) status of each family prior to home observation. This was accomplished through identification codes used to designate each status and through frequent contacts with each deviant family's therapist. Informed observers' and therapists' offices were adjacent so that both written and *vis a vis* sharing of observed changes in each family as a function of treatment with appropriate therapist response was convenient and frequent.All informed observers had access to each therapist's clinical notes regarding each family's treatment status. Furthermore, informed observers were made well aware of the intended effects and successful history of the child behavior therapy techniques employed (Patterson, 1970; Walter and Gilmore, in press; Wiltz, 1969) through reports at project staff meetings which they regularly attended.

By contrast, the uninformed observers had been excluded from discussions of research hypotheses, treatment progress, and individual cases. They had no access to case records. They could be regarded as totally "blind" regarding the treatment status of the families observed, except for one uncontrolled factor—the observation procedures changed as a family moved from baseline to intervention status. During baseline each family member was observed for ten minutes. During intervention, the deviant child was observed for 20 minutes and the other family members for five minutes each. Consequently, the uninformed observers knew some change had occurred in the status of the family being observed but would not have been aware of the predicted effects of that status on the family's behavior. Thus no way could the calibrating, or uninformed, observers be considered as knowledgeable about the research program, treatment procedures, and family status as the informed observers.

Dependent variable. The dependent variable in this study was the amount of deviant behavior recorded by the observers using the 30-category family interaction code. Fourteen of the codes were regarded as deviant. These were: command negative (CN); cry (CR); disapproval (DI); dependency (DP); destructiveness (DS); high rate (HR); humiliation (HU); indulgence (IN); noncomply (NC); negativism (NE); physical negative (PN); tease (TE); whine (WH); and yell (YE). The number of deviant behaviors recorded for all family members observed was determined for each of the paired observations in the sample. This constituted the raw data.

The raw data were corrected for observation time by dividing the total number of deviant behaviors for all family members per home observation by the number of five-minute observations made. This statistical transformation automatically corrected for differences in family size as observation time varied with family size. The resulting dependent variable is the *mean frequency of deviant behaviors per five minutes.* The number of deviant behaviors recorded by the informed observers was compared with the number recorded by the calibrating observer.

Observation conditions for separate studies of observer bias. *Simultaneous observations.* Since the conditions of observation have been shown to vary greatly depending upon whether an observer is overtly or covertly monitored (Reid, 1970; Romancyzk, et al., 1971), two separate evaluations of observer bias were conducted. In the first study reported below, one of the five informed observers was paired with a calibrating observer. The pair entered the home of the family to be observed together and *simultaneously* collected data on identical family interaction. They were well aware of each other's presence and, in fact, coordinated their observations by using the same 30-second signal to pace themselves during the home observation. They were spaced apart enough so that they could not view each other's protocol sheets, however, and had been instructed not to compare observations until they had been scored for agreement and recorded for computer processing.

Data for the study of simultaneous observations was limited to those instances where it was the calibrating observer's *first* contact with the family being observed. This reduced the possibility that she might infer selection or treatment status from familiarity with the family. No attempt was made to limit the number of contacts by the informed observers, who had usually seen the family several times prior to the simultaneous observation. Data from 12 pairs of simultaneous observations met these criteria. Seven were of normal families during baseline and five of deviant families in intervention. An insufficient number of simultaneous observations (N = 3) of deviant families in baseline were available to warrant inclusion in the data analysis.

Adjoining observations. In the second study reported below, the informed observer was unaware that her data would be in any way compared with that of other observations of the same family. This was accomplished by randomly selecting one of the two observations by informed observers which were in closest temporal proximity in days to an observation by the calibrating observer. As it turned out, two-thirds of the calibrating observer's observations preceded the observations by the informed observer, and the two adjoining observations were separated by no more than two days in over two-thirds of the cases.

Data for the study of adjoining observations was limited to those instances where it was the calibrating observer's *first* or *second* contact with the family being observed, again to limit familiarity with the family. Data from 30 pairs of adjoining observations from two different calibrating observers (17 pairs with JJ and 13 with KSt) met these criteria. Nine pairs of adjoining observations were made of normal families and 21 of deviant families during baseline. Unfortunately, adjoining observations of deviant families during intervention were not available as intervention observations occurred in pairs one month apart. A concurrent study (Shaw, 1971) required that the pair of observations in the intervention probe be conducted by the same observer.

Results

Constant error (Hypothesis I). In the studies of both simultaneous and adjoining observations, the reports of the calibrating and informed observers were compared on normal families to test Hypothesis I that there was no "constant error" in the calibrating observers' observations of deviant behavior before the opportunity for observer bias was introduced.

In the study of simultaneous observations the mean difference in number of deviant behaviors recorded per five minutes was .59, with the calibrating observer estimating less deviant behavior (Walker and Lev, 1953, p. 152; $t = 3.58$; $df = 6$; $p < .02$). The data are given in Table 1.

In the study of adjoining observations, the nine pairs of adjoining observations made of normal families were compared. The mean difference was .52 deviant behaviors per family observation with the calibrating observer again estimating less deviant behavior (Walker and Lev, 1953, p. 152; $t = .80$; $df = 8$; n.s.). The data can be found in Table 2.

Observer bias: Simultaneous observations (Hypothesis II). Five pairs of simultaneous observations were taken during intervention, when the observer's expectations were assumed to differ with respect to the treatment status of the families being observed. If the same difference in reports of deviant behavior hold for observations of both normal and deviant families, then the differences would be assumed due to constant error. If there were a significant interaction effect, one could assume a bias exists.

The mean difference between the report of the calibrating and informed observers was .46 deviant behaviors per five minutes, with the informed observer reporting the higher number of deviant behaviors. A comparison of the control and experimental results is presented in Figure 1.

The interaction between family status and observer status was not significant ($p < .05$) with a repeated measures analysis of variance (Kirk, 1968, p. 277). Hypothesis II under simultaneous obser-

Table 1 Mean Number of Deviant Behaviors Recorded per Five Minutes During Simultaneous Observations

	Family number	Family size	No. of 5 min. observations	Date observed	By informed observer	By calibrating observer
Normal Families in Baseline	81	5	10	10-21-69	3.5	2.7
	82	4	8	11-11-69	2.5	1.625
	83	4	8	11-18-69	1.0	0.0
	84	5	10	1-29-70	.1	.3
	85	6	12	1-26-70	.416	.167
	86	5	10	1-27-70	2.4	1.9
	87	5	10	2-18-70	2.1	1.2
Total					12.016	7.892
Mean					1.72	1.13
Deviant Families in Intervention	22	5	8	12-04-69	0.0	0.5
	27	4	7	9-11-69	1.857	1.428
	28	3	6	9-10-69	8.5	6.5
	29	5	8	10-30-69	0.75	0.25
	33	7	10	2-26-70	0.7	0.8
Total					11.81	9.48
Mean					2.36	1.90

vation conditions remains unsupported. A summary of the analysis of variance results for the simultaneous observation data is contained in Table 3.

Observer bias: Adjoining observations (Hypothesis III). Twenty-one pairs of adjoining observations were available for a comparison of calibrating and informed observer reports of deviant behavior in deviant families during baseline. The mean difference between calibrating and informed observer reports was .92 deviant behaviors per five minutes, with the informed observer reporting the larger number of deviant behaviors. A comparison of the control and experimental results is shown in Figure 2.

The interaction between family status and observer status in the case of adjoining observations was not significant ($p > .05$). Thus Hypothesis III failed to gain support. The analysis of variance results for the adjoining observations are summarized in Table 4.

Table 2 Mean Number of Deviant Behaviors Recorded per Five Minutes During Adjoining Observations

	Family number	Family size	No. of 5 min. observations	Date observed	By informed observer	Date observed	By calibrating observer
Normal Families in Baseline	71	5	10	2-05-69	6.6	2-04-69	2.7
	72	6	12	6-16-69	1.0	6-13-69	1.0
	73	4	8	7-01-69	1.125	7-02-69	1.625
	74	5	10	7-30-69	2.0	7-28-69	1.7
	75	7	14	7-29-69	1.285	7-30-69	0.357
	76	4	8	8-13-69	1.0	8-07-69	4.0
	80	6	12	10-27-69	2.916	10-24-69	0.583
	80	6	12	10-28-69	0.33	10-29-69	0.833
	82	4	8	11-07-69	1.5	11-06-69	0.25
Total					17.756		13.048
Mean					1.97		1.45
Deviant Families in Baseline	19	3	6	2-25-69	2.67	2-26-69	4.167
	21	4	8	3-05-69	4.625	3-04-69	1.0
	21	4	8	3-06-69	1.975	3-07-69	1.875
	22	5	10	3-05-69	0.9	3-06-69	0.2
	22	5	10	3-11-69	0.16	3-10-69	0.2
	23	5	10	3-18-69	0.1	3-24-69	1.0
	07	7	14	4-23-69	1.642	4-21-69	1.285
	26	7	14	4-15-69	2.071	4-16-69	3.071
	28	3	6	5-01-69	2.5	5-05-69	0.67
	29	5	10	5-08-69	1.7	5-06-69	0.5
	29	5	10	5-07-69	0.5	5-09-69	0.7
	30	3	6	1-16-70	2.67	1-14-70	1.33
	30	3	6	1-20-70	3.0	1-15-70	2.167
	32	5	10	1-21-70	2.4	1-19-70	1.1
	32	5	10	1-22-70	2.9	1-20-70	0.7
	34	4	8	2-13-70	9.75	2-11-70	1.5
	34	4	8	2-16-70	4.875	2-12-70	2.75
	36	4	8	3-18-70	1.75	3-16-70	3.625
	36	4	8	3-19-70	2.125	3-17-70	1.5
	38	4	8	5-01-70	3.875	4-28-70	3.0
	38	4	8	5-05-70	3.25	4-29-70	4.125
Total					55.778		36.465
Mean					2.66		1.74

Figure 1 **Simultaneous Observations of Deviant Behavior by Pairs of Informed and Calibrating Observers Where Observers Were Aware of Being Monitored**

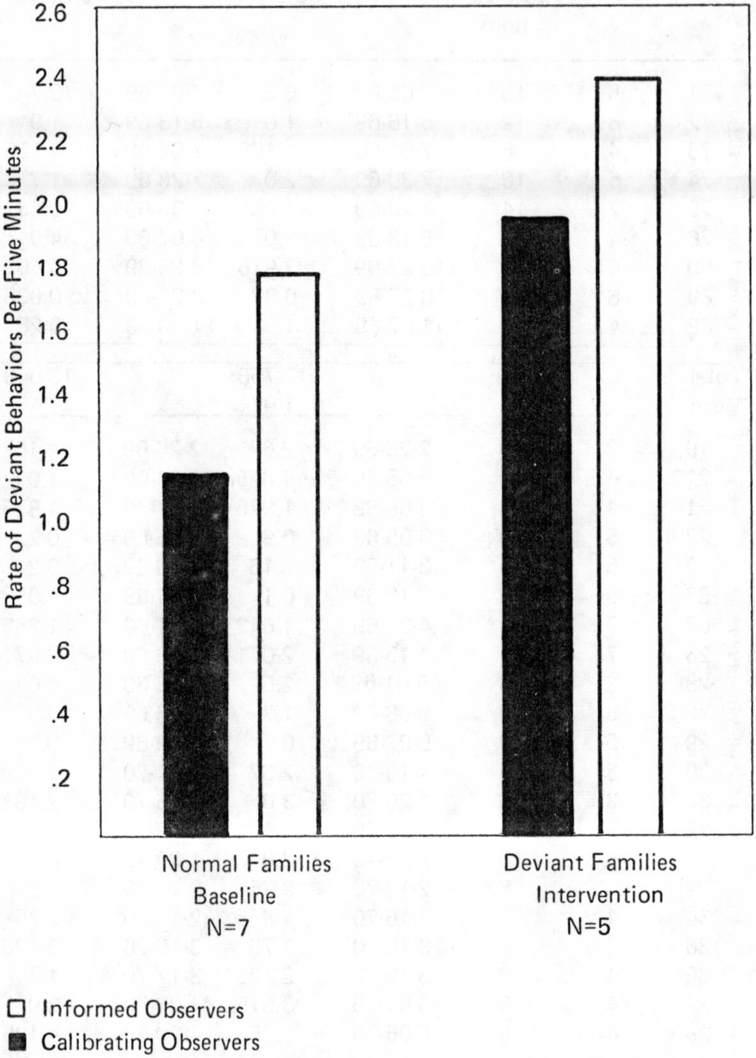

Table 3 Summary of the 2 x 2 Split Plot Analysis of Variance of Simultaneous Observations of Deviant Behavior (Corrected for Observation Time)

Source	SS	df	MS	F
Rows (Family status)	2.94	1	2.94	0.33
Subjects w. groups	89.23	10	8.92	
Columns (Observer status)	1.65	1	1.65	7.17*
Interaction	0	1	0	0.09
B X Subjects w. groups	2.30	10	0.23	

* $p<.05$

Table 4 Summary of the 2 x 2 Split Plot Analysis of Variance of Adjoining Observations of Deviant Behavior (Corrected for Observation Time)

Source	SS	df	MS	F
Rows (Family status)	2.963	1	2.963	0.88
Subjects w. groups	94.314	28	3.368	
Columns (Observer status)	6.557	1	6.557	3.003
Interaction	0.495	1	0.495	0.227
B X Subjects w. groups	61.139	28	2.184	

Figure 2 **Observations of Deviant Behavior by Pairs of Informed and Calibrating Observers Where Observations Were Made on Adjoining Days and Observers Were Unaware of Being Monitored**

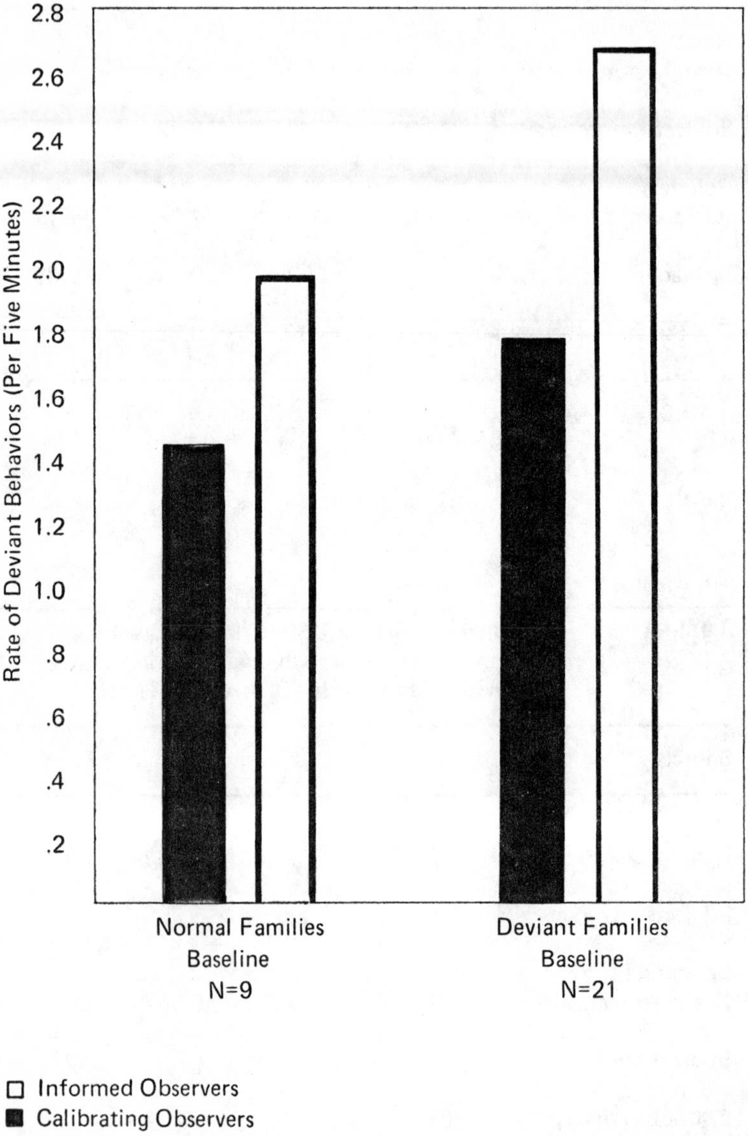

Discussion

Regarding constant error. The null hypothesis that informed and uninformed observers would not differ in their observations of deviant behavior in normal families was rejected by the results of the simultaneous observations study. The direction and magnitude of the difference in the study employing adjoining observations was the same, but not at a significant level.

This tendency of the calibrating observers to underestimate deviant behavior is assumed to reflect a constant error rather than a bias if the expectations of the informed and calibrating observers do not differ during observations of normal families. If any difference in expectations exists, it is logical that it would be the informed observers who would estimate less deviant behavior in the normal families so that the magnitude of constant error would be underestimated.

It is not clear what variables are responsible for the consistent tendency of the calibrating observers to underestimate deviant behavior, but several are apparent. First, the calibrating observers have less experience than the informed observers. Second, both calibrating observers had never been mothers, whereas most of the informed observers had been parents. Third, the calibrating observers averaged 17 years younger than the informed observers, suggesting a "generation gap" with more tolerance of deviant behavior by the calibration observers. Fourth, it is possible that having no awareness of the dependent variable, as was true of the calibrating observer, reduces the observer's vigilance with respect to the occurrence of the deviant behaviors. Related to this possibility is the finding of Kass and O'Leary (1970) that their control observers appeared to be less motivated and reported lower levels of deviant behavior than either of two groups of experimental observers during baseline observations. All four factors suggest more tolerance or less awareness of deviant behavior by the calibrating observers. Such factors would operate to depress the calibrating observers' reports of deviant behavior no matter what type of family was being observed, whether normal, deviant in baseline, or deviant in intervention.

Regarding observer bias. The hypothesis that informed observers would report less deviant behavior than an uninformed calibrating observer during intervention observations of deviant families remains unsupported under simultaneous observation conditions. The hypothesis that informed observers would report more deviant behavior than an uninformed observer during baseline observations of deviant families was unsupported under adjoining observation conditions.

One could argue that the differences obtained under adjoining observation conditions were in the predicted direction, although not significant. However, the relatively large error variance resulting from the use of adjoining observations would require an unusually large number of degrees of freedom to determine whether the family-observer interaction were reliable.

These results might lead to the conclusion that informing observers trained in multivariate behavior coding procedures as to the experimental hypotheses, family status, manipulation of the independent variable, etc., does not bias their data. However, this study has a number of limitations and possible alternate interpretations suggesting that these results are preliminary at best.

First, limiting the data to the first or second contact of the calibrating observer with a family resulted in relatively small sample sizes in both studies.

Second, an alternative interpretation of the data is possible. It was assumed that the magnitude of the constant error was independent of the absolute level of deviant behavior. If, in fact, the magnitude of observer error were *proportional* to the absolute rate of deviant behavior rather than a constant, the simultaneous observation data would suggest the presence of observer bias (see Figure 3). One could predict that since the calibrating observer's observations were 66% of the informed observer's during the normal control condition, the same proportional relationship should hold during the experimental condition. Such is not the case, as during observations of the deviant families in intervention, the calibrating observer reported 80% of the deviant behaviors seen by the informed observer. Were the same proportion to hold in the experimental condition as in the control condition, we could predict algebraically that the informed observer would have seen 2.88 rather than 2.36 deviant behaviors per five minutes. Such a difference in proportions (80% - 66%) might be regarded as a 14% bias on the part of the informed observers.

A comparable estimation of bias on the adjoining observation data suggests an approximate bias of 12%. However, a power curve analysis using a difference between proportions design has revealed that in the case of simultaneous observations, an N of 160 paired observations would be required to achieve significance with biases of this magnitude. With adjoining observations a considerably larger sample would be required due to the much greater error variance.[3]

Dawes (1970) cautions experimenters seeking significant interactions that much larger Ns are required for significant sprayed and monotonic interactions than for significant crossed interactions.

Figure 3 **Measurement of Observer Bias for the Simultaneous Observation Data Assuming Constant Observer Error is Proportional to Absolute Rates of Deviant Behavior**

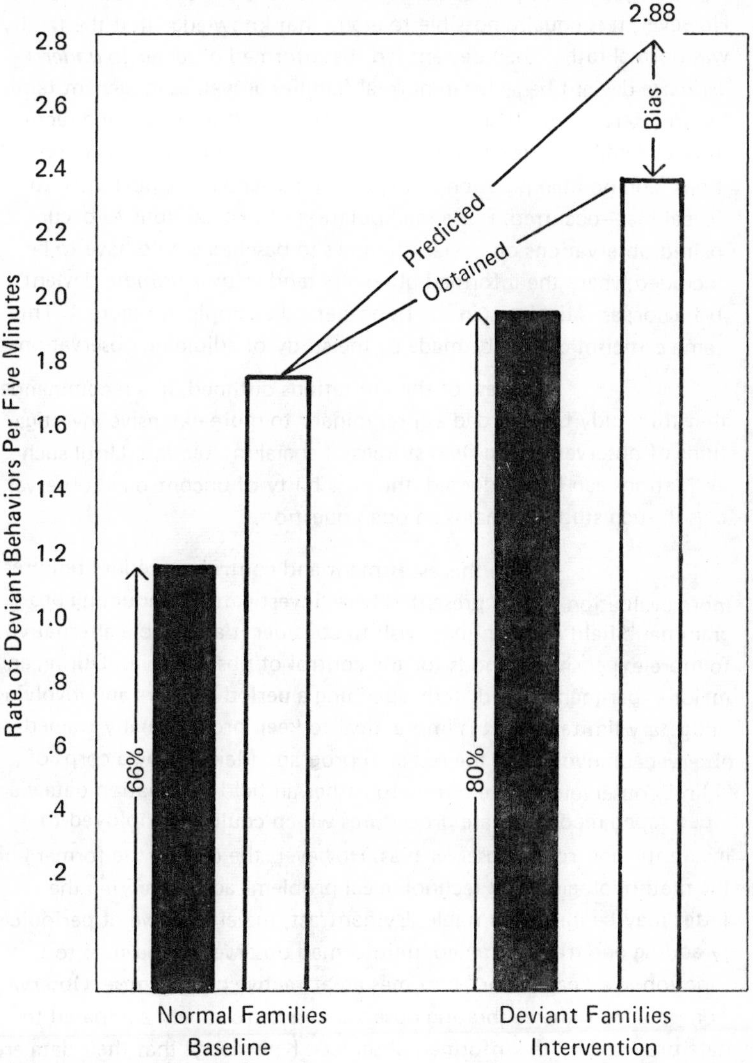

□ Informed Observers
■ Calibrating Observers

Hence, the severe limits imposed by the small sample in this study become more obvious.

Third, it can be argued that, in the study of simultaneous observations, no manipulation of observer expectations occurred. It will be recalled that both studies assumed that the observers' expectations did not differ during observations of *normal* families. However, it is equally possible to argue that knowledge that the family was normal rather than deviant led the informed observer to *underestimate* deviant behavior in normal families as well as in deviant families in intervention. If such is the case, the bias is in the same direction in both family status conditions in the study of simultaneous observations, and no manipulation of expectations—and no opportunity to reveal bias—occurred. For a manipulation of expectations to occur, paired observations on deviant families in baseline would have to be included where the informed observers tend to *overestimate* deviant behavior, as is depicted in the hypothetical example in Figure 4. This same criticism cannot be made of the study of adjoining observations.

In view of the limitations outlined, it is recommended that this study be regarded as preliminary to more extensive investigations of observer bias in field studies of social interaction. Until such evaluations can be conducted, the possibility of uncontrolled observer bias in such studies remains an open question.

While this assessment and control procedure requires more evaluation than is presented here, investigators conducting programmatic field research may wish to consider it as a viable alternative to more expensive methods for the control of observer bias. During any major experimental-field study spanning a period of years and involving budgetary limitations, it is impractical to keep professionally trained observers uninvolved in the research program. Maintaining a corps of "blind" observers or attempting to gather all field observation data via video taped recordings are procedures which could be employed to insure the control of observer bias. However, the cost of the former and the methodological and technological problems accompanying the latter may be insurmountable. By contrast, the alternative of periodically adding one freshly trained, uninformed observer to the staff to function as a "calibrator" becomes an attractive compromise. Observation data from the calibrating observer can be routinely compared to data provided by the informed observers. Knowledge that their data are open to scrutiny with respect to both observer agreement and bias should provide an incentive to the informed observers to maintain high standards of accuracy and objectivity.

Figure 4 **Hypothetical Comparison of Observations by Informed and Calibrating Observers Made Under All Treatment Conditions: A Complete Field Assessment of Observer Bias**

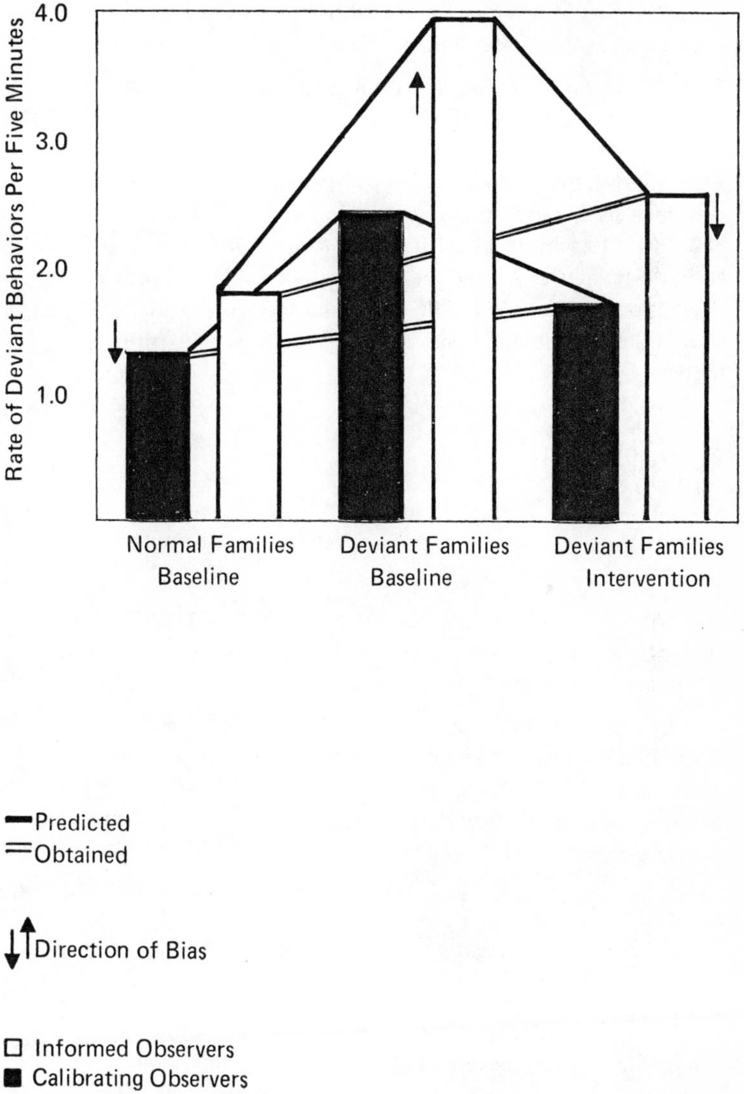

Footnotes

1. This study was supported in part by NIMH Grant MH 15985.

2. The author wishes to thank Gerald R. Patterson, Richard R. Jones, and John B. Reid for assistance with the data analysis and editing of this manuscript, with the author taking the sole responsibility for the content.

3. Further power curve analyses revealed that a bias of approximately 67% would be required before a test with N = 6 would achieve significance with simultaneous observations. Even assuming that observer error were constant rather than proportional and a two-way analysis of variance were used, the bias would again have to be about 67% to achieve a significant interaction with an N of 6. The author estimates that given the error variance obtained with simultaneous observations in the field, and the analysis of variance design, an N of 100 paired observations would be required to identify a bias of 15 to 25% beyond chance.

References

Azrin, N., Holz, W., Ulrich, R., and Goldiamond, I. The control of conversation through reinforcement. *Journal of the Experimental Analysis of Behavior*, 1961, *4*, 25-30.

Dawes, R. M. A recurring problem in M.A. and Ph.D. theses. Unpublished manuscript, Psychology Department, University of Oregon, 1970.

Johnson, S. M. and Bolstad, O. D. Methodological issues in naturalistic observation: Some problems and solutions for field research. In L. A. Hamerlynck, L. C. Handy, and E. J. Mash (Eds.), *Behavior change: Methodology, concepts, and practice.* Champaign, Ill.: Research Press, 1973.

Kass, R. and O'Leary, K. D. The effects of observer bias in field-experimental settings. Paper presented at a Symposium, "Behavior Analysis in Education," University of Kansas, Lawrence, Kansas, April, 1970.

Kennedy, J. L. and Uphoff, H. F. Experiments on the nature of extra-sensory perception: III. The recording error criticism of extra-chance scores. *Journal of Parapsychology*, 1939, *3*, 226-245.

Kent, R. N. Personal communication, 1972.

Kirk, R. E. *Experimental design: Procedures for the behavioral sciences.* Belmont, Cal.: Brooks/Cole, 1968.

Masling, J. Differential indoctrination of examiners and Rorschach responses. *Journal of Consulting Psychology*, 1965, *29,* 198-201.

O'Leary, K. D. and Kent, R. N. Behavior modification for social action: Research tactics and problems. In L. A. Hamerlynck, L. C. Handy, and E. J. Mash (Eds.), *Behavior change: Methodology, concepts, and practice*. Champaign, Ill.: Research Press, 1973.

Patterson, G. R. Intervention in the homes of pre-delinquent boys. Summary Progress Report MH 15985, May 31, 1970.

Patterson, G. R. and Cobb, J. A. A dyadic analysis of "aggressive" behaviors. In J. P. Hill (Ed.), *Minnesota symposia on child psychology*. Vol. 5. Minneapolis: University of Minnesota, 1971. Pp. 72-129.

Patterson, G. R., Cobb, J. A., and Ray, R. S. A social engineering technology for retraining the families of aggressive boys. In H. E. Adams and I. P. Unikel (Eds.), *Issues and trends in behavior therapy.* Springfield, Ill.: Charles C. Thomas, in press.

Patterson, G. R., Ray, R. S., Shaw, D. A., and Cobb, J. A. Manual for coding of family interactions. Document No. 01234, sixth revision, 1969. Available from ASIS National Auxiliary Publications Service, c/o CMM Information Service, Inc., 909 Third Avenue, New York, N. Y., 10022.

Pawlicki, R. Behaviour-therapy research with children: A critical review. *Canadian Journal of Behavioral Science*, 1970, *2*, 163-173.

Rapp, D. W. Detection of observer bias in the written record. Unpublished manuscript, University of Georgia, 1965.

Reid, J. B. Reliability assessment of observation data: A possible methodological problem. *Child Development*, 1970, *41*, 1143-1150.

Romanczyk, R. G., Kent, R., Diament, C., and O'Leary, K. D. Measuring the reliability of observational data: A reactive process. Paper presented at the Second Annual Symposium on Behavioral Analysis, Lawrence, Kansas, May 1971.

Rosenthal, R. *Experimenter effects in behavioral research*. New York: Appleton-Century-Crofts, 1966.

Rosenthal, R. and Fode, K. L. Three experiments in experimenter bias. *Psychological Reports*, 1963, *12*, 491-511.

Rosenthal, R., Friedman, C. J., Johnson, C. A., Fode, K. L., Schill, T. R., White, C. R., and Vikan, L. L. Variables affecting experimenter bias in a group situation. *Genetic Psychology Monographs*, 1964, *70*, 271-296.

Rosenthal, R. and Lawson, R. A longitudinal study of the effects of experimenter bias on the operant learning of laboratory rats. *Journal of Psychiatric Research*, 1964, *2*, 61-72.

Scott, P., Burton, R. V., and Radke-Yarrow, M. Social reinforcement under natural conditions. *Child Development*, 1967, *38*, 53-63.

Shaw, D. A. Family maintenance schedules for deviant behavior. Unpublished doctoral dissertation, University of Oregon, 1971.

Sheffield, F. D., Kaufman, R. S., and Rhine, J. B. A PK experiment at Yale starts a controversy. *Journal of the American Society for Psychical Research*, 1952, *46*, 111-117.

Skindrud, K. An evaluation of observer bias in experimental-field studies of social interaction. Unpublished doctoral dissertation, Univesrity of Oregon, 1972.

Smith, H. L. and Hyman, H. H. The biasing effect of interviewer expectations of survey results. *Public Opinion Quarterly*, 1950, *14*, 491-506.

Walker, H. and Lev, J. *Statistical inference.* New York: Holt, Rinehart and Winston, 1953.

Walter, H. I. and Gilmore, S. K. Placebo versus social learning effects in parent training procedures designed to alter the behaviors of aggressive boys. *Behavior Therapy*, in press.

Wiltz, N. A., Jr. Modification of behaviors of deviant boys through parent participation in a group technique. Unpublished doctoral dissertation, University of Oregon, 1969.

Behavioral Observation and Frequency Data: Problems in Scoring, Analysis, and Interpretation[1,2] 4

Richard R. Jones

Direct observations of ongoing behavior have become the data *sine qua non* of behavior modification research and practice. Historical antecedents of present-day observation procedures can be found in animal and human ecology (e.g., Hutt and Hutt, 1970), clinical practice in psychology (Raush, 1967), and early developmental research (Bijou, et al., 1969). As currently employed in many naturalistic settings, behavioral observation procedures are used to collect data on individual subjects, in contrast to assessment strategies designed for group studies of individual differences among subjects. This difference in focus between single subject and group assessment strategies may, under some conditions, produce different processes of measurement. As a result, scores derived from intraindividual kinds of assessment devices, e.g., some observational systems, may not be interchangeable with scores for the same constructs or behavioral categories derived from interindividual kinds of assessment instruments, e.g., psychological tests or inventories (Clemans, 1966; Hicks, 1970). The purpose of this chapter is to identify the differences in measurement properties for scores derived from naturalistic observation systems from those for scores derived from traditional psychometric tests, and, in so doing, point to some possible problems in the interpretation and analysis of behavioral observation scores when used in group studies of individual differences.

The measurement characteristics of behavioral observation scores may differ from psychometric test scores for at least three reasons: (a) temporal dependencies among observation raw scores, (b) comparability of assessment conditions under which observations are collected for different individuals, and (c) ipsatizing features of observation scoring procedures. Dependency in temporally ordered data has been a methodological problem of longstanding (e.g., Holtzman, 1963) which has recently been studied using techniques borrowed from disciplines other than psychology (Gottman, et al., 1969; Namboodiri, 1972). The comparability of assessment conditions is a well-known requirement for psychological scores when samples of subjects are studied. Finally, ipsative (as contrasted with differential) measurement properties have been recognized in traditional assessment research (Cattell, 1944; Clemans, 1966, Hicks, 1970), and now may be of concern in research dealing with observational data.

In large part, the kinds of methodological problems discussed under these three headings may not apply to studies in which single subjects rather than groups of subjects are the research focus. Researchers who have eschewed the need for inferential statistics and samples from populations of subjects in their functional analyses of behavior (e.g., Bijou, et al., 1969; Sidman, 1960) do not concern themselves with details of individual differences measurement. But students of behavior who seek generalizable laws of behavior through the nomothetic, as opposed to the idiographic, approach to psychological science, and use naturalistic observations in their search, should be aware of potential methodological pitfalls. These difficulties derive, in this writer's judgment, from the well-intentioned but often inappropriate application of traditional psychometric and statistical methods to behavioral scores based on naturalistic observations. What clearly is needed, and is now starting to be developed, is a methodology for treating intraindividually focused data as rigorously as is possible with interindividually focused measures (e.g., Gottman et al., 1969, Namboodiri, 1972). The reliance on visual or even intuitive analysis of behavioral data certainly will not hold up long under scientific scrutiny, except perhaps within rather limited professional circles. If nothing else, this chapter hopefully will give the reader an appreciation for what one writer sees as some of the measurement problems attendant on observation techniques, as well as a brief look at the ways in which some of these problems may be accommodated in future research.

Interindividual Dependencies Among Raw Observation Scores

A common unit for recording observations of ongoing behavior in naturalistic settings is a simple tally of the occurrence of preselected categories of behavior. Typically, an arbitrary partitioning of the time dimension is used to provide a frame of reference within which the behavioral observations can be recorded. As with virtually all kinds of psychological data, the user of observations is faced with the tasks of data reduction and data analysis. Inspection of the procedures employed to accomplish these tasks suggests that the methods for scoring and interpreting observational data come directly from traditional psychometric practice and theory. The purpose of this section is to consider some difficulties which seem to result from the application of traditional psychometric methods to the raw frequency data collected with many behavioral observation systems.

An important distinction between the direct observation procedures used in behavior modification research and more traditional kinds of assessment (e.g., tests) is that the former usually are carried out over numerous time samples, while the latter typically are obtained on single occasions. Therefore, time contributes a source of measurement variance unique to naturalistic observation (Holtzman, 1963). And, systematic fluctuations of behavior as a function of time have implications for psychological measurement procedures, as, for example, when observations are collected over a set of continuous time samples to obtain summary behavior scores for a subject.

Paradigm for Multibehavior Frequency Observations

To facilitate discussion, a general framework for conceptualizing multibehavior frequency observation systems will be presented. This paradigm represents the nucleus of virtually any naturalistic observation procedure which is used to collect behavioral frequency data. By simple extensions the paradigm can also represent observation data which result in duration, intensity, or latency measures. For the present, however, because of their ubiquitous position in behavioral research (Bijou, et al., 1969; Skinner, 1966; Yamamoto, et al., 1972), the paradigm will be used as a way of thinking about behavioral *frequency* data only.

Consider the display in Figure 1. The columns, B_1, B_2, B_3. . . .B_j. . . . .B_m, represent different behavioral categories in a multibehavior observation system, e.g., talking, hitting, yelling, attending, etc. Each behavioral category is unambiguously defined such that confusions in classifying observed behavioral events are at a minimum. Each of the rows, T_1, T_2, T_3. . . .T_i. . . . .T_n, represents the minimum time interval required by the observation system for the classification and recording of one, and only one, behavioral event from the set of "M" behavioral categories.

The arrangement of the columns in this paradigm is unimportant, but the arrangement of the rows is set by the order of the time intervals (T_i) as they occur in the "stream" of behavioral events encoded by the observation system. That is, the paradigm does not represent the phenomenology of naturally occurring behaviors if the order of the rows is changed. Time is a crucial ordering variable in the

Figure 1 **Paradigm for Displaying Occurrences of Behavioral Events Recorded by Naturalistic Observation Systems**

Behavioral Categories

Time Intervals	B_1	B_2	B_3	....	B_j	....	B_m	Total
T_1								0 or 1
T_2								0 or 1
T_3								0 or 1
....								
T_i								0 or 1
....								
T_n								0 or 1
Total	0 to N	0 to N	0 to N		0 to N		0 to N	N

paradigm, and this condition has implications for analysis of the observational frequency data which will be dealt with in subsequent sections.

By definition the length of an interval (T_i) in this paradigm is the minimum amount of time required for the recording of one, and only one, behavioral event. This is a reasonable definition for the purposes of the paradigm, but in practice intervals are specified in units of seconds, minutes, or sometimes even hours. Since the T_i is an arbitrary sectioning of the time dimension, the usual intervals of seconds or minutes can be viewed simply as combined adjacent intervals of the kind defined in the paradigm.

The number of behavioral events which can be re-recorded in an observation system may be specified, ranging from a "free form" procedure in which as many events are encoded as the recording apparatus (human and/or mechanical) can achieve, to a restrictive procedure in which the recording of one, and only one, event is required in each time interval. In principle, as the length of the time intervals is shortened, the observation system approaches a "free form" style. Also, with short intervals, physical incapabilities of the recording apparatus usually require the limit of recording only one behavior during each interval.

Behaviors are "scored" in this paradigm as follows. Since the behavioral categories are essentially mutually exclusive classes, and the paradigm requires that only one behavioral event be recorded for each of the "N" time intervals, the coding of data in any single row of the matrix can be given by "1" for the observed behavioral category and "0" for each of the other behavioral categories. This, of course, means that the sum of the entries in each row is limited to 0 if none of the behavioral categories occurred or 1 if a recordable behavior occurred. The sum for a column will range from 0 to N, meaning, respectively, that no events in the category occurred, or that all of the recorded events belonged to the same behavioral category.

For observation systems which permit recording more than one behavior during each time interval, the scoring procedure becomes a simple extension of the "zero/one" coding. For example, if the minimum time interval needed to record an instance of behavior "A" is ten seconds, and the observation system uses an interval of one minute, then a score for "A" during one interval could range from zero to six. The minute-long interval in this example is constructed simply by joining six adjacent ten-second intervals. Hence, any specified time interval can be thought of as comprised of one or more successive intervals of minimum length, as defined in the paradigm.

To review, observations are recorded as the occurrence of each of a set of categories of behavior along an arbitrarily segmented time dimension. Such raw data can be displayed as a matrix of zeros (nonoccurrence) and ones (occurrence), with the restriction that only one entry per time interval (i.e., row) can be a "1." Adjacent time intervals may be combined into larger, conventional time samples, such as seconds or minutes. When this is done in practice, the raw frequency scores may become larger than one if this suits the purpose of the data collection. Either way, the raw data take the form of frequencies of occurrence of each of the behavior categories during each of the ordered time intervals.

Scoring the Behavioral Observations

For most research or clinical uses of the kinds of observation data displayed schematically in Figure 1, some procedure for data reduction or summarization is required to make these numerous bits of information manageable. A common scoring procedure used to summarize such data is based on the sum of the entries in each column (Yamamoto, et al., 1972). This sum is the total number of occurrences of each of the "M" behaviors, collected over the "N" time segments. When this sum is divided by the number of time samples, rate measures are obtained (e.g., dividing by the number of minutes will give a behavior rate per minute for each category). Or alternatively, when the sum is divided by the total number of behaviors observed over all categories and time samples, proportion scores are obtained. Discussion of these conversion routines will be delayed until later sections; for now, consider the rationale underlying the sum-score procedure.

Apparently this behavior scoring procedure is based on measurement procedures which derive directly from traditional psychometric theory and practice. Scores from a large variety of psychological instruments are usually obtained by combining information from a set of separate assessment events. The information is often in the form of a structured response selected from alternatives provided on the instrument. The separate assessment events may be, for example, statements in a personality inventory, questions in an achievement test, or other kinds of discrete stimuli used to elicit subject responses. The essential reason for combining responses into a composite or summary score is that the psychological information contained in a single response to a single stimulus probably is insufficiently reliable for most statistical or analytical purposes. By combining responses to numerous stimuli, the robustness of psychological measures is enhanced. Thus, the rationales for adding frequencies of occurrence for behavioral categories over time samples, and for summing keyed responses to items from psychological scales, are essentially the same—measurement precision is increased as the number of summed bits of information is increased.

In terms of the paradigm in Figure 1, the parallel between the sum-scoring of observation frequency data and traditional psychometric scoring practices can be shown simply by changing the labels of the rows and columns. Figure 2 shows the observation data paradigm relabeled, where now the rows are items, not time segments, and the columns are attribute scales, not behavioral categories. As was true of the display in Figure 1, the arrangement of the columns is un-

Figure 2 Paradigm for Displaying Responses to Inventory Items Scored on Multiple Attribute Scales

Attribute Scales

Items	a_1	a_2	a_3	......	a_j	......	a_m
i_1							
i_2							
i_3							
⋮							
i_i							
⋮							
i_n							

important. But unlike the observation paradigm, the arrangement of the rows in Figure 2, i.e., items, also is unimportant, whereas the row or time interval arrangement was important in the observation paradigm. That is, serial dependency among the entries in adjacent items of the Figure 2 paradigm is not even a consideration, while it is for the entries in adjacent time segments of the observation paradigm in Figure 1.

This serial dependence interferes with the sum-score procedure used with observations for the following reasons. The sequence of separate observation scores, ordered by the time segments during which they are collected, form a time series. The scores in a time series may not be independent, as are the scores from other kinds of assessment data arrays, e.g., the responses to items in an attribute scale. Dependency among the scores in a time series can be evaluated by auto-correlation techniques. When all auto-correlations are zero, the time series is called stationary, i.e., the scores are independent of time. When auto-correlations are significantly larger than zero, the time series is called non-stationary, and the scores are, to varying degrees, dependent from one time segment to another. With stationary time series, the mean and variance of the distribution of scores are independent of time. This is not true when the time series is nonstationary. And, because of the dependence among scores in a nonstationary time series, the degrees of freedom in the distribution of points is less than in a distribution of independent scores.

The implications of serial dependency for behavioral scoring techniques used with observations collected over time are straightforward. Unless it can be demonstrated that a series of observations to be scored (i.e., summed, as in this example) is a stationary series, in which the scores are independent of time, then the sum-score procedure is an inappropriate use of the traditional psychometric model. The reason is that if trends or patterns exist as in a nonstationary series, the scores are not statistically independent. When this occurs, it is not theoretically possible to sample from any position in the time series and arrive at unbiased estimates of the mean and variance. Hence, contrary to suggestions that an individual's data can be viewed as a population of responses (Bijou, et al., 1969), some caution may be required in using traditional statistics with sets of serially dependent behavioral scores. With a stationary series in which scores are statistically independent, the classification of scores according to their temporal position in the series does not interfere (theoretically or practically) with the estimation of sample means or variances.

To illustrate the inappropriateness of this scoring procedure with time dependent observations in another context, consider the customary procedures for assessing the internal consistency or homogeneity of attribute scale scores. The split-half method of measuring internal consistency reliability requires the assumption that the items in one half of the scale (e.g., the odd items, or the first half of the items) are parallel, from a measurement standpoint, to the items in the other half. Further, it should be possible, according to the psychometric theory underlying these procedures, to sample sets of items from the scale in virtually any fashion and arrive at parallel scores. Now, when the data to be scored and checked for reliability are frequency counts of behaviors observed during sequentially dependent time samples, it is very likely that the split-half scoring methods will violate the assumption of parallelism in the possible subsets of time segments from which part scores could be derived. In other words, it seems very unlikely that one could sample subsets of time intervals from nonstationary series in virtually any fashion and arrive at parallel scores for the various samples. See Johnson's chapter in this volume for a review of various methods of assessing reliability of observations, including split-half procedures.

It is not difficult to construct examples to support these arguments when it is realized that cyclicity of behavior is a common phenomenon. Certainly variability of behavior over time is a particularly prevalent feature of human behavior, and often the variability will show discernable patterns or cycles. Suppose, for instance, that a child's irritability level reveals a morning-afternoon cycle which repeats daily. If observations were collected during a morning time sample and an afternoon time sample, and this sampling were repeated over days, the time series could likely show a cyclical pattern not unlike a sine function. Further, the auto-correlations would likely be significantly negative for lag one and significantly positive for lag two. In this hypothetical but not unrealistic example, the half of the observations scored from the morning clearly would not be parallel to the half scored from the afternoon. In fact, if an odd-even, split-half correlation were obtained, the relationship would be substantially negative, since all of the odd, or morning, scores would be low, and all of the even, or afternoon, scores would be high.

It may be that traditional ways of thinking about reliability estimation should be revamped for behavioral observation scores. Reliability "coefficients" perhaps should be based on the very characteristic of time series data which seemingly obviate the use of traditional methods. For example, as argued in the next section, the reliability of temporally ordered observations could be suspect unless significant auto-correlations are, in fact, found. That is, the behavior is predictable to some extent, given that an auto-correlational analysis shows the existence of serial dependency. For the behavior to be predictable, the scores must have some amount of reliability, generically. This idea, still just an idea, recasts the concept of reliability in time ordered behavioral data for the single case in terms of the subject's behavioral predictability.

Dilemmas in Scoring Behavioral Observations

It might be argued that sum-scoring of time series frequency data is defensible if lack of serial dependency can be shown. There are at least two logical dilemmas here. First, showing that serial dependency does not exist is akin to "proving" the null hypothesis. If all auto-correlations are shown to be not different from zero, it is possible, in fact parsimonious, to conclude that the basic data are so unreliable as to preclude the demonstration of serial dependency.

The second logical dilemma is more substantive in nature and related to the previous reconceptualization of reliability analysis for observation data. If in fact one could be convinced that serial dependency did not exist in a particular set of time series data, this would mean in effect that the subject's behavior is unpredictable. Statistically, the set of time ordered scores would be a set of totally unrelated, perhaps even random, numbers. Such a state of affairs in one's data is precisely the opposite of what would be desirable. Consider what total lack of serial dependency would mean. Simply stated, prediction of the subject's behavior from time sample to time sample would be impossible. Of course, knowing about other, concomitant individual or environmental events might enhance the likelihood of anticipating later scores in the behavioral series, but such sophisticated theoretical and methodological developments as multiple time series and environmental prediction scales are currently in their infancies. Unsatisfying as it may seem, the lack of serial dependency in time series data is not a desirable "out" for justifying the sum-scoring procedures outlined earlier. Instead, dependency seems necessary if behavioral predictability is to be realized. What is needed are methods for scoring serially dependent time series data which do not rely on the assumptions of classical test theory.

Unfortunately, it may well be that there are no existing scoring algorithms which can be used to summarize, in a single score, the important components of serially dependent time series data. A sum, or average, represents only one component, viz, level of the time series, and (as noted) completely ignores the time dependency in the set of scores, but also disregards the variability or scatter of the scores, or the overall slope of the series. These characteristics may just as likely show individual differences as does the level component. Alternative scores might include an index of serial dependence, e.g., auto-correlations, to compare the "predictability" of different subjects. Unfortunately, measures of scatter and slope characteristics suffer from the same methodological problems as do means when scores are not statistically independent.

Even if serial dependency were unimportant in scoring time series data, there is another inherent feature of behavioral research which, on logical grounds alone, seems to mitigate against the use of the traditional psychometric scoring procedures. Behavior theorists (e.g., Bijou, et al., 1969; Sidman, 1960; Skinner, 1966) and personality theorists (e.g., Mischel, 1968) alike argue that responses are largely under the control of external conditions of the environment. Stimulus controls, e.g., physical environmental factors and social interaction, are considered important determinants of the behavioral responses of subjects. But, environmental events in naturalistic settings are not static over time—to some extent they are unpredictable from occasion to occasion, particularly when the settings change in which behavior is observed. And yet, in much behavioral research, observations obtained from sequential time samples, which are very likely to occur under varying external environmental conditions, are simply added together as if the observed frequency scores were responses to a psychological inventory. The following section deals with this consideration in some detail.

Assessment Conditions for Observations vs. Tests

Psychological tests are designed to measure differences among persons for one or more behavioral attributes, while naturalistic observations are more often aimed at describing differences among behavioral attributes for one or more persons. In order for tests to provide comparable measures of individual differences, it is necessary that all subjects be tested under very similar assessment conditions. Hence, tests usually are administered during one occasion, in fairly restricted environmental settings, either to individuals or groups who respond to the same set of stimuli as others who take the test. By equating these assessment conditions, it is assumed that individual differences among resultant scores are largely due to variations in subjects' attribute status, rather than to variations in assessment conditions.

Naturalistic observations depart from this assessment model in several important respects, largely because they are focused on detailed descriptions of the ongoing behavior of individual subjects. Observations usually are collected over several time samples, under naturally occurring and hence varying environmental conditions, usually for one target individual at a time, and for several prescribed categories of behavior selected from the "stream of behavior." Often the assessment conditions under which observational data are obtained may be so obviously non-equivalent across different subjects that resultant behavioral scores are extremely unlikely to be comparable measures of individual differences among subjects. Even though assessment conditions do vary greatly among subjects, the resultant behavioral scores may be quite legitimately employed for intraindividual analyses, as in establishing the relative importance among the various behaviors in an individual's repertoire. In other cases, however, it may be argued legitimately that behavior scores could be treated as measures of individual differences when the assessment conditions surrounding the collection of the raw observational data are relatively invariant across subjects.

The importance of differences in assessment conditions lies in their effects on the behavior of the subjects being either tested or observed. If assessment conditions do affect behavior, whether in a testing or naturalistic observational setting, and the conditions vary among subjects, test scores or behavioral observations may not be comparable across subjects. To insure comparability of test scores among subjects, researchers in the experimental and psychometric traditions have imposed the aforementioned strict restrictions on the environmental conditions under which their subjects are examined. Observational data collected under restricted laboratory conditions seem to fit this tradition also.

But observational data collected in naturalistic settings do not. The assessment conditions under which ongoing behavior is observed and recorded typically will vary among subjects, if only because it is seldom feasible to observe all cases in a group study at the same time. Of course, none of this matters in single-subject studies, but it does matter when observational data are to be used in group studies in which individual differences among subjects are important.

It is this writer's contention that comparability of naturalistic observational data across subjects is extremely difficult to support, on logical, empirical, or statistical grounds. Nevertheless, researchers do employ observational data, e.g., behavioral frequency counts, in group studies. And, statistical methods employed and the psychological interpretations of results are borrowed directly from the experimental and psychometric traditions of psychological research. Since this common practice is not likely to be changed, for numerous complex reasons, those engaged in such research should at least be aware of the effects that the measurement properties of their data have on some analyses and interpretations of behavioral observation scores. Some of these considerations occupy the remainder of this chapter.

Ipsatized Observation Scores

As a way of introducing differences in the measurement characteristics of test vs. observation scores, consider the data in Table 1 which gives

Table 1 Hypothetical Raw Score Matrix

S	A	B	C	D	E	Total
1	8	16	38	94	474	630
2	9	13	31	56	306	415
3	6	15	27	68	477	593
4	1	15	29	38	402	485
5	2	12	28	47	594	683
6	2	17	40	80	558	697
7	1	10	49	29	549	638
8	3	15	23	45	522	608
9	1	16	39	25	336	417
10	9	14	30	26	375	454
Total	42	143	334	508	4,593	
Mean	4.2	14.3	33.4	50.8	459.3	

scores for 10 persons on each of five attributes (A through E). Even without knowing the specific procedures used to generate these data, it is clear that the five sets of scores have different units of measurement, since their means and variances differ widely. This is not a problem for comparisons between two or more scores within a single attribute, but if analyses of scores between attributes are desired, either for the same individual or among different individuals, the differences in measurement units between the attribute scores must be removed (Clemans, 1966).

For example, suppose the measures in Table 1 were ratings on a scale from 1 to 9 (attribute A), raw scores on a 20-item personality scale (attribute B), scores on two longer inventory scales (attributes C and D), and finally, College Board scores (attribute E). Neither inter- nor intraindividual comparisons between the attribute scores are appropriate unless the differences in units of measurement have been removed by equating the means and variances. It would be nonsense, for instance, to compare the first person's score of 8 on attribute A with his score of 474 on attribute E, or with the second person's score of 56 on attribute D. But such comparisons would be appropriate if the raw scores were converted to standard scores.

Now, suppose that the data in Table 1 are not ratings or scale scores but are frequencies for five behaviors derived from direct observations. The range and magnitude of these hypothetical scores are not atypical of frequency data which might be generated, say, by summing observations over several days of hour-long observation periods for each of five behavior categories. (Whether or not such summing is defensible is discussed in the first section of this chapter.) Interpreted as frequency data, A is clearly a low rate behavior (e.g., hitting) while E is a high rate behavior (e.g., talking).

The difference in means and variances indicate that the five sets of behavioral observation scores have different units of measurement, just as was true when these hypothetical data were presented as test scores.However, because frequency scores involve a different scale of measurement from test scores, some kinds of inter-individual comparisons are appropriate for the behavioral observation scores which were not justifiable for the test scores, in spite of the differences in units of measurement. Frequency scores have a precise and meaningful origin, viz, zero, while most test scores do not. In the traditional classification of measurement scales, frequency scores have the characteristics of ratio scales (Guilford, 1965), while test scores usually have the characteristics of either interval or ordinal scales.

Interpreting the hypothetical scores in Table 1 as behavioral frequencies, one could make the following kinds of comparisons among scores. Subject 1 exhibited twice as much of behavior B as behavior A (scores of 16 for B vs. 8 for A). These kinds of comparisons based on ratios of scores within and across both subjects and behaviors are quite appropriate from a measurement standpoint even though the score distributions have different means and standard deviations. It would seem, therefore, that behavioral observation frequency scores possess measurement properties that recommend them over more traditional kinds of interval or ordinal psychological measures, such as tests or rating scales, for interindividual comparisons of scores. However, the apparent superiority of observational frequency scores is clouded by the fact that the assessment conditions under which natural istic observational data are collected usually vary across subjects, as already noted.

Proportional Scoring of Observational Frequency Data

When assessment conditions vary across subjects, an often-encountered effect is that the total number of behavioral observations will vary from subject to subject. In Table 1 this situation is represented by the different total frequencies in the right-most column. Differences in the amount of time subjects are observed would be an obvious cause of different behavior totals. Alternatively, some settings may be more likely to elicit some behaviors than others. Also, some subjects may have higher activity levels than others. Numerous differences among assessment conditions, behavioral propensities of subjects, and the interaction of subjects and conditions can cause differences in the total amount of behavior recorded with naturalistic observation systems.

Users of behavioral frequency data have been quick to recognize that variations in total behavior across subjects interferes with valid interindividual comparisons among scores. For example, comparisons between the first two subjects' frequency scores for any of the five behaviors (in Table 1) should take into account the fact that about half again as much total data was obtained for the first subject than for the second. Logically, then, even though the ratio scales of measurement underlying the frequency scores permit direct comparisons of the scores, intersubject differences in total behavior clearly reduce the legitimacy of such comparisons.

To solve this problem, investigators often convert raw frequency data to proportions by dividing each subject's separate behavioral frequency scores by the total behavior score. To illustrate this "correction" procedure, Table 2 shows the proportion scores calculated from the raw frequency data in Table 1. Note that the effect of the adjustment of raw scores varies from subject to subject, depending on the magnitude of the total behavior score. For example, subjects 3 and 4 had identical frequency scores for behavior B (Table 1), but now have different proportion scores (Table 2). This, of course, is precisely the kind of adjustment that proportional scoring is designed to produce.

There are other features of the proportion scoring procedure worth noting. The rank order of raw frequency scores within an individual's profile is not changed by the proportion scoring procedure. This is most important for intraindividual analyses of an individual's behavioral repertoire. Of course, if the research interest is solely on within-subject study of behavioral scores, there may be no particular need to calculate proportion scores, since differences in total behavior between subjects would probably be irrelevant. The only value of proportion scores in single-subject studies would be to provide a

Table 2			Hypothetical Proportion Score Matrix			
S	A	B	C	D	E	Total
1	.013	.025	.060	.149	.752	.999
2	.022	.031	.075	.135	.737	1.000
3	.010	.025	.046	.115	.804	1.000
4	.002	.031	.060	.078	.829	1.000
5	.003	.018	.041	.069	.870	1.001
6	.003	.024	.057	.115	.800	.999
7	.002	.016	.077	.045	.860	1.000
8	.005	.025	.038	.074	.859	1.001
9	.002	.038	.094	.060	.806	1.000
10	.020	.031	.066	.057	.826	1.000
Mean	.008	.026	.061	.090	.814	.999

familiar metric, i.e., percentages, which in most contexts are more understandable than raw frequencies. In general, however, the effect of proportion scoring on intraindividual analyses is rather minimal.

But the effects of proportion scoring on some kinds of interindividual analyses may not be minimal. The most important effect of proportional scoring from the standpoint of such analyses is that proportion scores for each subject, unlike raw scores, are interdependent. In terms of a distinction offered by Cattell (1944), proportion scores are expressed in "ipsative" units. The salient feature of ipsative measures is that each score for a subject is not statistically independent of his scores for the other behaviors in the set of measures. Ipsative measures should be distinguished from differential measures, where the scores for an individual are dependent neither on other scores for that individual nor on the scores for other individuals. Frequency scores for behavioral observation categories may be differential measures. But when transformed to proportions these differential scores become ipsative measures. Before discussing the impact of this measurement distinction on interindividual analyses of behavioral observation scores, a simple illustration will serve to clarify further the differences between differential and ipsative measures.

Ipsative vs. Differential Measures

Suppose an assessment task required the measurement of several individuals on three characteristics, X, Y, and Z. Employing verbal reports either from the individuals themselves or from informed respondents, each individual could be assigned a *rating* on an appropriate scale for each of the characteristics, one at a time. This common procedure yields *differential* measurements for individuals on each of the three characteristics. The scores for an individual are free, procedurally, to vary independently of each other, and independently of the scores for other individuals. There are no constraints inherent in the measurement process which make an individual's score on one of the characteristics dependent on, or related to, his scores on the others. Of course, there may be empirical relationships among the three characteristics, e.g., in some samples of individuals, it may be that a high score on X will be associated with a low score on Y, but such relationships among the characteristics have nothing to do with any procedural aspects of the measurement process per se.

Now take the same illustrative assessment task, but this time each individual is to be *ranked* on the three characteristics. Unlike ratings, ranks for an individual do not vary independently of one another: if the individual is assigned the highest rank on one characteristic, the other characteristics must be assigned lower ranks. The ranking of the three characteristics in this example requires that the sum of the ranks be 6, i.e., 1 + 2 + 3. Clearly, an individual cannot obtain a rank of 1 (or 3) on all of the characteristics. Ranks are interdependent within the individual's score profile and illustrate ipsative measures.

Clemans (1966), Hicks (1970), and others have argued that differential and ipsative scores should not be interpreted as if they were equivalent forms of measurement. To illustrate using the preceding example, a rating of 3 on attribute X means that an individual has more of X than an individual with a rating of 2 on attribute X. Differential measures, such as the ratings in this example, can be interpreted in absolute terms without reference to the individual's status on other attributes in the set of measures. In contrast, two individuals' ranks of 3 and 2 on attribute A mean that the first individual ranks higher relative to his other ranks on the remaining two attributes than does the second individual relative to *his* other ranks. Thus ipsative measures, such as the rankings, should be interpreted only in a relative sense, i.e., in relation to the other measures in the set of attributes. It is entirely possible that an individual's rank on some attribute may be larger, relative to his other ranks, than another individual's rank on the same attribute, but that if differential measures of the attribute were obtained, the first individual actually might score lower on the attribute in absolute terms than the second individual (Clemans, 1966).

In examining the measurement characteristics of ipsative measures, Clemans (1966) assumes theoretically that underlying any set of ipsative measures there exists a set of absolute or differential measures.[3] In terms of the preceding examples, the set of ratings of the three individuals on the three characteristics would be the set of absolute or differential measures underlying the set of rankings of each individual on the attributes. Given a set of differential measures, Clemans shows that statistical transformations can be employed to create ipsatized measures. Such "generated" ipsative measures may or may not match ipsative measures obtained directly, e.g., rankings. The important point is that if the researcher collects differential measures and then opts to transform them into ipsative form, that is his perogative and the manipulation may well suit his purpose. However, when ipsatizing transformations are applied to raw differential measures, the interpretations of the resultant scores should change. The ipsatized scores should be interpreted in the relative sense, as described above, not in the absolute sense appropriate for differential measures.

Proportional Scores as Ipsative Measures

The parallels between the ratings and rankings in the preceding example and behavioral observation raw frequencies and proportion scores should be evident. The ratings and frequencies are examples of differential measures which can be appropriately interpreted in an absolute sense. The rankings and proportion scores are examples of ipsative measures which should be interpreted in reference to other scores in the set for each individual. If interindividual interpretations are desired, they should be presented as the relative strengths of scores within the set of scores for each of the individuals being compared. Appropriate kinds of interpretations of the frequency and proportion scores were presented in the earlier sections dealing with the hypothetical data in Tables 1 and 2.

From a measurement standpoint, an individual's set of proportion scores derived from observation frequencies are very similar to a set of rankings. The sum of a set of rankings is a constant for all individuals ranked on the same number of attributes, just as the sum of proportion scores is a constant for all individuals. As with ranks, an individual's set of proportion scores are not statistically independent, since high proportions on some behaviors must be accompanied by low proportions on others. With differential measurements, such as ratings or behavior frequencies, it is possible (although perhaps not likely) for an individual to score high, or low, on all behaviors, not just some as with rankings and proportion scores.

Another way to illustrate the dependency among sets of ipsatized scores involves the effect of deleting behavior categories on proportion scores for the remaining categories. Suppose one behavior category is dropped from a multicode data set (after observations have been collected) and the proportion scores are recalculated using the lowered total behavior frequency as the correction factor. Now the revised proportion scores differ from the original scores by varying amounts, depending on individual differences in the frequency of the deleted category. Or, suppose a category is simply not observed. Compared with observations including all categories, the total of all behaviors observed may differ, and therefore the proportion scores based on the total codes will differ.

In constrast, scores can be added to or deleted from a set of differential measures with no direct effect whatsoever on other scores. This is true of observational frequency scores so long as the addition or deletion of behavioral categories does not change the assessment conditions under which the required behaviors would have been observed. In the case of proportion scores, however, any changes in the measurement operations either at the time of scoring or during the actual observation sessions can result in changes in the subjects' scores.

Ipsatizing Features of Behavior Coding Systems

Proportion scores are derived ipsative measurements, in contrast to another form of score interdependency which originates at the data collection stage. The latter kind of interdependency in the raw data appears to be inherent in the data-generating procedures employed by some multibehavior code observation systems.

For either theoretical or practical reasons, most coding systems sample selectively from the stream of behavior, with the result that only a portion of the ongoing behavior is actually observed with the intent of recording its occurrence. This in itself does not directly affect the measurement characteristics of the observed behavior scores unless the coding system imposes priorities as to whether or not specific behaviors are to be recorded when several occur virtually simultaneously. For multicode observation systems, priority coding is necessary because of the practical problem of recording the occurrence of several behaviors which happen at once, i.e., within the same time sample. This procedural necessity means that frequencies for low priority behaviors will be different from what they would be if placed higher in the hierarchy, or if they were coded separately (i.e., not as one of several other codes in the same observation system).

Priority coding usually means that frequencies for low priority codes will tend to be lowered as the frequency of higher priority codes increases, particularly when the two classes of behavior tend to occur nearly simultaneously. This problem is especially acute when coders are restricted to recording only one behavior during each of numerous short time samples. The magnitude of low priority behavior scores will be dependent on the joint occurrence of low and high priority behaviors during the observation periods.

Time sampling constraints contribute to ipsativity in behavioral observation scores. Usually because of the physical difficulties inherent in trying to code all behavioral events from the stream of behavior, time samples partition the ongoing behavior into recordable units. Time samples of 60, 30, 15, and even 6 seconds are found in the observation literature. Coding systems which utilize time sampling often limit the number of behaviors that can be recorded during each sample, either for practical reasons or to increase the comparability of observations among subjects. When such restraints are imposed, priority coding may also be required. Observers typically will observe more behavior than the coding system allows them to record; hence there must be some basis for deciding which behavior to record. Thus there is an interaction between the problems created by priority coding and the time sampling constraints imposed on the observers' coding activities. Together these restrictions produce interdependencies among the recorded behavioral scores and thus generate partial ipsativity in the raw observational data.

In general, ipsative measures will be generated by a coding system in which the sum of the behavior category frequency scores tends to be a constant for all individuals, a primary characteristic of purely ipsatized measures (Clemans, 1966). A fairly common procedure required of coders by many observational systems results in similar or virtually identical frequencies of coded behaviors for all subjects observed during equivalent time periods. This procedure usually takes the form of a priority coding operation which prescribes which of two or more temporally proximal behaviors shall be coded in any one trial or coding interval (e.g., Barclay and Montgomery, 1968; Meichenbaum, et al., 1968; Patterson, et al., 1969). The observers record only one of a prescribed set of code categories during each specified time segment, even though more than one category of behavior may have occurred, and/or one behavior may have occurred more than once. The primary effect of this procedure is to remove from the subject's data protocol both the number and variety of actual behaviors which may have occurred. Hence, for any given observation period the heterogeneity of recorded behaviors is reduced by the priority restraint, and each individual is coded the same number of times.

Actual behavior in natural settings, however, varies both in frequency and kind from person to person. Unrestricted recording of behavioral events would tend to insure that all occurrences of observed behaviors would be included in the coded protocol. To the extent that priority restrictions are removed from an observational coding system, the raw frequency data should become less subject to ipsatizing influences. As the number of behavior categories is decreased there should be an accompanying decrease in the need for priority coding or arbitrary definition of time periods within which a coder must operate. In the limiting case where only one discrete behavior is recorded the resulting frequency scores will be clear instances of differential measures.

A Hypothetical Example

Consider an observational coding system[4] including, say, 25 behavior categories such as Play (PL), Talk (TA), and Work (WK). Trained observers code family interactions in the home for specified periods of time, regulated by a timing mechanism which partitions a five-minute observation into 10 thirty-second intervals. One family member is the observational target for each five-minute period and coders record sequences of behavioral interaction between the target and other family members. A sequence is defined as one interaction between the target subject and one or more family members. To code a sequence, the observer records both the appropriate behavior categories and the individual who performed each behavior. To reduce the need for multiple coding of temporally contiguous behaviors, the 25 behavior categories are grouped into an order hierarchy, such that if a first-order and a second-order behavior occur together, only the first-order behavior is coded.

For example, a sequence might be the target child talking to his mother who in turn talks to the child. This sequence would be coded—1TA 3TA—where the numbers 1 and 3 are labels for the target child and his mother respectively, and TA is the mnemonic symbol for talking. The coding instructions encourage observers to record one such sequence every six seconds, or an average of five sequences every 30 seconds.

The data collected for one target subject can be displayed in a 10-row by 25-column matrix, representing the 10 thirty-second intervals and the 25 behavior categories, respectively. The cell entries in this matrix are frequencies ranging from zero to five. The upper limit imposed by the coding system may be occasionally exceeded due either to the double coding of two behaviors within a sequence or to coding more than five sequences in one 30-second interval. In general, however, five behaviors are recorded from the set of 25 possible categories within each 30-second period. These five codes may represent five different behaviors or five occurrences of the same behavior. Collecting the counts over the 10 thirty-second intervals (ignoring temporal dependency for now) a total of 50 behaviors will usually be recorded for each subject, and these will be distributed among the 25 code categories in the form of frequency scores. This row vector of scores, the sum of which may range from 0 to 50, is the basic set of data generated by the coding system for each subject.

Consider now a typical data matrix of n rows (subjects) and m columns (the 25 behavior category scores). The sum of each row's frequency scores is a constant for all subjects (c = 50). The behavioral category measures are fully ipsatized, a condition brought about by the coding procedures used to generate the raw data from which the frequency scores are derived. Any behavioral observation and coding system which produces raw data points and frequency scores in a manner similar to this example probably will generate at least partially ipsatized measures also.

To clarify these points, consider the fictitious data displayed in Table 3. Four subjects were coded using the above procedures, and their frequency scores from the five-minute observation period were obtained. All of the first subject's behavior was coded as working (WK = 50). S_2 talked and worked equally (WK = 25; TA = 25). S_3 talked exclusively (TA = 50); and S_4 talked some (TA = 10), did not work (WK = 0), and engaged in two other behaviors (no. 2 =

Table 3 Hypothetical Ipsatized Scores for Four Subjects

	Behavioral Categories 1	2	3........	TA.....	WK.....	24	25	$\sum_{1}^{25}$
S_1				0	50			50
S_2				25	25			50
S_3				50	0			50
S_4		10		10	0	30		50

10, and no. 24 = 30). Note that each subject's scores total to 50, the constraint imposed by the coding procedures as described above. Since Work is a first-order behavior and Talk a second-order behavior, , WK was given coding priority over TA.

Interpreting these data interindividually, one might want to argue that S_2 is less of a talker than S_3, since their TA scores are 25 and 50, respectively. Assume for the moment that each of the 25 WKs for S_2 was actually accompanied by talking. Had the priority coding procedure not been followed, S_2 would have been given 50 TAs and 25 WKs—indicating that S_2 is not less of a talker than S_3; in fact, they are equally talkative. In this illustration, the coding system generates ipsative measures which lead to one interpretation of between-subjects differences, while the same information collected in differential measurement units would lead to another interpretation.

Consider another example. The low score of S_4 on TA does not mean necessarily that S_4 is less talkative than S_1, S_2, or S_3—only that S_4 produced two other codable behaviors in addition to talking, and this variety of coded behaviors necessarily depressed the TA frequency for S_4. This example should highlight the impact that experimental interdependence among ipsatized measures has on any interindividual comparisons. In effect, the coding system's constraints are such that behaviorally heterogeneous subjects will, of necessity, score lower on most or all behavior categories than behaviorally homogeneous subjects. If total output of behavior were allowed to vary across subjects, it might be the case that behaviorally varied subjects would produce higher frequencies in some categories than subjects whose behavior is less varied.

The possible difficulties imposed by ipsative measures of observed behavior may suggest revamping certain behavioral coding systems so as to generate differential measures which can be employed for both inter- and intraindividual analyses (Clemans, 1966). Redesigning coding schemes could involve removing arbitrarily defined time units or behavioral sequences which require priority coding of ongoing behaviors. In general, any system which will permit variations across subjects in the total number of behaviors recorded will "non-ipsatize" observational raw data. This may, however, produce unwanted variations in the raw data due to differences between coders or observational time periods across subjects. Some of these unwanted influences can be removed by statistical corrections, such as standardizing raw data within coders.

Realistically, changes in existing coding systems should be based on empirical and/or rational analyses of the extent to which the raw data are subject to the kinds of constraints which will produce either partially or fully ipsatized measures. To obtain an empirical test, behavioral frequencies could be collected two ways in the same sample—first by using a restricted coding system which is being tested for its ipsativity characteristics, and second, by obtaining simple unrestricted frequency counts of each behavioral category in the coding system. If the two procedures yield comparable scores both across and within subjects, problems with ipsativity probably can be discounted. If, however, interindividual comparisons of scores are not similar for the two sets of measures, caution may be required when interpreting the scores differentially, and changes in the coding procedures might be warranted.

Summary

It was argued that a useful conceptual and methodological distinction can be drawn between observational and testing procedures for collecting psychological data. Traditionally, the former strategy has been concerned with a comprehensive behavioral description for an individual organism, usually in the form of sequential time samples of single or multiple psychological characteristics or events. In contrast, testing procedures are concerned with psychological descriptions which are comparable among many individuals, usually in the form of single concurrent samples of responses to standardized stimuli.

The evolution of measurement and data analysis principles and procedures, such as those from classical test theory and various statistical inferential models, has been based on the assumption that psychological data are comparable among subjects. Subjects can be formed into samples for statistical analysis so long as each individual has been treated the same vis-a-vis measurement or experimental operations. When comparability among subjects does not hold, or when single subjects are the focus of psychological investigation, the measurement and statistical procedures designed for group data may be either inappropriately used or misleadingly interpreted.

Unfortunately, *n-of-1* research in psychology has occupied such an unpopular position that appropriate methods for the analysis of single subject data have not been as well developed or as quickly borrowed from other disciplines as has been true of methods for analysis of group data. Until recent emphasis in behavior modification research on both naturalistic observation data and single subject studies, the lack of analytic methods for intraindividual investigations has not been a particularly important concern. But a possible problem now seems to be evolving, brought about by the adoption of group analysis methods by single subject researchers, a development commendable for its appreciation of scientific rigor, but perhaps misguided in its enthusiasm.

This paper has reviewed several methodological problems which are sometimes encountered when users of single subject data apply traditional group-focused measurement and statistical procedures. The following three classes of problems were discussed and illustrated with hypothetical data: (a) intraindividual dependencies among behavioral observations; (b) interindividual incomparability of assessment conditions in observational data; and (c) ipsative versus differential measures derived from observed frequency data.

Footnotes

1. Paper presented at the Fourth Banff International Conference on Behavior Modification, Banff, Alberta, Canada, March 1972.

2. This study was supported by Grants MH12972 and MH15985 from the National Institute of Mental Health, United States Public Health Service.

3. The mathematically sophisticated reader is referred to Clemans (1966) for a detailed explanation of this point.

4. This hypothetical example draws extensively on a coding system designed by Patterson, et al. (1969). The intent is not to criticize arbitrarily what is clearly a well-conceived system, but to illustrate several points using an observational procedure which seems similar in several respects to other behavioral coding systems (e.g., Werry and Quay, 1969).

References

Barclay, J. and Montgomery, R. *Preliminary report: Evaluation of the effectiveness of Summer 1968 Title VI-A Teacher Training Institutes.* Castro Valley, Cal.: Skills Development and Research, Inc.

Bijou, S. W., Peterson, R. F., Harris, F. R., Allen, K.E., and Johnston, M. S. Methodology for experimental studies of young children in natural settings. *The Psychological Record,* 1969, *19*, 177-210.

Cattell, R. B. Psychological measurement: Normative, ipsative, interactive. *Psychological Review,* 1944, *51*, 292-303.

Clemans, W. V. An analytical and empirical examination of some properties of ipsative measures. *Psychometric Monographs*, 1966, *14*.

Gottman, J. M., McFall, R. M., and Barnett, J. T. Design and analysis of research using time-series. *Psychological Bulletin,* 1969, *72*, 299-306.

Guilford, J. P. *Fundamental statistics in psychology and education.* (4th ed.) New York: McGraw-Hill, 1965.

Hicks, L. E. Some properties of ipsative, normative, and forced-choice normative measures. *Psychological Bulletin*, 1970, *74*, 167-184.

Holtzman, W. H. Statistical models for the study of change in the single case. In C. W. Harris (Ed.), *Problems in measuring change.* Madison: University of Wisconsin Press, 1963.

Hutt, S. J. and Hutt, C. *Direct observation and measurement of behavior.* Springfield, Ill.: Charles C. Thomas, 1970.

Meichenbaum, D. H., Bowers, K. S., and Ross, R. R. Modification of classroom behavior of institutionalized female adolescent offenders. *Behavior Research and Therapy*, 1968, *6*, 343-353.

Mischel, W. *Personality assessment.* New York: Wiley, 1968.

Namboodiri, N. K. Experimental designs in which each subject is used repeatedly. *Psychological Bulletin*, 1972, *77*, 54-64.

Patterson, G. R., Ray, R. S., Shaw, D. A., and Cobb, J. A. Manual for the coding of family interactions. Unpublished manuscript, Oregon Research Institute, 1969.

Raush, H. L. Naturalistic aspects of the clinical research method. *Human Development,* 1967, *10*, 155-169.

Sidman, M. *The tactics of scientific research: Evaluating experimental data in psychology.* New York: Basic Books, 1960.

Skinner, B. F. Operant behavior. In W. K. Honig (Ed.), *Operant behavior: Areas of research and application.* New York: Appleton-Century-Crofts, 1966.

Werry, J. S. and Quay, H. C. Observing the classroom behavior of elementary school children. *Exceptional Children,* 1969, *35*, 461-470.

Yamamoto, K., Jones, J. P., and Ross, M. B. A note on the processing of classroom observation records. *American Educational Research Journal,* 1972, *9*, 29-44.

TWO

Section Two: Conceptual Issues

TWO

Introduction

L. A. Hamerlynck

The second generation of research and practice in behavior modification (Stuart, Chapter 9) would appear to be examining several of its basic assumptions or givens. Some assumptions which are under examination in this section are:

1. Ethics and motivation
2. Power of reinforcing consequences
3. High base rate of prerequisite behaviors for intervention
4. Generalization of training programs

The chapters in this section overlap in their discussion of the assumptions in question. The reader will find four suggestions for alternative or supplemental views for the old assumptions:

1. Control of Behavior (Davison, Stuart, Reid and Hendriks)
2. Stimulus Control (Patterson)
3. Classroom Survival Behaviors (Hops and Cobb)
4. Contingent and Precise Training (Reid and Hendriks, Hops and Cobb, Patterson)

Control of Behavior

I strongly suspect that this issue is overdue for consideration by all behavior modifiers, if only because of the impact of *Beyond Freedom and Dignity* (Skinner, 1971). The issue of control and counter-control is not new as evidenced by the psychoanalytic concept of resistance. B. F. Skinner has devoted separate discussions to the question of counter-controlling of social control institutions, i.e., religion, politics, education, psychotherapy, etc. in *Science and Human Behavior* (Skinner, 1953). In this section Davison discusses the problem of counter-control in therapy and research. He details the issue with regard to history, clinical experience, and the literature in related disciplines. His concluding questions should be seriously considered by the researcher as well as the therapist.

Stuart extends the discussion of counter-control into the arena of ethics, and he examines the question with specific reference to the interaction of scientific vigor and therapeutic goals. Stuart provides a framework for all scientist/practitioners to examine their dual roles in their interaction with other human beings. Finally, the issue is again found in subtle but real form in the Reid and Hendriks paper. They discuss the failure of an intervention with a boy who stole. There is other substance to their paper, but in terms of control of human behavior they provide vivid clinical evidence for partial explanation of counter-control during intervention. Their experience is best summarized by Ogden Lindsley's prescription for Ideal Mental Health Services—"When you pass the behavioral buck—make it contingent!" (Lindsley, 1969).

It would be simplistic to expect that we can resolve the question of control and counter-control just with Lindsley's prescription, particularly in environments where the therapist or researcher does not have positive consequences available. However, I am sure that a significant determinant to unexplained variability in our research and practice is due to the fact that we forget to assure that significant consequences are made contingent upon the behaviors involved. Within a positively reinforcing system, the moral issue of control of human behavior is significantly reduced, as the controller must provide or give consequences defined by the client or subject. Perhaps this is the accurate empathy, non-possessive warmth and genuineness described by Truax (1963)?

Stimulus Control

There is probably a very close relationship between the methodological problems of data collection and analysis and the fact that the accounting for antecedent behaviors in complex interactions is still of low rate in the literature. Researchers and clinicians generally pay attention to the consequences of behaviors rather than to the events preceding the behaviors. The usual data system precludes such analysis as it includes the behavior and then the consequence in close continguity. Patterson and his colleagues have developed an observational system with data analysis procedures which permits them to look at the complete behavioral event network—Antecedent Events, Targeted Behavior, and Consequent Events.

Recall that Patterson has examined questions about aggressive behaviors within classrooms, homes, and institutions. Then add the fact that many aggressive behaviors are episodic as well as having relatively low base rates. How can a data system for research and intervention attend *only* to the consequences of a deviant behavior and offer adequate explanation and prescription? Patterson has shown it cannot. To understand and do something about a child who "sets fire to one car per week—on the average" requires a data base *including antecedent events* or we risk mentalistic constructs. Patterson has accepted the empirical question, and the promise is considerable.

I urge the reader to pay careful attention to the notation system and also to become familiar with the data collection procedures. The consequences are exciting.

Classroom Survival Behaviors

A common prescription to teachers is, "Ignore deviant behavior and pay attention to appropriate behavior." When the deviant behavior is obviously inappropriate for the classroom such as high-rate "talk out," the prescription is excellent. Validity or confirmation is also likely when the task is locked into the teaching situation. However, problems arise when the task requirements have not been mastered by the child and/or the teacher is unable to define the task requirements and their prerequisites.

Hops and Cobb describe their work in developing a typology of pretask and task-specific behaviors for survival in classrooms. Also included in the paper is evidence of the significance of precise training of individuals acting as agents of change, i.e., teachers. In summary, the authors have offered evidence of the direction and probable results to behavior modification if we avoid the unquestioning expectancy that children know how to be taught or that teachers realize their noninstructional requirements.

Pinpoint Training for Intervention

I recently reviewed a manuscript describing a program of intervention for emotionally disturbed children. The triadic model of Tharp and Wetzel was used with the parents acting as the therapists (Tharp and Wetzel, 1969). The investigators reported some fine changes but simultaneously stretched the assumption of generalization of training to the breaking point. Two sentences were used to describe how the parents were trained utilizing a programmed text. Most investigators and clinicians would not "trust" such a hopeful procedure (nor expect editors to forgive). However, a serious weakness in the science and technology is the acceptance of general or non-specific training of agents of change. We also commit the mistake of failing to provide for the maintenance of established behaviors.

Hops and Cobb describe how they worked with teachers for the survival behaviors study. Patterson gives some of the details in training the family of a deviant child and then shows where they probably failed in training and support.

Reid and Hendriks, in their paper discussing differential characteristics of stealers and non-stealers, describe their clinical experience with counter-controlling parents in training. They also describe how Patterson, Reid, and Cobb, acting as therapists, handled the problem. It is strong evidence of the need for incentives and pinpointed training.

Lindsley, O. Comment during discussion at the First Banff International Conference in Behavior Modification, Banff, Alberta, Canada, March 1969..

Skinner, B. F. *Beyond freedom and dignity*. New York: Knopf, 1971.

Skinner, B. F. *Science and human behavior*. New York: MacMillan, 1953.

Tharp, R. G. and Wetzel, R. J., *Behavior modification in the natural environment.* New York: Academic Press, 1969.

Truax, C. B., Effective ingredients in psychotherapy: An approach to unravelling the therapist-patient interaction. *Journal of Counseling Psychology*, 1963, *10*, 256-264.

Counter-Control in Behavior Modification[1]

5

Gerald C. Davison

The distance between theory and practice is frequently discussed in scientific circles, and there is no dearth of such discussion in our own field (e.g., London, 1964; Lazarus and Davison, 1971). While important for the scientist, this disjunction between what we say at the abstract level and what we do at the applied level is particularly important in clinical work. Largely through experiences over the past several years in training graduate students and postdoctoral fellows in clinical behavior therapy, I have become acutely aware of and occasionally uncomfortable with the distance between theory and practice. Indeed, it is when one tries to explain to a trainee why he behaved as he did in a given clinical situation that the weaknesses and limitations of available conceptual schemes become clear.

Many areas relate to this topic, and we have considered some of these in an earlier paper (Lazarus and Davison, 1971). Discussion here will be restricted to what may be termed counter-control, that is, the extent to which a client may resist the efforts of a therapist to change him. This issue has been discussed far too little, though it is likely that skillful practitioners and astute researchers are not unaware of the problem. Hopefully it will be useful to make the issue more explicit and to look into some selected areas of the social sciences for ideas and data not typically regarded within the purview of behavior modification.

Counter-Control in Current Behavioral Techniques

In a recent film (Davison, et al., 1971), a homosexual client wishing to change had to be persuaded by the therapist to employ a rather unusual and somewhat difficult therapy procedure. While it is unnecessary here to go into the details of the technique (see Davison, 1968; Marquis, 1970), what is noteworthy for the present purposes is the point at which the client refused initially to follow the therapist's instructions. The therapist was faced with the choice either of switching gears entirely or else, believing that he should persist, persuading the client to go along with the procedure. There is little doubt that it is at this juncture that many novice behavior therapists either lose their clients entirely or are otherwise severely handicapped in attempting to help them change. For if a client is not willing to go along with the therapeutic strategy, treatment as a whole can become problematical.

To give some other examples from current behavior therapy techniques, consider how much cooperation from the client is necessary for most of the procedures available to us (with *perhaps* the exception of operant shaping procedures with institutionalized patients, though some possible problems with these are noted at the end of this paper). Systematic desensitization, for example, requires that the client generate a vivid image, that he do it at a particular point in time and for a certain period of time, and that he attempt to relax himself while confronting the fantasied scene. An uncooperative or unwilling client can obviously sabotage the procedure. Another procedure, covert sensitization, entails the imagined association of negative feelings with stimulus situations which are deemed by the client and the therapist to be undesirably appealing. Here again the client can readily defeat whatever beneficial goals the technique is capable of achieving. Along similar lines, I have previously (Davison, 1970) raised questions about contingency management procedures where the client remains in ultimate control of whether he is going to use a particular technique or device which, *if utilized,* would indeed change his behavior. For example, the cigarette box devised by Azrin and Powell (1968) requires that the smoker abide by the agreement to take cigarettes only from this pack. Clearly, he is free to take cigarettes from other sources if he so desires. To the extent that he takes cigarettes exclusively from the specially designed case, which provides cigarettes only after a specified period of time has passed, his smoking rate will *necessarily* be reduced. And finally, the technique described in the Davison, et al. (1971) film requires that the patient masturbate at home to certain pictorial stimuli in a prescribed fashion; obviously extensive cooperation and motivation is required here as well.

Hopefully these examples will suffice to support my basic thesis that nearly everything we do in behavior modification requires the active cooperation of the client. This is especially true when the therapist cannot be present whenever the problematic behavior may occur, and/or when the therapist's presence cannot ensure the forcing out of a particular response at any given time. Let me reiterate that I am sure most people are not unaware of these issues (surely non-behavior modifiers are sensitive to them). What is not clear to me, however, is how adequately we have conceptualized this problem and, indeed, to what extent we have formally dealt with it in our writing and our clinical teaching.[2]

Social Science and Counter-Control

Several areas of social science seem to offer something of value to behavior modifiers with respect to the topic of counter-control.

Brehm's Theory of Psychological Reactance (1966)

For several years Brehm and his co-workers have studied experimentally what happens when a person is led to believe that he is free in a particular choice situation and is then threatened with or actually deprived of that freedom. In other words, what happens when an individual perceives himself to have choice and then sees this choice threatened, restricted, or eliminated by an external authority?

Numerous reactance theory experiments have shown several factors to be important in how hard a person works *against* an influence attempt. Among these factors are the importance of the freedom for satisfying certain needs, the proportion of freedoms eliminated, and the amount of pressure to comply where elimination of freedom is threatened.

What happens when reactance is aroused? There seems to be an increased desire to engage in the behavior, an increased desire to have the tabooed object, an increased tendency actually to engage in the behavior, and an increased tendency to encourage another person to engage in the eliminated or threatened behavior. In other words, what one as an agent of change wants *not* to happen may well happen *because* of the influence attempt.

As with all analogue work, we must of course beware lest we attribute too much external validity to such findings, and certainly Brehm and his associates are sensitive to this. For the subjects in these experiments are college undergraduates, and the behaviors manipulated would seem to be of far less personal importance than what clients bring to us. Furthermore, Brehm points to an important qualifying condition that would seem to be of great relevance in our clinical work, namely, the extent to which a person perceives himself as already having given up a certain degree of freedom even before encountering the agent of change. That is, once subjects volunteer for an experiment, they seem more or less to have put themselves at the disposal of the experimenter, perhaps very much in the same fashion as the voluntary therapy client does with his therapist. Under such conditions, less reactance would be aroused.[3]

Like Festinger (1957), whose theory was overextended and misapplied, Brehm cautions against using reactance theory to explain data collected for other purposes; I recognize that I run the risk of doing just that. It seems of heuristic value, however, to alert behavior therapists to an area of social psychology which suggests that, under circumstances which may be analogous to clinical situations, people will behave opposite to the intent of the therapist.

Bandura (1969) and the Concept of "Self-Arousal"

In his brilliant review of behavior modification, Bandura (1969) has recently placed considerable emphasis on what he terms "self-arousal" and other self-initiated factors as playing important roles in several behavior therapy procedures. Perhaps it is with respect to aversive "conditioning" procedures that he invokes the concept most often, because of the paucity of evidence that stable conditioned aversive reactions can be built into human beings. However, to the extent that one believes the clinical data must one attempt to rationalize the apparent improvement that can be brought about with sensibly and sensitively engineered aversive conditioning regimens.

In discussing aversion therapy, Bandura mentions Freund's (1960) classic study in which, among other things, he found that markedly fewer homosexuals referred for therapy by the courts or coerced by relatives achieved changes in a heterosexual direction than those who seem to have come on their own accord, and who presumably were more desirious of change. Bandura is keenly aware of how aversion therapy can be sabotaged, e.g., by clients

> . . . failing to attend to the attractive stimuli and to produce accompanying imagery. They can fake signals at crucial points in the procedure where the therapist usually depends upon guidance from the client. They can even reverse the direction of counter-conditioning by conjuring up heterosexual imagery while undergoing unpleasant stimulation (Bandura, 1969, p. 519).

It may be, however, that Bandura is not entirely consistent in his awareness of the counter-control problem, for in the very same chapter, in discussing Antabuse treatment of alcoholics, he differentiates such treatment from aversive conditioning with the following statement:

> In the case of disulfiram, abstinence is maintained on a chemical basis. As long as the pills are taken regularly, the potent physiological consequences of drinking serve as a powerful deterrent (Bandura, 1969, p. 546).

Bandura seems to be emphasizing too little the phrase "as long as the pills are taken regularly," for it seems that *this* is the essence of Antabuse therapy, the chemical antagonism between the drug and alcohol being of relatively secondary (though probably significant) importance. How does the therapist convince the client to stay on the pills? How are resistances handled? Given the necessary commitment to take Antabuse, how important actually is the client's knowledge that a drink will lead to severe discomfort?

London (1969) and Client-Activity in Therapy

One of our few behavioral colleagues who for some time has written about the active role clients play in psychotherapy and behavior therapy is Perry London, whose many writings over the past several years (e.g., 1964, 1969) have stressed the advisability of viewing a therapy patient as indeed a very active member of the therapeutic dyad. To quote from a recent informal communication from London:

> To talk about control in psychotherapy, it is not merely true that clients *can* play an active role in whether they will be shaped, but rather perhaps that they cannot be shaped at all if they disdain an active role. If one were to judge by the technical literature, it seems questionable how much of anything is ever learned incidentally, that is, without deliberate or at least conscious attention. One would have to then conclude that the best bet therapeutically would be always to enlist the client's active awareness of the entire process as much as you possibly can. If anything, it would suggest that when I want to use a classical conditioning process, I would use it most effectively by persuading the client in advance to orient himself emotionally to the stimulus situation I will confront him with—obviously the very thing we are doing, without always recognizing its technical aspects, when we have people rehearse a therapeutic episode at home, or when we put them through the regimen of desensitization. The client's load in his own shaping, in other words, is always terribly active,

whether he articulates it or not, whether he (and the therapist) are aware (verbally) of it or not.[4]

Kelman's Work in Attitude Change (1958)

There is a voluminous literature in social psychology on attitude change; with few exceptions (e.g., Bandura, 1969; Goldstein, et al., 1966; Kanfer and Phillips, 1970; Mischel, 1968) this literature is largely ignored by behavior therapists. Consider Kelman's thinking with regard to "compliance," "identification," and "internalization." Compliance can occur under conditions of continued surveillance by the influencing agent, or in our own terms, while the contingencies responsible for the change in the first place are still in effect. Identification is said to refer to behavioral change somewhat less tied to such surveillance, though remaining importantly a function of the original agent of change in that the person continues his new behavior in order to maintain a satisfying relationship with the agent. Both compliance and identification are seen by Kelman to depend upon the communicator's control over rewards and punishments and hence, to my mind, are most closely related to our current state of development in behavior modification, where the problem of transfer remains a vexing one. The third process of attitude change, according to Kelman, is internalization, or, in our own language, the situation wherein new behavior is said to be intrinsically reinforcing, and thereby under less control by the external agent of original influence.

In a study designed to test some of above notions, Kelman exposed black college students in 1954 to a communication which argued that it would be good to maintain some private black colleges as all-black institutions in order to preserve black history and identity. What was varied was the description of the source, ranging from portraying the communicator as the president of a foundation funding the college in which the students were enrolled (thereby controlling rewards extensively) to a professor of history, who was in no controlling relationship to the students. Attitudes were measured under varied conditions of perceived surveillance by the communicator. As expected, for those who heard the compliance communication (that is, where the communicator was described as holding financial power over the college), attitude change was greatest under conditions where students believed that this man would see their answers. In contrast, the so-called internalization subjects (those who thought a professor had made the remarks), showed equivalent attitude change whether or not they thought he would see their answers.

Of course, no single experiment resolves an issue, and this particular study has been criticized by several social psychologists (e.g., Kiesler, et al., 1969). Furthermore, Kelman was concerned more with verbal statements of opinion and attitude than with the more overt behavioral measures with which we tend to be concerned. Nonetheless Kelman's line of research does not seem unrelated to what behavior therapists should be concerned with.

Altercasting (Weinstein, 1969).

Sociologists are also concerned with how to change people; the unfortunate divisions arising from professional allegiances and separate jargon probably account for the infrequent cross-fertilization between sociology and behavior modification that could contribute to theoretical growth in both fields. As an example, consider Weinstein's (1969) writings on altercasting (related to Goffman's "presentation of self," 1959). For example, I say to my friend, "Dan, you're a buddy, lend me five dollars." In altercasting terms, what I have done is cast Dan (alter) into the role of a buddy, reminding him in this particular situation that he is a friend, a status which I can be relatively sure he wishes to maintain; then I suggest that intrinsic to this role is the loan of five dollars. For him to refuse the loan would threaten the existence of the buddy relationship, which he hopefully wishes to maintain. In sociological terms, I am casting alter in such a way as to restrict his lines of action, that is, the behavior that he is free to engage in.

This thinking seems to relate to behavior therapy in a number of ways. For example, there are times when a client resists a particular line of questioning or set of suggestions. At this point, it is often useful to gently remind the client of the nature of the therapeutic relationship so as to cast him more explicitly into the role of "someone who trusts the therapist." Presumably, the client is there to change, but he may sometimes need reminding of this role relationship.

Erickson and Haley on "Utilization Techniques" in Hypnosis

From the above we can see that many people for different reasons believe that a given behavioral change attempt cannot in itself be adequately understood outside of how the interaction is construed by the person who is to be changed. Milton Erickson (1959) and Jay Haley (1963) have for many years written on the importance of analyzing the power struggle which seems intrinsic to a dyadic relationship in which one person is trying to get the other to do something. In my own teaching of clinical graduate students and postdoctoral fellows at Stony Brook, I have found it very useful to use Haley's communications analysis as it bears on hypnosis, particularly Milton Erickson's utilization techniques. I find in this way that it is possible to make students more attentive to the intricacies of any relationship which involves an influence attempt.

Erickson and Haley advise that the hypnotist, especially with resistant subjects, utilize whatever behavior the subject exhibits at any given time as a kind of "foot-in-the-door" in order to gain increasing control. For example, in an arm-levitation induction, the subject is told to look at his right hand as it rests on his leg. It is suggested that minute muscle twitches, not yet visible, may soon become visible. Almost inevitably *some* kind of movement occurs, and the hypnotist must be very careful to comment on it. He reminds the subject that this is precisely what was supposed to happen and then suggests that perhaps additional movement will take place. For reasons that, quite frankly, are not entirely clear to me, one can frequently get the hand moving up off the pant leg without the subject indicating or feeling that *he* is lifting it up. With suggestions to enter a hypnotic trance, the subject usually begins to behave and feel in ways which can be labelled "hypnotic." The important empirical principle is that the hypnotist couch suggestions in such a way as to enable/constrain the subject to construe *anything* that happens as being due to the hypnotist's suggestions. Thus, my trainees are told not to say things like "your hand will rise" but rather, "perhaps you will soon note a tendency for your hand to rise." If the hand does not rise, one must be able at least to imply that it was not supposed to anyway.

A further consideration, from Haley, is the non-symmetrical nature of the hypnotic relationship. The client is not free to do or say certain things and still maintain the hypnotic relationship. Thus, if a subject does not look at his hand when he is told to at the beginning of an induction, he is in essence denying the asymmetry of the relationship, denying that he is there to be hypnotized. This would itself become something to be dealt with, and, if one is in a clinical situation, the therapist would do well to attend to why the client is not willing to cooperate. Perhaps the client is afraid of losing control, or does not trust the therapist; there are any number of other nontrivial possibilities that cannot be ignored.

A recent study by Davis (1971) bears on this issue in an interesting way. Davis examined verbal conditioning in the power terms that Haley suggests and produced an effect inconsistent with much of the verbal conditioning literature. Subjects were found to emit more verbal behavior on a target topic when the experimenter first disagreed with what the subject was saying and then agreed; the verbal conditioning effect was greater in this condition than one in which the experimenter either agreed or disagreed all the time. These results were discussed by Davis in terms of the subject preferring a relationship where he did not see himself manipulated, that is, in a one-down relationship to the experimenter. And, this low profile of manipulation was apparently more readily achieved when the interviewer could be seen as behaving not consistently, leading the subject to perceive himself as having power over the experimenter rather than vice versa. It may be that greater behavioral change can be achieved if the manipulative aspects of the situation are played down, at least for certain kinds of subjects or clients.*

Rotter, Kelly, and Attribution Theory

Another line of thought related to counter-control can be alluded to here without, however, going into the detail that it merits. For many years Rotter (1966) has proposed that in understanding human learning we pay attention to the extent to which the person perceives his actions as leading to particular consequences in contrast to seeing consequences coming his way without his playing any appreciable role in earning the reward. Rotter's internal-external locus of control is receiving increased attention in behavior modification, and I believe we may see some worthwhile research relating this personality dimension to various kinds of behavioral change.

An emphasis on the person's view of the world can be seen in George Kelly's personal construct theory (1955), and we are seeing a welcome resurgence of interest in this line of thinking (e.g., Mischel, 1968, 1971). For example, though not taking off explicitly from Kelly, it was demonstrated (Geer, et al., 1970) that nonveridical perceived control over aversive stimulation led to significantly less stress in human subjects than aversive stimulation perceived as being uncontrol-

* Following preparation of this paper, I came upon a lovely experiment by Patterson, et al. (1968) on "Negative Set and Social Learning." With normal children, they illustrated a significant tendency to behave contrary to the open influence attempts of a model, the oppositional tendency diminishing markedly when the model was absent. Their results, as well as their recommendation that mediational constructs such as negative set appear necessary to account for certain failures of behavior change attempts, are entirely consistent with my main theme. An earlier study by Cowan, et al. (1965) with "autistic" children likewise demonstrated an oppositional tendency that worked against behavior control.

lable, when the actual amount of shock was the same. The study was instigated by the growing animal literature on control and helplessness (Seligman, et al., in press) long neglected since the original Mowrer and Viek (1948) study. In these animal experiments, control was defined strictly on the basis of the experimenter's arrangement of events rather than the subject's perception of them. The suggestion of Geer, et al. (1970) was that human beings draw conclusions about what is happening to them, that these conclusions do not always mesh with externally defined reality, and that under certain circumstances these perceptions might even override external reality. A significant part of the author's current research program is directed to related questions within attribution theory (e.g., Davison and Valins, 1969; Davison, et al., 1972).

"Kol Nidre" Effect

During the Spanish Inquisition of the 14th Century, it was decreed that all Jews either convert to Catholicism or else be banished or executed. There was widespread conversion among the Jews to Catholicism, and some of the best practicing Catholics in the country were former Jews. The only problem for the Spanish Church was that the Jews did not *really* convert. Indeed, apparently they were only further strengthened in their faith, and each year, on the evening preceding the Day of Atonement (Yom Kippur), small groups of "Catholics" met in great secrecy and sang together a prayer from the 7th Century called "Kol Nidre," which in Hebrew means "all our vows." The prayer came to be construed as a statement to God that the vows taken during the year were not to Him, and were therefore not really binding. With such powerful contingencies in effect, the Jews were able to change their behavior to such a degree as to render themselves indistinguishable from the prevailing majority. However, this tremendous degree of external control failed to take into satisfactory account other variables that might enter into whether a person will change in a basic way, in this case, probably the degree to which people regard the changes required of them as being legitimate. Though some very good behavior modification work is done in institutional settings (especially the work reported by the Oregon and Kansas groups), there are not only empirical problems (e.g., Davison, 1969), but perhaps a "Kol Nidre" problem as well. It may be worth looking for.

Concluding Comments: Stimulus-Response Analysis

At least implicit in the above speculative observations is the possibility that even a mediational stimulus-response analysis cannot handle much of the clinical and research data that as behavior modifiers we have carved out as our legitimate domain.** No doubt we could translate much of the above into stimulus-response terms, perhaps in the same fashion as Dollard and Miller (1950) did to Freud's second theory of anxiety. For we behavior therapists are as resourceful as our psychodynamic friends in construing the entire human and animal world in the terms we choose to use at any given time. But what does a stimulus-response analysis tell us about the issues I have raised? In what sense can we honestly say that thinking in even mediational stimulus-response terms will get us to focus on what I am suggesting is important in present clinical practice even if not yet in our conceptualizations? Can we most effectively transmit our clinical skills to our students and colleagues while staying with our current metaphors? Does learning theory get us to talk to sociologists, to anthropologists, or to communications analysts? Does it encourage us to think about the person as an active agent, a source of control that can sometimes run counter to our therapeutic intents? Do we gain appreciably in explanatory and predictive power by invoking concepts like "instructional stimulus control" and "secondary reinforcement"? And, finally, are we perhaps not running the risk of getting better and better at talking about less and less, while we ought to be attempting to talk about more and more and adapting/adopting concepts that are heuristically valuable and of greater educational utility?

** If by "stimulus-response analysis" we mean "antecedent-consequent analysis," then there is no difference of opinion, for I remain as deterministic as those who would not invoke mediational, sometimes cognitive concepts as explanatory fictions. The issue is what the causal network is made out of.

Footnotes

1. Preparation of this paper was facilitated by NIMH grant MH 14 577-03 and American Cancer Society grant ET-25A. For their critical comments and suggestions, I wish to thank several friends and colleagues: John H. Gagnon, Norman Goodman, Michael J. Mahoney, John Monahan, and G. Terence Wilson. For their sake, I assume responsibility for the final form of this paper.

2. In addition to the writers to be cited below, Arnold Lazarus and Gordon Paul, whose clinical work I am fortunate to be very familiar with, have discussed counter-control problems though they usually refer to them as part of the "nonspecifics." In a sense, with reference to Lazarus' most recent position statements as enunciated in his *Behavior Therapy and Beyond* (1971), I am trying to bring some of the "beyond" back within a more formal conceptual framework.

3. On the other hand, in a recent review of subject effects in laboratory research, Weber and Cook (1972) discuss various roles which volunteer subjects can adopt, including that of the recalcitrant subject who contributes to the "screw you effect" (Masling, 1966).

4. London, personal communication, March 1972.

References

Azrin, N. H. and Powell, J. R. Behavioral engineering: The reduction of smoking behavior by a conditioning apparatus and procedure. *Journal of Applied Behavior Analysis,* 1968, *1*, 193-200.

Bandura, A. *Principles of behavior modification.* New York: Holt, Rinehart and Winston, 1969.

Brehm, J. W. *A theory of psychological reactance.* New York: Academic Press, 1966.

Cowan, P. A., Hoddinoth, B. A., and Wright, B. A. Compliance and resistance in the conditioning of autistic children: An exploratory study. *Child Development,* 1965, *36*, 913-923.

Davis, J. D. *The interview as arena.* Stanford: Stanford University Press, 1971.

Davison, G. C. Elimination of a sadistic fantasy by a client-controlled counterconditioning technique: A case study. *Journal of Abnormal Psychology*, 1968, *73*, 84-90.

Davison, G. C. Appraisal of behavior modification techniques with adults in institutional settings. In C. M. Franks (Ed.), *Behavior therapy: Appraisal and status.* New York: McGraw-Hill, 1969.

Davison, G. C. Critical notice: Review of Patterson and Gullion, and Homme et al. *Behavior Therapy*, 1970, *1*, 124-131.

Davison, G. C., Liebert, R. M., and Sobol, M. *Behavior therapy for homosexuality.* Psychological Cinema Register, 1971, 16 mm. film.

Davison, G. C., Tsujimoto, R., and Glaros, A. Attribution and the maintenance of behavior change in falling asleep. Unpublished manuscript, State University of New York at Stony Brook, 1972.

Davison, G. C. and Valins, S. Maintenance of self-attributed and drug-attributed behavior change. *Journal of Personality and Social Psychology*, 1969, *11*, 25-33.

Dollard, J. and Miller, N. E. *Personality and psychotherapy.* New York: McGraw-Hill, 1950.

Erickson, M. H. Further clinical techniques of hypnosis: Utilization techniques. *The American Journal of Clinical Hypnosis,* 1959, *2*, 3-21.

Festinger, L. *A theory of cognitive dissonance.* Stanford: Stanford University Press, 1957.

Freund, K. Some problems in the treatment of homosexuality. In H. J. Eysenck (Ed.), *Behavior therapy and the neuroses.* New York: Pergamon Press, 1960.

Geer, J. H., Davison, G. C., and Gatchel, R. I. Reduction of stress in humans through nonveridical perceived control of aversive stimulation. *Journal of Personality and Social Psychology*, 1970, *16*, 731-738.

Goffman, E. *The presentation of self in everyday life.* Garden City, N.Y.: Anchor Books, 1959.

Goldstein, A. P., Heller, K., and Sechrest, L. B. *Psychotherapy and the psychology of behavior change.* New York: Wiley, 1966.

Haley, J. *Strategies of psychotherapy*. New York: Grune and Stratton, 1963.

Kanfer, F. H. and Phillips, J. S. *Learning foundations of behavior therapy.* New York: Wiley, 1970.

Kelly, G. A. *The psychology of personal constructs.* Vols. 1 and 2. New York: Norton, 1955.

Kelman, H. Compliance, identification, and internalization: Three processes of attitude change. *Journal of Conflict Resolution,* 1958, *2*, 51-60.

Kiesler, C. A., Collins, B. E., and Miller, N. *Attitude change.* New York: Wiley, 1969.

Lazarus, A. A. *Behavior therapy and beyond.* New York: McGraw-Hill, 1971.

Lazarus, A. A. and Davison, G. C. Clinical innovation in research and practice. In A. E. Bergin and S. L. Garfield (Eds.), *Handbook of psychotherapy and behavior change*. New York: Wiley, 1971.

London, P. *The modes and morals of psychotherapy.* New York: Holt, Rinehart and Winston, 1964.

London, P. *Behavior control.* New York: Harper & Row, 1969.

Marquis, J. N. Orgasmic reconditioning: Changing sexual object choice through controlling masturbation fantasies. *Journal of Behavior Therapy and Experimental Psychiatry*, 1970, *1*, 263-271.

Masling, J. Role-related behavior of the subject and psychologist and its effects upon psychological data. *Nebraska Symposium on Motivation*, 1966, *14*, 67-103.

Mischel, W. *Personality and assessment*. New York: Wiley, 1968.

Mischel, W. *Introduction to personality*. New York: Holt, Rinehart and Winston, 1971.

Mowrer, O. H. and Viek, P. An experimental analogue of fear from a sense of helplessness. *Journal of Abnormal and Social Psychology,* 1948, *43*, 193-200.

Patterson, G. R., Littman, I., and Brown, T. R. Negative set and social learning. *Journal of Personality and Social Psychology,* 1968, *8*, 109-116.

Rotter, J. B. Generalized expectancies for internal versus external control of reinforcement. *Psychological Monographs,* 1966, *80,* Whole No. 609.

Seligman, M. E. P., Maier, S. F., and Solomon, R. L. Unpredictable and uncontrollable aversive events. In F. R. Brush (Ed.), *Aversive conditioning and learning*. New York: Academic Press, in press.

Weber, S. J. and Cook, T. D. Subject effects in laboratory research: An examination of subject roles, demand characteristics and valid inference. *Psychological Bulletin*, 1972, *77*, 273-295.

Weinstein, E. A. The development of interpersonal competence. In D. A. Goslin (Ed.), *Handbook of socialization theory and research.* Chicago: Rand McNally, 1969.

Changes in Status of Family Members as Controlling Stimuli: A Basis for Describing Treatment Process[1]

6

G. R. Patterson

Both individual case studies (Wolf, et al., 1964; Zeilberger, et al., 1968) and those involving larger samples (Wahler and Erickson, 1969; Patterson, et al., 1968; Tharp and Wetzel, 1969; Patterson, et al., 1972b) showed that parents can be trained to effectively apply social learning principles to alter the behavior of their own problem child. Presumably these changes are brought about by changes in the reinforcing contingencies provided for the problem child's deviant behavior. When the child displays a deviant response, the parent is trained to introduce either an extinction or a punishment contingency. It is hypothesized that consistent arrangements of this kind would result in eventual changes in the status of certain agents and agent behaviors as discriminative stimuli for deviant child behaviors.

It was demonstrated in previous analyses that specific activities of family members increased the probability of the problem child's responding in a deviant manner (Patterson and Cobb, 1972; in press). These analyses showed that, for the younger boy, immediately impinging social stimuli apparently determine much of his ongoing social behaviors. While no analyses of sequential dependencies in social interactions have identified the mechanisms which provide given social stimuli with such control features, it is assumed that reinforcement would be one important contributor. Within this context, it is assumed that certain behaviors, when dispensed by a family member, are also associated with rich schedules of positive or negative reinforcers for specific deviant child behaviors. In effect, the behavior of the agent signifies which deviant child behavior, if any, is likely to be reinforced at that time. Some agents reinforce such behaviors on very lean schedules, or not at all, and the child learns not to display the behaviors in the presence of that agent. Generally, each family agent tends to reinforce at least a few deviant responses, and certain of his behaviors signal when such a reinforcer is likely to occur. Presumably an effective family treatment program should not only alter the reinforcing contingencies provided by family members for the deviant behaviors of the problem child but should also reduce the frequency with which they present these behaviors that signify the availability of reinforcers.

The present report outlines a method for analyzing the status of stimuli which control deviant child behaviors. The data requisite for such an analysis are extensive samplings of sequential interactions such as those found among family members. The procedures have been used previously to identify networks of social stimuli controlling classes of noxious responses exhibited by aggressive and normal boys (Patterson and Cobb, in press). In the present study, pre- and post-treatment data were collected in the home of an extremely disruptive boy. Analyses of these data were used to illustrate shifts in stimulus control produced by a family intervention program.

Analysis of Stimulus Control—General Considerations

Given sequential data collected along some known time base, one can proceed in the manner of ecologists (Barker, et al., 1962) to specify the frequencies with which certain events precede, or covary with, certain behaviors. However, such simple frequency counts do *not* necessarily identify controlling stimuli. For example, given that a certain setting such as "school" takes up two-thirds of the observations, it is likely to be identified as a major antecedent for any given target behavior under study.

The definition of "controlling stimulus" used in the present report and the series of across-subject analyses which preceded it (Patterson and Cobb, 1972; in press) requires that the occurrence of the antecedent stimulus (A_i) be associated with an increase in the probability of the target response (R_j). In this sense, then, a frequent antecedent may or may not be a "controlling stimulus." To determine the status of a stimulus, it is necessary first to tabulate its occurrence as an immediate antecedent for all non-target behaviors as well as its occurrence as antecedent for the target behavior. Comparing the latter conditional probability $p(R_j/A_i)$ to the former $p(R_j/\text{Non-}A_i)$ makes it possible to discriminate between events which are simply antecedents and those which control behavioral events. For example, given that Sister Tease occurred as an immediate antecedent for Brother's Hit on ten occasions and the total sample of Sister Tease events was 30, then $p(R_j/\text{Sister Tease}) = .30$. Comparing this figure to the base rate, or probability, for R_j given all other antecedents provides the basis for making a decision about stimulus control. For example, given that

$p(R_j$/All Non-Sister Tease) was .002, one would conclude that Sister Tease was a controlling stimulus.

In the present study, a time interval of six seconds was used for the collecting of observations (Patterson, et al., 1969); hence the problem involved predicting what would happen from one six-second interval to another. Subject and environmental events were arranged sequentially in six-second intervals along a time line. Antecedent events were analyzed to determine their contribution to increasing the probability that R_j would occur in the immediately following time interval. Those which significantly increased the probability that R_j would occur were, by definition, significant controlling stimuli; they were labeled "facilitating stimuli" (S^F). An antecedent could acquire the status of an S^F as a result of its association with reinforcement, repeated contiguous association, and cognitive or instinctual processes. It was hypothesized that the S^Fs controlling deviant behavior would be altered as a function of treatment.

A Study of Stimulus Control of Deviant Behavior

A 29-category code system was used to collect data in 48 observation sessions during baseline, eight during intervention, and two following intervention. The data were collected as part of the evaluation for treatment of a family of a high-rate aggressive boy.

The baseline data were analyzed twice to determine the networks of stimuli controlling each of 14 noxious behaviors. The first analyses identified those family members whose presence served as S^Fs for each of the noxious behaviors displayed by Denny, the aggressive boy. A second analysis was carried out to identify those behaviors, across agents, which served as S^Fs for each of the noxious behaviors.

During treatment the parents were trained to alter the reinforcing contingencies for certain deviant and prosocial behavior displayed by the problem child and by his sister. These intrusions were designed to reduce the rates of the deviant behaviors. It was assumed that they would also alter the status of both the parents and the sister as S^Fs for noxious behaviors displayed by the boy. *These changes in stimulus control should be reflected in two ways: (1) there should be a decrease in the density with which family members present these S^Fs to Denny and (2) there should be a reduction in the magnitude of control exerted by those S^Fs which were presented.*

Method

The target child. Denny was referred to the Project by his parents, who in turn had been urged to do so by the school. This six-and-a-half year old boy was reported to be unmanageable in the first grade classroom. In addition to frequent temper tantrums which involved his throwing objects about the room, he was disruptive to other children. He seldom responded to requests by the teachers and was making little progress in his academic subjects. He performed at the 16th percentile or less on the Wide Range Achievement Test for reading, spelling, and arithmetic.

His father reported that he was impossible to live with at home. His noncompliance, temper tantrums, teasing, hyperactivity, and constant conflict with family members was making life miserable for his mother and his three-year-old sister. He tended to yell at a very high rate; his normal inflection was an irritating nasal whine. Often he would wander away from home for hours; such excursions would be followed by complaints of his stealing from stores and neighbors. Denny was being treated by 10 mg. b.i.d. of Ritalin, but this appears to provide only minimal behavioral effects.

The father was taking a course as an auto mechanic; the mother worked in a local factory. They lived in a modest but well-appointed home. When Denny returned from school, he was to go to a neighbor's home where he was "supervised" until one of his parents returned later in the afternoon.

The father was a mild-mannered, cooperative man, 29 years old. He seemed genuinely concerned about his family and eager to begin the training program. He described himself as warm and permissive in his interactions with Denny. His MMPI profile was '4379518–3:2:17. The mother was a silent, timid, withdrawn woman, 27 years of age. Her MMPI profile was '0398714–4:3:15. She seemed very confused by Denny's behavior and reported often feeling very angry. She was taking tranquilizers for her "tension."

Observations. Denny and his family were observed in their home for 12 days of baseline. Each day three sessions of approximately 60 minutes' duration were arranged. One was held at 7:00 to 8:00 in the morning, one at 2:15 to 3:15 in the afternoon, and a third at 4:00 to 5:00 in the evening. During these three sessions, Denny was the "target subject" for the entire period. Each day there was also a fourth session at 3:15 to 4:00 in which each family member was the target subject for two, five-minute segments. During this session all family members were required to be present; the TV set was turned off, and no guests were present. None of these structuring requirements was introduced for the three earlier sessions each day.

During intervention, eight days of observation data were collected; two consecutive sessions occurred immediately following the parents' reading of the programmed textbook, at four and eight weeks of training, and at termination. While the case was not deemed ready for termination, it becamse a necessity when the parents decided to move to another city where the father had obtained employment. Two weeks following termination, the parents kindly allowed the observers to collect two additional days of observation data.

The observers received intensive training in using a 29-category coding system (Patterson, et al., 1969) designed specifically to describe aggressive behaviors and the stimuli which probably control them. Approximately every sixth second the observer sampled either the behavior of the target subject or the behavior of whichever family member(s) was interacting with him. The data offer a continuous sequential account of these interactions.

Observer drift. Reid (1970) found that observers showed an immediate drop in reliability following training when placed in a situation which they believed to be unmonitored. For this reason, bi-weekly training sessions were held in which the five observers viewed video tapes of very complex interactions among members of deviant families. A recent report by DeMaster and Reid (in preparation) showed this procedure to be effective in ameliorating the "observer drift" phenomenon.

The continuous retraining has also led to very high levels of agreement among the observers. The average agreement was 85% during the period covered in the present report. To count as an agreement, events had to be coded correctly by subject number, coding category, *and* in the proper sequence. Percent agreement was obtained from the total number of events for which both observer were in agreement divided by the total number of events recorded by both observers.

Observer bias. The importance of observer bias has been noted by Rosenthal (1966). Scott, et al. (1967) showed that the therapist was biased in observations of client behaviors. However, a comparable effect was not obtained by Skindrud (1972a), who analyzed the field observations from 16 problem and 10 non-problem families. The professional observers had knowledge of which families were problem and which were not, and also whether the sessions with the problem families were in the baseline period or the treatment period. Their data were compared to that obtained by calibrating observers who had none of this information. The analysis showed no bias toward recording higher rates of deviancy in problem families or in recording lower rates during treatment. Similarly, more carefully controlled laboratory studies by Skindrud (1972b) showed no bias as a function of instructional set or information.

Observer presence effects. Presumably, the observers' presence functions as a social stimulus which has some impact upon family interaction; however, the nature and magnitude of this effect has proved difficult to determine. Two studies compared family interaction patterns obtained when mothers surreptitiously observed their own families to data obtained when observers came into the home. No significant effects of observers' presence were detected, either for rates of social interaction (Harris, 1969; Hoover and Rinehart, 1968) or for rates of deviant child behaviors (Patterson and Harris, 1968). However, it should be noted that the size of the samples and the variability inherent in the data would have mitigated against identifying anything other than very large effects. The Harris analysis did reveal, though, that the observers' presence was associated with greater unpredictability in the behavior of family members (Harris, 1969).

In a study by Johnson and Lobitz (1972) parents were given instructions to "make their child look good" or "make their child look bad" on alternate nights of observation. The data for child behavior showed marked shifts as a function of this instructional set. This suggests the possibility that observer presence *could* produce variations in the set which the parents have to make their family look good or look bad.

Stimulus control analysis. For the present analysis, noxious behaviors exhibited by boys between the ages of three and 14 were identified. These included: Command Negative (CN), Cry (CR), Disapproval (DI), Dependency (DP), Destructiveness (DS), High Rate (HR), Humiliate (HU), Ignore (IG), Noncomply (NC), Negativism (NE), Physical Negative (PN), Tease (TE), Whine (WH), and Yell (YE).

Dependent variable. The dependent variable used throughout the analysis was the probability of occurrence for a given noxious response. The base rate value $p(R_j)$ was calculated for each of the 14 responses; this was calculated by tabulating the total number of events that Denny exhibited and dividing this sum into each of the summed R_js. Only those noxious behaviors exhibited by Denny were included where the same family member was coded as providing both the antecedent and consequence for the behavior.

Facilitating stimuli. Each of the 29 categories displayed by other family members was analyzed to determine the frequency with which it occurred as an antecedent for Denny's behaviors, excluding his non-social responses—Work, Self-Stimulation, and No Response. Then the conditional probability $p(R_j/A_i)$ was calculated based upon the frequency with which each of the events occurred as an antecedent for each of the 14 noxious behaviors. For purposes of comparison, when calculating the base rate pR_j of a particular behavior, the contribution of an event as an antecedent for R_j was subtracted from the total number of events exhibited, providing a corrected base rate value $p(R_j/\text{Non-}A_i)$. The identification of a controlling stimulus, then, involved comparing the corrected base rate value to the conditional probability value. To facilitate the decision, a chi-square analysis was used. When appropriate, corrections were made for continuity, or, if the Ns were small, Fisher's exact chi-square was used.[2] Those antecedents which produced conditional probability values greater than the base rate values, and for which the chi-square values were significant at $p < .10$, were said to be S^Fs, or significant controlling stimuli.

Even though identified as significant, an S^F's contribution to prediction might be trivial. For example, given that a significant stimulus occurred very infrequently, then the contribution of such an antecedent might be severely limited. For this reason, the information contained in the conditional probability of R_j given the presence of the antecedent stimulus $p(R_j/A_i)$ was combined with the information about the base rate for the S^F. Summing the compound probabilities resulting from multiplying $[p(R_j/A_i)]$ $[p(A_i)]$ for each of the code categories would account for all of the information available for $p(R_j)$, i.e., sum to 1.00.

Controlling stimuli, then, may have two characteristics. They may be "significant," in which case they are S^Fs, or they may be "nonsignificant," and their compound probabilities may be of different magnitudes. It is important to keep in mind that these two characteristics are not necessarily related. An antecedent stimulus that occurred only once but was followed by a Hit would generate a conditional probability $[p(\text{Hit}/A_i)]$ of 1.00. The chi-square analysis would identify such a variable as nonsignificant. Similarly, the compound probability $[p(\text{Hit}/A_i)]$ $[p(A_i)]$ would be extremely low, and thus either process would identify such a variable as of limited value. While all high-rate antecedents are likely to have relatively high compound probability values, the chi-square analyses may or may not prove them to be significant. Therefore, a two-step process was necessary to determine controlling stimuli. Both steps were a necessary, but neither a sufficient, condition for defining an antecedent variable.

Intervention. Most of the family training procedures used to teach Denny's parents have been described in previous publications (Patterson, et al., in press). The parents were required to read programmed materials outlining the social-learning-based techniques in *Families* (Patterson, 1971). Then they were trained by video tapes of their own family to pinpoint, observe, and tabulate the occurrence of a target behavior, for example, Yell. When the parents had collected several days of baseline data, a program was initiated which consequated non-yelling behaviors with social reinforcement and a point system, while at the same time consequating Yell with Time Out. The skills required to carry out this, and the other programs, were modeled and supervised by the experimenters. When the parents had made considerable progress in bringing Denny's behavior under control at home, they "earned" the additional therapists' time required to intervene in the classroom. These classroom procedures have been described by Patterson, et al. (1969, 1972a).

The total investment of therapist time for the home and school intervention was 94.7 hours. This included intake interview, telephone calls, travel time, and all contacts with family members or school personnel. When two staff members were in attendance, the time for both was included in the estimate.

Results

The baseline, intervention, and follow-up data were analyzed to determine which of Denny's deviant behaviors, if any, showed changes following intervention. The data, expressed as frequency of events per minute, were calculated for each of the three phases of the study. The intervention data were sampled during the entire period rather than just at termination. Also included were data from parents' daily reports of occurrence of problems identified as being of concern to them. These data were obtained on each day that observations were collected in the home.

Comparing the baseline and intervention data showed a modest reduction in the overall level of deviant behaviors. Reductions occurred for 10 of the R_js. At follow-up there was an overall reduction of about 50% from baseline level; reductions at follow-up were obtained for 11 of the 14 problem behaviors.

Table 1 Changes in Denny's Behavior During Intervention and Follow-up

Experimental Condition	Mean occurrence of referral symptoms per day	Rate of Noxious Responses (R_j) per Minute															
		CN	CR	DI	DP	DS*	HR	HU	IG	NC*	NE*	PN*	TE*	WH	YE*	Total	Mean
Baseline	69%	.0044	.0245	.0708	.0019	,0164	.0123	.0035	.0007	.0453	.0030	.0039	.0030	.0326	.0243	.2466	.0176
Intervention	50%	.0019	.0237	.0549	-0-	.0050	.0075	-0-	.0006	.0474	.0025	.0050	.0056	.0343	.0131	.2015	.0144
Follow-up	50%	.0012	.0095	.0213	.0012	.0047	-0-	.0012	-0-	.0498	-0-	.0095	.0083	.0201	.0071	.1342	.0096

* Behaviors targeted by parents during training

Table 2	Stimulus Control Networks for Denny's Noxious Responses	
Noxious Response (R_j)	**Number of Significant S^Fs**	**Percent of $p(R_j)$ Accounted for by Summed Compound Probabilities**
Command Negative (CN)	4	40.6
Cry (CR)	4	56.6
Disapproval (DI)	4	67.4
Dependency (DP)	2	74.8
Destructive (DS)	1	70.4
High Rate (HR)	2	50.9
Humiliate (HU)	2	46.8
Ignore (IG)	1	66.7
Noncomply (NC)	2	98.0
Negativism (NE)	2	84.8
Physical Negative (PN)	3	58.9
Tease (TE)	1	54.0
Whine (WH)	5	88.0
Yell (YE)	3	55.3

Analysis of stimulus control. The baseline data were analyzed for each of the 14 noxious responses (R_js) to identify the network of stimuli controlling the behaviors. Those facilitating stimuli (S^F s) found to be significant for each R_j are listed in Appendix A, together with their base rates, conditional probability values, and compound probabilities.

As summarized in Table 2, each of the noxious responses was defined by at least one facilitating stimulus. Several, such as Whine, Disapproval, Cry, and Command Negative, were defined by extensive networks of four and five stimuli.* The extent to which the controlling stimuli accounted for a specific R_j was specified by first summing the compound probabilities for the network of S^F s for that response. This sum was divided into the base rate probability for the R_j. The resulting percentages are listed in column 2.

The analysis showed that information about "significant" antecedents occurring in the immediately prior time interval accounted for a surprising proportion of the base rate information about *every* one of the R_js. It would seem that, for Denny, much of the information needed to predict his behavior is to be found in a small number of immediately impinging, *external* social stimuli. The behaviors of other family members set the occasion for much of his obnoxious behavior.

Behaviors such as Noncomply, Negativism, Whine, and Dependency seemed to be well-defined by the network of S^Fs in that three-fourths, or more, of the information in the base rates for those R_js was accounted for.**

Reduction in the number of stimuli which are S^Fs. It was hypothesized that changes in rate for the noxious behaviors displayed by Denny would be accompanied by alterations in the density with which controlling stimuli were presented to the child. The stimulus control analysis was carried out separately for baseline, intervention, and follow-up. The number of S^Fs for each noxious response during each condition are presented in Table 3. The summed base rate values for the entire network of S^Fs are also listed for each R_j in each condition.

The data showed that during baseline 36 stimuli were found to be significant in controlling the 14 noxious behaviors displayed by Denny. In many instances the same antecedent stimuli could control a variety of responses. During intervention only five of the baseline set of S^Fs continued to control his behavior. During follow-up there were seven. However, during both conditions, some new S^Fs acquired status as controlling stimuli, nine during intervention and two during follow-up. The overall reduction in the number of S^Fs constituted support for the hypothesis that treatment changed the number of S^Fs effective in facilitating Denny's deviant behaviors.

---

* The data in the current analysis were provided by only a single target subject and used both chained and unchained interactions (see Patterson and Cobb, in press, for definitions of these terms). One might expect there to be little relation between findings obtained in the present analysis as compared to that previously obtained when using 55 problem boys and only those data from "unchained" interaction. The stimulus networks obtained in the two analyses were compared to determine whether some similarities did in fact exist. The data showed that for the 13 noxious responses common to both analyses, at least half of the facilitating stimuli were the ***same*** behavioral events for eight of the variables. This suggests some modest generalizability of the earlier across-subjects findings for networks of controlling stimuli.

** In the across-subjects analyses reported earlier (Patterson and Cobb, in press) there was a nonsignificant correlation of .49 ($p < .10$) between $p(R_j)$ and the proportion of the R_j accounted for by the S^Fs. The comparable correlation for the present data was .17 (n.s.). These findings suggest that stimulus control response definitions were only partially related to the adequacy of the sampling of response events and perhaps more related to the appropriateness of the variables being sampled as determinants.

Table 3 Changes in Density of Controlling Stimuli

Noxious Response(R_j)	$\lesseqgtr p(A_i)$ Baseline	Number of $S^F s$	$\lesseqgtr p(A_i)$ Intervention	Number of $S^F s$ Old (Baseline)	Number of $S^F s$ New	$\lesseqgtr p(A_i)$ Follow-up	Number of $S^F s$ Old (Baseline)	Number of $S^F s$ New
CN	.0716	4	.0589	0	0	.0294	0	0
CR	.2781	4	.2355	0	0	.2333	2	0
DI	.3939	4	.4552	0	3	.3304	1	0
DP	.3829	2	.4483	0	0	.3115	0	0
DS	.1885	1	.1174	0	0	.1327	0	0
HR	.1905	2	.1174	1	0	.1338	0	0
HU	.0507	2	.0444	0	0	.0260	0	0
IG	.0488	1	.0444	1	0	.0260	0	0
NC	.1032	2	.1268	2	0	.1006	2	0
NE	.3350	2	.4039	0	0	.2855	0	0
PN	.1261	3	.0956	0	2	.2949	0	1
TE	.1185	1	.1174	1	3	.1327	1	0
WH	.5103	5	.5707	0	0	.4501	1	0
YE	.3469	3	.4134	0	1	.2937	0	1
Total		36		5	9		7	2

Changes in the frequency with which S^Fs presented. Even though subsequent to baseline there were *fewer* stimuli significant in controlling behavior, it was possible that those which did remain were presented at higher rates. For this reason, the data for stimulus density ($p(A_i)$ data in Table 3) were of special interest. It was assumed that following treatment there would be reductions in the frequency with which S^Fs were presented to the problem child when comparing baseline to intervention and follow-up data.

A comparison of the baseline and intervention data showed a reduction in the summed base rate values for the network of stimuli controlling eight of the noxious responses and *increases* in density for six of the responses. Such shifts during intervention suggested a limited effect during the earlier stages of treatment. The comparison of baseline to follow-up data showed more clearcut improvements in that the densities of controlling stimuli were reduced for 11 of the responses. The fact that these probabilities had decreased for so many of the noxious responses provided support for the hypothesized impact of family intervention procedures upon the densities of controlling stimuli. It should be noted, however, that the fact that these densities remain at what seem to be substantial levels would bespeak a poor prognosis for this family. These data would suggest that treatment was not completed.

Comparing S^Fs found during either phase, there was a decrease from baseline to intervention in the conditional probability values $p(R_j/A_i)$ in 26 instances; they remained the same, or increased, in 21 (see Appendix A). The comparable values for the follow-up data were 32 and 15. These trends suggest that the majority of the controlling stimuli were losing their "pulling power" in that their occurrence was associated with lowering values for the probability that R_j would occur. In effect, all three analyses of stimulus control were in agreement. There were fewer S^Fs, and those which did persist occurred at lower rates and with reduced power. The analyses showed that as a result of the treatment program, the behavior of family members is less likely to set the occasion for Denny's deviant behaviors.

Changes in agent status. The stimuli discussed in the preceding section consisted of behaviors presented by one or more family members. Perhaps certain agents were more likely than others to reinforce some R_js. But it was hypothesized that, for whatever reason, the mere presence of some agents would be associated with an increased probability of occurrence for each R_j. Each problem behavior might have a different agent or set of agents contributing to its occurrence.

The data were analyzed to determine the contribution of each of the family members as antecedent stimuli for Denny's behavior. These data are summarized in Table 4.

During baseline, the mother interacted the most with Denny; she served as an antecedent for the bulk of his deviant behaviors as well. Her unique status continued throughout the experiment. While efforts were made to teach her to be more contingent, it is clear that the training program had only a small effect on her status as a controlling stimulus for deviant behavior. She continued to serve as an antecedent for most of Denny's noxious behaviors. These analyses were also in keeping with our clinical impressions to the effect that she changed only slightly.

The father reduced both his general interaction rates with Denny and eventually the frequency with which he served as either antecedent stimulus or S^F for deviant behaviors. The stimulus control data showed that during treatment he temporarily became involved as a key S^F for much of Denny's noxious behavior. The observers' notes for the period stated that he often served in the role of remedial reading instructor. This shift in role may account for some of the increase in S^F status. However, both the father and the mother seemed to be monitoring the sister's initiations to Denny, and his reactions to her, but largely ignoring their own unique contributions to his behavior![3] A process analysis such as this, if it had been available during intervention, would have emphasized the importance of closer supervision for *both* mother and father in *their own* interactions with Denny.

Probably the major impact of the treatment program was reflected in the altered status of the younger sister. Although she had previously served as an S^F for the largest number of Denny's noxious behaviors, this was dramatically altered during intervention and follow-up. It is interesting in this regard that as her interactions with Denny presumably became more pleasant she almost doubled her rate of social interaction with him.

Summary

The data showed the parents to be only moderately effective in reducing the rate of deviant child behaviors for their problem child. It had been predicted that their efforts to alter the contingencies maintaining these behaviors would be accompanied by changes in the status of the external stimuli which controlled his noxious responses. The analysis of stimulus control during baseline, intervention, and follow-up supported this hypothesis.

Table 4 **Changes in Agent Status**

Experimental Condition	Denny's Behavior	Proportion of Denny's Behaviors for which Agent was Antecedent			Number of Denny's Deviant Behaviors for which Agents were Facilitating Stimuli (S^Fs)			
		Father	Mother	Sister	Father	Mother	Sister	Total
Baseline	Deviant Behavior	31.2	46.4	22.3	2	4	6	12
	Total Interaction	31.2	44.8	24.0				
Intervention	Deviant Behavior	42.1	44.3	13.6	5	2	1	8
	Total Interaction	26.2	41.9	31.9				
Follow-up	Deviant Behavior	19.5	56.6	23.9	1	3	1	5
	Total Interaction	11.6	42.5	45.9				

There were changes from baseline through follow-up in the *number* of social behaviors which served as controlling stimuli for noxious behaviors. As treatment progressed, those stimuli which did significantly control deviant behavior were also presented at *lower densities.* Presumably, these changes were brought about in large part because of the parents' success in altering the behaviors of the younger sister that had served to facilitate the occurrence of responses from the problem child.

The stimulus control analysis showed that the actual status of the parents, particularly the mother, had actually changed little. This finding suggests that the treatment program was incomplete.

The results suggest that analysis of stimulus control may constitute a subtle description of changes in family structure produced by intrusions such as family intervention programs. Conceivably, such analysis, if carried out during treatment, could serve to identify areas of difficulty which might not be immediately apparent even to the trained clinician.

Appendix A Networks of Controlling Stimuli for Noxious Responses During Baseline, Intervention, and Follow-up

Antecedent	Baseline			Intervention			Follow-up		
Event	$p(A_i)$	$p(R_j/A_i)$	$[p(A_i)][p(R_j/A_i)]$	$p(A_i)$	$p(R_j/A_i)$	$[p(A_i)][p(R_j/A_i)]$	$p(A_i)$	$p(R_j/A_i)$	$[p(A_i)][p(R_j/A_i)]$
Command Negative p(CN) .00439									
Compliance	.00971	.0476*	.00046	.0082	.0000	.0000	.0023	.0000	.0000
Cry	.00115	.2000*	.00023	.0000	.0000	.0000	-0-	.0000	.0000
Disapproval	.04880	.0190*	.00093	.0044	.0141	.00062	.0260	.0000	.0000
Noncomply	.01179	.1373*	.00162	.0063	.0000	.0000	.0011	.0000	.0000
Sister's presence		.0106*							
Cry p(CR) .02452									
Attend	.18852	.0552*	.01041	.1174	.0745	.00874	.1327	.0000	.0000
Command Negative	.02059	.0674*	.00139	.1149	.1053	.00125	.0817	.0145	.00119
Physical Negative	.00300	.3077*	.00093	.0013	.0000	.0000	.0059	.2000*	.00119
Tease	.00393	.2941*	.00116	.0019	.0000	.0000	.0130	.2727*	.00356
Father's presence		.0481*							
Disapproval p(DI) .07078									
Disapproval	.04880	.1848*	.00902	.0444	.1690	.00749	.0260	.0455	.00119
Ignore	.00693	.1667*	.001157	.0050	.1250	.00062	.0059	.0000	.0000
Talk	.33402	.1080*	.036086	.4039	.0587	.02372	.2855	.0456*	.01303
Tease	.00393	.2353*	.00093	.0019	.0000	.0000	.0130	.0000	.0000

Appendix A, continued

Antecedent Event	Baseline $p(A_i)$	Baseline $p(R_j/A_i)$	Baseline $[p(A_i)][p(R_j/A_i)]$	Intervention $p(A_i)$	Intervention $p(R_j/A_i)$	Intervention $[p(A_i)][p(R_j/A_i)]$	Follow-up $p(A_i)$	Follow-up $p(R_j/A_i)$	Follow-up $[p(A_i)][p(R_j/A_i)]$
Attend	.18852	.0712	.01342	.1174	.0957*	.01124	.1327	.0179	.002370
Comply	.00971	.0952	.00093	.0082	.3846*	.00312	.0023	.0000	.0000
Whine	.00046	.0000	.0000	.0007	1.0000*	.00062	-0-	.0000	.0000
Mother's presence		.0723*							
Sister's presence		.0724*							
Dependency p(DP) .00185									
Disapproval	.04880	.0095*	.00046	.0444	-0-	.0000	.0260	.0000	
Talk	.33402	.0028*	.00093	.4039	.0000	.0000	.2855	.0041	.00119
Mother's presence		.0031*							
Destructiveness p(DS) .01642									
Attend	.18852	.0613*	.01157	.1174	.0213	.0025	.1327	.0089	.00119
Sister's presence		.0512*							
High Rate p(HR) .01226									
Attend	.18852	.0258*	.00486	.1174	.0213*	.00249	.1327	.0000	.0000
High Rate	.00185	.7500*	.00139	.0000	.0000	.0000	.0011	.0000	.0000
Receive	.00092	.0000	.0000	.0019	.3333*	.00062	.0011	.0000	.0000
Sister's presence		.0280*							
Humiliate p(HU) .00346									
Disapproval	.04880	.0284*	.00138	.0444	-0-	.0000	.0260	.0000	.0000
Humiliate	.00185	.1250*	.00023	.0000	.0000	.0000	.0000	.0000	.0000
Sister's presence		.0106*							

Antecedent Event	Baseline $p(A_i)$	Baseline $p(R_j/A_i)$	Baseline $[p(A_i)][p(R_j/A_i)]$	Intervention $p(A_i)$	Intervention $p(R_j/A_i)$	Intervention $[p(A_i)][p(R_j/A_i)]$	Follow-up $p(A_i)$	Follow-up $p(R_j/A_i)$	Follow-up $[p(A_i)][p(R_j/A_i)]$
Ignore p(IG) .00069									
Disapproval	.04880	.0095*	.00046	.0444	.0141*	.00062	.0260	-0-	.0000
Father's presence		.0015*							
Noncomply p(NC) .04533									
Command	.08252	.4482*	.037011	.1149	.3696*	.04245	.0817	.5362*	.04384
Command Negative	.02059	.3596*	.0074	.0119	.4211*	.00499	.0189	.3125*	.00592
Mother's presence		.0671*							
Negativism p(NE) .0030									
Negativism	.00092	.2500*	.00023	.0000	.0000	.0000	.0000	-0-	.0000
Talk	.33402	.0069*	.00231	.4039	.0031	.00125	.2855	-0-	.0000
Mother's presence		.0067*							
Physical Negative p(PN) .00393									
Cry	.00115	.2000*	.00023	.0000	.0000	.0000	.0000	-0-	.0000
Disapproval	.04880	.0237*	.00116	.0444	.0141	.00062	.0260	.0000	.0000
Play	.07610	.0122*	.00093	.0512	.0000	.0000	.2689	.0088	.00237
Attend	.18852	.0049	.00093	.1174	.0213*	.0025	.1327	.0268	.00356
Laugh	.0030	.0000	.0000	.0038	.1667*	.00062	.0047	.0000	.0000
Yell	.00162	.0000	.0000	.0019	.0000	.0000	.0023	.5000*	.00119
Sister's presence		.0116*							

Appendix A, continued

Antecedent Event	Baseline $p(A_i)$	Baseline $p(R_j/A_i)$	Baseline $[p(A_i)][p(R_j/A_i)]$	Intervention $p(A_i)$	Intervention $p(R_j/A_i)$	Intervention $[p(A_i)][p(R_j/A_i)]$	Follow-up $p(A_i)$	Follow-up $p(R_j/A_i)$	Follow-up $[p(A_i)][p(R_j/A_i)]$
	Tease p(TE) .0030								
Attend	.18852	.0086*	.00162	.1174	.0106	.00125	.1327	.0268*	.00356
Disapprove	.04880	.0047	.00023	.0444	.0282*	.00125	.0260	.0455	.00119
Noncomply	.01179	.0000	.0000	.0063	.1000*	.00062	.0011	.0000	.0000
Sister's presence		.0068*							
	Whine p(WH) .03261								
Attend	.18852	.0552*	.01041	.1174	.0266	.00312	.1327	.0179	.00237
Disapproval	.04880	.0806*	.00393	.0444	.1127	.00499	.0260	.0909	.00237
Humiliate	.00185	.1250*	.00023	.0000	-0-	.0000	.0000	-0-	.0000
Ignore	.00693	.1333*	.00093	.0050	.0000	.0000	.0059	.0000	.0000
Talk	.33402	.0395*	.01319	.4039	.0526	.02122	.2855	.0415*	.01185
Father's presence		.0430*							
Mother's presence		.0418*							
	Yell p(YE) .02428								
Comply	.00971	.1190*	.00116	.0082	.0769	.000624	.0023	.0000	.0000
Physical Negative	.00300	.1538*	.00046	.0013	.5000	.000624	.0059	.0000	.0000
Talk	.33402	.0353*	.01180	.4039	.0170	.00687	.2855	.0041	.00119
Tease	.00393	.0588	.00023	.0019	.3333*	.000624	.0130	.0909	.00119
Physical Positive	.00879	.0000	.0000	.0113	.0000	.0000	.0071	.1667*	.00119
Mother's presence		.0294*							

Footnotes

1. The preparation of this report was facilitated by MH grants MH 10822, MH 15985, and Career Development Award MH 40, 518.

Many of the ideas presented here were developed as a result of extended discussions about stimulus control with R. Ziller, H. Hops, J. Cobb, R. Jones, and J. Reid. The writer is particularly grateful to R. Jones for his critical response to an earlier version of this manuscript.

2. As pointed out by R. Ryder, the fact that the events *within* code classes *may not* be independent would violate one of the fundamental assumptions underlying the use of the chi-square statistic. This, in turn, would pose a major problem in the interpretation of the statistic. Currently we are testing the validity of the independence assumption by carrying out auto-correlational analyses for each code category.

3. There was an across-response correlation of +.27 (n.s.) between $p(R_j)$ and the summed $p(A_i)$ for each of the 14 R_js during baseline. Evidently, the density of controlling stimuli is only partially responsible for determining the relative rate of occurrence for an R_j.

References

Barker, R. G., Gump, P., Campbell, W., Barker, L., Willems, E., Friesen, W., LeCompet, W., and Mikesell, E. Big school—small school. O.E.O. Project No. 594, Progress Report, 1962.

DeMaster, B. and Reid, J. B. Effects of feedback on observer reliability. University of Wisconsin and Oregon Research Institute, in preparation.

Harris, A. Observer effect on family interaction. Unpublished doctoral dissertation, University of Oregon, 1969.

Hoover, L. K. and Rinehart, H. H. The effect of an outside observer on family interaction. Unpublished manuscript, Oregon Research Institute, 1968.

Johnson, S. and Lobitz, G. Demand characteristics in naturalistic observation. Unpublished manuscript, University of Oregon, Psychology Department, 1972.

Patterson, G. R. *Families: Applications of social learning to family life.* Champaign, Ill.: Research Press, 1971.

Patterson, G. R. and Cobb, J. A. A dyadic analysis of "aggressive" behaviors. In J. P. Hill (Ed.), *Minnesota symposia on child psychology*. Vol. 5. Minneapolis: University of Minnesota, 1972. Pp. 72-129.

Patterson, G. R. and Cobb, J. A. Stimulus control for classes of noxious behaviors. In J. F. Knutson (Ed.), *The control of aggression: Implications from basic research*. Chicago: Aldine-Atherton, Inc., in press.

Patterson, G. R., Cobb, J. A., and Ray, R. S. Direct intervention in the classroom: A set of procedures for the aggressive child. In F. W. Clark, D. R. Evans, and L. A. Hamerlynck (Eds.), *Implementing behavioral programs for schools and clinics.* Champaign, Ill.: Research Press, 1972. Pp. 151-201. (a)

Patterson, G. R., Cobb, J. A., and Ray, R. S. A social engineering technology for retraining the families of aggressive boys. In H. E. Adams and I. P. Unikel (Eds.), *Issues and trends in behavior therapy.* Springfield, Ill.: Charles C. Thomas, in press.

Patterson, G. R. and Harris, A. Some methodological considerations for observation procedures. Paper presented at the meeting of the American Psychological Association, San Francisco, September 1968.

Patterson, G. R., Ray, R. S., and Shaw, D. A. Direct intervention in families of deviant children. *Oregon Research Institute Research Bulletin*, 1968, *8*, No. 9.

Patterson, G. R., Ray, R. S., Shaw, D. A., and Cobb, J. A. Manual for coding of family interactions. Document No. 01234, sixth revision, 1969. Available from: ASIS National Auxilliary Publications Service, c/o CMM Information Service, Inc., 909 Third Ave., New York, N. Y. 10022.

Patterson, G. R., Shaw, D. A., and Ebner, M. J. Teachers, peers, and parents as agents of change in the classroom. In F. A. M. Benson (Ed.), *Modifying deviant social behaviors in various classroom settings.* Eugene, Oregon: University of Oregon Press, 1969, No. 1. Pp. 13-47.

Reid, J. B. Reliability assessment of observation data: A possible methodological problem. *Child Development,* 1970, *41,* 1143-1150.

Rosenthal, R. *Experimenter effects in behavioral research.* New York: Appleton-Century-Crofts, 1966.

Scott, P. M., Burton, R. V., and Yarrow, M. R. Social reinforcement under natural conditions. *Child Development*, 1967, *38*, 53-63.

Skindrud, K. Field evaluation of observer bias under overt and covert monitoring of observer reliability: Two preliminary studies. Paper presented at the Fourth Banff International Conference on Behavior Modification, Banff, Alberta, Canada, March 1972. (a)

Skindrud, K. An evaluation of observer bias in experimental field studies of social interaction. Unpublished doctoral dissertation, University of Oregon, 1972. (b)

Tharp, R. and Wetzel, R. *Behavior modification in the natural environment.* New York: Academic Press, 1969.

Wahler, R. G. and Erickson, M. Child behavior therapy: A community program in Appalachia. *Behavior Research and Therapy*, 1969, *7*, 71-78.

Wolf, M., Mees, H., and Risley, T. Application of operant conditioning procedures to the behavior problems of an autistic child. *Behavior Research and Therapy,* 1964, *1*, 305-312.

Zeilberger, J., Sampen, S., and Sloane, H. Modification of a child's problem behaviors in the home with the mother as therapist. *Journal of Applied Behavior Analysis*, 1968, *1*, 47-53.

Survival Behaviors in the Educational Setting: Their Implications for Research and Intervention[1] 7

Hyman Hops and Joseph A. Cobb[2]

A major focus of CORBEH, the Center at Oregon for Research in the Behavioral Education of the Handicapped, is the prevention and remediation of behaviors which are incompatible with successful social and academic functioning in educational settings. The wide variety of behaviors which children emit are conceptualized as forming two broad classifications: *educational survival skills* and *academic responses.* Educational survival skills are distinct from academic responses and are defined as a group of behaviors which act to increase the probability of successful functioning in any educational setting. Two subgroups of survival skills are conceptualized: *social* and *academic*. The former, consisting of such responses as smiling, greeting, and cooperative play, are components of positive social interaction among students and their teachers. The latter subgroup is composed of behavioral categories assumed to be prerequisites for correct academic responding. Examples of these would be looking at the reader or arithmetic page and following the teacher's instruction.

The second broad group of behaviors consists of the precise academic responses related to curriculum content. High achievement, for example, involves high rates of correct responding to specific academic materials. It is likely, however, that minimal levels of survival skills are required before such high rate responding can be performed. The present model assumes, therefore, that adequate levels of survival skills and academic responding are *both* required for successful performance in the educational environment.

The CORBEH conceptualizes both groups of behaviors as primarily under environmental control through the behavior of the teacher and the peer group. It is believed that an ongoing interactive process occurs such that the levels of students' survival skills and academic responses affect and are affected by the responsiveness of the environment. An effective remedial approach presumably would have to involve the child's social agents.

To answer questions arising out of such conceptualizations, the CORBEH adopts an empirical research model based upon a sequence of hypothesis testing. For example, the development of an efficient and effective program of remediation based upon the above conceptual model would require some preliminary investigations. First, the analysis of a broad range of children's classroom behaviors would be conducted to determine their relationships with both social and academic success. This initial step could consist of observing many children in regular educational settings and then correlating the observation data with a primary external criterion such as math achievement (Cobb, 1969, 1970, 1972). An alternative initial investigation might be the manipulation of hypothesized remediation variables to test their effectiveness within an experimental classroom setting (Walker, et al., 1971).

The second and crucial step in the empirical model would be to validate the correlational and/or experimental findings in the normal educational environment. Two questions would be asked at this juncture: (1) In the real world setting, was there a significant change in the previously specified behaviors of children as a direct result of the remediation program? (2) Have the data demonstrated the existence of a causal relationship between the specified behaviors and the academic criterion variables?

This chapter illustrates the use of the empirical model to answer one of the questions arising from our formulations: Is there a causal relationship between specific academic survival skills and reading achievement in the regular first-grade classroom? A review of the relevant research literature will be presented, followed by an outline of the intervention procedures used in the study. Data, collected in the natural educational environment, will be examined to test the hypothesis that training in survival skills will result in an increase in reading achievement.

Research on Academic Achievement and Classroom Survival Behavior

Reading Achievement

Reading achievement in children has been studied in relation to a complex array of social, physiological, and psychological variables. These have included the socioeconomic status of the child's family, sex of the child, mental capacity (Cobb, 1969; Gray, 1970), performance on a wide variety of perceptual-motor tasks (de Hirsch, et al., 1966), early anoxia (Corah, et al., 1965), brain damage (Reed, et al., 1965), emotional disturbances (Gray, 1960; Balow, 1966), and personality factors (Cobb, 1969). The discovery of any such relationships has been criticized as being irrelevant for use by the teacher in the regular classroom for increasing achievement (Bateman, 1966, 1967; Engelmann, 1967). The knowledge that etiological factors such as early anoxia or brain damage are responsible for low achievement may be more important for prevention rather than remediation. Manipulating genetic and physiological variables is beyond the domain of the educator. The assumption that perceptual-motor deficiencies must be dealt with before reading achievement can be improved has been based on equivocal findings (Halliwell and Solan, 1972). It has been criticized by Adelman and Feshbach (1971). Meikle and Kilpatrick (1971) found that reading achievement could be increased by direct instruction without concomitant gains in related perceptual-motor tasks.

Although some form of emotional disturbance has been found in academic underachievers, Balow (1966) argues that it is difficult to determine the causal direction of this relationship. The treatment of emotional disorders had no affect on school performance in children of grades three through six as compared with an untreated control group (Ashcraft, 1970). Moreover, both groups fared significantly worse than the average expected gain per year over a five-year follow-up period. Cobb (1969) reviewed a number of studies in which personality variables were manipulated in an attempt to increase academic achievement of elementary school students; none of the studies produced evidence of increases in achievement following personality changes.

Correlational Studies

More recently, there has been an increased emphasis on investigating relationships between academic achievement and those behaviors that children emit in the classroom which can be observed objectively, and which are potentially under the teacher's control. In a five-year predictive study, Meyers, et al. (1968) demonstrated significant relationships between behavioral ratings in kindergarten and scores on the subtests of the California Test of Achievement in the fifth grade. The behavioral rating on Attention was the most powerful predictor for three of the criterion subtests and the fourth and fifth best predictor for two others. The average correlation between all six of the subtests and the rating on Attention was .36. In another study by Lahaderne (1968), observers rated the attending behavior of sixth-grade children over a two-month period. The correlations with various standardized achievement tests ranged from .39 to .51.

The studies of Meyers, et al. and Lahaderne used broad global ratings which may have included a number of irrelevant behaviors that masked the true relationship between specific response classes and achievement. In a major replication of these studies, Cobb (1970) was able to identify specific behavioral classes which were predictive of achievement. First-graders in three elementary schools were observed during reading and arithmetic periods. Rates of various behaviors were obtained and analyzed via a stepwise multiple regression procedure. The results showed that higher correlations could be obtained using independent, discrete behavioral categories than by using a composite score of total appropriate behaviors. Two behaviors, Look around (LO) and Compliance (CO) produced a correlation of .42 with arithmetic as opposed to .31 with total appropriate behavior. In reading achievement, the combined score was correlated at .42 whereas two component behaviors, Attending (AT) and Volunteering (VO), produced a correlation of .59.

The behaviors demonstrated to be powerful predictors of achievement were conceptualized as academic survival skills necessary, but not sufficient, for successful academic functioning (Cobb, 1970, 1972). They were not academic behaviors per se, but, rather, the first components in a chain of correct academic responding. Staats (1968) has argued that "Formal education depends heavily on the prior establishment in the child of a repertoire of social discriminative stimuli that will control his attentional behaviors, and other motor behaviors as well" (p. 509). The work of Cobb has attempted to precisely define those child behaviors that must be under the teacher's control if her teaching is to be effective. Three precise behavioral categories were identified for each subject area. For reading they were AT, VO, and LO, the latter a negatively related behavior; for mathematics they were AT, LO, and CO.

The implications of these findings are clear. All children, regardless of ability level, must first be taught the prerequisite skills that will enable them to take advantage of educational opportunities offered in the classroom. Each child must learn to look at the book before he can learn to read from it, whether it be a basal or phonics reader. Intervention procedures are, therefore, required which will facilitate the teaching of necessary survival skills prior to teaching the academic task itself.

Behavior Change

Little doubt remains that children's classroom behavior can be changed. Many studies have amply demonstrated that behaviors presumed appropriate for the classroom setting can be accelerated and those behaviors considered inappropriate, and in competition with the former, decelerated. These studies have been carried out in *regular* (Cobb, et al., 1971) and *special education* (Hops, 1971) classrooms.Both *social* (Becker, et al., 1967; Hall, et al., 1968) and *nonsocial* or token reinforcers (Hewett, et al., 1969; Kuypers, et al., 1968; Walker, et al., 1971) have been used with *group* (McAllister, et al., 1969; Packard, 1970; Schmidt and Ulrich, 1969), and *individual* contingencies (Glavin, et al., 1971; Patterson, et al., 1969). Successful interventions have been carried out by focusing directly on the behavior of the *targeted* children (Coleman, 1970; Schwarz and Hopkins, 1970) or by modifying *teacher* (Hall, et al., 1968; Thomas, et al., 1968; Cossairt, et al., in press) and/or *peer* behavior (Walker and Buckley, in press).

Many of the reported studies have involved only the behavior of a single student treated individually. The expense of focusing on individuals using extra personnel may not be justified. It has been suggested that a more practical and effective procedure would be to place the control of the entire classroom in the hands of the teacher by using group contingencies (Hall, et al., 1968). Packard (1970) proceeded to develop a device which would allow the constant monitoring of all of the children in a class and yet be simple, economical, and reliable. Using a clock-light mechanism and group contingencies, teachers of four different classrooms from kindergarten through grade six were taught to increase the amount of classroom "Attention." Based on the aforementioned rationale and Packard's findings, the clock-light mechanism was utilized in the present study.

Although the ease with which changes in children's classroom behavior can be achieved has been demonstrated, there has been little attention to solving the problem of maintenance. Patterson, et al. (1972) have argued that reprogramming the total social environment may result in continued social reinforcement of appropriate responses by the social agents even after the experimenters have departed and tangible reinforcement is no longer used. Tangible or nonsocial reinforcement can be used during the intervention procedure to make the social praise and attention of the social agents more powerful reinforcers, as was demonstrated by Walker, et al. (1972). By involving both teachers and peers, Patterson, et al. (1972) obtained effective maintenance of appropriate behavior in targeted children for periods of six months to two years. Walker and Buckley (in press) found that a maintenance procedure which included the peers was more successful than a limited teacher training procedure. Cossairt, et al. (in press) found that instruction and feedback without social praise was unsuccessful in modifying teacher behavior. The current study, therefore, implemented a teacher training program using experimenter instruction, cueing, modeling, feedback, and praise. The teacher then trained the students using similar techniques backed up by group reinforcement contingencies.

Behavior and Achievement

Lipe and Jung (1971) have suggested that simply focusing on increasing appropriate behavior in the classroom is insufficient. They state, "There is a need for a clear and empirically demonstrated rationale relating such behaviors to measured achievement" (p. 274). Unfortunately, there has been almost no attempt to partial out the direct effects of increases in attention, time on task, or survival skills on academic achievement. In most studies on achievement changes, the treatment variables have been so confounded as to make the relationships between behavioral and academic improvement nonspecifiable. In two major studies utilizing token economies (Hewett, et al., 1969; Walker, et al., 1971), the use of innovative curriculums plus contingent social and non-social reinforcement makes it impossible to determine the independent effects of behavioral changes. In fact, the Hewett, et al. study produced only minor increases in reading achievement, with no significant differences between the control and experimental conditions.

A Study on the Relationship Between Survival Skills and Reading Achievement

The present study was an attempt to demonstrate that not only does a relationship exist between survival skill behaviors and achievement, but, more specifically, that increases in the former will directly result in concomitant increases in scores on standardized reading achievement tests. *The main hypothesis, therefore, states that students who receive training in survival skills will make significantly greater gains in reading achievement than the control students.*

Method

Subjects. The subjects were all of the children in three regular first-grade classrooms in a school district of approximately 21,000 students. By random selection, one classroom was designated as control (N = 20) and the other two as experimental (N = 42).

Achievement tests. As part of an overall reading battery, the Gates-MacGinitie Reading Readiness and Primary A were administered prior to and approximately four to six weeks after the intervention program. For each administration, a mean score was obtained for each child based on standard scores on the Readiness test and the two subtests of the Primary A, Vocabulary and Comprehension.

Observations. During each week in which achievement testing occurred, observations were made of classroom behavior during reading periods for five consecutive days. An interactive coding system developed by Cobb and Hops (1971) was used to record the behavior of all of the children in a pre-arranged fashion. Each student was observed for two continuous eight-second intervals before the observer went on to the next child on the list. After the entire group had been sampled, the observer returned to the first child and began the sequence again. In this way, the behavior of each student was sampled several times during each observation session.

Four full-time and six part-time observers were used in the study. Each new observer was trained until an 85% or greater agreement with an experienced observer was reached on three occasions. Observer reliability was calculated by dividing the total number of agreements by the total number of agreements and disagreements. Reliability data was collected systematically between various pairs of observers throughout the study. Based upon 19 paired observations, the range of reliabilities was 85% to 99% with a mean of 94%.

Cobb (1970) reported correlations between first-grade reading achievement and three survival skills—Attending (AT), Volunteering (VO), and Look around (LO)—of .45, .59, and −.41, respectively. For the present study, AT was divided into two new independent behavior categories, Attending (AT) and Work (WK). To compute the level of survival skills for each student during each observation period, the frequency of LO was subtracted from the summed frequencies of AT, VO, and WK. This figure was divided by the total frequency of all behaviors to give the proportion of time a child engaged in survival skill activities.

Intervention. The details of the intervention program are presented in another paper (Cobb and Hops, 1972) and will be briefly outlined here. All of the procedures took place in the regular classroom with the experimenters acting as consultants to the teachers. The model was based on the work of Packard (1970), Patterson, et al. (1972), and Walker, et al. (1971). Packard developed a clock-light mechanism which allowed the teacher to observe the behavior of the entire class and record the total amount of time the entire group was engaged in "Attending" behavior. Walker, et al. demonstrated that a token economy program could be effectively utilized to increase the amount of appropriate behavior in acting-out children, and Patterson, et al. found consistent long-term gains after social agents had been involved in the overall program.

The teachers were taught to monitor the entire group individually and to use a new set of social behaviors including the increased use of praise for survival skill behavior. To train the teachers, the experimenters frequently praised them for correct responding and, in addition, used modeling, cueing, and daily feedback during the initial stages. All of these actions were faded out as the proportion of time the children engaged in appropriate behavior increased. Readings which coincided with various aspects of the training program were assigned from two programmed textbooks, *Living With Children* (Patterson and Gullion, 1968) and *Modifying Classroom Behavior* (Buckley and Walker, 1970).

Components of the child-training program which were taught to and utilized by the teachers included: (1) the pairing of social and nonsocial reinforcers to enhance the power of social reinforcement when used alone (Walker, Fiegenbaum, and Hops, 1971); (2) vicarious reinforcement, which acts to increase the rate of appropriate behavior in nontask-oriented children and provides more frequent opportunities for the teacher to dispense praise to *all* children contingently. Rather than disapprove the inappropriate behavior of low functioning students, the teacher publicly praises *other* children's appropriate behavior, a situation which tends to elicit appropriate behavior in the low rate students who, then, can be contingently praised as well; (3) shaping procedures so that the criterion for reinforcement is adjusted upwardly as the group demonstrates increased performance levels; and (4) the fading of nonsocial reinforcers as the children progressed. The total period of intervention was 20 school days, and the total consultant time required in each classroom was approximately 12 hours.

Results

To demonstrate the existence of a causal relationship between survival skills and academic achievement, it was necessary to show a concomitant change in both variables such that the group making the greatest gains in achievement would also make the greatest increases in survival skills.

Table 1 Mean Proportion of Survival Skills and Mean Standard Scores for Reading Achievement for Experimental and Control Groups at Baseline and Post-Intervention

Group	Survival Skills				Reading Achievement			
	Baseline		Post-Intervention		Baseline		Post-Intervention	
	M	SD	M	SD	M	SD	M	SD
Experimental (N = 42)	.57	.11	.69	.12	48.4	6.0	60.3	6.6
Control (N = 20)	.63	.09	.66	.12	52.5	7.5	60.0	8.3

Table 1 shows the mean baseline and post-intervention levels of survival skills and achievement for the experimental and control students. The mean proportion of the experimental group's survival skills at the outset was .57, which increased to .69 following intervention, a gain of .12; in contrast, the controls began at .63 and gained only .03. Thus the experimental group, having begun at a lower level than the controls, surpassed them on the post-intervention measure. A two-way analysis of variance with repeated measures on one factor (Winer, 1962, p. 302) indicated significant treatment ($F = 37.75$, $df = 1/60$, $p < .0005$) and interaction ($F = 8.80$, $df = 1/60$, $p < .005$) effects, providing statistical evidence that the experimental group gained more in survival skills than did the control.

Similar findings were obtained from the analysis of the achievement data, which showed significant treatment ($F = 287.93$, $df = 1/60$, $p < .0005$) and interaction ($F = 10.65$, $df = 1/60$, $p < .005$) effects. The experimental children had lower baseline (48.4 vs. 52.5) and higher post-intervention (60.3 vs. 60.0) scores, gaining significantly more standard score points in reading achievement (11.9 vs. 7.5) than the controls.

The data were consistent with the main hypothesis that an increase in survival skills would lead to a similar increase in academic achievement. However, the repeated measures analysis of variance has been criticized for use with groups differing on initial status (Werts and Linn, 1971). To obviate the possible confounding of baseline levels and treatment effects, a post hoc analysis using a matching technique was employed (Cobb and Hops, 1972). All experimental subjects within $\pm$ 1.33 standard score units on baseline achievement and $\pm$ .05 proportion on baseline survival skills of any control subjects were selected for further analysis. The matching criterion was met by 12 control and 16 experimental subjects.

The results were consistent with the findings for the larger group. With more evenly matched mean survival skill scores and standard deviations, as shown in Table 2, the experimental group gained .18, more than three times the .05 increase of the control group. Again, significant treatment ($F = 48.71$, $df = 1/26$, $p < .0005$) and interaction ($F = 11.38$, $df = 1/26$, $p < .005$) effects were obtained.

The achievement gains were highly similar to those of the larger group. The treatment ($F = 142.62$, $df = 1/26$, $p < .0005$) and interaction ($F = 11.32$, $df = 1/26$, $p < .005$) effects were both significant. The data in Table 2 shows that the experimental group gained almost twice as much academically (11.8 vs. 6.4) as the control group. Thus the post hoc analysis indicated that the differential gains obtained in the analysis of the entire groups were not simply a function of initial status.

Discussion

The empirical model developed by the CORBEH for the investigation of key variables related to successful social and academic functioning is considered germane to the realization of our goals. The research process, as practiced in the Center, for the most part, follows a progressive series of orderly, logical steps. At each step in the process, hypotheses are critically tested with hard data.

The critical test of the validity of the research process always occurs in the natural environment. Sidman (1960) argues that the generality of data is one of the three most important questions in the evaluation of experimental findings. In the real world, correlated variables can be tested functionally for the causal direction of the relationship. In addition, variables shown to be effective under controlled conditions can be tested for their efficacy under natural conditions. The results answer a number of theoretical questions, generate new hypotheses in a progressive feedback process, and, most important, provide essential data for the evaluation and development of remedial procedures.

The practical implications of the results of this study are clear: first grade teachers can be trained to increase the level of students' survival skills so that reading achievement can be improved.

Table 2 **Mean Proportion of Survival Skills and Mean Standard Scores of Reading Achievement for Matched Experimental and Control Groups at Baseline and Post-Intervention**

Group	Survival Skills				Reading Achievement			
	Baseline		Post-Intervention		Baseline		Post-Intervention	
	M	SD	M	SD	M	SD	M	SD
Experimental (N = 16)	.59	.06	.77	.08	50.1	7.1	61.9	6.4
Control (N = 12)	.63	.06	.68	.09	51.7	6.9	58.1	8.4

The set of intervention procedures used in the study may be a useful model for the variety of professionals who act as consultants to teachers. In the study, the consultant's time in the classroom averaged slightly more than one-half hour per child. Combined with the minimal effort required of the teacher, it would appear that such procedures can be easily introduced into the educational environment with effective results.

A number of related research questions are still to be answered. For example, it may be argued that increases in achievement may be obtained through curriculum intervention without concomitant increases in survival skills. It is highly probable, however, that a minimum level of survival skills may be required before *any* curriculum intervention program would be effective. If children do not attend to the teacher or follow instructions, it is unlikely that even the best designed curriculum would have significant effects. Further analyses of two years of extensive data collection will be conducted in attempts to answer these and other important questions.

The present paper was an attempt to illustrate the approach used by the CORBEH in solving educational problems; perhaps the findings have made a small but significant contribution to our understanding of the relationship between survival skills and achievement.

Footnotes

1. This research was supported by Contract No. NPECE-70-005, OEC 0-704152(607), Bureau of Educationally Handicapped, U. S. Office of Education.

2. Hyman Hops, Ph.D., is a research associate at the Center at Oregon for Research in the Behavioral Education of the Handicapped, University of Oregon. Joseph A. Cobb, Ph.D., held a joint appointment as research associate at the Center at Oregon for Research in the Behavioral Education of the Handicapped, University of Oregon, and at Oregon Research Institute.

References

Adelman, H. S. and Feshbach, S. Predicting reading failure: Beyond the readiness model. *Exceptional Children*, 1971, *37*, 349-354.

Ashcraft, C. Later school achievement of treated and untreated emotionally handicapped children. *Proceedings of the 78th Annual Convention of the American Psychological Association*, 1970, *5*, 651-652.

Balow, B. The emotionally and socially handicapped. *Review of Educational Research*, 1966, *26*, 120-133. Washington, D. C.: American Educational Research Association.

Bateman, B. D. Learning disorders. *Review of Educational Research, 26*, 93-119. Washington, D. C.: American Educational Research Association.

Bateman, B. D. Three approaches to diagnosis and educational planning for children with learning disabilities. *Academic Therapy Quarterly*, 1967, *2*, 215-222.

Becker, W. C., Madsen, C. H., Arnold, C. R., and Thomas, D. R. The contingent use of teacher attention and praise in reducing classroom behavior problems. *Journal of Special Education*, 1967, *1*, 287-307.

Buckley, N. K. and Walker, H. M. *Modifying classroom behavior: A manual of procedure for classroom teachers.* Champaign, Ill.: Research Press, 1970.

Cobb, J. A. The relationship of observable classroom behaviors to achievement of fourth grade pupils. Unpublished doctoral dissertation, University of Oregon, 1969.

Cobb, J. A. Survival skills and first grade academic achievement. Report No. 1, December 1970, University of Oregon, Contract No. NPECE-70-005, OEC 0-70-4152(607), Bureau of Educationally Handicapped, U. S. Office of Education.

Cobb, J. A. Relationship of discrete classroom behaviors to fourth-grade academic achievement. *Journal of Educational Psychology*, 1972, *63*, 74-80.

Cobb, J. A. and Hops, H. Coding manual for subject/peer/teacher sequential interactions in academic survival skill settings. Report No. 4, September 1971, University of Oregon, Contract No. NPECE-70-005, OEC 0-70-4152(607), Bureau of Educationally Handicapped, U. S. Office of Education.

Cobb, J. A. and Hops, H. Effects of academic survival skill training on low achieving first graders. Report No. 12, June 1972, University of Oregon, Contract No. NPECE-70-005, OEC 0-70-4152 (607), Bureau of Educationally Handicapped, U. S. Office of Education.

Cobb, J. A., Ray, R. S., and Patterson, G. R. Increasing and maintaining appropriate classroom behavior of aggressive elementary school boys. Paper presented at the meeting of the Second Annual Symposium on Behavior Modification, Lawrence, Kansas, May 1971.

Coleman, R. A conditioning technique applicable to elementary school classrooms. *Journal of Applied Behavior Analysis*, 1970, *3*, 293-297.

Corah, N. L., Anthony, E. J., Painter, P., Stern, J. A., and Thurston, D. L. Effects of perinatal anoxia after 7 years. *Psychological Monographs*, 1965, *79*, No. 3.

Cossairt, A., Hall, R. V., and Hopkins, B. L. The effects of experimenter's instructions, feedback, and praise on teacher praise and student attending behavior. *Journal of Applied Behavior Analysis*, in press.

Engelmann, S. Relationship between psychological theories and the act of teaching. *Journal of School Psychology*, 1967, *2*, 93-100.

Glavin, J. P., Quay, H. C., Annesley, F. R., and Werry, J. S. An experimental resource room for behavior problem children. *Exceptional Children*, 1971, *38*, 131-137.

Gray, W. S. Reading. In C. W. Harris (Ed.), *Encyclopedia of educational research.* (3rd ed.) New York: MacMillan, 1960, 1086-1135.

Hall, R. V., Lund, D., and Jackson, D. Effects of teacher attention on study behavior. *Journal of Applied Behavior Analysis*, 1968, *1*, 1-12.

Halliwell, J. W. and Solan, H. A. The effects of a supplemental perceptual training program on reading achievement. *Exceptional Children*, 1972, *38*, 613-621.

Hewett, F. M., Taylor, F. D., and Artuso, A. A. The Santa Monica Project: Evaluation of an engineered classroom design with emotionally disturbed children. *Exceptional Children*, 1969, *35*, 523-529.

de Hirsch, K., Jansky, J. J., and Langford, W. S. *Predicting reading failure: A preliminary study.* New York: Harper & Row, 1966.

Hops, H. The school psychologist as a behavior management consultant in a special class setting. *Journal of School Psychology*, 1971, *9*, 473-483.

Kuypers, D. A., Becker, W. C., and O'Leary, K. D. How to make a token system fail. *Exceptional Children*, 1968, *35*, 101-109.

Lahaderne, H. M. Attitudinal and intellectual correlates of attention: A study of fourth-grade classrooms. *Journal of Educational Psychology*, 1968, *59*, 320-324.

Lipe, D. and Jung, S. M. Manipulating incentives to enhance school learning. *Review of Educational Research*, 1971, *41*, 249-280.

McAllister, L. W., Stachowaik, J. G., Baer, D. M., and Condermon, L. The application of operant conditioning techniques in a secondary school classroom. *Journal of Applied Behavior Analysis*, 1969, *2*, 277-285.

Meikle, S. and Kilpatrick, D. L. Changes in perceptual, motor and reading test scores in a remedial reading group. *Canadian Psychologist*, 1971, *12*, 254-269.

Meyers, C. E., Atwell, A. A., and Orpet, R. E. Prediction of fifth-grade achievement from kindergraten test and rating data. *Educational and Psychological Measurement*, 1968, *28*, 457-463.

Packard, R. G. The control of "classroom attention": A group contingency for complex behavior. *Journal of Applied Behavior Analysis*, 1970, *3*, 13-28.

Patterson, G. R., Cobb, J. A., and Ray, R. S. Direct intervention in the classroom: A set of procedures for the aggressive child. In F. W. Clark, D. R. Evans, and L. A. Hamerlynck (Eds.), *Implementing behavioral programs for schools and clinics.* Champaign, Ill.: Research Press, 1972.

Patterson, G. R. and Gullion, M. E. *Living with Children.* Champaign, Ill.: Research Press, 1968.

Patterson, G. R., Shaw, D. A., and Ebner, M. J. Teachers, peers, and parents as agents of change in the classroom. In F. A. M. Benson (Ed.), *Modifying deviant social behaviors in various classroom settings.* Eugene, Oregon: Department of Special Education, College of Education, University of Oregon, 1969, Monograph No. 1, 13-48.

Reed, H. B. C., Jr., Reitan, R. M., and Klove, H. Influences of cerebral lesions on psychological test performances of older children. *Journal of Consulting Psychology,* 1965, *29*, 247-251.

Schmidt, G. W. and Ulrich, R. E. Effects of group contingent events upon classroom noise. *Journal of Applied Behavior Analysis*, 1969, *2*, 171-179.

Schwarz, M. L. and Hawkins, R. P. Application of delayed reinforcement procedures to the behavior of an elementary school child. *Journal of Applied Behavior Analysis*, 1970, *3*, 85-96.

Sidman, M. *Tactics of scientific research*. New York: Basic Books, 1960.

Staats, A. W. *Learning, language, and cognition.* New York: Holt, Rinehart and Winston, 1968.

Thomas, D. R., Becker, W. C., and Armstrong, M. Production and elimination of disruptive classroom behavior by systematically varying teacher's behavior. *Journal of Applied Behavior Analysis*, 1968, *1*, 35-45.

Walker, H. M. and Buckley, N. K. Programming generalization and maintenance of treatment effects across time and across settings. *Journal of Applied Behavior Analysis*, in press.

Walker, H. M., Fiegenbaum, E., and Hops, H. Components analysis and systematic replication of a treatment model for modifying deviant classroom behavior. Report No. 5, November 1972, University of Oregon, Contract No. NPECE-70-005, OEC 0-70-4152 (607), Bureau of Educationally Handicapped, U. S. Office of Education.

Walker, H. M., Mattson, R. H., and Buckley, N. K. The functional analysis of behavior within an experimental class setting. In W. C. Becker (Ed.), *An empirical basis for change in education*. New York: Science Research Associates, 1971.

Werts, C. E. and Lynn, R. L. Causal assumptions in various procedures for the least squares analysis of categorical data. *Psychological Bulletin*, 1971: *75*, 430-431.

Winer, B. J. *Statistical principles in experimental design.* New York: McGraw-Hill, 1962.

Preliminary Analysis of the Effectiveness of Direct Home Intervention for the Treatment of Predelinquent Boys Who Steal[1]

8

John B. Reid and A. F. C. J. Hendriks

Between 1967 and 1971, Patterson and his colleagues at Oregon Research Institute carried out a systematic series of investigations aimed at developing social-learning-based home intervention procedures for the treatment of hyper-aggressive children (Patterson, et al., 1967; Patterson, et al., 1968; Patterson and Reid, 1970; Patterson, et al., in press; Patterson and Reid, in preparation). As a result of this series of studies, a set of social learning techniques were developed, articulated, and cross-validated. The data from these experiments indicated that highly aggressive, pre-adolescent boys could be treated effectively in their homes by training their parents to use social learning child management procedures at an average cost of 25 to 28 professional hours per family.

An analysis of all treatment cases for which complete and high-quality home observation data were available at least through termination of treatment (N = 25) revealed that although the intervention was quite effective on the average, those boys who were reported to steal (N = 14) were helped less by the project than were those boys who were not reported to steal (N = 11).[2]

It is the purpose of this paper: (1) to describe some differences observed among stealers, non-stealers, and a group of matched controls in the 1967-1971 sample; (2) to compare the parents of these stealers, non-stealers, and controls; and (3) to describe our initial impressions of a new treatment sample of children whose primary referral problem was stealing rather than social aggression. No attempt will be made to present a set of intervention procedures for the modification of stealing behavior. Rather, we will attempt to suggest some directions in which we are moving in the search for set of such procedures.

Comparison of Stealers, Non-stealers, and Controls

Subjects

The subjects were members of 54 families studied at Oregon Research Institute between 1967 and 1971.

Treated families (N = 27). Each of the families was referred for treatment because at least one male child was reported to be exhibiting high rates of aggressive behavior. During intake screening, 14 boys were reported to steal and 13 were not. The behavior of each member of the 27 families was coded during 12 to 20 five-minute observations in the home over two to four weeks during the baseline investigation (for details of the observation procedures see Patterson, et al., 1969). Home observation data through the termination of treatment are also presently available for 25 of the 27 families (14 stealers, 11 non-stealers).

Control families (N = 27). These families were matched with the 27 treatment families on relevant demographic variables. The boys in these control families, however, were not seen by the parents as having adjustment problems. By offering a monetary incentive, it was possible to collect baseline observation data on each of these families in the same manner as was done for the treated families.

Relevant demographic information on the total subject sample is presented in Table 1. As can be seen from inspection of these data, the groups are quite comparable.

Differences among Stealing, Non-Stealing, and Normal Boys*

Response to intervention (stealers vs. non-stealers). Of the 27 cases accepted for treatment, complete observation data, from baseline through termination of treatment, are presently available for 25 cases. Data from these cases are presented in this section. The most obvious difference between stealers and non-stealers in the sample treated at Oregon Research Institute was in their response to the intervention procedures. The observational measures of the treatment outcome are reported in detail elsewhere (Patterson and Reid, in preparation; Patterson, et al., in press) and consisted of a comparison of an average of seven days of baseline data with the same type of observation data collected at termination of treatment.

Using a success criterion of 33% reduction in the rate of deviant behavior from baseline (see Patterson, et al., in press), six of the 14 stealers compared to nine of the 11 non-stealers were categorized as successes. Thus the procedures were approximately twice as effective for non-stealers as for the stealers in this sample.

Comparing the reduction in rate of deviant behavior from baseline to termination, non-stealers showed a mean reduction of

* Henceforth, the term ***stealer*** refers to boys in treatment for social aggression who also steal; ***non-stealer*** refers to boys in treatment for social aggression who do not steal; ***normal*** refers to boys in the control group.

Table 1 Demographic Information on Stealers, Non-stealers, and Normals in Subject Sample

Variable	Normals (N = 27)	Stealers (N = 14)	Non-Stealers (N = 13)
Age of referred child	Mdn = 8 Rng 5-11	Mdn = 8 Rng 5-14	Mdn = 8 Rng 6-11
Number of siblings	Mdn = 3 Rng 2-6	Mdn = 3 Rng 2-6	Mdn = 3 Rng 2-6
Number families with father absent	9	5	4
Socio-economic level*	Mdn = 4 Rng 1-7	Mdn = 4 Rng 2-7	Mdn = 4 Rng 1-6
Birth order of referred child	Mdn = 2nd Rng 1st-6th	Mdn = 2nd Rng 1st-7th	Mdn = 2nd Rng 1st-6th
Grades ahead or behind in school for age**	Mdn = 0 Rng -1 to +1 year	Mdn = 0 Rng -1 to +1 year	Mdn = 0 Rng -1 to +1 year

*Based upon a system provided by Hollingshead and Redlich (1958) with class 1 denoting higher executive or professional, class 4 clerical, and class 7 unskilled laborer.

** No fine-grain data are available on the achievement or intellectual abilities of these children.

.461 deviant behaviors per minute, while stealers showed a mean reduction of .171. The difference between these rates was highly significant ($t = 3.45$, $df = 22$, $p < .001$). Combining both groups, a strong and significant positive relationship was found between rate of total deviant behavior during baseline and the magnitude of reduction of deviant behavior at termination of treatment ($r = +.642$, $df = 23$, $p < .001$).

In summary, these findings show that: (1) children referred for treatment of social aggression who also steal were helped significantly less than the non-stealers; (2) the higher the rate of deviant behavior demonstrated by a child, the more likely he will respond to the social-learning-based treatment offered at Oregon Research Institute.

General Social Behavior of Stealers, Non-stealers, and Normals

In an attempt to better understand the differences between stealers, non-stealers, and normals, the baseline data for the entire sample (14 stealers, 13 non-stealers, and 27 normals) were more completely analyzed and compared.

As mentioned previously, 12 to 20 five-minute observations were made of each member of all 54 families during the baseline period. The observation code used (Patterson, et al., in press) provided a running narrative account of the behavior of a given subject in terms of 29 categories and all of the reactions of other family members to him in terms of the same categories. Correlational analyses showed that only a subset of these 29 codes were sufficiently reliable to warrant further analysis. This subset, along with the Spearman-Brown corrected estimates of split-half reliability for fathers, mothers, and referred children, is presented in Table 2.

The codes presented in Table 2 were then combined into two rational categories: positive-friendly and negative-coercive behaviors. From the data pool, it was possible to calculate the mean rate per minute at which these two larger classes of behaviors occurred for each relevant member of each family.

Data on the occurrence of positive-friendly and negative-coercive behaviors for the three groups of boys are presented in Table 3. The normal boys, as would be expected, produced the lowest rates of negative behaviors; non-stealers produced the highest rates, and the stealers fell about midway between. Considering the positive behaviors, the normals produced the highest rates, as expected, but the stealers scored below non-stealers. These findings suggest that even though stealers appear to be in less conflict with their families in terms of observable negative-coercive behavior, they are in greater conflict with their families if rate of positive social interaction is used as the index.

General Social Behavior of Parents of Normals, Stealers, and Non-stealers

Data on the occurrence of positive-friendly and negative-coercive behaviors for the parents in the three groups are presented in Table 4.

In line with the boys' behaviors, mothers of normal boys produced the lowest rates of negative-coercive behaviors, mothers of non-stealers produced the highest, and mothers of stealers were intermediate. In terms of positive-friendly behaviors, the mothers again

Table 2 **Behavioral Categories Used in the Analysis of General Social Behavior**

Behavioral Categories	Reliability (Spearman-Brown Estimate)* Referred Boys	Mothers	Fathers
Positive-friendly behaviors			
Attention to other family members (AT)	.53	.55	.60
Compliance to requests from other family members (CO)	.80	.54	.55
Friendly laughing (LA)	.37	.63	.52
Playing with others or alone (PL)	.67	.74	.64
Talking to other family members (TA)	.41	.70	.55
Useful household work (WK)	.75	.67	.29
Negative-coercive behaviors			
Commands to other family members (CM)	.38	.84	.61
Angry commands to other family members (CN)	.81	.89	.70
Cry (CR)	.95	**	**
Disapproval of others (DI)	.79	.77	.65
Destruction of property (DS)	.63	**	**
Humiliation of other family members (HU)	.85	.70	.50
Ignoring initiation of others (IG)	.43	.77	.10
Non-compliance to requests (NC)	.77	.51	.62
Subtle negativistic behaviors (NE)	.71	.81	.57
Physical assaults on others (PN)	.55	.77	.77
Teasing (TE)	.52	.92	.50
Whine (WH)	.77	**	**
Yelling at others (YE)	.85	.62	.05

*All reliabilities are based on a correlation of the first half and the second half of baseline.

**Absence of entry indicates that this behavior was never observed to occur in the group.

parallel their sons: mothers of normals highest, mothers of stealers lowest, and mothers of non-stealers in between. Thus, with the mothers' behavior we again find the possibility of a curious paradox. If overt

Table 3 **Mean Rate Per Minute of Positive-Friendly and Negative-Coercive Behaviors of Boys in the Subject Sample**

	Normals	Stealers	Non-Stealers	F	p
Positive-Friendly Behaviors	7.18	6.29	6.84	2.46	.10
Negative-Coercive Behaviors	.30	.57	.75	4.31	.05

Table 4 **Mean Rate Per Minute of Positive-Friendly and Negative-Coercive Behaviors of Parents in the Subject Sample**

	Normals	Stealers	Non-Stealers	F	p
Positive-Friendly Behaviors					
Mothers	8.66	7.31	8.19	4.35	.05
Fathers	6.67	6.79	5.82	1.55	n.s.
Negative-Coercive Behaviors					
Mothers	.63	.77	1.07	4.55	.05
Fathers	.43	.43	.62	1.44	n.s.

negative behavior is the criterion, families of non-stealers appear most disturbed; if level of positive social interaction is the measure, families of stealers seem the worst.[4]

Analysis of data on the fathers did not yield significant between-group effects; however, inspection of Table 4 suggests that: (a) fathers in all groups interact less with their families than do mothers, (b) fathers of non-stealers demonstrate lower rates of positive behaviors and higher rates of negative-coercive behaviors than do fathers in the other two groups, and (c) fathers of stealers behave like fathers of normals on both dimensions.

Analyses of Observation Data: Summary and Tentative Conclusions

The observation data indicate that predelinquent boys who steal did not respond as well to the social-learning-based treatment provided at Oregon Research Institute as did those who did not steal. The analyses of general social behaviors in the families studied provide some clues as to why this is the case.

Stealers do not exhibit high rates of observable out-of-control behaviors. The finding that stealers tended to exhibit less deviant behavior than did non-stealers is a factor that alone might account for the relative inefficiency of a program designed to modify high-rate deviant behavior. However, at least two other possibilities exist. First, the stealers may be exhibiting high rates of anti-social behavior, but only outside the home setting; second, stealers may be "sneaky" and "shut down" deviant behavior while the observers or behavior modifiers are present. Although the second alternative is entirely possible and would argue against our general model of treatment for this type of client in out-patient settings, it fits neither our clinical impressions nor parent report, nor can its validity be checked with our current data collection technology. The first alternative, that stealers cause trouble primarily outside the home, does fit our clinical impressions, parent report, and the perceptions of neighbors and community agencies. It is a hypothesis which helps to resolve the apparent discrepancy between referral information (i.e., high rates of deviant behavior) and our observation data (i.e., low rates of such behavior). If true, it suggests that the reason the parent training program produces minimal results is that there is little deviant behavior occurring within the actual home setting upon which the parent of the stealer can work. Finally, if it is true that the referred stealer causes little trouble at home, it is possible that the community is more immediately punished by his behavior than are the parents. Thus, the parents may refer the child for treatment primarily to appease the school counselor or to get the juvenile authorities off their backs. Were this the case, it would follow that the parents may be motivated to refer the child but relatively unmotivated to actually work to change him. This is in contradistinction to the parents of non-stealing children who are punished daily and at a high rate by their children's behavior. The idea that parents of stealers are relatively unmotivated to change or control their children has gained some measure of support in our subsequent work with stealers and will be discussed further in the final section of this report.

Families of stealers demonstrate low rates of positive-friendly behaviors. Although fathers' data, which have low stability (see Table 2), did not discriminate among the three groups, there was a clear pattern for the mothers and children in the stealer group to exhibit fewer positive social behaviors than those in the other two groups. These findings suggest that stealers and their families are rather distant, having only loose social ties with one another. One possible implication is that the parents of stealers may not have powerful social reinforcers at their command to be systematically and effectively employed within the social-learning treatment paradigm. This low rate of positive, and negative, social exchange gives the picture of a rather boring family climate, which may in fact serve to motivate the child to seek out his developmental experiences and positive reinforcers in unsupervised, extra-family settings.

Current Experience with Treatment of Stealers

Since the completion of work with the families discussed in the previous sections, we have switched our focus to the exclusive study and treatment of families of children who steal. Twenty-seven referrals have been made to our project since the transition. Only five of these referrals actually began treatment.** The primary reason for the dismal response to our offers of treatment has been lack of parental motivation to make the commitments necessary for involvement in the project. The typical pattern was as follows. The parents phone to request treatment immediately following the child's being apprehended for stealing; they either miss the intake appointment or cancel it with one of the following explanations—the problem has ceased to exist, one of the parents (usually said to be the father) refuses to cooperate, or the parents have reconsidered the incident and now feel that the child was unjustly accused. The message behind these cancellations appears quite clear: The parents were upset at the time the child was apprehended, but after that incident had blown over there is little motivation to enter treatment. There is also a marked level of family disorganization characterizing these cases. The children in the families are typically unsupervised for long periods each day, and the working schedules of the parents, both mother and father, tend to keep most of them from spending much time with their children.

The five families actually entering treatment have been quite difficult to treat. They tend to be very slow in completing their assignments and miss or cancel appointments at a high rate. Problems of this magnitude were not encountered in our previous work on social aggression. In fact, it has taken a rather extensive modification of our treatment strategies to effect a change in these new families.

Strategies developed in work with three of the five cases being treated in this series appear to offer some promise. G. R. Patterson began working with one of the cases and found that he was

** It is important to note that this sample of stealers differs from that described in the previous sections in that the members of the present sample were referred specifically for the modification of stealing behaviors. The stealing of the former sample was considered secondary to social aggression problems.

able to obtain only token cooperation from the parents. After several weeks of frustration, he instituted a parenting salary of $60 per month, contingent upon parental cooperation in treatment. This intervention effected a dramatic change in the progress of treatment. The parents are now collecting data, running programs, and producing change in the child's behavior. It may well be the case, as previously suggested, that the parents have little motivation to work on the problem, but by giving them an extrinsic set of reinforcers, they may be treated as effectively as the families of non-stealing aggressive children.

The senior author began work with a different family and encountered problems similar to those confronted by Patterson. That is, the parents seemed unable to monitor the child's behavior, execute programs effectively, or generally get involved in treatment. A different sort of strategy was implemented in this case. Each time the child was caught stealing he was immediately taken by the therapist to the local detention facility where he was kept for a period of three to 24 hours. The child was not permitted to participate in the normal institutional activities during these "time-outs," but rather was put to work cleaning windows or washing walls. At the end of the isolation period, the father had to leave work or home to retrieve his son. This was quite aversive to the father, who wanted the son institutionalized. However, the child ceased getting apprehended for stealing after the fourth time-out, and the father began to monitor the child's behavior and to manage the prescribed programs in a verbalized effort to keep the therapist from "bugging" him. Although the stealing was modified and the observation data showed that the child had halved his rate of deviant behavior, the parents terminated treatment and relinquished custody of their son to the juvenile authorities. Again, it appears that external contingencies may be necessary in teaching such parents to take control of their sons.

J. A. Cobb, working with another case, initially met with this lack of motivation and inability of parents to exert control over the suggested programs. After numerous discussions with the parents, he discovered that they were simply unprepared to deal with the more deviant behaviors emitted by their son. He "switched gears" and had the parents work on the shaping of pro-social behaviors. Effectively, he was shaping the parents to take control of their children, starting on very simple, non-threatening behaviors, then working up to dealing with aggression and stealing. At this point, the parents have achieved a good measure of control over their son who, incidently, has apparently stopped stealing. Rather than employing external contingencies, Cobb achieved success by beginning at a much more primitive level of parent-skill training than has heretofore been necessary with families treated at Oregon Research Institute.

Thus, one of the approaches we feel may be necessary is to teach the members of these families to relate more closely and positively with each other before instituting programs to eliminate undesirable behaviors. Clinically, we have seen an incredible level of family disorganization and diffusion, a near-total absence of enjoyable family activities, and a lack of general parenting skills in these families. These clinical impressions are consistent with the findings of low levels of positive and negative interactions for the families of stealers reported in the previous sections of this report.

It is felt that a successful treatment of stealers will have to involve at least the following steps: an initial, external incentive for the family to change; extensive training in intra-family relations of a general nature; training the parents to monitor or track their children; and finally programs to alter the stealing itself. At this point we are still "experimenting" with variations on the home intervention approach. Until a way can be found to get more of the referred families to actually enter and participate in treatment, the conclusions reached in this paper must remain speculative.

Footnotes

1. This study was supported by Grants MH 10822 and MH 15985. The authors wish to thank J. A. Cobb, R. R. Jones, and G. R. Patterson for their critical readings of earlier drafts of this paper.

2. Information on stealing was provided by parents during the intake procedure.

3. For negative-coercive behaviors, non-stealers are significantly higher than normals ($t = 2.524$, $df = 38$, $p < .025$); the difference between stealers and normals is not significant ($t = 1.438$, $df = 39$, $p > .10$), nor is the difference between stealers and non-stealers ($t < 1.0$). For positive-friendly behaviors, stealers are significantly lower than normals ($t = 2.412$, $df = 39$, $p < .025$); the difference between non-stealers and normals is not significant ($t < 1.0$). The differences between stealers and non-stealers on these two dimensions are not significant. (Means are presented in Table 3.)

4. For negative-coercive behaviors, mothers of non-stealers are significantly higher than mothers of normals ($t = 3.367$, $df = 38$, $p < .01$) and higher than mothers of stealers ($t = 2.632$, $df = 25$, $p < .025$); the difference between mothers of stealers and mothers of normals is not significant ($t < 1.0$). For positive-friendly behaviors, mothers of stealers are significantly lower than mothers of normals ($t = 3.062$, $df = 39$, $p < .01$); neither the difference between mothers of non-stealers and normals ($t = 1.228$, $df = 38$) nor between mothers of stealers and mothers of non-stealers ($t = 1.521$, $df = 25$, $p > .10$) is significant. (Means are presented in Table 4.)

References

Hollingshead, A. B., and Redlich, F. C. *Social class and mental illness.* New York: Wiley, 1958.

Patterson, G. R., Cobb, J. A., and Ray, R. S. A social engineering technology for retraining the families of aggressive boys. In H. E. Adams and I. P. Unikel (Eds.), *Issues and trends in behavior therapy*. Springfield, Ill.: Charles C. Thomas, in press.

Patterson, G. R., McNeal, S., Hawkins, N., and Phelps, R. Reprogramming the social environment. *Journal of Child Psychology and Psychiatry*, 1967, *8*, 181-195. Also in R. Ulrich, T. Stachnik, and J. Mabry (Eds.), *Control of human behavior*. Vol. 2. Glenview, Ill.: Scott, Foresman, 1970. Pp. 237-248.

Patterson, G. R., Ray, R. S., and Shaw, D. A. Direct intervention in families of deviant children. *Oregon Research Institute Research Bulletin*, 1968, *8*, No. 9.

Patterson, G. R., Ray, R. S., Shaw, D. A., and Cobb, J. A. Manual for coding of family interactions. Document No. 01234, sixth revision. Available from: ASIS National Auxilliary Publications Service, c/o CMM Information Service, Inc., 909 Third Avenue, New York, N. Y. 10022

Patterson, G. R. and Reid, J. B. Reciprocity and coercion: Two facets of social systems. In C. Neuringer and J. L. Michael (Eds.), *Behavior modification in clinical psychology*. New York: Appleton-Century-Crofts, 1970. Pp. 133-177.

Patterson, G. R. and Reid, J. B. Intervention for families of aggressive boys: A replication study. Oregon Research Institute, in preparation.

Notes on the Ethics of Behavior Research and Intervention

9

Richard B. Stuart

Many of the papers presented in this exciting book reflect the fact that behavior modification has entered the second generation of its young life. The germination of the movement began with laboratory investigations of the behavior of infrahuman organisms. The principles of the functional analysis of behavior which were the fruit of this early period laid the groundwork for the first generation of behavior modification studies—those concerned with validating the emergent principles for work with human subjects. We have now moved into the second generation reflecting concern with the development of more refined research strategies and more innovative service delivery techniques. O'Leary's concern with group designs, Skindrud's attention to observer bias, and Patterson's analysis of the facilitating conditions of problematic behavior as critical mediating variables all represent a rapid escalation in the perfection of our research methods. The effort of Hops and Cobb to find the constituent behaviors requisite to academic problems and of Reid and Hendriks to find explanation for the comparative lack of success in the service rendered to selected client groups shows dramatic movement beyond the passive acceptance of gross outcomes to a new level of the creative use of data. Finally, the application of sophisticated procedures for marital interaction displayed by Weiss, Hops, and Patterson, LoPiccolo and Lobitz's elaboration of strategies for the treatment of sexual disturbance, plus the demonstration by Fixsen, Phillips, and Wolf of the creation of a microcosmic democracy to aid the resocialization of delinquent youth all reflect the flowering of the work of clinicians in the movement.

As these new directions begin to bear fruit, it is likely that the challenge to behavior modifiers from both lay and professional communities will be intensified. Acknowledging the fact that behavior is being and will continue to be controlled, this challenge is likely to be focused upon the question of whether behavior should be controlled and upon the ethics of behavioral research and practice. The question of whether behavior should be controlled is beyond the scope of this paper and can be the subject of only brief comment. Confronted by daily exposure to massive conditioning programs pairing male companionship with cleaning fluids, masculinity with the speedy driving of sleek eight cylinder, four-on-the-floor phallic extensions, and femininity with the replacement of human odors with eau de anticeptics, it is clear that the molding of our thoughts and feelings is the object of a very sophisticated and concerted effort. Some take a laissez faire attitude toward this situation, believing that the fruits of the conditioning are good, that those which are not so good will be pruned out by differential public acceptance, and that any effort to control the brain benders would concentrate too much power in the hands of a few. Those who believe that these culture-shaping forces should be planfully managed assert that the system has yielded many ill effects ranging from the courtship of violence to the pursuit of drugs, that the very power of the technology precludes the exercise of popular choice, and that the best (albeit not fail-safe) means of ensuring public control of the forces which mold our minds is recallable elected officials with this control.

Concern with the ethics of behavioral research and control is attributable to a variety of factors. With the growing investment of the federal government in health and social science research, investigators in search of subjects have been invading social organizations with increasing intensity, Research projects have grown in size, leading to greater management complication with its resulting likelihood of subject abuse, and the literally astronomical growth in the power of technology has immeasurably raised the possibility of harm to experimental subjects. The burgeoning of large-scale studies involving high risk procedures have led to countless allegations of abuse such as the following:

1. Scores of Chicano women became pregnant as a result of receiving placebos in place of the birth control pills which they thought they were taking. They were the unknowing participants in a study of the psychological and physiological side effects of the contraceptive drug in question (Associated Press, March 17, 1972).

2. At least 28 men died or suffered needlessly from the effects of syphilis through a study of the long-term effects of the disease. The 400 men who volunteered to forego treatment in 1932 were offered free transportation to and from the hospital for periodic examination, free treatment for diseases unrelated to syphilis, free hot lunches, and free burial in exchange for allowing the disease to run its course (Associated Press, July 26, 1972).

3. Several dozen junior high school students began using or intensified their use of drugs as a result of their participation

in a drug education experiment designed to test the hypothesis that drug education is iatrogenic in its effect (Stuart, in press).

Each of these studies is justified by its investigator and sponsor in terms of the good to the community stemming from its conclusions. A considerable amount was learned about the depressive and hematological effects of a certain population control drug, a good deal of information was collected about the longitudinal course of an illness which has since been brought under effective means of control, and the general unquestioning acceptance of drug education programs has been halted. Failure of the first study might have permitted millions of women to suffer serious birth control side effects, failure to conduct the second study might have exposed countless men and women to mercury-arsenic treatment which could have had more harmful side effects than the illness which it was supposed to treat, and failure to conduct the final study might have allowed millions of children to be turned on to drugs in the name of drug use prevention. The outcome of each of these studies involves a certain amount of gain for the general community. On the other side of the ledger, however, is the cost to the individuals involved in each of these studies—the necessity to cope with unwanted pregnancies and children, with incapacitating illness and possibly death, and with the odious concomitants of drug use as it becomes abuse.

Under what conditions are these gains worth making? In modern societies there is little questioning of the right of governments to subvert the rights of citizens for the good of the community—witness taxation and conscription as just two examples. The relevant question thus relates to the conditions under which individual rights can be set aside in the name of the commonwealth. Three criteria are commonly used. First, the Neuremberg Code set the requirement that all research subjects must volunteer with no constraint for participation in experiments which they fully understand, with full knowledge of any harmful side effects. Unfortunately this requirement is not always scrupulously met, and when it is respected many factors limit its being perfectly respected. For example, many psychological and drug studies are carried out without the knowledge of their subjects to avoid the confounding of results by the Hawthorne effect—a change of behavior attributable solely to the subjects' knowledge that they are participating in an experiment. For example, if students in a classroom knew that their behavior was being studied, this knowledge would be very likely to profoundly influence what they do. Other psychological studies deliberately misinform subjects of the intent of the investigation on the assumption that they would modify their behavior if they knew what was being monitored. For example, Braver and Stuart (in press) told subjects that they were studying expressive styles, when the real objective of having husbands and wives rate each other and opposite-sexed others was to determine whether spouse-spouse interaction was more or less positive than spouse-stranger interaction. If spouses knew that their interaction was the object of study, they would be very likely to change their interaction by trying to behave in a socially desirable manner. Finally, many investigators simply cannot anticipate all of the possible hazards of participation in research. Obviously true with drug studies, even behavioral measures which use punishment, for example, might lead to highly damaging escape or counteraggression behaviors. For these reasons informed consent may not fulfill its promise.

The second and third ethical requirements both require highly subjective judgements. The second requires that the benefits of the research outweigh the risks. The obvious problem here is that before conducting an experiment one can only estimate on an a priori basis what its benefits might be, while the final reckoning of costs to the subjects can only be made long after the experiment is completed. At the extremes, it is easy to say that the prolonged social isolation of children to determine whether they are more gregarious when they have had minimal social contact would involve an overbalance of subject costs over possible returns, while the human testing of a carcinoma vaccine which has been extensively tested in animals would clearly show a preponderance of benefits over costs. But the injection of live cancer cells in dying cancer patients to determine the latency of antibody formation (as was done in New York in 1964) is much more clearly in a gray area.

The third criterion requires that the validity of an experiment must be determined by an independent group. Predicated upon the assumption that researchers who have vested interests in their own programs loose objectivity, it is assumed that independent judgments by outside evaluators will be less biased. But professionals are no less limited by their personal prejudices than anyone else. A psychoanalytically oriented group of research reviewers might look askanse at the most conservative effort to provide appropriate academic material and accelerating consequences for task oriented behavior, while partisans of behavior modification might condone the use of potentially damaging procedures in the service of small technological advances.

The three ethical guarantees—informed consent, determination of the benefit/cost ratio, and validation by external professional peers—are obviously not infallible protection. In practical terms, the operationalization of these guarantees involves decision making at six critical choice points. These will now be the subject of discussion.

Ethical Choice Points in Research Design

Ethical choices occur at six stages of the research process. The first two are selection of research goals and intervention methods. If the goals of a research undertaking do not meet stringent ethical requirements, no amount of care subsequently can correct the evil. If the methods used do not pass an ethical test, they have no value for society.

To contrast the ethics of goal and method selection, the work of Cotter (1970) can be compared with that of Fixsen, Wolf, and Phillips (Chapter 10, this volume). Both studies involved work with nonvoluntary clientele, the former with Vietnamese mental patients and the latter with delinquent youth. Both studies were carried out in institutional settings, a mental hospital and a family group home, respectively. Cotter's goals were to place his patients in servitude in Green Beret agricultural teams, while Fixsen and his associates sought to return their subjects to their natural communities in the shortest possible time. The mental patients were subjected to a negative reinforcement paradigm involving electroconvulsive therapy or starvation, while Fixsen's team created a group living environment based essentially upon the use of positive reinforcement. In the mental hospital, patients were coerced to accept administrative dictates, while in the group home subjects had an opportunity to influence most features of the methods to which they were exposed.

It is doubtful that Cotter's study could have been carried out in a situation in which a high value is placed upon human life—all lives—or that it could be carried out in an environment in which community control was possible. Funded by a foreign government with a maximum of geographical, cultural, and political remoteness from the research cite, no checks upon the researcher's practice was possible. In contrast, Fixsen, et al. drew both their values and the bulk of their funding from the community in which their work was both a research project and a service. Because of their dependence upon local funding, they were open to constant scrutiny, an invaluable check upon the acceptability of their goals and practices and license for their continuation.

The third ethical choice point arises in the matter of subject selection. Here the work of Walker and Hops (Chapter 11, this volume) can be contrasted with that of LoPiccolo and Lobitz (Chapter 13, this volume). The former team, in agreement with the teacher, selected 12 subjects who evidenced withdrawn behavior in elementary school classrooms. LoPiccolo and Lobitz solicited volunteer couples facing problems of sexual adjustment. Walker and Hops' subjects were exposed to an ingenious intervention aimed at increasing their skills in eliciting social reinforcers from peers and teachers. LoPiccolo and Lobitz's subjects were offered an equally creative treatment, but one which is adapted from more customary efforts to modify sexual behavior. The elementary school children were thus subjected to a novel intervention program for which neither they nor their parents volunteered, while the marital couples underwent a more conventional service for which they volunteered. The first procedure comes close to raising a serious ethical issue, while the latter appears safely within the realm of ethical acceptability. The justification for the first procedure might well be twofold: (1) the teachers are the acknowledged agents of social control in the classroom, and they are the sole arbiters of those who will and will not receive special treatment; and (2) the procedures were simply more skillful applications of the same type of interventions which the teachers would have used anyway. Should the parents of any of the children involved have chosen to raise issue with the inclusion of their children in the Walker and Hops research, however, it is doubtful that these defensive statements would hold very much weight in the court of public opinion, particularly if the parents alleged that their children's privacy was invaded, that their children were exposed to the secondary deviance consequences of labeling, or that their children suffered some iatrogenic effects.

The fourth choice point for ethical determination is the area of research design. O'Leary and Kent (Chapter 2, this volume) have pointed out that single subject designs, which have been invaluable in the generation of support for the principles of the functional analysis of behavior, suffer from at least two limitations: (1) some intervention techniques are so powerful that they may not be subject to reversal (leading to falsely negative conclusions); and (2) subject selection for these studies is typically biased and restricted so that the generalization gradient of the results is small or unknown. To these criticisms can be added the ethical consideration of what effect the reversal process might have upon the child subject inasmuch as it systematically exposes him to great inconsistencies in the behavior of important agents of social influence. (Multiple baseline studies offer some advantage in this regard; see Risley, 1969.)

O'Leary and Kent suggest that control group designs are a mandatory next step for behavior modifiers. This suggestion has varied ethical implications. Control group designs necessarily involve withholding from a randomly chosen group of subjects a treatment which the experimenter believes to be effective. In human service research, these subjects generally have either applied for or been referred for treatment to overcome a behavioral problem. Some of the subjects might be assigned to a placebo condition in which they are exposed to what is believed to be innocuous contact with the experimenter, contact chosen because it has no behavior change value. This procedure is effective only if the subjects find the placebo credible. Other subjects might be placed in "wait list control" conditions in which they are told that treatment is not now available but will be offered at a later date. The wait list deception is used out of recognition that many so-called untreated controls often set out to find their own treatment elsewhere, leaving the experimenter with a comparison between known and unknown treatment rather than with the presence or absence of treatment. When it is effective, however, the control condition preserves the "pristine" quality of the control subjects whose only contact with the experimenter is for pretest purposes, and often even this can be avoided in large sample studies through the use of post-test only designs.

The disadvantages of both the placebo and untreated control group designs are twofold. Most seriously, subjects are deceived into thinking that they are to receive the needed help while their problems increase—as marital conflict rises to the point of marital disolution, as adolescent deviance mounts to the point of exclusion from the community, and the like. Less dramatic but no less serious are the emotional consequences of subjects realizing that they have been deceived or their disenchantment with human service organizations in general as a result of their poor experience as control subjects.

The pros and cons of control group designs are summarized in Table 1.

The use of contrast groups and control group monitoring procedures can mitigate some of the problems inherent in the control group procedure. Contrast groups employ procedures which, like the focal experimental procedure, have some reasonable expectation of success. The contrast conditions might be factorial components of the focal procedure or they might be quite separate and distinct procedures. For example, a study of services to delinquents based upon behavioral

Table 1	Some Pros and Cons of Control Group Designs
Pro	**Con**
1. Control group designs allow determination of whether a particular treatment is better than none.	1. a. It is rare that subjects in social science research are ever truly "untreated." b. Clinicians rarely ask the question: "Should I use your treatment or none at all?"
2. The absolute effectiveness of a method can only be tested through control group designs.	2. This implies that the distribution of results in social science research is linear or bimodal. Results typically show curvilinear relationships which require multiple data points unobtainable through pretest—post-test control group designs.
3. It is unethical to offer to the public treatments which have not been fully validated.	3. It is unethical to deceive those who seek out treatment, reducing the likelihood that they will be treated elsewhere.
4. Experimental resources are limited and can only be offered to a small proportion of applicants anyway.	4. More subject related basis for resource allocation could be used.

contracting might contrast differing durations of service (a factorial comparison) or might compare the focal procedure with techniques aimed at arousing adolescents' self-awareness. The liability in this procedure is that if the groups fail to yield significant differences, the researcher is hard-pressed to say whether the subjects would have been better off if they had been spared participation in either treatment condition. The asset in this procedure is that all subjects receive at least some service, and the question answered by the design is one commonly asked by practitioners: "Which of two procedures should I use?"

The monitored control group procedure requires that subjects who are randomly assigned to a control condition must be continuously monitored throughout the period of employment as controls. The monitoring is designed to detect any serious deterioration which might lead the subjects or the community to suffer in unintended ways. For example, in a study of services to delinquents, control subjects can be included in activity groups which meet infrequently and are believed to have no therapeutic value. Through these contacts researchers can determine whether controls have increased deviance patterns which might be personally or socially harmful. Any such subjects could then be offered immediate service. The liability of this procedure is that it decreases the likelihood of positive experimental findings by deleting the most negative cases from the control group. The assets of this procedure are that the subjects are offered a modicum of protection and the experimental results are likely to be more conservative, often a virtue given the overzealous claims of many researchers.

The final two choice points at which ethical considerations are important are found in the selection of which data to report and how and when to disseminate research results. Skindrud (Chapter 3, this volume) as well as Johnson and Bolstad (Chapter 1, this volume) have shown that "all that is reported is not reliable"—that the observational data obtained through behavioral experimentation can in many cases be confounded by artifacts of the data collection process. Inattention to this kind of detail can lead to the publication of false findings, and the mettle of any researcher is tested when confronted at the end of a year or two of hard labor with unnoticed defects in his procedures. The same can be said for the failure to report negative results. For those of us who feel that a part of behavior modification is a social and scientific "movement" it is tempting to hide unflattering outcomes. But publication of these data in a manner demonstrated by Reid and Hendriks (Chapter 8, this volume) both places our procedures in a more credible context and provides a stimulus for the development of means of resolving unsolved problems.

The selection of channels for the distribution of research results is also an ethically important decision, although one not often considered in this regard. By and large, professionals communicate their results to other professionals at meetings not attended by the public, or in journals which are little-read even by professionals. It is ethically stronger to present research results to the general public which in most instances bears the cost, serves as subjects, and is the ultimate consumer of the service. This, of course, would require professional researchers to learn new styles for more effectively communicating their procedures and results, and it might possibly, too, require the development of new outlets. But as long as research is cloaked in "technicalese" secrecy, canons of professional ethics will remain ill-served.

Ethical Considerations in Behavior Modification Practice

The ethics of service delivery begin with the requirements that therapists not misrepresent themselves, that clients must be protected from exploitation, and that the services offered must afford the maximum possible benefit at the least cost to the client. The growing volume of malpractice suits attests to the failure of many therapists to subscribe to these requirements as scrupulously as they might.

Several of the papers included in this book also have important implications for the ethics relating to service delivery. Davison's (Chapter 5) clinical demonstration of the exercise of clients' options for countering the control sought by therapists is an excellent case in point. In this undertaking Davison showed an abiding respect for his clients' right to accept or reject any intervention procedure offered. To aid this decision, the therapist was encouraged to feed back to the client the precise outcome of the use of each technique. This responsiveness to client wish and to the empirical outcome of each procedure represents the highest level of ethical regard for those receiving behavioral service.

LoPiccolo and Lobitz, and Weiss, Hops, and Patterson also describe the use of treatment contracts with the client. A contract specifying the privileges and responsibilities of both therapists and clients is an important means of at least explicating the goals and procedures to be used.

Despite the apparent safeguards afforded by the contracting procedure, however, it is not without its limitations. Merely making the client aware of the objectives and techniques of treatment, and securing his consent to both, do not legitimate the use of any procedure which the therapist might wish to employ. First, the demand characteristics of the therapeutic situation give the therapist even more control over his client than the experimenter has over his subject. In addition, faced with intense personal misery, the clients may be inclined to agree to procedures which they would reject in more cogent moments. Furthermore, some procedures are frankly violations of statute or ordinance. For example, a client cannot be allowed to contract to perform illegal acts in the name of mental health. Finally, some procedures clearly go beyond both local and professional custom. This last consideration is the gray area because it includes the forefront of clinical innovation. At the same time, however, it is the client in these instances who is exposed to the untoward consequences of therapeutic failure and the therapist who triumphs along with the client from clinical success. Therefore, while contracting provides some protection against violations of clients' rights, it is not a guarantee that these rights will be respected.

Other considerations should also enter into a code of ethical practice for behavior modifiers. For example, therapists might be enjoined from charging their clients for the administration of procedures which are regarded as experimental (the problem here being to determine when a procedure has been fully validated for clinical use), or therapists might be required to request payment for only that treatment which has been successful (the problem here being the determination of success). When treatment is conducted in training settings, it is questionable whether it is ethical to offer clients treatment by students unless they agree to accept such treatment (which, of course, can exceed the excellence of professional practice and always is rendered with greater hopefulness and enthusiasm). Finally, it might be an ethical requirement that therapists expose their biases to their clients before undertaking treatment. For example, a study presently in progress has shown that marriage counselors who have not undergone divorce are more likely to have clients whose marriages are sustained. Clients advised that their therapists are or are not inclined to view divorce as an acceptable solution to marital trouble might be able to make wiser choices among therapists. If it were possible to identify a salient list of attitudes such as these, it might be well to inform clients in advance of the value climate to which they will be exposed.

Moving beyond direct therapist-client contracts to other forms of service—those instigation procedures in which mediators are instigated by a therapist to promote changes in the behavior of the client target, or intervention procedures in which the behavior modifier assumes control of the microsocial environment himself—another ethical issue is raised. Here the ultimate goal is a change in the behavior of a person who, by definition, is not a party to any therapeutic contract. In these situations, ethics is served only when the intervention procedure used clearly conforms to the prevailing custom, when the procedures and results are monitored by a third party, and when the target of behavior change is a "minimal goal." Minimal goals seek to strengthen behavior which is mandatory if the client is to preserve his rights as a citizen. For example, if an adult jeopardizes his rights by assaulting a young child or if continuation of a youth's schooling is jeopardized by repeated delinquent acts, the development of prosocial behavior may be sought even without client consent. However, when the goals are "optional," that is, when they go beyond the production of minimally required social behavior, client consent would seem to be mandatory. For example, in the first illustration if the goal were not only to produce different behavior toward young children but also to promote appropriate heterosexual approach behavior, or in the second illustration if the goal were to promote academic excellence, the consent of the targets must be secured.

Summary

In this brief paper, more issues were raised than were solved. As evidenced by the material presented in this book, behavior modifiers seem to be moving toward new levels of excellence in research and practice. But these escalations also pose new ethical dilemmas for the field. The use of more rigorous experimental procedures may fulfill one ethical requirement but violates another: the empirical basis for intervention procedures is strengthened although at some considerable cost to the rights of subjects. By the same token, as the clinical procedures become more potent, so, too, does the possibility of infringement upon the client's rights. Failure to attend to these ethical implications of progress could, over time, prove harmful both to society and to behavior modification. Unfortunately, the decisions which have to be made are arbitrary in many instances. The *summum bonum*, the highest good, which is the object of ethics, has as many different definitions as it has beholders, and an analysis of the immediate and long-range benefits and costs of any research or clinical procedure must necessarily be decided in the public forum through an interaction of professionals and laymen together. The decisions which will be made through these exchanges will at best represent a compromise between "the ethics of personal conscience" and "the ethics of social responsibility" of both professional and layman alike (Hogan, 1970). Because the alternatives which one may choose for himself in private do not coincide with his public choices, some conflict will inevitably result from the public exposure of private ethical decisions.

References

Braver, J., and Stuart, R. B. Reactions to spouses and strangers: A test of marital satisfaction. *Family process*, in press.

Campbell, D. T. and Stanley, J. T. *Experimental and quasi-experimental designs for research.* Chicago: Rand McNally, 1963.

Cotter, L. T. Operant conditioning in a Vietnamese mental hospital. In R. Ulrich, T. Stacknik and J. Mabry (Eds.), *Control of human behavior: Volume 2.* Glenview, Ill.: Scott, Foresman, 1970.

Hogan, R. A dimension of moral judgement. *Journal of Consulting and Clinical Psychology*, 1970, *35*, 205-212.

Risley, T. R. Behavior modification: An experimental-therapeutic endeavor. In L.A. Hamerlynck, P. O. Davidsen, and L. Acker, *Behavior modification and ideal mental health services.* Calgary: University of Calgary, 1969.

Stuart, R. B. Drug education: Pushing or preventing? *Journal of Abnormal Psychology*, in press.

THREE

Section Three: New Applications and Developments

THREE

Introduction

Lee C. Handy

In the following section of four chapters the emphasis is on application or, if vou will, actual delivery of services to the ultimate direct consumer. It will quickly become apparent that many of the issues raised in the preceding sections are further exemplified in the following papers. This would seem especially true regarding behavioral observation difficulties and, obviously, control of behavior. Also, further application of Patterson's work on stimulus control (Chapter 6) to the types of endeavors reported here would seem particularly fruitful.

The papers presented here are of particular interest and relevance in that we have a relatively new and increasingly recognized powerful approach to behavior change tackling a number of society's most grievous problems. Fixsen, Wolf, and Phillips' paper describing Achievement Place illustrates an exemplary approach to the remediation and subsequent prevention of crime and delinquency. Walker and Hops have addressed themselves to the very important issue of increasing social skills aimed at the prevention of social withdrawal, a critical concern in our increasingly highly socialized environments. The problem of marital discord and its concomitant difficulties has plagued society unabatedly, and it is this concern that Weiss, Hops, and Patterson have tackled. LoPiccolo and Lobitz present a promising approach to the treatment of sexual dysfunction, a continually vexing problem which in the past has contributed much to human misery.

The chapters appear in an order which could roughly fall on the following continua: from most structured to least structured, and from most imposed goals to least imposed goals. Both continua would seem to be highly related to Stuart's comments regarding selection of research goals and intervention methods and also subject selection (Chapter 9). Another characteristic of interest in these chapters is the high degree to which all of the treatment strategies meet the criterion of allowing for the monitoring of treatment affect upon an individual (or individuals) in relationship to the therapeutic goal. On a larger scale this same process can be seen to be operating profitably in what Weiss, et al. (this volume) have phrased as ". . . the continual interplay between case study and technique building" which I believe is characteristic of all of the work reported here.

Fixsen, Wolf, and Phillips' outstanding work with Achievement Place in dealing with pre-delinquent, delinquent, and dependent-neglected boys, in its six years of operation and development, has achieved the stature of a milestone in such endeavors. They have described the development and present status of this program in a most practical and useful manner. The three major basic components of the treatment program—the point system, the social behavior of the teaching parents, and the semi-self-government system—are all dealt with in detail as well as the general and specific goals of the program. It is suggested that a major factor in the continued successful development of Achievement Place has been the integration of evaluative procedures at three levels: program, progress, and procedure.

Walker and Hops report an attempt to develop a procedure for treatment of social withdrawal which meets their stated criteria of: effective, economical, relatively independent of teacher monitoring, facilitating acquisition of social interaction skills, and providing opportunity for rehearsal and development through interaction with relevant peers. Their procedure of symbolic modeling in combination with individual, group, and individual-group reinforcement contingencies has produced some very desirable results. Theirs is an excellent paper with promising implications.

The danger of implicit assumptions leading to discord by default in marriage relationships has long been recognized. Weiss, Hops, and Patterson present an intervention program which directly attacks such difficulties. Based upon the ability to assess the present state of affairs and determine what is maintaining the undesirable behavior, their (re)educational package and its subsequent evaluation contains several stimulating and practical components. Two of these are: (1) the emphasis on utilizing communication skills outside as well as within the marital dyad in producing increased personal satisfaction, and (2) the use of observational data in assessment and evaluation of outcome as well as the usual types of self-report techniques. May their efforts be rewarded.

Much of the currently popular literature dealing with sexual dysfunction therapies has suffered greatly from lack of attention to scientific or experimental rigor. Certainly the program being developed at Oregon by LoPiccolo and Lobitz is a major thrust in the direction of remedying this situation. While admittedly in the developmental stage, their work has much of immediate practical value to the practitioner in this area. It is of interest to note that the procedures reported here (with promising results) have been adopted by Dr. N. Wagner* at the University of Washington with an interesting modification. Wagner reports considerable success in improving marital relationships without screening for unrelated marital difficulties, suggesting that perhaps successfully coping with the specific sexual difficulties is a positive catalyst on the marriage relationship in general. LoPiccolo and Lobitz's extremely brief statement regarding the conceptualization of sexuality seems to be a point well taken.

Taken as a group these papers certainly qualify as excellent examples of ". . . innovative service delivery techniques" as referred to by Stuart in the preceding chapter.

*Personal communication May 5, 1972.

Achievement Place: A Teaching Family Model of Community-Based Group Homes for Youth in Trouble[1,2,3]

10

Dean L. Fixsen, Montrose M. Wolf, and Elery L. Phillips

Introduction

In 1966, Lee Robins published a book entitled *Deviant Children Grown Up* in which she described a longitudinal study of 524 Caucasian children who had been referred to a St. Louis mental health clinic between 1924 and 1930. At the time of referral the children were all 18 years old or younger with a median age of 13 years, and all had an IQ of 80 or above, with a median IQ of 95. Of the total 524 referrals, 406 were referred for antisocial behavior and 118 were referred for other reasons. Of the boys, 30% were referred for theft, 18% for incorrigibility, 10% for learning problems, 8% for sex offenses, and 7% for running away. For the girls, 28% were referred for incorrigibility, 17% for sex offenses, 12% for theft, 11% for running away, and 10% for learning problems. The remaining percentages of boys and girls were those not categorized by referral problems. Robins also studied 100 control subjects who were matched with the referral group with respect to race, age, sex, IQ, and socio-economic status. On the basis of elementary school records, the control subjects had not been referred to a mental health clinic and had no record of expulsion from school or transfer to a correctional institution during their elementary school years.

In a most ambitious effort Dr. Robins and her staff began locating, contacting, and interviewing the subjects to conduct a follow-up study. Of the 624 subjects, 591 (92%) were contacted and interviewed 30 years after they had been referred to the mental health clinic. Robins presents a wealth of information in her book and excellent summaries of the data. In one summary she stated:

> We had expected that children referred for antisocial behavior would provide a high rate of antisocial adults, but we had not anticipated finding differences invading so many areas of their lives. Not only were antisocial children more often arrested and imprisoned as adults, as expected, but they were more mobile geographically, had more marital difficulties,

> poorer occupational and economic histories, impoverished social and organizational relationships, poor Armed Service records, excessive use of alcohol, and to some extent, even poorer physical health. The control subjects consistently had the most favorable outcomes, and those referred for reasons other than antisocial behavior tended to fall between the two. . . For antisocial boys the risk of future arrests was 71%, with almost half having frequent arrests and almost half having been incarcerated. For antisocial girls, the risk of divorce was 70% and for boys 50%. . . antisocial behavior in childhood apparently predicts no specific kind of deviance but rather a generalized inability to conform and perform in many areas (Robins, 1966, pp. 68, 70, 73).

When Robins and her staff looked into the histories of the youths who had been referred for antisocial behavior, she found that most of the youths,

> . . . in addition to a history of juvenile theft, had a history of incorrigibility, running away from home, discipline problems in school and, having been held back at least one grade by the time they appeared in the clinic, most of them never even graduated from elementary school. More often than other patients, they were described as aggressive, reckless, impulsive, slovenly, enuretic, lacking guilt, and lying without cause.
>
> Ordinarily referred to the clinic about age 14, the history of behavior problems dated back an average of 7 years, beginning early in the school history. Before passing Juvenile Court age, almost four out of five appeared in court and more than half were sent to a correctional institution. Most of them had directed antisocial behavior toward their parents and teachers, and. . . they were also involved in offenses against business and strangers (Robins, 1966, p. 293).

Robins' findings indicate that children who display antisocial behavior are very likely to become adults who display similar antisocial behavior. These results place added emphasis on the need to find effective treatment methods for redirecting the lives of antisocial youths. On the basis of her follow-up data, Robins noted that placing children in a reformatory or institution apparently had less effect on their future antisocial behavior than leaving them with their seemingly incompetent parents. However, neither alternative had much effect on subsequent antisocial behavior. This result is particularly disturbing since most juvenile judges have only two alternatives for disposition: placing an adjudicated youth in an institution, or placing him on probation where he remains with his parents. As an alternative, Robins suggested having the schools take a more vigorous "parental" role in "preventing truancy, supervising completion of assignments, and in controlling the use of leisure time by children with early antisocial behavior" (Robins, 1966, p. 219). The use of "residential family institutions" was another possibility presented by Robins. Thus, Robins' recommendations for treatment centered on developing alternatives that would assume the role of responsible parents.

These recommendations correspond with a recent trend away from building new institutions and toward developing community-based treatment programs. The 1970 White House Conference on Children gave one of the highest priorities to developing community-based programs. The 1970 President's Committee on Mental Retardation recommended taking the retarded out of institutions and normalizing their lives in community treatment programs. The states of California and Washington have an incentive program that pays up to $4,000 to a community for each youth who was eligible but not sent to a state reformatory. The state of Massachusetts is currently undertaking a program to remove all but 50 youths from state institutions for delinquents and place them in community-based treatment programs such as group homes. The trend toward community-based treatment is also evident in Sweden and Denmark where community programs care for almost all their antisocial and retarded youths (Wolfensberger, 1970). Although the success of these programs in terms of redirecting the lives of delinquent youths has yet to be established, it is already apparent that they are less expensive to operate and more humane than most institutions.

In Kansas we are currently developing a model community-based treatment program for antisocial youths. We call it the *teaching-family model* group home. The group home is a large, older home that has been renovated to accommodate six to eight youths in trouble and one set of teaching-parents who administer the program and live with the youths. The teaching-parents are professionals specifically trained for their job and paid a professional salary at the level of public school teachers. The teaching-parents have the explicit responsibility for teaching the deviant youths the self-care, social, academic, and community-living skills necessary for them to become successful citizens in the community. Although the teaching-parents are directly responsible for carrying out the objectives of the treatment program, the goals of the program are determined by the community or neighborhood in which the group home is located. In this way the goals of each program can reflect the unique characteristics and customs of the community.

The details of the teaching-family model are presented in *The Teaching-Family Handbook* (Phillips, Phillips, Fixsen, and Wolf (in press).

The teaching-family model is based on Achievement Place, a group home for delinquent, pre-delinquent, and dependent-neglected boys in its sixth year of operation. The 25 youths who have been adjudicated and placed in Achievement Place were, on the average, 13 years old, in the seventh grade in school; their achievement tests placed them in the third grade, and they had an average IQ of 95. Seventy-seven percent of the youths came from families with income under $5,000 per year, 76% had been suspended from school one or more times, 60% had failed one or more grades, and 94% had been classified as school behavior problems, 60% as emotionally disturbed, and 35% as slow learners. Fifty-three percent of the youths had failed probation, and the youths averaged 2.2 police contacts and 1.9 court contacts prior to coming to Achievement Place.

The cost of purchasing and renovating the Achievement Place facility was $50,000, or about $6,000 per bed compared to a cost of about $20,000 to $30,000 per bed to construct a large institution. The average yearly operating cost per boy was about $4,100 in 1971 compared to about $9,500 per boy at the reformatory in Kansas. The principal savings in operating costs at Achievement Place is in personnel. Most state institutions hire ward attendants who work on a shift basis to supervise the youths. Additional personnel include psychiatrists and psychologists to treat the youths, social workers to work with the parents, teachers to operate their school, maintenance men, cooks, secretaries, bookkeepers, and other administrative personnel. Many of the people hired by an institution are necessary only because of the large size of the facility, the large number of youths served, and the distance from the youths' homes to the institution. At Achievement Place and other group homes based on the teaching-family model, an unpaid Board of Directors handles the money and the administration of the group home, and the teaching-parents carry out the treatment and supervisory functions.

The Achievement Place Treatment Program and Treatment Goals

The treatment program at Achievement Place consists of three basic parts: (1) a point system (token economy) in which the youths earn points for appropriate behavior, lose points for inappropriate behavior, and exchange points for various privileges available in most group homes; (2) the social behavior of the teaching-parents who provide contingent positive and negative feedback to the youths, instruct the youths in appropriate behavior, provide the youths with opportunities to practice newly learned behaviors, and act as a model for appropriate behavior; (3) a semi-self-government system whereby the youths judge each other's behavior and provide consequences for both appropriate and inappropriate behavior, all under the supervision of the teaching-parents.

The point system and the social behavior of the teaching-parents will be discussed in this section, and the self-government system will be discussed in a later section.

The Point System

In any treatment or training setting there are various trainee or subject or patient behaviors that are of interest to the staff, and there are a number of privileges controlled by the staff that are of interest to the trainees. The staff may want the trainee to stop cursing, hitting others, cheating, and picking his nose and to start having more eye contact, displaying better manners and greeting skills, and volunteering to help. The trainee may want the staff to grant permission for him to see his girl friend, call his mother, watch television, have extra dessert, and avoid his daily chores. In many treatment or training settings the relationship between what the trainee does and what he gets is not well structured and depends, to a large degree, upon the momentary behavior of the trainee and the whims of the staff. In other settings where this relationship is better structured it is often difficult to provide privileges for small improvements in behavior or to grant a privilege for many small improvements over a period of time. A point system introduces a degree of structure that allows the trainee to earn or lose points that represent small pieces of privileges. If a privilege sells for 1,000 points and a youth earns 100 points, he has earned one-tenth of that privilege. By engaging in nine other "100-point behaviors" the youth can earn permission to use that privilege. Thus, the point system provides powerful consequences that can be given contingent upon a youth's performance of minor behaviors as well as behaviors of major importance. And, the point system provides a structure that states specifically the relationship between the trainee behaviors required by the staff and the staff permissions requested by the trainees.

Point systems or token economies have come into rather widespread use since Ayllon and Azrin (1965, 1968) described their system for training chronic psychotic patients at Anna State

Hospital. The point system is an administrative arrangement that establishes the privileges available to the youths, sets the prices (in points) for the privileges, determines when the privileges may be purchased, and establishes the type of point system to be used (i.e., whether the youths can make points and not lose any, can start with a daily total and lose points and not make any, or can both make and lose points). The particular behaviors for which the youths can earn or lose points are determined by the goals of the program and not by the point system. The manner in which the points are given or taken away from the youths is dependent upon the social behavior of the teaching-parents and not the point system.

Privileges. The privileges (listed in Table 1) that can be earned by the youths at Achievement Place are readily available in most homes. Except for allowance and bonds, the privileges consist of permission to engage in or to avoid certain activities and add nothing to the cost of the treatment program. The *basics* privilege gives the youth permission to use the radio, telephone, tools, or recreation room, and to go outdoors. The *snacks* privilege permits the youth to have a snack (cookies or candy or fruit and kool-ade or coke or milk) after school and before bedtime. The youth must ask the teaching-parents' permission to use this privilege and must describe the snack he wishes to prepare. The *TV* privilege permits the youth to watch television almost anytime. The basics, snacks, and TV privileges are difficult for the teaching-parents to monitor and are relatively "weak" when compared to some of the other privileges. Therefore, the youths are required to purchase the basics, snacks, and TV privileges in that order before hometime or other privileges can be purchased. The *hometime* privilege permits the youth to go to his natural home from Friday evening to Sunday evening and to attend extra-curricular activities at school, go downtown, and visit friends during the week. The youth must obtain permission from the teaching-parents (or parents during the weekend) before this privilege can be used. The youths are required to purchase the hometime privilege after basics, snacks, and TV because the goal of the treatment program is to return the youth to his natural family. Requiring the youth to purchase this privilege before the remaining privileges helps guarantee the youth's continued exposure to all of the problems of getting along in his natural home at a time when the teaching-parents can help solve those problems. This allows the teaching-parents to discover the parent-child problems that exist for each youth and to work with the youth and his parents to remedy those problems before the youth completes the treatment program at Achievement Place.

Table 1 **Privileges That Can Be Earned by the Youths at Achievement Place**

Privilege	Cost in Points (Weekly)
Basics	5,000
Snacks	3,000
TV	3,000
Hometime	6,000
Out of Saturday Work	6,000
Out of Weekly Work	12,000
Allowance $1 First	3,000
Allowance $1 Second	6,000
Bonds	1,500
Special First	Variable
Special Second	Variable

Basics, snacks, TV, and hometime are activities that each youth can gain access to by paying points. However, there are restrictions on the use of each privilege not unlike those found in most homes. For example, the basics privilege permits the youth to use the tools to repair his bicycle, but if he does not return the tools to their proper place he may lose that privilege for a short time or lose points. Similarly, abuse of the telephone or snacks privileges may result in loss of the privilege or loss of points. Thus, the youths may use any privilege they purchase, but the abuse of any privilege may still result in consequences for them.

There are two privileges that allow the youths to avoid work. The *out-of-Saturday-work* privilege allows the youth to avoid returning to Achievement Place on Saturday morning to help with household cleanup and maintenance tasks for which the youths do not earn points. These tasks include cleaning the garage, raking leaves, painting, and repairing household items. The *out-of-weekly-work* privilege permits the youth to avoid doing a major household cleaning task that each boy is assigned to carry out one day each week. The weekly jobs include mopping and waxing the kitchen and dining room floors, dusting and cleaning the windows in the living room, and vacuuming the rugs. The youths earn 7,000 points for properly completing each weekly job, but if a youth purchases the out-of-weekly-work privilege he does not earn these points.

The *allowance* privilege entitles the youth to one or two dollars allowance per week depending upon whether the youth buys one or two allowances. The money is simply given to the youth on the day points are exchanged for privileges. The purchase of *bonds* does not give the youths any immediate privileges. Rather, bonds are accumulated (an unlimited number of bonds can be purchased each week) to purchase clothing or gifts or to purchase advancement through the treatment program. When bonds are used to purchase clothing or merchandise, the youth and the teaching-parents negotiate an exchange rate of bonds per dollar. If the youth wishes to purchase clothing he needs badly, the exchange rate is usually about one bond or less per dollar. However, if the youth wants blue and white striped jeans that have a red flag on the seat of the pants, the exchange rate might be as high as five bonds per dollar. Bonds can also be accumulated to purchase onto the merit system, the final step in the treatment program before returning the youth to his natural home. A youth must pay 100 bonds to purchase onto the merit system. The *special* privileges can be purchased by a youth to engage in some privilege not covered by the ones listed in Table 1. The youth usually describes what he wants to do, and he and the teaching-parents negotiate a price for the speical privilege.

Prices of privileges. The number of points the youths pay for each privilege is listed in Table 1. The cost of the first four privileges combined is 17,000 points per week, or an average of 3,400 points per day for the five weekdays. The prices of the privileges are relatively constant from month to month. The main exception is that the price of basics is increased from 5,000 to 10,000 points during the summer months when the boys are not in school and have increased opportunities to earn points.

Table 2 shows the youths' frequency of purchasing each privilege during a 15-week period. The boys purchased the basics, snacks, and TV privileges 72 times each out of 78 opportunities and the hometime privilege 71 out of 78 opportunities. Since the youths were required to purchase these four privileges first, these data indicated that only 6 times out of 78 opportunities some youths did not have enough points at the end of a week to purchase basics or any other privilege; during 4 of the 15 weeks one youth did not have enough points to buy any privileges, and during 1 of the 15 weeks two youths did not have enough points. However, during 10 of the 15 weeks all of the youths had enough points to purchase the first four privileges. The out-of-Saturday-work privilege was purchased 52 times out of 78 opportunities,

Table 2 **Frequency of Purchase of the Privileges Available at Achievement Place During a 15-Week Period***

Privilege	Total Times Purchased/ Total Opportunities	Percentage
Basics	72/78	92%
Snacks	72/78	92%
TV	72/78	92%
Hometime	71/78	91%
Out of Saturday Work	52/78	67%
Out of Weekly Work	0/78	0%
Allowance $1 First	15/78	19%
Allowance $1 Second	12/78	15%
Bonds	49/78	63%
Special First	5/78	6%
Special Second	0/78	0%

*from June, 1971 to October, 1971

and the bonds privilege was purchased 49 times out of 78 opportunities. The remaining privileges were purchased less than 25% of the time.

The frequency of purchase gives a general idea of the relative popularity of the privileges but, since the point prices of the privileges vary, another index is the number of points spent by the youths to purchase the privileges. Table 3 shows the total number of points spent by all of the youths to purchase each privilege during the same 15-week period. The youths spent the largest number of points for bonds which could be used to purchase advancement onto the merit system. During these 15 weeks the youths purchased 390 bonds, or an average of 5 bonds per week per youth.

In addition to selling the privileges at the stated prices, the teaching-parents also require the youths to maintain a certain daily point total in order to engage in those privileges. Thus, if the required daily point total is 3,000 points and a youth does not have 3,000 points at the end of the day, the next day he cannot engage in the privileges he has purchased. As soon as the youth earns the required total the next day, he regains the use of his purchased privileges. It should be noted that the youth does *not* pay for his privileges twice. He only has to maintain a certain daily point total to continue to use the privileges he has purchased. This requirement was established after the teaching-parents noted that some youths earned very few points

Table 3 **Total Number of Points Spent By All the Youths for Each Privilege During a 15-Week Period***

Privilege	Total Points Spent
Basics	345,000
Snacks	207,000
TV	207,000
Hometime	408,000
Out of Saturday Work	312,000
Out of Weekly Work	------------
Allowance $1 First	45,000
Allowance $1 Second	72,000
Bonds	585,000
Special First	70,000
Special Second	------------

*from June, 1971 to October, 1971

during the first few days of the week and then attempted to earn all of the points they needed during the last day or two of the week. The daily point requirement helped solve this problem by requiring the youths to earn a minimum number of points each day to retain their privileges for the next day.

Purchasing privileges. The point system is an artifical but necessary part of the treatment program. The teaching-parents teach each new boy that comes into the program the essentials of the point system by placing the youth on an hourly-point-system. On the *hourly-point-system* the youth earns points for three hours and then exchanges the points for privileges that can be used during the next three-hour interval. After the youth comes under the control of the point system, the three-hour exchange interval is lengthened to six hours for several intervals and finally to a 24-hour interval or a daily-point-system. On the *daily-point-system* the youth earns points during one day and, before bedtime, purchases privileges that can be used the following day.

The purpose of the hourly- and daily-point-systems is to get the youth "hooked" on earning points, that is, to teach the youth the connection between earning points and receiving privileges for doing so. The frequent exchanges of points for privileges facilitate the learning of this connection. However, the teaching-parents soon place the new youth onto the *weekly-point-system* where he earns points for five days and, on Friday evening, purchases privileges that can be used during the next seven days (including the weekend). On the weekly-point-system, points are still directly contingent upon the youth's behavior, but the purchase of privileges is delayed from one day to seven days. This is to prepare the youth for the final system, the *merit system*, where all the privileges are free but the youth's behavior is still evaluated to make sure he maintains an adequate level of appropriate behavior. The merit system provides only social feedback to the youth and thus is a much less artificial system of maintaining the youth's behavior.

Type of point system. The goal of most treatment programs is to produce significant changes in the trainee's or patient's behavior while, at the same time, providing a pleasant environment in which the trainee can live. These two general treatment goals are sometimes incompatible when some consequence which is unpleasant to the trainee must be used to produce a change in his behavior. Often, a treatment environment results in a compromise of each general goal so that some more or less aversive consequences are occasionally applied but attempts are also made to maximize the reinforcers available to the trainee. These general treatment goals should be considered when any point system is devised.

The point system at Achievement Place is a "positive and negative system" in which the youths earn points for appropriate behavior and lose points for inappropriate behavior. The point system is also very flexible in that there are nearly unlimited ways the youths can earn points. These two aspects of the program are important because if a youth loses a large number of points he has the opportunity to make up the lost points in order to buy the privileges that are sold at a fixed price. Thus, loss of points does not necessarily mean loss of privileges, but it does mean that the youth who lost the points will have to engage in additional point-making activities to purchase the privileges he wants. The youths generally have made up their lost points as indicated in Table 3, which shows that over 90% of the youths purchased the first four privileges each week.

The fact that the youths can lose points indicates that the Achievement Place treatment program depends partially on mild punishment. However, the flexibility of the point system allows the youths to readily make up the lost points, so the youths seldom lose any significant privileges. It would appear that the aversiveness of a point system could be better measured by the degree of success that the participants have in earning the privileges rather than by the presence or absence of contingent point losses. Thus, at Achievement Place mildly aversive consequences are used to produce significant changes in the youth's behaviors, but a flexible point system is also used to maximize the privileges available to the youths each week.

Teaching-Parent Social Behavior

As we indicated in a previous section, the point system is an administrative arrangement or tool that can be used by the teaching-parents. Once the administration, bookkeeping arrangements, and materials needed to use the point system are established, the use of the point system is determined by the social behavior of the teaching-parents. In general, if the teaching-parents can modify or maintain a youth's behavior by providing social consequences for that behavior, they do so. For behaviors that are not initially sensitive to social consequences, the teaching-parents provide point consequences as well. Thus, the degree to which the point system is needed is determined by the quality of the teaching-parents' social behavior and the severity of the youths' problems.

The importance of the teaching-parent's social behavior becomes apparent when the data on the number of point transactions are taken into account. Table 4 shows the average number of point transactions per day for each boy for points earned and points lost during a 15-week period. Points were involved in a total of about eight interactions a day between the teaching-parents and each youth. Since the teaching-parents interact with the boys several hundred times each day, the interactions involving points comprise only a relatively small portion of the total.

Many social skills are needed by the teaching-parents. Perhaps the most important of these is being able to interact in a positive way with the youths. The teaching-parents must be friendly, constantly praising appropriate behavior, providing positive feedback, smiling, joking, etc. They must make requests in a positive way. They should not sound as though they are demanding, threatening, or challenging the youth when they make a request. Rather, the request should be given in a friendly, matter-of-fact way that sounds as though the teaching-parent is confident the youth will carry it out.

The teaching-parents must provide constant feedback to the youths. They need to monitor the youth's behavior carefully and provide positive feedback to the youths at every opportunity. The positive feedback can be smiles, jokes, an arm around the shoulder, giving points, or a praise statement such as "The yard looks great since you mowed it." By practicing the delivery of genuinely enthusiastic praise statements and other positive feedback, the teaching-parents can demon-

Table 4 **Average Number of Point Transactions Per Boy Per Day for Points Earned and Points Lost During a 15-Week Period***

	Average Number Transactions/Day	Range (Average for all Boys)
Points Earned	6.7	5.7–8.2
Points Lost	1.5	1.2–2.1

*from June, 1971 to October, 1971

strate examples of appropriate behavior and provide powerful positive reinforcement essential for a happy home and a successful program. The teaching-parents also need to provide negative feedback to the youths contingent upon inappropriate behavior. Examples of negative feedback are frowning, finger shaking, a firm grip on the shoulder, taking off points, and correction statements such as "That's aggressive talk; we don't say things like that around here." When a teaching-parent gives negative feedback he should also carefully explain to the youth what he has done to deserve the negative feedback and demonstrate to the youth another, appropriate way of behaving in the situation. The teaching-parents then ask the youth to practice the appropriate way of behaving and deliver positive feedback to the youth for doing so.

Some Achievement Place Goals

The general goals of Achievement Place are to improve the youths' social, academic, and self-help skills sufficiently to make them successful citizens who can hold a job, stay out of trouble with the authorities, and lead a pleasant life. Of course, these are general, long-term goals of the program which can only serve as a guide for establishing goals that can be realized more immediately.

The immediate social behavior goals of Achievement Place include teaching the youths to cooperate, help others, greet adults, have good manners, discuss issues without arguing or fighting, resolve problems by helping each other, carry out instructions, smile in the face of adversity, display a good sense of humor without hurting others with practical jokes or cruel teasing, and get along in a family situation without being rowdy, threatening others, pouting or sulking, lying, cheating, or stealing. The academic behavior goals include keeping the youths in school, improving their social behaviors in school so they will not be suspended, and improving homework and report card grades. The self-help behavior goals include teaching the youths how to cook, iron their clothes, take a shower, brush their teeth, clean house, do minor household maintenance and repair tasks, use tools properly, and organize their time to complete the tasks assigned to them.

These and other treatment goals are further defined to include a definition of the behavior, some examples of behaviors that would earn or lose points, and the probable number of points that would be earned or lost. These defined goal behaviors are available to the youths. An example of one defined goal behavior, helping others, is given below.

> *Goal behavior: Helping others.* The goals of the Achievement Place program include teaching youths to be thoughtful, courteous, and aware of the needs of people around them. They are encouraged and rewarded for offering to help, i.e., helping another boy with a homework problem, taking coats of guests, caring for a baby, etc.
>
> When a youth offers to help without a prior request, it is worth more points. However, if he willingly and eagerly agrees to help after being asked this is in his favor when points are paid.
>
> It is almost impossible to name all the ways of helping another person, and they all vary in the length of time and effort required. Therefore, time spent helping often must determine the number of points earned.
>
> The boys are especially encouraged to help people in the community. We want the local citizens to be impressed with the Achievement Place program. Therefore, the boys are highly paid when given praise from people from the community. If a boy does a "good deed" for someone, such as changing a tire or helping a person cross the street, and the teaching-parents only hear about it from the youth, the boy

(if he has a history of honesty) is given points (1,000 to 2,000 points). The following list gives examples of these behaviors and the points made or lost for each.

Behaviors	Points made or lost
Brought luggage in for guests	+300 to +500 points
Helped a lady or older person change a flat tire	+2,000 points
Did not willingly help someone in need	–500 to –1,000 points
Took someone's coat or got them an ashtray (this involves a small effort but should be rewarded)	+300 points
Entertained a baby for two hours or helped another boy with a difficult puzzle	+1,000 to +1,500 points per hour

Self-Government

One important aspect of the Achievement Place treatment program is the self-government system. There are many advantages to having a self-government component in the treatment program. The youths learn how to cooperate to reach some agreed upon goal, how to elect and change their leaders, how to be good (fair, just) leaders, and how to develop rules and to live under those rules. They become skilled in assigning appropriate consequences for violations of the rules, and they become aware observers of their own behavior and the behavior of others. The teaching-parents value the self-government system because assignment of large fines is a group decision, the youths help enforce the rules they make by reporting violations of the rules to the teaching-parents and thereby help change the behavior of their peers, griping and complaining about the treatment program is reduced since the rules and consequences for rule violations are approved by the peer group, and in the spirit of self-government the youths help one another with learning tasks such as homework, speech correction, manners, greetings, etc. Even though this is only a partial list of the advantages of a semi-self-government system, it can be seen that the system plays an important role in the treatment program.

Establishing A Self-Government System

Because most of the youths in the program originally do not have the skills necessary for a self-government system to function, the teaching-parents must carefully educate the youths in the self-government process. When starting a program the teaching-parents set a time each day for a *Family Conference.* Dinner is a convenient time since both teaching-parents and the youths are usually together at this time and the Family Conference will not have to compete with other activities. Initially the Family Conference should be used to explain the rules of the home to the youths. Each *rule* can be specified, the *reasons* or natural consequences for each rule can be given, and the *point consequences* for breaking each rule can be stated. During these first few Family Conferences the teaching-parents should play the role of the *benevolent dictator.* That is, they should tell the youths what the current rules are and only ask whether they understand them, not whether they like them or approve of them. The teaching-parents at this time are obligated to set up rules for which they have good reasons. Arbitrary rules should be avoided since they will reduce the youths' confidence in the fairness of the system. When several rules have been established and the reasons for the rules explained to the youths, the teaching-parents should carefully note each rule infraction that occurs each day. Points should be removed throughout the day whenever a rule violation occurs. Then at the Family Conference all rule violations should be reviewed, perhaps by having each boy review his own rule violations for the group. The teaching-parents should also discuss and quiz the youths occasionally about the reasons for each rule. By these means the youths learn the rules of the home and the reasons for those rules.

After the youths have demonstrated that they can live under a system of rules (this usually requires a few months when a new program is first being established), a rule violation each day can be used for discussion at the Family Conference. The teaching-parents can describe to the youths the situation and the misbehavior that occurred and ask for their opinion of whether a rule violation occurred. For training purposes, the first few misbehaviors that are described should be clear violations of a long standing rule familiar to all. If, as they should, the youths agree (by a show of hands) that a rule violation occurred, the teaching-parents should ask the youths to tell the reasons why that rule was established. By this time the youths should be able to give the teaching-parents good reasons for the rule which relate to the natural consequences for engaging in that behavior, i.e., safety, reputation of the home, health, law, or peer's or teaching-parent's rights.

If on several occasions the youths have all agreed that the behaviors the teaching-parents described were rule violations and if the youths have given appropriate reasons for the rules when they were asked, they are then ready for the next step toward self-government. The teaching-parents can then not only ask the youths' opinions of whether a rule violation occurred and the reasons for the rule, they can also ask the youths to set the consequence for violating the particular rule (the youths should already be familiar with the possible penalty for that particular rule) and then ask the boys to decide what the consequences should be in this particular case. The teaching-parents should give the boys feedback after each suggested consequence. Some suggestions will be "too high," some "too low," and some will "sound about right." The final consequence, however, must have the teaching-parents' approval before it is levied. This procedure should be carried out at each Family Conference for several weeks so the youths will gain experience in establishing consequences for their peers' rule violations. By helping establish consequences, under the direction of the teaching-parents, they will also learn about the relative seriousness of various rule violations.

Along with the *appropriate consequence training*, the teaching-parents should begin teaching the youths how to establish and modify rules. To do this, the teaching-parents can capitalize on the complaints the youths have concerning one another. With six to eight youths living together there will be complaints about trespassing, use of one another's belongings, teasing, threats, arguing, etc. From the beginning the teaching-parents should help the youths establish rules to govern the behaviors they complain about. The teaching-parents can ask the youths why they think the behavior is inappropriate, what potential harm it could do the youth, and what kind of rule they think should be established. The youths will often make rules that are overly harsh or restrictive. However, the teaching-parents can point out the potential consequences of the rule and suggest alternatives to the youths. Pointing out that *all* the youths have to live by the same rule is usually sufficient to make most rules fair. The final rule, of course, must have the approval of the teaching-parents before it becomes binding.

With each Family Conference the youths will become more experienced in making new rules, modifying old rules, recognizing rule violations, and setting consequences for rule violations. The final step toward self-government is peer reporting of rule violations. When the youths are allowed to make their own rules, the teaching-parents can encourage the youths to report any infractions of the rules. Since the rules being broken are those the youths have established, it is usually easy to point out how it is in their best interests to take an active part in enforcing the rules. To encourage peer reports, the teaching-parents initially can give points to the youth who reports any rule violation. If an infraction of an important rule occurred and several of the youths were aware of the violation but did not report it (and the teaching-parents have good evidence of this), the teaching-parents can also levy large point fines to the youths for not reporting.

Peer reporting should not be confused with "ratting" or "stool pigeon" types of behavior. "Stool pigeons" are those who report their peers' misbehavior to local school or law enforcement authorities who then use the information in ways that are beyond the control of the youth who reported. Peer reporting, on the other hand, occurs where misbehavior is reported to the teaching-parents who then ask, during a Family Conference, for the youths' decision on what to do about the misbehavior. Thus, a peer reporter maintains some control over the consequences of his report.

Self-government, then, consists of training the youth in several skills. The youths have to become experienced in: (a) establishing new rules and modifying old rules, (b) giving reasons for each rule, (c) recognizing the behaviors that violate each rule, (d) reporting rule violations, and (e) establishing consequences for rule violations.

Teaching these skills requires time and programmed effort on the part of the teaching-parents. The skills, however, are made up of specific behaviors that are sensitive to social and point consequences and, as such, can be taught with a systematic program.

Once all of the self-government skills have been trained, the trial procedure is as follows:

Trial Procedure

1. Identify which trial you are talking about, then ask for a discussion of the incident.
   a. Have the person who reported the violation describe what happened.
   b. Ask the accused youth if he committed the rule violation.
   c. Ask for further discussion of the incident.
2. Ask the youths, "Is he guilty or innocent?"
   a. Have the youths raise their hands to vote on guilt or innocence.
   b. If there are any dissenting votes, call for further discussion and vote again. (The teaching-parents have final authority.)

3. If he is guilty, ask the youths, "What consequences do you want to apply?"
   a. Ask for a discussion of the possible consequences.
4. Have the youths vote, by raising their hands, for the consequence more or less decided upon.
   a. Before the vote, the teaching-parents should summarize the consequences so it is clear what they are voting on. (If the teaching-parents disagree with the youths' decision, they can ask the youths to accept *responsibility* as described below.)

Normally, the teaching-parents will agree with the youths' decision on consequences for a rule violation. If, however, the youths insist on a consequence that is, in the teaching-parents' judgment, too low, the youths can vote to accept *responsibility* for any future violations of the rule by that youth. Thus, if the same youth violates the same rule again in the future, the group will lose a number of points designated by the teaching-parents.

Once all of the self-government skills have been taught, the teaching-parents can eliminate many of the less important rule violations (used for training purposes) from discussion at the Family Conferences. However, rule violations that result in fines of more than 3,000 points should be brought up routinely at the Family Conference and subjected to the approval of the youths via the trial procedure.

Procedure Evaluation: An Example

The development and continued refinement of the Achievement Place program is the result of a commitment to evaluation of the program at all levels. There are at least three important levels of evaluation. First, a program can be evaluated in terms of the behavior of the youths five or ten or fifteen years after they graduated. If the youths become successful citizens who are an asset to their families and the community, and if they are measurably better than other comparable groups of youths who received some other treatment, the program would be successful. This type of *program evaluation* is very important. Unfortunately, program evaluation does not provide the program staff with information about the effectiveness of specific treatment procedures, and it requires a long period of time between application of the treatment and evaluation of the effects of the treatment.

A second, more immediate form of evaluation is *progress evaluation.* This method of evaluation is concerned with the progress of each youth toward his individual behavior goals. Since the goals of the program are spelled out in objective terms, it is possible for the teaching-parents to evaluate daily a boy's progress. When there is no progress the teaching-parents can immediately try another procedure and again watch the boy's record for signs of progress. Thus, progress evaluation allows the teaching-parents to adjust the program to the individual differences of the boys in a systematic manner.

Although progress evaluation allows a more immediate evaluation of a treatment procedure, it cannot provide the data necessary for evaluating the effectiveness of specific treatment procedures. It is necessary, therefore, to carry out a third level of evaluation, *procedure evaluation*. Procedure evaluations are concerned with the carefully measured effects of a specific, well described procedure on a specific, objectively defined behavior of a youth. To demonstrate the reliable effects of a procedure, reversal or multiple-baseline designs are used (Baer, et al., 1968; Wolf and Risley, 1970).

An example of procedure evaluation is the research we carried out recently on the self-government system (Fixsen, et al., in press). The teaching-parents at Achievement Place spent about one year informally trying out and evaluating many possible self-government procedures to supplement the manager system (see Phillips, Wolf, and Fixsen, in press, for a detailed description of the manager system). The result of this informal investigation was the self-government system described above. We then carried out a formal investigation to evaluate the effects of the system on one behavior, the participation of the youths in discussions of consequences for rule violations at the Family Conference.

Definition of the Behavior

"Participation in discussion" was defined as a youth suggesting alternatives, adding information, or making a statement that was directly related to the discussion taking place. In each case, a youth had to do more than agree with what had already been said.

Observation of the Behavior

Each Family Conference was video taped. Each evening the boys would set up the video tape equipment, tape the evening meal where the Family Conference was held, and dismantle the equipment after dinner. The next morning an observer would replay the video tape and record the names of the boys who participated one or more times in discussions of guilt or consequences. The number of boys attending each trial varied from four to seven, so these observations were converted to the percentage of boys participating in each discussion.

Reliability of Observation

For four trials during the experiment inter-observer agreement was measured by having a second observer simultaneously and independently record participation from the video tapes. The two observers' records were compared for agreement of recording each boy's name for each trial, and the percent agreement was calculated by dividing the total number of agreements x 100 by the total number of agreements plus disagreements. Inter-observer agreement for participation was 100%, 92%, 100%, and 100% for the four trials. This high percentage of inter-observer agreement indicates that the definition of participation was sufficiently objective to permit reliable observation by two independent observers.

Experimental Conditions

Trial-set consequences. In this condition the teaching-parents recorded any reported rule violation that would likely result in at least a 3,000 point fine. No consequences for the rule violation were actually delivered before the trial by the teaching-parents, however. At the Family Conference, the teaching-parents would call a trial on the boy accused of violating the rule, and the boy's peers would decide his guilt or innocence and what consequence to deliver, if any. The trial procedure used was that described in the above section on Self-Government.

Pre-set consequences. In this condition the teaching-parents recorded any 3,000 point, or more, rule violation and delivered a consequence to the boy *at that time*, i.e., before the trial. At the Family Conference the teaching-parents would call a trial on the boy accused of violating the rule, and the boy's peers would decide his guilt or innocence and what consequence to deliver, if any. The only change in the trial procedure in this condition was that the teaching-parents would tell the group how many points they had already fined the boy before asking for a discussion of the consequences. The boys were free to modify any pre-set consequence, and the group decision on consequences took precedence over the teaching-parents' pre-set consequence.

Unfair consequence probe. The teaching-parents made every attempt to pre-set consequences that were fair and appropriate to the rule violations that occurred. For two trials, however, the teaching-parents set a consequence that was ten times greater than what they considered to be fair.

Preference Probe. Near the end of this experiment, and after the formal data collection was terminated, the boys were asked on several trials whether they preferred to have the teaching-parents pre-set the consequences for rule violations or to have the consequences decided entirely by trial decision. The preference measure was taken for nine trials that had Pre-Set Consequences and for three trials that had Trial-Set Consequences. The preference question was asked sometimes before a trial and sometimes after a trial was completed. The boys voted for the alternative of their choice by raising their hands.

Results

Figure 1 shows the percentage of boys who participated in each trial decision on consequences. During the first Trial-Set Consequence condition where the teaching-parents did not pre-set consequences and the peers decided the consequence for rule violations in the trial, there was a median of 80% of the boys participating in each trial. When the teaching-parents began delivering consequences before each trial in the Pre-Set Consequence condition, the percentage of participation dropped to a median of 40%. When the Trial-Set Consequence condition was reinstated the percentage of boys participating in the trial decision increased to a median of 83% and immediately decreased to a median of 0% when the teaching-parents once again began pre-setting consequences.

The Unfair Consequence Probe (indicated by the arrows in Figure 1) occurred during the second Pre-Set Consequence condition. As shown in Figure 1, the percentage of participation increased sharply when the teaching-parents pre-set a consequence that was judged by them to be inappropriate to the rule violation.

On 12 occasions the boys were asked whether they preferred the Trial-Set Consequence condition or the Pre-Set Consequence condition. The boys' preference *after* four Pre-Set Consequence trials was unanimously in favor of pre-set consequences. Their preference *before* five Pre-Set Consequence trials was unanimously in favor of pre-set consequences on four trials and in favor of trial-set consequences on one trial. The boys' preference before and after all three Trial-Set Consequence trials was in favor of trial-set consequences.

In the Pre-Set Consequence condition there was an opportunity to compare the consequences pre-set by the teaching-parents with the consequences agreed upon by the boys. These data are shown in Table 5. Of 53 Pre-Set Consequence trials, the boys agreed

Figure 1

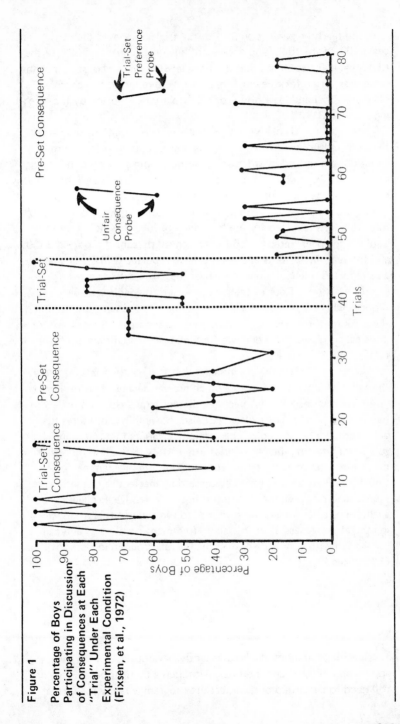

Percentage of Boys Participating in Discussion of Consequences at Each "Trial" Under Each Experimental Condition (Fixsen, et al., 1972)

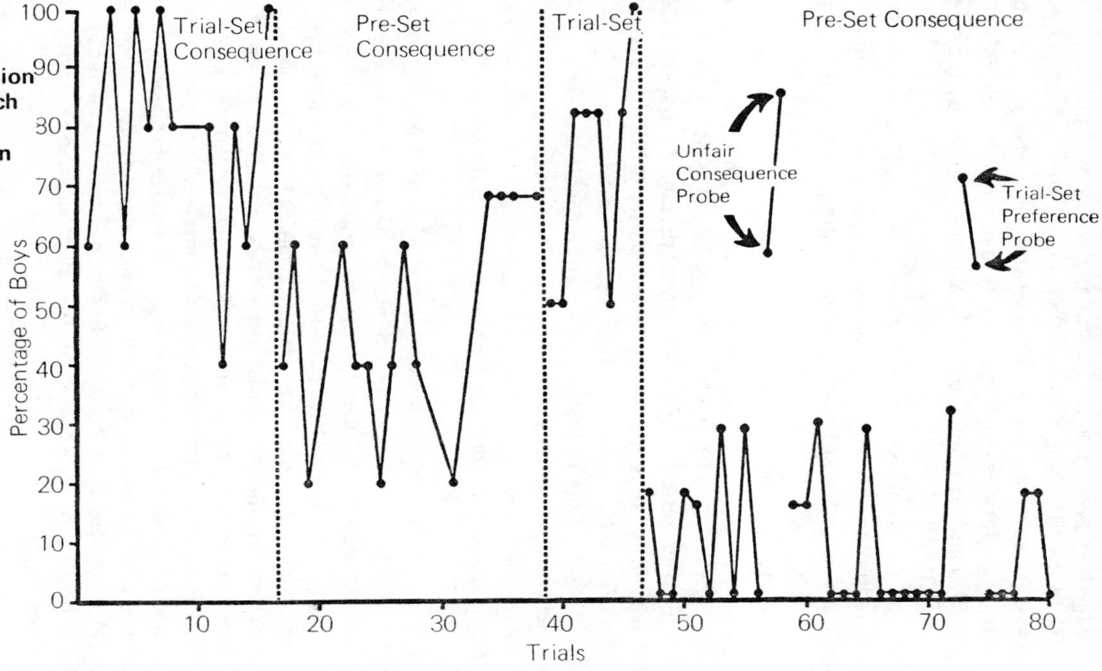

with the teaching-parents on 62% of the trials, increased the consequences on 6% of the trials, and decreased the consequences on 32% of the trials. Table 5 also shows that the boys left the pre-set consequence the same most often for rule violations that were reported by school officials (83%) and least often for rule violations reported by the teaching-parents (31%).

Table 6 gives the types of rule violations reported by the peers, school personnel, teaching-parents, and parents. The rule violations are ranked in order of seriousness from stealing to not being prompt. Of the first four types of rule violations, the peers reported a majority of the rule violations in three of the four categories and reported as many as the school personnel in the third. Thus, of the 27 rule violations reported for the four most serious rule violations in Table 6, the peers reported 15 (52%), school personnel reported 8 (29%), and the teaching-parents and parents each reported 2 (8%). The peers also reported rule violations in each of the seven categories.

Four of the peer-reported rule violations were self-reports, where a youth reported a rule violation he had committed. Of these four self-reported violations, one was for stealing, two were for physical aggression, and one was for violation of Achievement Place rules.

These data indicate that the youths participated in the self-government system to a much greater degree when they were given full responsibility for deciding the consequences for a peer who had violated a rule. The experiment also shows that procedures that are informally developed can be formally evaluated to determine their role in maintaining the behavior of interest. By evaluating the specific procedures comprising a treatment program, the program can be continually refined and improved by discarding ineffective or inefficient aspects and retaining those features that are effective. Procedure evaluations offer immediate feedback to the treatment staff concerning the effectiveness of their specific treatment procedures and can be conducted with very little cost to the overall program in terms of time or finances.

Dissemination

The teaching-family model is sufficiently developed to allow general application in other communities. Although a number of refinements still need to be carried out, we feel the program is ready for further

Table 5 Changes in the Teaching-Parents' Pre-Set Consequences by the Peers' Trial Decisions (Fixsen, et al., 1972)

Rule Violations Reported By		Change in Pre-Set Consequences by Trial Decision		
		Increase	Same	Decrease
Peers	No.	2	12	5
	%	11%	63%	26%
School Officials	No.	---	15	3
	%		83%	17%
Teaching-Parents	No.	1	4	8
	%	7%	31%	62%
Parents	No.	---	2	1
	%		67%	33%
Totals	No.	3	33	17
	%	6%	62%	32%

replication. To accommodate the expansion of the teaching-family model, we are developing a small, experimental education program for teaching-parents to give them the skills to operate and evaluate professionally run group homes for antisocial youths. We are also training Ph.D. level personnel who will be able to start teaching-family group homes and education programs for teaching-parents outside of Kansas. The development of these training programs is critical to successful dissemination of the model since the professional teaching-parents are the key to the success of the program.

Our experience has shown that adequate sources of financing are currently not available for starting group home treatment programs. The cost of the facility in Kansas has ranged from $35,000 to $60,000 for purchase, renovation, and furnishings for a large, older home. For each group home we have been associated with, these costs were paid from donations contributed by civic groups and individuals in the community. For many medium to large size communities this has not been an insurmountable problem, but for small communities it is almost impossible to raise enough money even for a down payment on a house. Thus, widespread dissemination of community-basedl group homes will require funding for facility costs from federal or state sources.

Footnotes

1. The research and development of the Achievement Place program was made possible by grants MH 16609 and MH 20030 from the National Institute of Mental Health (Center for Studies of Crime and Delinquency) to the Bureau of Child Research and the Department of Human Development, University of Kansas.

2. A film, *Achievement Place*, which describes this program, can be obtained on loan from the Audio Visual Center, Univesity of Kansas, 6 Bailey Hall, Lawrence, Kansas 66044.

3. Portions of this article were reprinted with permission from the *Journal of Applied Behavior Analysis.*

References

Ayllon, T. and Azrin, N. H. The measurement and reinforcement of behavior of psychotics. *Journal of the Experimental Analysis of Behavior*, 1965, *8*, 357-383.

Ayllon, T. and Azrin, N. *The token economy: A motivational system for therapy and rehabilitation*. New York: Appleton-Century-Crofts, 1968.

Baer, D. M., Wolf, M. M., and Risley, T. R. Some current dimensions of applied behavior analysis. *Journal of Applied Behavior Analysis*, 1968, *1*, 91-97.

Fixsen, D. L., Phillips, E. L., and Wolf, M. M. Achievement Place: Experiments in self-government with pre-delinquents. *Journal of Applied Behavior Analysis*, in press.

Phillips, E. L., Phillips, E. A., Fixsen, D. L., and Wolf, M. M. *The teaching-family handbook*. Champaign, Ill.: Research Press, in press.

Phillips, E. L., Wolf, M. M., and Fixsen, D. L. An experimental analysis of governmental systems at Achievement Place. *Journal of Applied Behavior Analysis*, in press.

Table 6 Types of Rule Violations by Peers, School Personnel, Teaching-Parents, and Parents (Fixsen, et al., in press)

Type of Rule Violation	Rule Violation Reported By				
	Peers	School	Teaching-Parents	Parents	Totals
Stealing	3 (75%)	1 (25%)	-----------	-------------	4 (5%)
Cheating	2 (67%)	1 (33%)	-----------	-------------	3 (4%)
Physical Agg.	5 (38%)	5 (38%)	2 (15%)	1 (9%)	13 (16%)
Verbal Agg.	5 (72%)	1 (14%)	-----------	1 (14%)	7 (9%)
School Rules	5 (20%)	18 (72%)	2 (8%)	-------------	25 (31%)
Ach. Pl. Rules	9 (47%)	---------------	10 (53%)	-------------	19 (24%)
Promptness	1 (11%)	1 (11%)	4 (45%)	3 (33%)	9 (11%)
Totals	30 (38%)	27 (24%)	18 (22%)	5 (6%)	80 (100%)

President's Committee on Mental Retardation. *Residential services for the mentally retarded.* Washington, D. C.: U. S. Government Printing Office, 1970.

Robins, L. *Deviant children grown up*. Baltimore, Md.: Williams & Wilkins, 1966.

Wolf, M. M. and Risley, T. R. Reinforcement: Applied research. In R. Glaser (Ed.), *The nature of reinforcement.* Columbus, Ohio: Charles E. Merrill, 1970, 310-325.

Wolfensberger, W. The principle of normalization and its implications to psychiatric service. *American Journal of Psychiatry*, 1970, *127:3,* 291-296.

The Use of Group and Individual Reinforcement Contingencies in the Modification of Social Withdrawal[1]

11

Hill M. Walker and Hyman Hops

During recent years, a number of studies have dealt with the problem of social withdrawal in children and adults (Allen, et al., 1964; O'Connor, 1969; Guerney and Flumen, 1970; Milby, 1970). Social withdrawal has usually been defined in terms of low rates of social interaction, an interaction referring to a reciprocal involvement between two or more persons (O'Connor, in press; Whitman, et al., 1970).

The process of social interaction provides for the acquisition, rehearsal, and eventual strengthening of essential social skills. As such, it has been advocated as a critical prerequisite for much of a child's behavioral development (Whitman, et al., 1970). Thus, the absence of or extremely low rates of social interaction may actually retard such development.

A variety of treatment procedures have been used for increasing the frequency and duration of social interactions. Specific treatment techniques include *adult social reinforcement* (Allen, et al., 1964; Milby, 1970), *adult social reinforcement plus priming* (Buell, et al., 1968; Baer and Wolf, 1970; Hart, 1968), *symbolic modeling* (O'Connor, 1969), *symbolic modeling, shaping, and symbolic modeling plus shaping* (O'Connor, in press), *social reinforcement plus tangible reinforcement* (Kirby and Toler, 1970; Whitman, et al., 1970), and *client centered play therapy* (Guerney and Flumen, 1970). The effectiveness of these procedures in modifying isolate behavior has been clearly validated.

The majority of studies on social withdrawal have used natural social reinforcers such as praise, approval, and attention to increase rate of social interaction. Few studies have used token reinforcement procedures for this purpose. This may be due, in part, to the easy availablity of adult social reinforcement in such settings as preschools, classrooms, and institutions where social withdrawal studies are often conducted. In addition, the use of reinforcers natural to the setting in which social interaction is expected to generalize may facilitate maintenance of increased social interaction rates after formal treatment is terminated.

Several studies have described less direct methods of increasing social interaction rate than the simple reinforcement of social initiations with adult attention. For example, Buell, et al. (1968) used social reinforcement of a child's motor skills as a tactic to increase her rate of social contact with other children. The subject was socially reinforced for using outdoor play equipment. This resulted in an increased proximity to peers using the same equipment. Consequently, increases were produced in social interaction rate with peers as well as in other collateral child behaviors.

In a study by Kirby and Toler (1970), a five-year-old boy with a low rate of interaction with his nursery school classmates was induced to pass out candy as a tactic to increase his rate of interaction with them. The study was designed to minimize the time and effort required of the teacher in achieving this goal. The rationale for the tactic was twofold: (1) by dispensing a reinforcing stimulus to his peers, it was conceivable that the target subject would acquire conditioned reinforcing properties which would make his classmates more inclined to interact with him; and (2) dispensing the candy would serve as a priming device which would stimulate increased social interactions with his classmates. The procedure proved to be highly effective and required very little investment of teacher time. In addition, it demonstrated peer reinforcement contingencies to be a powerful resource for modifying isolate behavior.

O'Connor (1969) has demonstrated that reinforcement procedures are not absolutely essential for the modification of social withdrawal. By using a symbolic modeling procedure (a film) depicting positive social consequences for interacting with peers, he showed that the level of social interaction of preschool isolates could be increased to the level of their nonisolate classmates. A comparable group of isolates who saw a control film did not increase their social interaction rate. The actual amount of invested time in this treatment procedure was minimal (23 minutes), and no teacher time was required to administer the treatment. Although the long-term maintenance of social interaction rate following such treatment needs to be evaluated, the effectiveness and economy of the symbolic modeling procedure is impressive.

In summary, there appear to be some effective treatment procedures available for modifying social withdrawal which do not rely upon adult social reinforcement. Such procedures may be especially valuable for regular classroom teachers who generally do not have the time to selectively reinforce and monitor the behavior of withdrawn children over long periods of time.

Additional research is needed to develop social withdrawal treatment procedures that are effective, economical, and relatively independent of teacher monitoring. Procedures are also needed that simultaneously facilitate the acquisition of social skills required in social interaction as well as provide opportunities to rehearse and develop those skills through increased peer interaction. O'Connor (1969) has suggested that the exclusive use of reinforcement procedures to increase social interaction rate may produce difficulties if the withdrawn child has not learned the necessary social skills required to initiate and maintain social interactions with other children.

The present study investigated the effects of a symbolic modeling training procedure combined with three different reinforcement contingencies for modifying social withdrawal. Following training in social interaction skills, the withdrawn child and/or his peers were reinforced with tokens (points) contingent upon an increased rate of social initiation. A separate experiment was conducted to evaluate the effects of each contingency. Experiment I evaluated training combined with an individual reinforcement contingency, experiment II, training combined with a group reinforcement contingency, and experiment III, training combined with an individual-group reinforcement contingency.

Method

Subjects

The primary criterion for subject selection was a low rate of social interaction relative to other peers in the same classroom. Initially, a group of subjects was selected on the basis of their scores on the social withdrawal subscale of the Walker Problem Behavior Identification Checklist (WPBIC) (Walker, 1970).

The WPBIC, a classroom screening instrument for identifying children with behavior problems, was completed on 1,067 children in grades one, two, and three in the local school district as part of a separate normative study. Twelve subjects were selected from this sample for more systematic and intensive observation. Each of the selected subjects had scores on the social withdrawal subscale that were greater than one standard deviation from the standardization mean. Items making up this subscale consisted of such behaviors as, "tries to avoid calling attention to himself," "does not engage in group activities," "has no friends," "doesn't protest when others hurt, tease, or criticize him," and "does not initiate relationships with other children."

All 12 subjects were systematically observed in their regular classrooms to determine whether their social interaction rates corresponded with the teachers' ratings on the WPBIC. Of the sample of 12 subjects, three were selected who emitted the lowest observed rates of social interaction relative to their peers.

Settings

The three experiments were conducted in regular elementary classrooms. Observations were recorded across instructional periods. Classroom activities sampled during observation periods included teacher- and peer-led discussion sessions, individual seat work, and other relatively unstructured group and individual activities.

No observations were recorded during recess or lunch periods or during other activities outside the classroom setting. Transitions during class time involved only those situations in which the class was changing from one subject activity to another.

The three experiments were carried out in three separate elementary schools. The subjects were enrolled in grades one and two. Each subject's teacher cooperated with the experimenters in implementing the contingencies and carrying out the study.

Observation and Recording

A behavioral coding system was developed for observing and recording social interactions in this study. An interaction was defined as a reciprocal social exchange between two subjects. Two elements were required for an interaction to be coded: a directed social stimulus (initiation) by one subject and an observable response to that stimulus by another subject. Thus, initiations that were ignored were not recorded as interactions.

The coding system consisted of ten behavior categories and provided a sequential account of social interaction between a target subject and his or her peers.[2] It was possible to derive the antecedents as well as consequences of social interactions from this code. The code also provided for measuring the duration of interactions in seconds. Although antecedent and consequence data were recorded for each interaction, only frequency and duration of social interaction and number of different peers interacted with were used as dependent variables in this study.

An observer recorded the behavior of the subject only when an interaction occurred. The identity and initial response (social stimulus) of the child initiating the interaction was noted on an appropriate space on the observation form. A stopwatch was also activated simultaneously to record the duration of the interaction. The subsequent behaviors of the subjects engaged in the interaction were observed and recorded until the interaction was terminated. The stopwatch was depressed as soon as the final response in the interaction was recorded. Observation sessions averaged 30 minutes in length. No more than one 30-minute session was recorded per day.

The observation form consisted of two sections. The top half provided space for general identifying information on the subjects and the classroom setting. The lower half was used for recording social interactions. Space was also provided to allow recording of the class activity and the duration of each interaction.

Examples of the behavior categories are: *cooperative*—referring to cooperative behavior during work or play; *work alone*—referring to solitary or parallel play/work; *attend*—an individual observing the behavior of another for longer than five seconds; *positive physical*—physical contact that is affectional; *negative physical*—physical aggression designed to injure or inflict pain.

A second observational procedure was developed for the purpose of collecting normative data on the rate of social interaction for all peers in each of the three classrooms. The procedure involved recording the total number of social interactions occurring in the classroom during an observation period and dividing this figure by N/2, half the total number of children in the classroom. (Dividing by N/2 assumes that at least two subjects have to be interacting for an interaction to be coded.) This figure, subsequently divided by time, constituted the mean rate per minute of social interaction for the entire class. The same classroom activities were sampled during collection of the group social interaction data as were sampled during data collection on the individual target subject's interactions. However, these two sets of data were never collected simultaneously.

The estimate of group social interaction rate was used for three purposes in the present study: (1) to provide a standard measure for comparing overall social interaction rate across the three classrooms, (2) to serve as an additional baseline for evaluating the effects of each contingency upon the target subjects, and (3) to give an index of the stability of social interaction rate over time for subjects in each of the three classrooms.

Reliability

Two graduate students were trained to use the coding system for recording social interactions between the subjects and their peers. An arbitrary criterion for acceptable inter-observer reliability was set at five consecutive interactions with 80 percent or better agreement. Agreement was calculated by dividing the total number of agreements by the total number of behaviors recorded by both observers. Behaviors recorded by only one observer were tallied as disagreements. No observer data were utilized until this criterion was achieved.

Reliability was also estimated on duration of social interaction. Pearson product moment correlations were computed between the duration scores of the two observers over a series of simultaneous recordings. The mean correlation for six consecutive sessions was 0.96 (see chapters by Johnson and Bolstad and by Jones).

Correlations, however, do not take into account the possibility of differences in the levels of the scores. For example, it is possible for one observer to systematically over- or underestimate the other, thereby creating high correlations based on scores at differing levels. Therefore, a t-test was calculated for the difference between the means for the six observations and found to be nonsignificant.

A third observer was trained to collect social interaction rate data on all peers in each of the three classrooms. This observer did not use the observation form described above but simply tallied social interactions as they occurred. Prior to the collection of the normative data, two reliability checks were held between this observer and one of the two observers trained to collect individual interaction data. Since the total frequency per unit of time was the main consideration in this data collection procedure, percent agreement was calculated by dividing the smaller number of interactions recorded by an observer by the larger number recorded by the other for each session. The reliability coefficients obtained for the two sessions were .82 and .93, respectively.

Design

As mentioned earlier, most studies of social withdrawal and isolate behavior have directly reinforced social interactions between the withdrawn child and his peers. As a rule, contingent teacher attention has been the reinforcing stimulus used to increase social interaction rate in these studies. The effectiveness of this approach has been impressive (Allen, et al., 1964; Milby, 1970; and Whitman, et al., 1970). However, in these studies, the withdrawn child is generally able to produce external reinforcement for himself by simply initiating social interactions with other children. As a result, neither the withdrawn child nor his peers are required to appreciably alter the quality of their *interactive* behavior in order to meet the requirements of the reinforcement contingency. The initiation and maintenance of social interactions are usually sufficient to produce reinforcement on a nearly continuous reinforcement schedule.

The purpose of this study was to provide either the withdrawn child and/or his peers with training in specific social interaction skills and then to make reinforcement indirectly contingent upon the use of those skills in increasing the rate of social interaction. That is, rather than initiating to other children, the target subjects would have to be skilled enough to get other children to initiate to them. In experiment I, for example, the withdrawn subject was given training in social interaction skills using a symbolic modeling procedure developed by O'Connor (1969). Immediately following the training, a reinforcement contingency was implemented in which the withdrawn subject could earn one point for each interaction that resulted from a peer initiating to her. Initiations by the withdrawn subject to peers did not result in reinforcement. When a required number of points were earned, they were exchanged for a preselected backup reinforcer.

Experiment II was the reciprocal of experiment I. In this experiment, the withdrawn subject's peers were given training in social interaction skills (using the same procedure) and then a contingency was impelemented in which the peer group could earn one point for each initiation by the withdrawn subject to any peer. Initiations by peer group members to the withdrawn subject did not produce reinforcement. When a required number of points was earned, they were exchanged for a preselected group reinforcement for the entire class.

Experiment III was a combination of experiments I and II. For example, the withdrawn subject could earn a point whenever any peer initiated to her. Conversely, the peer group could earn one point whenever the withdrawn subject initiated to any peer. Both the peer group and the withdrawn subject were required to earn a predetermined number of points before they could be exchanged for the respective backup reinforcers. In addition, *both* the peers and the withdrawn subject had to achieve their respective point totals before either could exchange their points. The withdrawn subject exchanged her points for a preselected individual reinforcement, while her peers exchanged theirs for a preselected group reinforcement.

Experiment I: The Use of Individual Token Reinforcement to Increase Social Interaction Rate

The effectiveness of a particular reinforcement contingency in increasing social interaction rate may depend, in part, upon the nature of the social withdrawal. For example, there may be a considerable discrepancy between the withdrawn child and his peers in the rate with which they initiate social interactions with each other. In such cases, withdrawn children who have low rates of initiating to their peers may require different interventions than those who have high rates but whose peers make few social initiations.

The withdrawn subject in experiment I had a mean rate of initiating social interactions with her peers, during baseline$_1$, that was significantly greater than the mean rate of her peers' initiation to her (.13 vs. .09 per minute; $t = 2.89$, $df = 15$, $p < .02$). Thus, a reinforcement contingency was implemented for this subject which was designed to increase the rate with which her peers initiated to her.

Procedure

The experiment followed an ABAB design (Bijou, et al., 1969) in which baseline and experimental conditions were alternated. The withdrawn subject for experiment I was a second grade, female student.

Baseline$_1$. A total of 16, 30-minute observation recordings were taken on the subject's behavior over a two-month baseline period. During this period, she was not informed that recordings of her behavior were being made.

The classroom teacher knew that the child had been selected as a withdrawn subject and that an intervention program was planned. However, she was not informed as to its purpose or design during this period.

Reinforcement period 1. Immediately after stable baseline estimates of the subject's peer interaction rate were obtained, one of the *E*s met with her during a lunch period. The child was informed that she had been observed for some time by an observer who had noted that her social interaction rate was quite low. In addition, she was told that the experimenters would like to help her increase her interactions with her classmates.

A 23-minute color film depicting a series of social interactions between nursery school children, used in a previous study (O'Connor, 1969), was shown to the child. The film and soundtrack covered various ways of initiating social interactions with others, in a step-by-step fashion, continually emphasizing the positive value of such behavior. In the film, nursery school children who engaged in social interactions were socially reinforced by their peers and the commentator.

The *E* tested the subject to make certain she was able to reiterate some of the statements made in the film. The child was then informed that a backup reinforcer, of her own choice, would now be made contingent upon initiations to her by peers. Specifically, she was told that she would earn one point for each initiation made to her by a classmate during the time the observer was in the room. When she had acquired 50 points she could exchange them for the preselected tangible reinforcer. The child chose two pet white rats and a cage as her first selection.

A paper "thermometer" chart was placed on her desk with a top level of 50 points. The first observation occurred immediately after the film was shown. After each observation, the observer told the child how many points she had earned during that period, and the "thermometer" was filled in a cumulative fashion.

Baseline$_2$. Observations during this phase were collected on five days over a two-week period. However, the subject was not informed about the number of interactions, and no reinforcement contingencies were programmed.

Reinforcement period 2. The same *E* met with the subject again and reviewed the behaviors necessary for increasing social interactions, as presented in the film. A 50-point reinforcement contingency was again established. The subject's choice of a backup reinforcer during this phase was two Barbie Dolls to add to her collection.

Results

Figure 1 contains the total interaction rate per observation session for the withdrawn subject and intermittent samples of the overall peer interaction rate during the four phases of the experiment.

The withdrawn subject's (S_1) average interaction rate per minute with her peers during the four phases of experiment I was as follows: baseline$_1$, .22; intervention$_1$, .59; baseline$_2$, .36; and intervention$_2$, .71. The overall interaction rate for the entire class across the four phases was .44 and ranged from .26 per minute to .70 per minute. Thus, S_1's interaction rate was below the mean of her peer group during the baseline phases and well above this figure during the two experimental phases.

Figure 1 **Total Interaction Rate Per Observation Session**

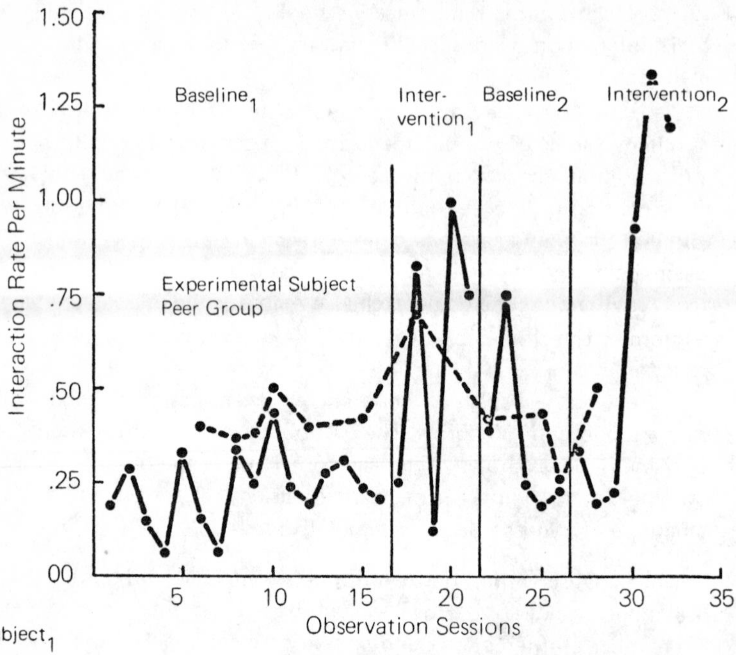

Subject$_1$

Inspection of Figure 1 reveals that in addition to increasing overall interaction rate, the intervention procedures had a considerable effect upon S_1's session-to-session variability. For example, her interaction rate varied from .06 to .44 per minute across the baseline$_1$ sessions. However, during intervention$_1$ her rate varied from .13 to 1.00 per minute. During baseline$_2$ the range was from .19 to .75, and during intervention$_2$, from .19 to 1.35.

S_1's mean rate during baseline$_2$ did not return to her pre-intervention rate of .22. However, Figure 1 indicates that the subject's interaction rate during the last three sessions of baseline$_2$ approximated her rate during the last six sessions of baseline$_1$. The relatively higher rates during the first two sessions of baseline$_2$ may reflect generalization (over time) of treatment effects from the prior phase.

Conversely, there was only a minor increase in the subject's interaction rate during the first three sessions of intervention$_2$. This was followed by a substantial increase during the last three sessions of this phase. The initial low rate may have been due to the subject having to relearn the skills necessary to increase her peers' initiations during this period.

Figure 2 **Interactions Resulting From Peers Initiating to Subject**

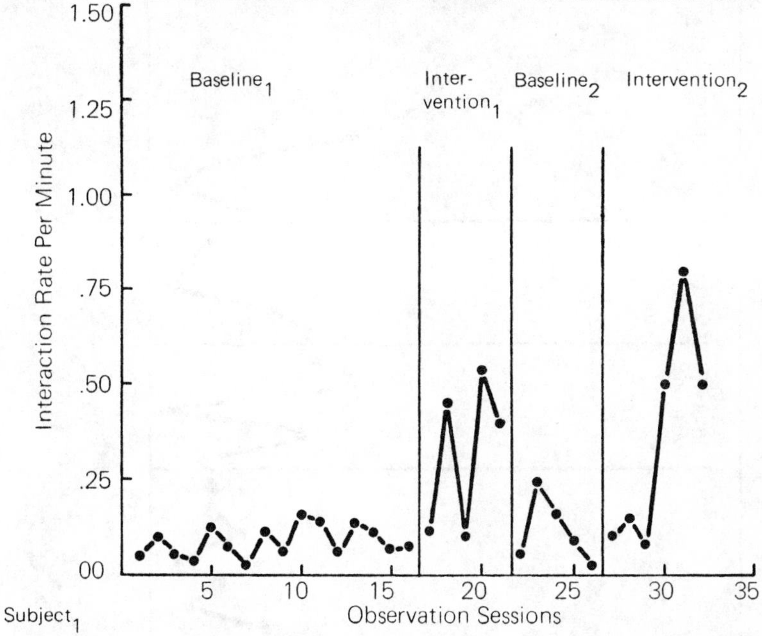

Figures 2 and 3 contain S_1's social interaction rates which resulted from peers initiating to her (Figure 2) versus her initiating to peers (Figure 3). In Figure 2, the mean social interaction rates during the four phases were, respectively, .09, .32, .15, and .36.

In Figure 3, the mean rates were .13, .27, .21, and .35. The intervention procedures thus increased the peers' initiations to the subject as well as her initiations to them. There was also an increase in the reciprocity of the two initiation rates during intervention. For example, there were considerable discrepancies between the rates during baseline phases (.09 vs. .13 for $baseline_1$ and .15 vs. .21 for $baseline_2$). This is in contrast to the intervention phases where the rates were more nearly balanced (.32 vs. .27 for $intervention_1$) and .36, vs. .35 for $intervention_2$).

Figure 4 contains the number of different peers with whom the withdrawn subject interacted during the observation sessions. These data were collected during the last six sessions of $baseline_1$ and during all sessions of the remaining three phases. The mean number of different peers interacted with across the four phases were, respectively,

Figure 3

Interactions Resulting From Subject Initiating to Peers

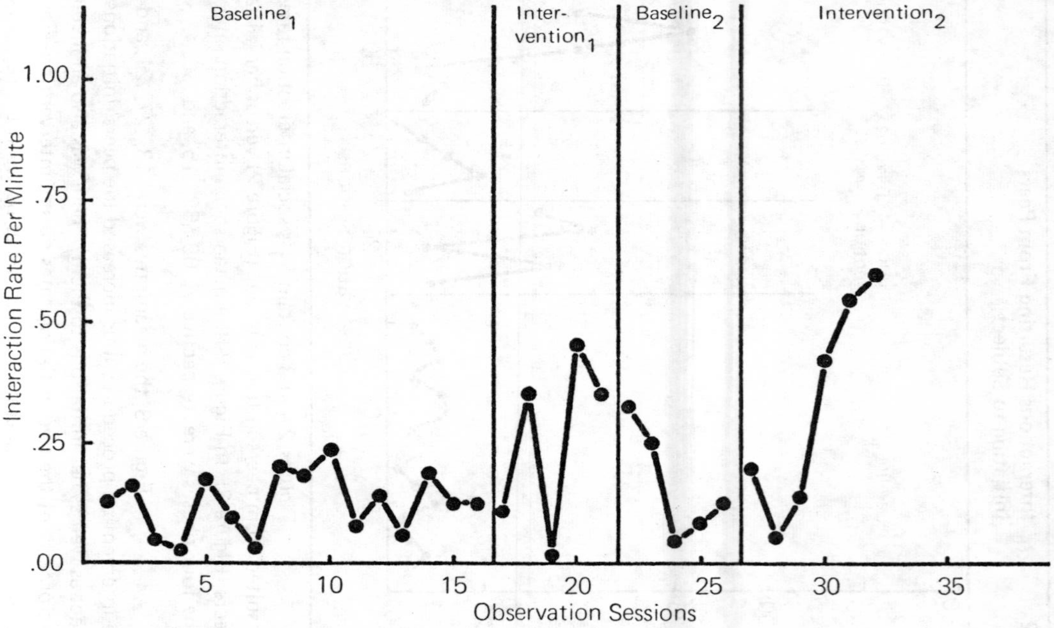

Subject$_1$

Figure 4 **Number of Different Peers Interacted With During Each Observation Session**

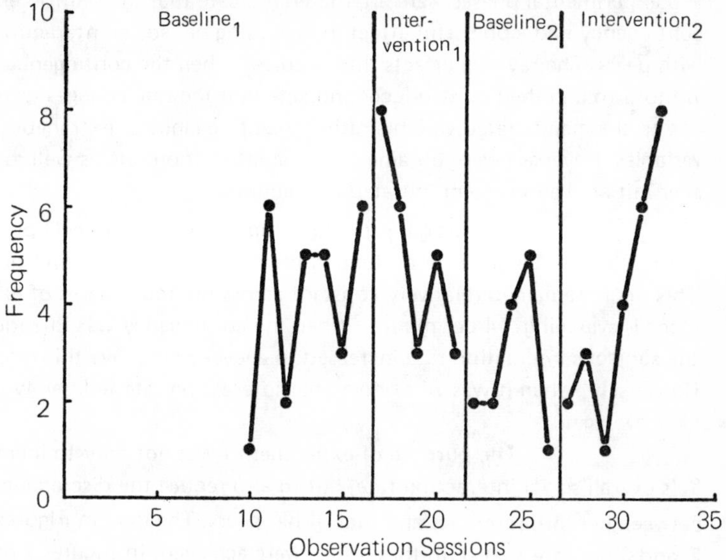

Subject1

4, 5, 2.8, and 4. Although the mean differences between phases do not appear to validate a systematic increase during interventions 1 and 2, the data in Figure 4 suggest that there was an increasing trend during these phases. This was especially true during intervention$_2$. Such an increase would be an artifact of the reinforcement contingency since the subject was not required to interact with different peers in order to produce reinforcement.

The duration (in seconds) of interactions occurring during each observation session were recorded for the withdrawn subject and her peers. Duration data were recorded for both peer initiated and subject initiated interactions.

The mean duration of interactions across the four phases of experiment I were 16 seconds for total interactions, 15 seconds for subject initiated interactions, and 17 seconds for peer initiated interactions. There was no systematic trend for the interactions to increase or decrease in length as baseline and experimental phases were implemented. Thus, the duration of social interactions, whether initiated by the subject or her peers, proved to be a relatively insensitive measure of the effects of the reinforcement contingency in experiment I.

Discussion

The changes that occurred in S_1's social interaction rate when baseline and experimental phases were alternated indicate that the reinforcement contingency had a powerful effect in increasing her social interactions with peers. The reversal effects that occurred when the contingency was withdrawn and then reintroduced indicate that the rate changes were due to the manipulated variable rather than to chance or extraneous variables. Reversals were obtained in total interaction rate as well as in peer initiated and subject initiated interactions.

The overall rate of peer interaction (Figure 1) provided a further baseline for evaluating the reinforcement contingency. This figure remained relatively constant across the four phases of experiment I, averaging .44 per minute. When the contingency was introduced, the subject's interaction rate increased to a level well above this rate. Conversely, when it was withdrawn, her interaction rate fell below the class average.

The purpose of experiment I was not only to increase S_1's overall social interaction rate, but to also reduce the discrepancy between her initiation rate and that of her peers. The data in Figures 1, 2, and 3 indicate that both these goals were achieved. In Figures 2 and 3, the peers' rate of initiation to the subject was very similar to the rate with which she initiated to them during the intervention phases. In fact, the peer initiation rate exceeded S_1's initiation rate during intervention$_1$. However, in the next baseline phase when the contingency was withdrawn, the peer initiation rate was again well below that of S_1 (as in baseline$_1$). During intervention$_2$, the rates were nearly identical, thereby replicating the effect obtained in intervention$_1$.

Although S_1 did not receive token reinforcement for increasing her initiation rate to peers (only for peer initiations to her), her initiation rate showed an increase whenever the reinforcement contingency was in effect. Presumably, this was a "priming" technique that S_1 used to increase the frequency of peer initiations to her. Although increases in the two rates occurred concurrently, it was not possible to determine whether S_1's increased initiation rate actually accounted for the increased peer initiation rate.

It was also not possible to precisely determine the effects of the symbolic modeling procedure in increasing S_1's interaction rate. If the film alone accounted for the increases in S_1's social interaction rate, there should have been no decrease in rate when the reinforcement contingency was withdrawn during baseline$_2$. Presumably, the reinforcement contingency alone could also have accounted for the increased rate. However, another experiment would be required to answer this question.

It seems more likely that some interaction between the symbolic modeling and reinforcement contingency produced the increase in social interaction rate. For example, several sessions were required for the interaction rate during baseline_2 to return to baseline_1 levels. This may have been due to the earlier strengthening of those skills acquired by S_1 through the symbolic modeling procedure. That is, even though peer initiated interactions no longer produced reinforcement for S_1, the strengthened behaviors continued to be emitted for two sessions until they extinguished.

During intervention_2, the reinforcement contingency was in effect for three sessions before its effect upon interaction rate was clearly demonstrated. This may have been due to the subject's having to relearn the skills required to increase her peers' initiation rate to her. It was not possible to confirm or deny this hypothesis from data collected in experiment I. However, it is interesting to note that the peer initiation rate did not show an increase until S_1 increased her rate of initiating interactions (see Figures 2 and 3).

It does appear, however, that the subject increased the range of peers with whom she interacted as well as her interaction rate with them, even though reinforcement was not made contingent on increasing the number of different peers. She could have simply increased the initiation rate of only one or two subjects and achieved the same effect. However, it would be more likely that a higher overall peer initiation rate would be achieved if a larger number of subjects were initiating to her.

The data in Figure 4 suggest that the subject did increase the number of different peers she interacted with during interventions 1 and 2, but this behavior pattern did not maintain when reinforcement was terminated in baseline_2. The frequency increased again, however, when the reinforcement contingency was reintroduced during intervention_2.

Measures of the duration of social interactions were recorded during experiment I since the experimenters wished to determine what effect, if any, an increased rate of social interaction would have upon duration. These data indicate that an increased social interaction rate had no appreciable effect upon the length of social interactions. There did not appear to be any systematic increase in the duration of social interactions as a function of either baseline or experimental conditions.

The duration of subject initiated interactions closely approximated the duration of peer initiated interactions (15 seconds vs. 17 seconds). This balance was not appreciably affected by the intervention procedures.

It would seem that an optimal strategy for increasing social interaction rate would be to keep the length of such interactions brief. That is, interactions of long duration would tend to compete with an increased frequency. Apparently, the reinforcement contingency did not significantly alter the length of S_1's social interactions with her peers.

In summary, the intervention procedures in experiment I appeared to have a positive effect for the withdrawn subject in terms of increased social interaction rate and the number of peers with whom she interacted. There was little effect upon duration of social interactions. The procedures also reduced the discrepancy between subject initiated and peer initiated interactions.

Experiment II: The Use of Group Token Reinforcement to Increase Social Interaction Rate

In contrast to experiment I, the withdrawn subject's rate of initiation to her peers in experiment II was significantly below that of her peers' rate of initiation to her (.05 vs. .13 per minute: $t = 5.10$, $df = 31$, $p < .001$). Thus, a reinforcement contingency was implemented for this subject which was designed to increase the rate with which she initiated to her classmates.

Procedure

The same ABAB design was used in this experiment. The subject for experiment II was a first grade female.

Baseline$_1$. Thirty-two, 30-minute observation recordings were taken on this subject's behavior over a two-month baseline period. Conditions in this phase were identical to those in experiment I.

Reinforcement period 1. The subject was asked to leave the room on the pretext of having to make up some work she had missed during a recent absence. At the same time, the rest of the class was taken to a projection room in the school where a brief discussion was held about the low rate of the subject's social interaction with peers.

The *E* indicated that a film would be presented to show them some ways of helping the subject increase her social interaction rate with them. The same film used in experiment I was shown, and a further discussion was held to insure that the children understood the principles and techniques presented. In addition, they were informed that a reinforcer of their choice would become available when the subject had made 25 social initiations to them during scheduled observation periods. A list of possible group reinforcing events was contributed by the class and placed on the board. A vote was used to decide which event would be selected. The selected reinforcement was a trip to a new mall and a visit to a local ice cream parlor.

The classroom teacher provided a clown's face, with a paper tape protruding from the clown's mouth on which was recorded the number of points earned by the class. After each observation period, the observer informed the class about the number of points that had been earned, and the clown's "tongue" was pulled out an equivalent length. During this experimental phase, the subject was not informed that any reinforcement contingency had been established.

Baseline$_2$. During this phase, regularly scheduled observations continued to be taken. However, the class was given no information about the number of interactions occurring, and no reinforcing consequences were programmed.

Reinforcement period 2. At the beginning of this phase, a second discussion was held with the class to review material contained in the film. The contingency was again explained and discussed. On this occasion, the subject remained in the room and listened to the discussion about her social behavior.

The number of points required for the reinforcing stimulus was raised from 25 to 50 points during this reinforcement period. The previous point level was considered too low since the subject was now aware of the reinforcement contingency and could respond to it without the peers' initial intervention. Suggestions were again made about possible backup reinforcers, and the class chose to have an ice cream party in the classroom after reaching the required point level.

Results

Figure 1 contains the social interaction rate of S_2 with her peers, and intermittent samples of the overall peer interaction rate across the four phases of the experiment. During experiment II, the overall rate of social interaction averaged .39 per minute and ranged from .22 to .60

Figure 1

Total Interaction Rate Per Observation Session

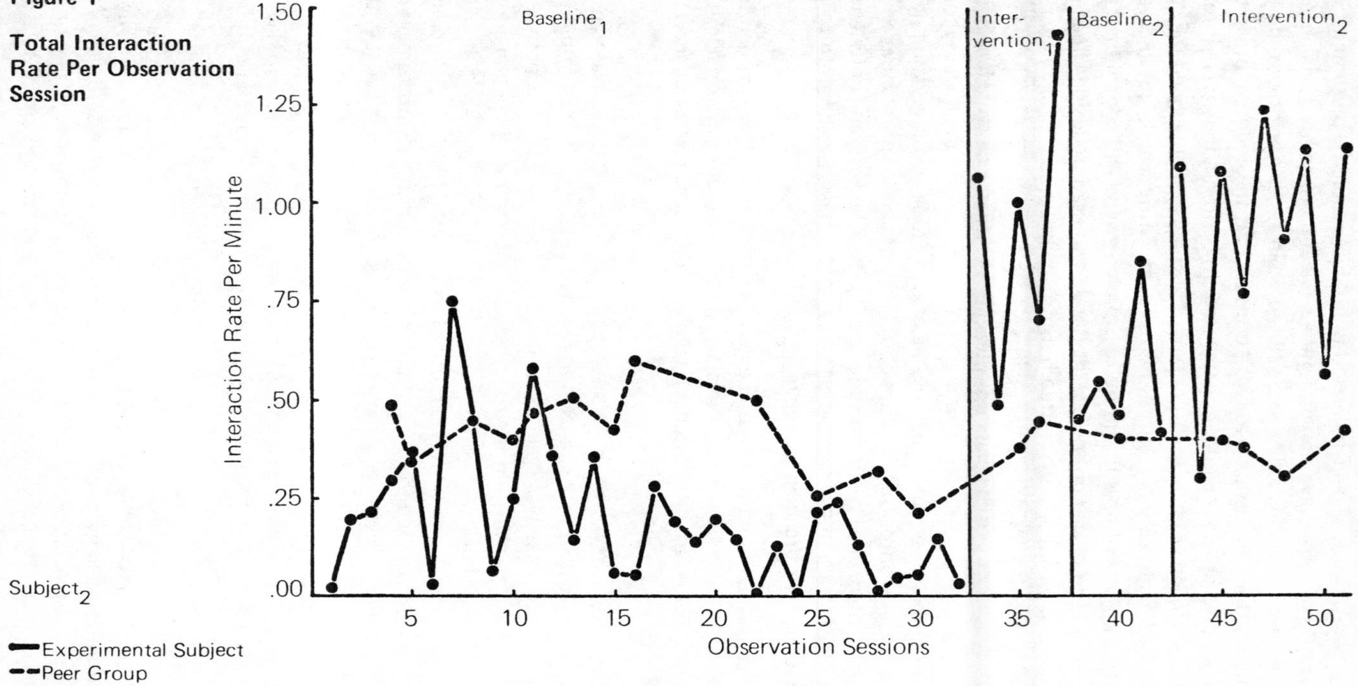

interactions per minute. This compares with a mean rate of .44 per minute and range from .26 to .70 for S_1's peer group.

The mean rates of S_2's social interaction for each of the four phases of experiment II were as follows: baseline$_1$, .18; intervention$_1$, .93; baseline$_2$, .55; and intervention$_2$, .91. S_2's interaction rate increased dramatically during intervention$_1$. The rate decreased during baseline$_2$ and increased again when the reinforcement contingency was reintroduced in intervention$_2$.

Both interventions 1 and 2 increased S_2's social interaction rate to levels well above the mean of her peer group. Although her rate decreased during baseline$_2$, it did not return to baseline$_1$ levels but maintained above the class average for the five observation sessions.

S_2's interaction rate was highly variable during the first 15 observation sessions of baseline$_1$. During the last 17 sessions of baseline$_1$, however, her interaction rate was much lower and much less variable. Although data are not available, the observers did note that a large proportion of the subject's interactions during the first 15 days occurred with a single peer who sat close by. This had been arranged by the teacher, who was concerned about the subject's low interaction rate. The data indicate, however, that this "intervention" had very short-term effects.

As with S_1, the intervention procedure increased S_2's session-to-session variability as well as her interaction rate. For example, S_2's interaction rate varied from .00 to .75 during baseline$_1$ and from .39 to .58 during baseline$_2$. During the intervention phases, the range increased substantially, from .49 to 1.42 during intervention$_1$ and from .29 to 1.23 during intervention$_2$.

Figures 2 and 3 contain, respectively, the rates of interaction resulting from peer initiations and subject initiations. Figure 2 indicates that there was a substantial increase in the peer initiation rate to S_2 whenever the reinforcement contingency was in effect. Since experiment II was the reciprocal of experiment I, the peers were never reinforced for initiating to the subject. However, S_2's peers apparently increased their initiation rate to her in order to stimulate increased social initiations by her. S_1, in experiment I, appeared to use the same technique to increase the rate of peer initiations to her. The mean rate of peer initiations to S_2 during the four phases of experiment II were .13, .73, .39, and .62.

The data in Figure 3 demonstrate the effects of the reinforcement contingency upon S_2's initiation rate. The baseline$_1$ data indicate that there were 14, 30-minute observation sessions in which S_2

Figure 2

Interactions Resulting From Peers Initiating to Subject

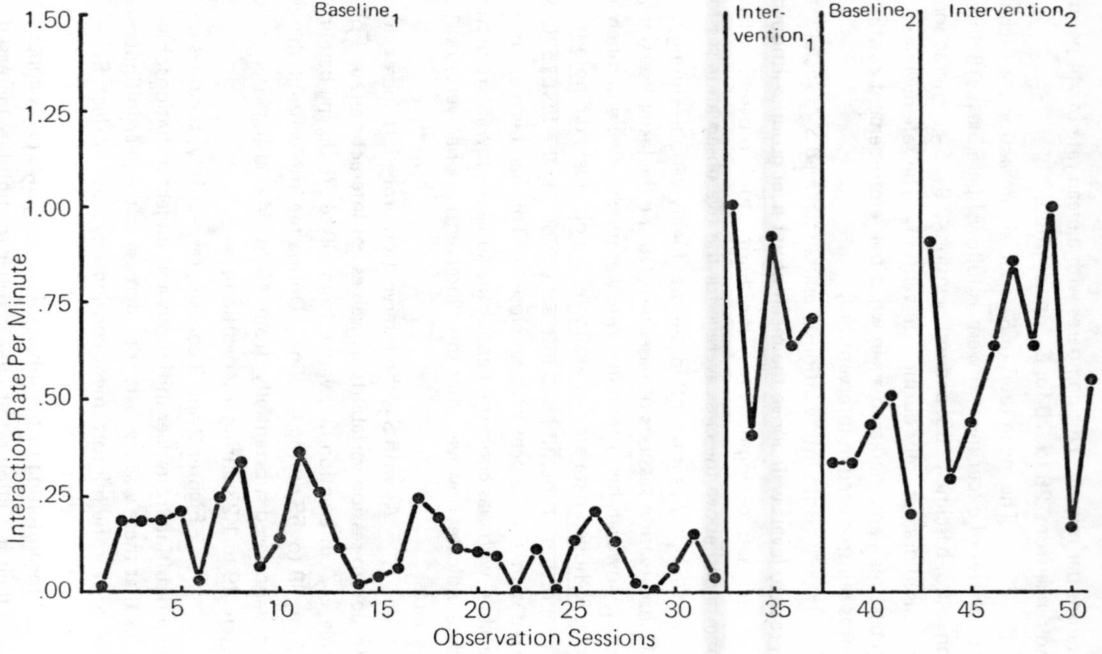

Subject$_2$

Figure 3

Interactions Resulting From Subject Initiating to Peers

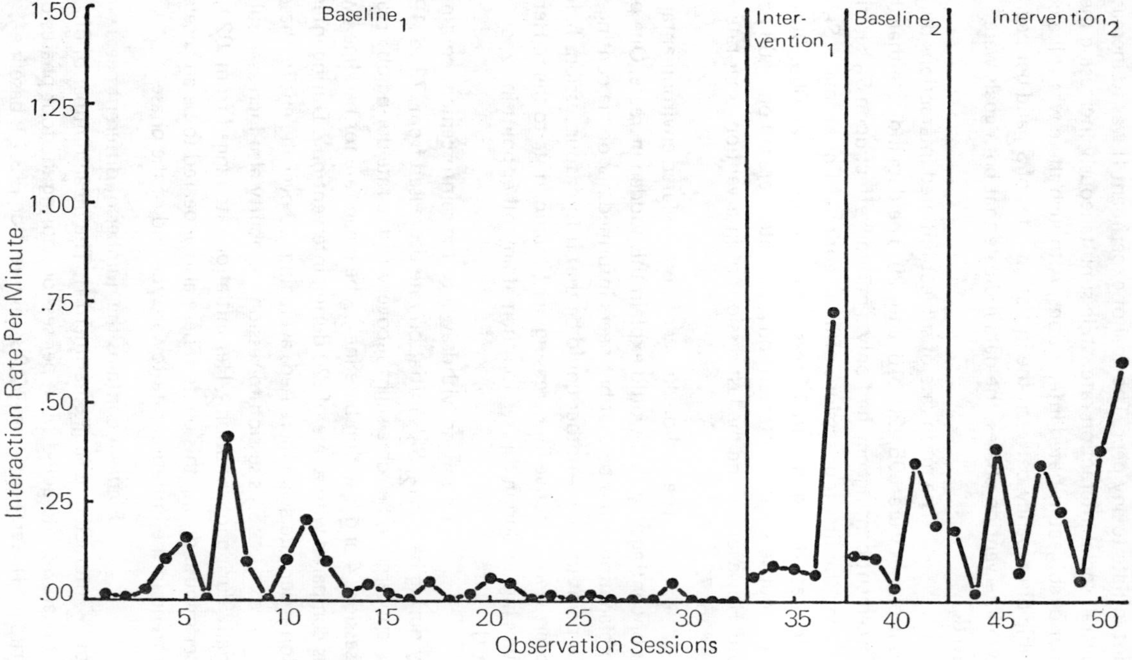

Subject$_2$

did not initiate to any peer. The goal of experiment II was to increase her overall social interaction rate while simultaneously increasing the number of subject initiated interactions. Although there was still a considerable discrepancy between the initiation rates of S_2 and her peers in the two intervention phases, the data indicate that both goals were achieved.

The mean rate of subject initiated interactions during the four phases were: .05, .20, .16, and .29. The data indicate that the reinforcement contingency had only a minimal effect upon S_2's initiation rate during the first four sessions of intervention$_1$. For example, S_2's initiation rate during the last 11 sessions of baseline$_1$ was .009. During the first four sessions of intervention$_1$, her rate averaged only .08 per minute. However, during the last sessions of intervention$_1$, her rate increased to .73.

The authors know of no correlated environmental event or contingency that would explain this sudden increase. One possible explanation could be that her peers informed her of the contingency at this point in time. Another could be that it took four sessions before the peers were effective in increasing her initiation rate to them. Her rate was higher during this session than at any other point in experiment II.

Following withdrawal of the reinforcement contingency during baseline$_2$, S_2's initiation rate decreased from .73 to .12. There appeared to be some slight recovery of the rate during observation sessions 4 and 5 within baseline$_2$. The mean rate for baseline$_2$ was .16 as compared with a rate of .20 during intervention$_1$. During intervention$_2$, her rate again increased, averaging .29 over the entire phase.

S_2's session-to-session variability also increased substantially during intervention$_2$. Her initiation rate ranged from .02 to .60 per minute during this phase. There also appeared to be an accelerating trend in the initiation rate toward the end of the phase.

Figure 4 contains the number of different peers with whom S_2 interacted during experiment II. The mean number of different peers S_2 interacted with, per session, during the four phases of experiment II were: baseline$_1$, 2.23; intervention$_1$, 3.20; baseline$_2$, 2.00; and intervention$_2$, 3.22. During the two baseline phases, the average was 2.15, and during the two intervention phases, 3.21.

Thus, it appears that the intervention procedures in experiment II also increased the number of different peers with whom S_2 interacted. This replicates a similar result obtained with S_1 in experiment I.

Figure 4

Number of Different Peers Interacted With During Each Observation Session

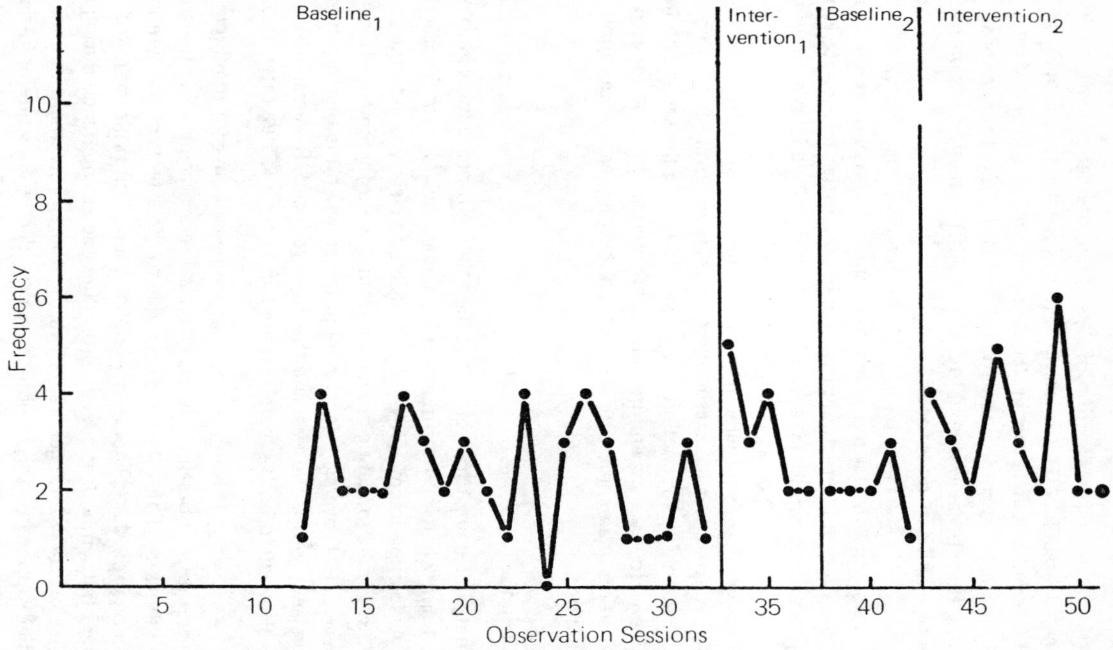

Subject$_2$

The duration of S_2's social interactions with peers averaged 16 seconds. This is identical to the average length of S_1's social interactions. The average length of interactions initiated by S_2 was 17 seconds, as compared with 15 seconds for S_1. Interactions resulting from peers initiating to S_2 averaged 15 seconds, in contrast to an average of 17 seconds for S_1.

As in experiment I, the length of peer initiated interactions was very similar to the length of subject initiated interactions. Also, duration of interaction proved to be insensitive to the intervention procedures, a finding replicating results obtained in experiment I.

Increased length of social interactions appeared to be correlated with S_2's initially high interaction rate during the first half of baseline_1. There was a corresponding decrease in duration of interactions when S_2's interaction rate decreased during the second half of baseline_2. However, when interaction rate increased during the two intervention phases, there was no concomitant increase in duration of interactions.

Discussion

The data in Figure 1 indicated that the treatment procedures in interventions 1 and 2 had a powerful effect in increasing S_2's social interaction rate. As in experiment I, it was not possible to clearly isolate the effects of the symbolic modeling procedure from the reinforcement effects. However, clear reversal effects were obtained when the reinforcement contingency was withdrawn and then reintroduced. Reversal effects were obtained in both subject initiated and peer initiated interactions.

It is interesting that the peers' rate of initiating to S_2 did not return to baseline_1 levels when the reinforcement contingency was withdrawn. This may have been due to the effects of the symbolic modeling procedure. That is, peer social interaction skills, acquired through the symbolic modeling procedure and strengthened during intervention_1, may have generalized to the nonreinforcement period. Further support for this hypothesis is provided by S_2's rate of initiation to peers during baseline_2. Her initiation rate of .16 was well above her rate of .05 in baseline_1. For whatever reason, it is encouraging to note that the initiation rate of S_2 to her peers did not return to baseline_1 levels when reinforcement was withdrawn.

However, the number of different peers S_2 interacted with per observation session did return to its baseline_1 level when the reinforcement contingency was removed. When the contingency was reinstated, the number per session increased. The means for interventions 1 and 2 were nearly identical (3.20 vs. 3.22).

Thus, the increased interaction rate appeared to generalize from reinforcement to nonreinforcement periods to a much greater extent than did the range of peers with whom S_2 interacted. A similar effect was also obtained for S_1 during experiment I.

The data on the duration of S_2's interactions with her peers replicates results obtained with S_1 in experiment I. The mean duration across all four phases were identical for S_1 and S_2. The close similarity between the duration of subject initiated and peer initiated interactions also replicates results obtained with S_1.

The treatment procedures in experiment II were effective in increasing S_2's overall interaction rate with her peers. However, the procedures seemed to have a greater effect upon peer initiation rate than upon subject initiation rate. This is a particularly interesting finding since peers did not receive external reinforcement for initiating to S_2.

The intervention procedures did increase S_2's initiation rate well above her baseline$_1$ rate of .05 per minute. However, the treatment effect in intervention$_2$ seemed to be much more effective and more consistent than it was in intervention$_1$. This may have been due to S_2's awareness of the reinforcement contingency in intervention$_2$, whereas she may not have been aware of it during intervention$_1$. In fact, Figure 3 shows that, during intervention$_1$, her rate of interaction due to her own initiations remained at baseline$_1$ levels until the fifth session. The results of intervention$_2$ indicate that the reinforcement contingency in intervention$_1$ may have had a greater immediate impact upon S_2's behavior if she had been made aware of it at the beginning of the phase.

It should be pointed out that the authors cannot certify that S_2 *was not* aware of the contingency from the beginning of intervention phase 1. Her peers could have informed her of the procedure on the first day it was implemented. However, anecdotal information provided by the observers suggested this was not the case. They reported that S_2 seemed to be somewhat overwhelmed by the sudden increase in peer initiations toward her after the contingency was implemented. This may have acted to temporarily suppress an increase in her initiation rate to peers.

In summary, the peer reinforcement contingency combined with the symbolic modeling procedure appears to be an effective technique for modifying social withdrawal. Its effectiveness in increasing subject initiated interactions may be greater if the withdrawn child is informed of the contingency in advance along with the peer group. However, another experiment would be required to verify this assumption.

Experiment III: The Use of Individual-Group Token Reinforcement to Increase Social Interaction Rate

The withdrawn subject in this experiment had an extremely low rate of social interaction with her peers. Both her initiation rate to peers and their initiation rate to her were very low and not significantly different from each other (.01 vs. .02 per minute, $t = 1.57$, $df = 21$, n.s.).

The purpose of experiment III was to investigate the combined effectiveness of the procedures used in experiments I and II. It appeared that the combined set of procedures would be most appropropriate for a withdrawn child whose peer initiation rate was approximately equal to the peers' rate of initiation to her.

Procedure

An ABAB design was again used to evaluate the reinforcement contingencies. The withdrawn subject for experiment III was a second grade female.

Baseline$_1$. Twenty-three, 30-minute observation recordings were taken on this subject's behavior over a two-month baseline period. Conditions in this phase were identical to those in experiments I and II.

Reinforcement period 1. The purpose of experiment III was simultaneously explained and discussed with the entire class, including the subject. The film was shown and a review discussion followed as in experiments I and II.

In this experiment, however, a double, interlocking reinforcement contingency was established. The subject could earn an individual, preselected reinforcer after her peers had made 75 social initiations to her during regularly scheduled observation periods. The class could earn its preselected group reinforcement after the subject had made 25 social initiations to her peers. The completion of *both* contingencies was required before either of the reinforcers could be dispensed.

Two "thermometer" charts were placed on the wall of the classroom, one for each of the contingencies. After each observation period, the observer announced the number of points earned by the subject and by the class. The point totals were subsequently recorded on the wall charts.

The subject chose a Johnny Cash record as her selection. The class, after much discussion and a series of votes, decided upon a trip to the downtown mall with a stop at a popular ice cream parlor.

Baseline$_2$. During this phase, regularly scheduled observations were continued. However, no points were awarded and no reinforcement contingencies were programmed.

Reinforcement period 2. During this phase, the subject matter of the film and the purpose of the program were again discussed with the subject and her peers. The same reinforcement contingencies were also reestablished. During this reinforcement period, the subject chose a pet white rat and a cage as a backup reinforcer. The class decided upon a picnic in a nearby park. Wall charts were set up to record the awarding of points, as before.

Results

Figure 1 contains the social interaction rate of S_3 with her peers during the four phases of experiment III. The overall peer interaction rate is also plotted in Figure 1; this averaged .28 throughout experiment III and ranged from .16 to .37 per minute.

S_3 had an extremely low rate of interaction with her peers during the baseline$_1$ phase of experiment III. No social interactions occurred between her and any of her peers during 12 of the 23 sessions in which she was observed. Her total interaction rate during baseline$_1$ averaged .03 per minute.

There was a substantial increase in S_3's total interaction rate during intervention$_1$ followed by a sharp decrease during baseline$_2$. There was another parallel increase in rate during intervention$_2$. Her interaction rate during intervention$_1$, baseline$_2$, and intervention$_2$ was, respectively, .76, .25, and 1.05.

As in experiments I and II, S_3's interaction rate during interventions 1 and 2 was increased to levels considerably above the mean interaction rate of her peers. During baseline$_2$, her mean rate (.25) was slightly below the average peer interaction rate (.28). This replicates the result obtained in experiment I with S_1. In contrast, S_2's interaction rate in experiment II maintained well above her peers' interaction rate during baseline$_2$.

Figure 1 Total Interaction Rate Per Observation Session

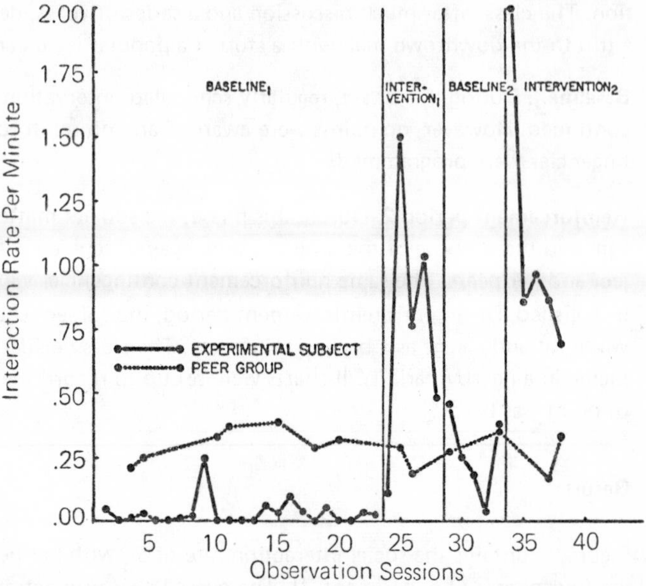

Subject$_3$

In both interventions 1 and 2, there was a sharp increase in S_3's total interaction rate shortly after the intervention procedures were implemented. For example, during the second observation session of intervention$_1$ and during the first session of intervention$_2$, S_3's rate was 1.48 and 1.99, respectively. However, in both interventions, the rate leveled off to a mean figure of approximately .90 interactions per minute. The rate remained fairly stable from this point until the end of each intervention.

The increase in session-to-session variability during intervention phases was most clearly demonstrated for S_3. For example, her interaction rate varied from .00 to .25 during baseline$_1$ and from .02 to .47 during baseline$_2$. During intervention$_1$, her rate varied from .11 to 1.48 and during intervention$_2$, from .69 to 1.99.

Figure 2 shows the rate of peer initiated interactions and Figure 3 the rate of subject initiated interactions. The mean rate of peer initiated interactions during the four phases of experiment III were: baseline$_1$, .02; intervention$_1$, .60; baseline$_2$, .15; and intervention$_2$, .89. The corresponding rates for subject initiated interactions were: baseline$_1$, .01; intervention$_1$, .16; baseline$_2$, .10; and intervention$_2$, .16.

Figure 2 Interactions Resulting from Peers Initiating to Subject

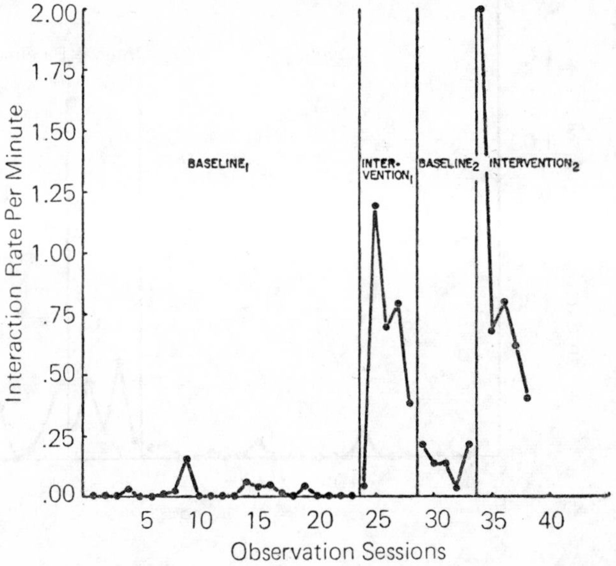

Subject$_3$

By examining Figures 2 and 3, it is clear that the major portion of S_3's increased interaction rate during interventions 1 and 2 was accounted for by peer initiated interactions. Thus, the initial increase in rate that was followed by a relatively stable leveling off period can be attributed largely to peer initiated interactions.

S_3's initiations to peers increased from a rate of .01 per minute to .16 per minute during intervention$_1$. The rate decreased to .10 during baseline$_2$ and again increased to .16 during intervention$_2$. There was a much greater proportional increase in rate for peer initiated interactions than there was for subject initiated interactions.

S_3's rate of subject initiated interactions increased in session-to-session variability as well as in overall rate. There appeared to be no systematic trend in the data during intervention$_1$. However, her rate during intervention$_2$ was much less variable and showed an accelerating trend.

Figure 4 gives the number of different peers S_3 interacted with during each observation session. The mean number of different peers interacted with per session was substantially increased during each of the phases as follows: 1.14, 6.60, 4.40, and 6.20.

Figure 3 **Interactions Resulting from Subject Initiating to Peers**

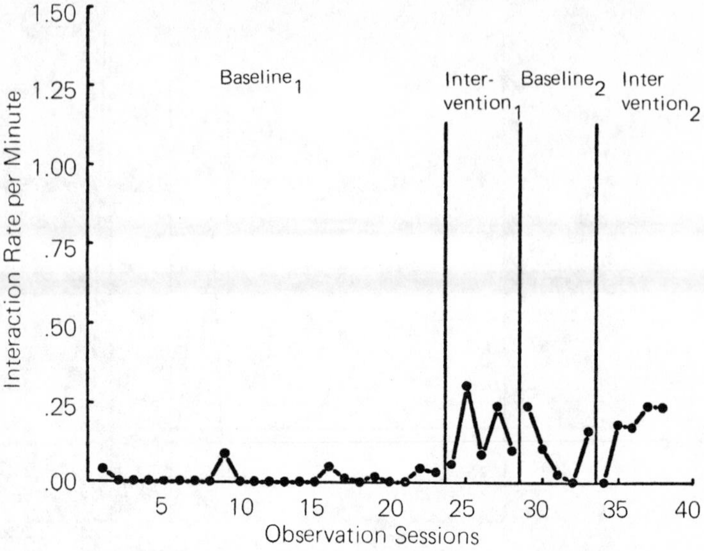

Subject$_3$

The number of different peers S_3 interacted with per session was substantially increased during interventions 1 and 2. Although there was a decelerating trend during baseline$_2$, the baseline$_1$ frequency was not recovered during this phase. This is in contrast to S_1 and S_2 whose frequencies did return to baseline$_1$ levels (or below) during baseline$_2$.

S_3's social interactions were of a much shorter average duration than those for S_1 and S_2. Her interactions averaged only 11 seconds over the four phases of experiment III. Subject initiated interactions averaged 10 seconds, and peer initiated interactions averaged 12 seconds. Thus, the balance between the length of subject initiated and peer initiated interactions was replicated for S_3.

Discussion

As in experiments I and II, clear reversal effects were obtained whenever the reinforcement contingency was withdrawn and then reintroduced. However, neither subject initiated nor peer initiated interaction rates returned to their baseline$_1$ levels when the contingency was withdrawn

Figure 4 **Number of Different Peers Interacted With During Each Observation Session**

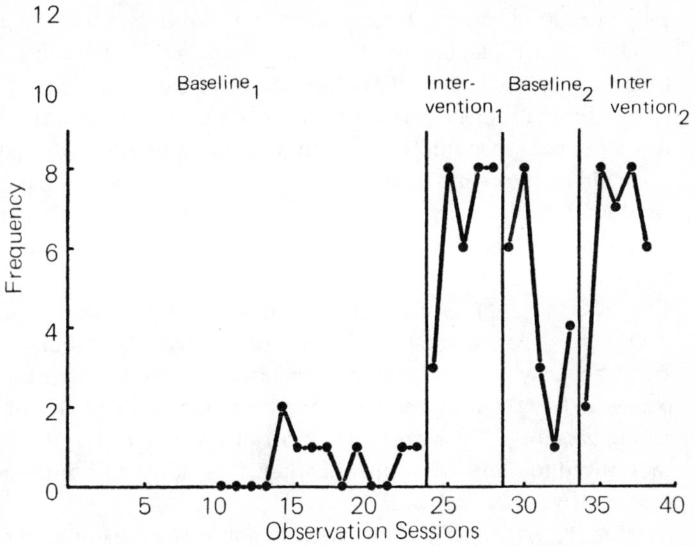

Subject$_3$

during baseline$_2$. This result may or may not have been due to the effects of the symbolic modeling procedure.

The primary effect of the reinforcement contingency in experiment III was to increase S_3's rate of social interaction with her peers. The contingency produced a much higher rate of peer initiated interactions than subject initiated interactions. This result may have been due to the way in which the contingency was established. That is, the peer group had to initiate 75 interactions with S_3 while she had to initiate only 25 interactions with her peers in order to meet the requirements of the contingency. This automatically built in a higher peer initiation rate than subject initiation rate.

The contingency requirements were divided 75-25 instead of 50-50 since the experimenters felt it was unrealistic to require S_3 to initiate 50 interactions before she could exchange her points for the backup reinforcer. Her extremely low rate of initiation to peers in baseline$_1$ made such a requirement seem unfeasible. However, if the reinforcement requirements of the contingency had been set up equally, it might have reduced the discrepancy between the rate of subject initiated and peer initiated interactions during interventions 1 and 2.

The differences in the rates of interaction initiated by the subject compared with her peers had a further effect which is reflected in the decelerating trend in the total social interaction rate which occurred halfway through each intervention period. The peers quickly ran off the number of initiations required for the subject's reinforcement and subsequently reduced their rates of initiations as they waited for the subject to reach the criterion necessary for both reinforcers to be dispensed. It is interesting to note, however, that the peers did not stop initiating, even though further responses from them would not result in any more points. Presumably, their initiating behavior was maintained in order to stimulate the subject to further initiations to them.

The reinforcement contingency also greatly increased the range of peers that S_3 interacted with during intervention periods. This frequency averaged 6.40 per session during the two intervention phases and 4.40 during baseline$_2$, compared with a frequency of 1.14 during baseline$_1$. The increased number of peers S_3 interacted with generalized to nonreinforcement periods (baseline$_2$) to a much greater extent than for S_1 and S_2.

The generalization to nonreinforcement periods may have been due to the interlocking nature of the reinforcement contingency in experiment III. In experiments I and II, the reinforcement contingency was specific to either the subject or the peer group, a condition which could have accounted for the substantially lower frequency of peers that S_1 and S_2 interacted with during interventions 1 and 2. S_3, on the other hand, interacted with a much larger number of peers during the intervention periods. As a result, the increased frequency may have been much slower to extinguish for S_3.

The authors were unable to determine empirically whether S_3's initially low interaction rate was related to the relatively brief duration of her interactions with peers. Interactions initiated by S_3 as well as interactions initiated by peers were of a much shorter duration than those of S_1 and S_2.

The mean duration of peer initiated interactions showed an increase from 6 to 8 seconds during intervention$_1$. However, the duration continued to increase during baseline$_2$ (15 seconds) and intervention$_2$ (17 seconds). This result suggests that the increase was related to the reinforcement contingency in only a very general way, if at all.

The mean duration of subject initiated interactions showed an increase drom 6 to 17 seconds during intervention$_2$. However, there was no increase over baseline$_1$ in the duration of interactions in intervention$_1$. The increase during intervention$_2$ is equally difficult to relate to the reinforcement contingency alone.

It would have been interesting to determine if the increased duration of both subject and peer initiated interactions during intervention$_2$ would have maintained indefinitely following withdrawal of the reinforcement contingency. If this were the case, it would suggest that the increased duration was being maintained by variables whose operation may have been stimulated but not controlled by the reinforcement contingency.

For example, it is likely that the range of S_3's social skills was more limited than that of the other two subjects; during baseline$_1$ her rate of interaction was extremely low, demonstrating that she rarely practiced such behaviors. Presumably, the deficiency in those skills necessary to *maintain* social interaction resulted in shorter durations of interactions for S_3. The film and the initial reinforcement period may have had the effect of providing cues about social interaction and motivating her to practice such behaviors; in fact, the peers' increase in initiations forced her to do so. One can only speculate that the increased practice and presumed increase in her reinforcing power finally resulted in increased durations during intervention$_2$.

In summary, the intervention procedures in experiment III produced dramatic increases in S_3's overall interaction rate. The reinforcement contingency in experiment III appears most appropriate for changing the isolate behavior of extremely withdrawn children.

General Discussion

The results of experiments I, II, and III indicate that all three interventions were effective in increasing social interaction rate. Although the combined procedures in experiment III produced the most dramatic changes in interaction rate, the interventions in experiments I and II also achieved the therapeutic goals for which they were designed.

However, some unexpected effects resulted from application of the reinforcement contingencies in experiments I and II. For example, in experiment I, S_1's rate of initiating to peers was increased as was her peers' rate of initiating to her, even though S_1 was never reinforced for initiating to peers. Similarly, in experiment II, S_2's peers greatly increased their rate of initiating to her even though they were never reinforced for doing so. The contingencies also increased the number of different peers with whom the withdrawn subjects interacted. Thus, the effect of the intervention procedures was to change the behaviors to which they were directly applied and to also produce concurrent changes in social behaviors to which they were never applied. These reinforcement contingencies would appear to have more therapeutic impact, and possibly more enduring effects, than those that only produce changes in the behavior classes to which they are directly applied. An example of the latter may be reinforcement dispensed for simply initiating to others.

The reinforcement contingencies in this study were programmed so that neither the withdrawn child nor her peers could receive reinforcement for simply initiating to each other. In order to meet the requirements of the contingencies, either the withdrawn child and/or her peers had to alter their interactive behavior so as to facilitate an increased initiation rate of the other. The specific processes that the subjects and their peers used to achieve this goal are of major interest. Unfortunately, it was not possible in this study to precisely determine what these processes were.

It could have been that the withdrawn subjects and their peers systematically applied skills acquired through the symbolic modeling procedure to selectively reinforce and strengthen each other's initiation rates. However, the authors have no evidence to demonstrate that this was actually the case. It is possible that the same effects could have been achieved with the reinforcement contingencies alone, without the symbolic modeling procedure.

An alternative hypothesis is that the withdrawn subjects and their peers did not employ specific therapeutic techniques but simply became more "attentive" and socially responsive to each other. It may be that such consequences were delivered contingent upon social initiations during intervention phases and noncontingently during baseline phases. Again, it was not possible to confirm or discomfirm this hypothesis in the present study.

A third hypothesis is that S_1's increased rate of initiating to her peers accounted for the reinforcement effect(s) in experiment I. Conversely, the increased rate of initiating to S_2 by her peers accounted for the reinforcement effect(s) in experiment II. The data in experiment I indicate that there was a high correlation between S_1's initiation rate and the increase in her peers' initiation rate. Similarly, in experiment II, S_2's increased initiation rate was highly correlated with an increased rate of peers' initiation to her. In spite of these covariant relationships, it was not possible to establish that one rate increase either caused or was caused by an increase in the other.

When peers respond to a reinforcement contingency or a symbolic modeling procedure by increasing their interaction rates with each other, it would appear important to determine which behavior changes (of the peers involved) are functionally related to the increases in rate. The identification of such parameters could conceivably provide information on how social withdrawal develops and is maintained in young children.

This question is also related to the maintenance of increased social interaction rates following termination of formal treatment procedures. If the behavior changes that control increased social interaction rates are maintained, either artificially or naturally, then the interaction rates themselves should maintain. Until these variables are identified, alternative procedures will have to be used to achieve generalization of increased social interaction rates both across time and across settings.

In each of the three experiments, the rate of interaction during the second baseline period remained considerably above the level of $baseline_1$. The apparent increase in generalization across time may have been due simply to the observers' presence. During the $intervention_1$ period, the presence of an observer also signaled the availability of tokens for social initiation. During $baseline_2$, even though reinforcers were no longer dispensed, the observers may have become conditioned stimuli for social interaction as a result of their earlier pairing with powerful reinforcers. In experiments I and III, however, the data indicate that whatever was accounting for increased social interaction rates at the beginning of the second baseline period quickly began to lose its effectiveness. If the generalization effect was due to the stimulus control of the observers, then it appears that more pairings would be required for longer periods of maintenance.

It may be that if the treatment procedures are left in effect long enough, social interactions will become intrinsically reinforcing, and the increased rate will maintain automatically. Unfortunately, it is not known how long the treatment procedures have to be in effect for this result to occur, if in fact it ever will.

An increased social interaction rate, if maintained long enough, could possibly stimulate the operation of other variables that would maintain the rate. For example, a study by Baer and Wolf (1970) indicates that the preschool social environment can function as a natural community of reinforcement for maintaining behaviors that have high enough rates to enter this sytem. These investigators used a combined priming and social reinforcement technique to increase a withdrawn child's interaction rate with his peers. The treatment procedure was then systematically withdrawn and reintroduced over time until withdrawal no longer produced a reversal effect. That is, the interaction rate maintained at the same level but unsupported by the treatment procedures. Presumably, the rate was being maintained by reinforcers available within the preschool environment. However, the systematic withdrawal and reintroduction of the treatment program, which was in itself a fading-scheduling procedure, could also have contributed to the maintenance of the increased rate.

Additional research is needed to program indefinite maintenance of increased social interaction rates following termination of formal treatment procedures. The identification and use of natural communities of reinforcement is one potential method for accomplishing this task. Another important technique is the scheduling of reinforcements, whether contrived or natural, during treatment so as to delay the process of extinction. Methods of gradually fading out the treatment procedure may be yet another method for achieving this goal.

Numerous studies have demonstrated that a technology is available for increasing social interaction rate. However, the question of whether over the long term these effects generalize across settings, and to other persons not involved in treatment has not been clearly answered. If such is not the case, a similar technology needs to be developed for achieving generalization.

The present study also evaluated the feasibility of using token reinforcement procedures to modify isolate behavior. Tokens (points) were very effective in increasing social interaction rate for all three subjects. However, the extent to which the increased rate maintains following withdrawal of tokens is a largely unanswered question. It is possible that social interaction rates would maintain better following the use of natural social reinforcers such as praise and adult or peer attention than they would following the use of contrived reinforcers during treatment. However, this also appears to be an empirical question that has not been clearly answered.

If, as Baer and Wolf (1970) suggest, an extremely low rate of behavior prevents entry into a natural community of reinforcement, then it appears that the specific techniques used would be relatively unimportant as long as a reliable increase in rate is achieved. Once this has occurred, the natural reinforcement system in the environment would support the behavior and thereby maintain it. However, it is not known to what level the rate must be increased nor how long it must be maintained at that level before the natural reinforcement system "locks in" and supports the behavior indefinitely. All the above assumes a rather direct, unconfounded relationship between the rate of the behavior in question and its becoming "locked in."

In conclusion, the symbolic modeling procedure combined with the three reinforcement contingencies appeared to have substantial impact and considerable generality in modifying social withdrawal. The combined individual-group reinforcement contingency is powerful and seems to be most appropriate for changing the behavior of withdrawn children who have extremely low rates of social interaction. The individual reinforcement contingency in experiment I seems most appropriate for increasing the rate of peer initiations to the withdrawn child. Conversely, the group reinforcement contingency in experiment II seems appropriate for increasing the withdrawn child's initiation rate to peers. However, the effectiveness of this contingency appears to be increased if the child, as well as the peer group, is informed of the nature of the contingency in advance.

Footnotes

1. The authors wish to express appreciation to Edward Fiegenbaum, Margaret Glim, Cliff McKeen, and Linda Levy for their efforts in implementing the study, collecting data, and reviewing the manuscript.

2. A copy of the manual describing the observation and scoring procedures for recording individual social interactions as well as normative data can be obtained from the authors.

References

Allen, K. E., Hart, B., Buell, J. S., Harris, F. R., and Wolf, M. M. Effects of social reinforcement on isolate behavior of a nursery school child. *Child Development*, 1964, *35*, 511-518.

Baer, D. M. and Wolf, M. M. The entry into natural communities of reinforcement. In R. Ulrich, T. Stachnik, and J. Mabry (Eds.), *Control of human behavior*. Glenview, Ill.: Scott, Foresman, 1970, 319-324.

Bijou, S. W., Peterson, R. F., Harris, F. R., Allen, K. E., and Johnston, M. Methodology for experimental studies of young children in natural settings. *The Psychological Record,* 1969, *19*, 177-210.

Buell, J., Stoddard, P., Harris, F. R., and Baer, D. M. Collateral social development accompanying reinforcement of outdoor play in a preschool child. *Journal of Applied Behavior Analysis*, 1968, *1*, 167-173.

Guerney, B. F., Jr. and Flumen, A. B. Teachers as psychotherapeutic agents for withdrawn children. *Journal of School Psychology*, 1970, *8*, 107-113.

Hart, B. M., Reynolds, N. J., Baer, D. M., Brawley, E. R., and Harris, F. R. Effect of contingent and non-contingent social reinforcement on the cooperative play of a preschool child. *Journal of Applied Behavior Analysis*, 1968, *1*, 73-76.

Hopkins, B. L. Effects of candy and social reinforcement, instructions, and reinforcement schedule learning on the modification and maintenance of smiling. *Journal of Applied Behavior Analysis*, 1968, *1*, 121-129.

Kale, R. J., Kaye, J. H., Whelan, P. A., and Hopkins, B. L. The effects of reinforcement on the modification, maintenance, and generalization of social responses of mental patients. *Journal of Applied Behavior Analysis*, 1968, *1*, 307-314.

Kale, F. D. and Toler, H. C., Jr. Modification of preschool isolate behavior: A case study. *Journal of Applied Behavior Analysis*, 1970, *3*, 309-314.

Kirby, F. D. and Toler, H. C., Jr. Modification of preschool isolate behavior: A case study. *Journal of Applied Behavior Analysis*, 1970: *3*, 309-314.

Milby, J. B., Jr. Modification of extreme social isolation by contingent social reinforcement. *Journal of Applied Behavior Analysis*, 1970, *3*, 149-152.

O'Connor, R. D. Modification of social withdrawal through symbolic modeling. *Journal of Applied Behavior Analysis*, 1969, *2*, 15-22.

O'Connor, R. D. The relative efficacy of modeling, shaping, and the combined procedures for the modification of social withdrawal. *Journal of Abnormal Psychology*, in press.

Walker, H. M. *Walker problem behavior identification checklist.* Los Angeles, Cal.: Western Psychological Services, 1970.

Whitman, T. L., Mercurio, J. R., and Caponigri, V. Development of social responses in two severely retarded children. *Journal of Applied Behavior Analysis*, 1970, *3*, 133-138.

A Framework for Conceptualizing Marital Conflict: A Technology for Altering It, Some Data for Evaluating It[1]

12

Robert L. Weiss, Hyman Hops, and Gerald R. Patterson

Relationships called marriage pose interesting, seductive, and troublesome challenges to those working within a behavioral framework. To understand continuing intimate adult relationships within a social learning framework requires first of all a translation of strongly held subjective truths into functional person-setting utility statements. It is alleged that marital behaviors, perhaps more than most other behaviors, are determined by cognitive factors, so that a suggestion that spouses might track their daily exchanges of rewards and punishments is tantamount to introducing a foreign language. Yet this may be an accurate reflection of how the system functions, namely, that a considerable amount of mutual training in vagueness has indeed taken place and that for most adults living together in a marital relationship, assumptions and expectations about the spouse overshadow the data at hand. Lederer and Jackson refer to the *Mirages of Marriage* (1969), and of course other communications-oriented marital therapists have made similar observations (cf. Olson, 1970). Unlike the relatively simpler case with children where situational control of behavior seems to be more direct, adult relationships called marriage appear to be less explicitly under the control of peers and community, or at least there are greater difficulties in pinpointing the nexus of positive situational control.

The purpose of this paper is to summarize the nature of an assessment and intervention package developed by the writers over the past three years at the University of Oregon and the Oregon Research Institute. The focus largely is on the clinical approach although the research track of our work will be introduced in an attempt to illustrate the interplay between applied setting and the research questions that arise therefrom. Related behavioral approaches may be found in the papers of Liberman (1970), and Stuart (1969a, 1969b).

Conceptual Overview

At this stage of our work we are concerned primarily with ongoing marital dyads and not with questions of initial attraction or mate selection. Like walking in on the middle of a movie, the marital therapist encounters already well established dyadic repertoires of considerable complexity.

Oversimplifying, three main areas are of concern in a behavioral approach to marital dyads: (a) the partners exchange affectional behaviors, (b) they problem solve over a wide range of specifics including distribution of resources, and (c) they engage in behavior-change attempts toward one another. At any given time, one or more of these dimensions may be salient so that a total rehabilitation program would necessarily provide training in skills germane to all dimensions.

We assume that marital conflict is the result of faulty behavior-change operations (Patterson and Hops, in press), and that the partners attempt to bring about immediate change in one another largely through aversive control. Their problem is to either accelerate or decelerate some behavioral rate in the other, but because prior training stressed coercive or aversive control the partners readily shape one another by the singular use of these techniques. Over time the partners learn to terminate the aversive manding behavior of the other person by change, but the process is based upon a negative reinforcement paradigm. The aversive manding behavior is strengthened by the behavior of the other which turns off the manding, thus increasing the probability that a comparable form of aversive manding will occur in the future.

One focus of this intervention package is to provide appropriate training in behavioral principles. Because the partners usually fail to label contingencies governing their mutual behaviors, and because persons generally are untrained in making discriminations within a behavioral environment, they rely heavily upon a cognitive-motivational model of behavior. Thus "intent," "motivation for good or bad," "attitude," etc., are all invoked to "explain" the behavior of the other. The Oregon program stresses S^D training, or pinpointing, both in terms of teaching partners to utilize a behavioral denotative vocabulary and to track sequences of behavior-consequence-behavior.

At this point the program takes an additional step not included in communications-oriented approaches. Once established, communication skills can persist only if care is taken to build in payoffs for their occurrence. While there may be inherent reinforcing effects in the reciprocal exchange of behaviors based upon these skills (for example "consideration" may be positively rewarding), it is still necessary, over the long run, to insure that reinforcing props are available in the setting. We assume, therefore, that for training in communication skills to be effective over time, it is necessary to provide the partners with a system of reinforcing exchanges so that the trained skill behaviors will occur at a higher rate. To this end we specifically train couples in the use of contracting and negotiation skills. The objective is to provide them with a vehicle for bringing about behavior change which has considerable face validity, i.e., it is equitable for both partners, with benefits for keeping one's contractual obligation and penalties for failing to do so.

Because of the explicit commitment to the use of reinforcing contingencies, our approach also stresses the availability of satisfactions outside of the particular dyad. Attention is paid to how the spouses utilize recreational facilities in the community, the degree to which they make use of "self-improvement" projects, or, in other words, any evidence for expanding their repertories of social behaviors which may increase the likelihood of positive payoff for them. In this system it would not be sufficient to train the spouse in the use of a particular communication skill if at the same time there was no change in the utilization of this skill outside of the dyad.

To summarize, we offer an approach which explicitly trains married couples in the use of behavior change principles, such as shaping, use of positive (not aversive) control, pinpointing, and contingency management. These techniques are combined with specific training in problem solving behaviors. Finally, by paying attention to sources of rewards and pleasures both within the dyadic relationship and from the community at large, we train the partners to exchange reinforcing behaviors with one another. Contracting and negotiating skills are the main vehicles for bringing about these behavioral changes between the spouses.

This procedurally focused account can be formalized somewhat by looking at the underlying concepts. The Oregon approach has much in common with social psychological concepts of exchange, reciprocity, and behavioral economics. One aspect of S^D training—labelling functional relationships in one's environment—is the use of behavioral utilities (cf. also Knox, 1971). Before one can enter into negotiation proper one must have a utility hierarchy of response costs and benefits. Some changes, because of their high response costs, should be reinforced more heavily than others of lesser cost. Each individual in the dyad must be able to assign utility or value to his or her behaviors. Whereas it may have been assumed that dishwashing was one person's role—an implicit assumption or expectation—it might now be viewed as a behavior having utility and therefore exchangeable for some other behavior from the spouse.

The present approach is also similar to social psychological approaches in its emphasis on situational or state determination of behavior (cf. Mischel, 1969). We are more concerned with restructuring the day-to-day environment of our clients than we are with their motivational histories or their need systems. It is a working hypothesis that therapeutically significant determinants of behavior lie in the causal day-to-day variations in behavioral exchanges, and global states, such as mood, follow upon reinforcement scheduling rather than from internal vicissitudes. Lewinsohn's work with depression follows similar assumptions (Lewinsohn and Shaffer, 1971).

In all of the above one is confronted with an assessment problem of considerable scope. A functionally oriented behavioral approach requires ongoing measurement of behavior in contexts (Weiss, 1969) rather than the more traditional assessment of traits or enduring structures within persons. It has become necessary to develop techniques for objectifying reinforcing exchanges, problem solving skills, and variations in daily rewards and punishments. We turn next to a consideration of the assessment approach utilized in this program.

Assessment of Marital Conflict

In a behavioral approach to marital therapy, assessment and intervention are two sides of the same coin. Any procedure for objectifying change is elevated to the status of "assessment device" if it is used repeatedly with clinical cases. It should be noted that assessment techniques serve both as independent and dependent variables; in some of our research, couples are selected on the basis of behavioral samples of conflict, and treatment outcomes are evaluated in terms of post-intervention administration of these same assessment procedures. (A helpful listing of traditional instruments may be found in Strauss, 1969). This section describes the kinds of procedures we have developed and presents some of the research which supports the use of these devices. Focus on the intervention package itself will be held for the later sections of this chapter.

Self-Report Techniques

In addition to using a well-known traditional marital adjustment scale (Locke and Wallace, 1959), we have developed two self-report survey type instruments and a third self-report, quasi-observational procedure for coding Pleasurable and Displeasurable events.

The Locke-Wallace scale provides a measure of reported marital dissatisfaction and has been included to allow coordination between our sample of cases and others mentioned in the literature. For example, in two studies (Birchler, 1972; Vincent, 1972) a sample of distressed couples was drawn using as one criterion of distress a Locke-Wallace score of less than 90. In a study by Wills and Weiss (1972) the Locke-Wallace scale was used to *exclude* apparently distressed couples so that only couples with scores above 100 were included.

The Willingness to Change (W-C) scale was developed to pinpoint conflict areas by asking each spouse to indicate on a seven point scale whether his (her) partner should engage in specific activities *much less, no change,* or *much more*. ("Spouse should keep the house clean," "Spouse should want to have sexual relations with me," and "Spouse should help with housework when asked" are examples.) A conflict score is obtained by summing the scale values for each spouse separately. Deviations from "no change" indicate reported dissatisfaction and presumably reflect attempts at behavior change. To date the W-C has proven most useful in providing a common starting ground for spouses to pinpoint instances of conflict about changing the behavior of the other.

The Marital Activities Inventory:Alone, Together, Others (MAITAO) samples 85 common recreational, self-enhancing, affectional, or utilitarian activities which could be engaged in alone or with another person, whether spouse or nonspouse. Examples include playing cards, sunbathing, discussing family problems or marital conflicts, going to a museum or an exhibit, etc. In each instance the respondent is asked to estimate the frequency of occurrence of the event (alone, with spouse, and with others) during the past month. This survey samples the range of activities available to the spouses and provides an indication of the relative amount of time spent in mutually satisfying activities versus that spent in activities by self and with nonspouse others. Initial validity for this approach has been obtained from the Birchler-Vincent study of distressed and nondistressed couples, where it was found that distressed, relative to nondistressed, couples reported a significantly lower mean percentage of recreational activities with spouse ($p < .005$). This finding indicated that the distressed couples were avoiding mutual activities. The two groups did not differ significantly in absolute range of activities, suggesting that by our criterion of marital distress these were not greatly isolated or withdrawn individuals.

The last of the self-report techniques, the Pleasurable-Displeasurable count (P's and D's) reflects our concern with assessing the rate at which rewards and punishments are exchanged between spouses. Drawing from a universal checklist of P's and D's—or almost universal!—couples indicate which spouse behaviors they find pleasing or displeasing. P's and D's must reflect behaviors or behavioral consequences which originate from one spouse and are directed toward the other spouse. Acts of God, prearranged exchanges, or gifts from others, are not to be included. Examples range from "Spouse came home on time," "Spouse called just to say hello," "We cuddled in bed," to "Spouse mimics me," "Spouse drank too much," etc. P's and D's can be categorized into instrumental and affectional behaviors and outcomes. The former refer to utilitarian outcomes, where some action was taken to accomplish an end (making a meal, taking out garbage, etc.). Affectional P's and D's more often refer to overt displays of love and affection such as "Spouse kissed me" or "Spouse preoccupied when with me." In either case the *consumer* labels the behavior as pleasing or displeasing.

The recording of P's and D's is done on a daily basis from either a specially compiled list (with write-in options) for a given couple, or from a spouse observation check list including a wide range of P's and D's, many of which are not specific to a spouse. Whenever possible we strive for ongoing recording through all phases of treatment, but in all instances P's and D's are collected during baseline prior to intervention and also after intervention.

Of all the self-report assessment techniques used in the project we have done more empirical work on the P's and D's, and while unanswered questions remain, there are data which support this particular technique.

One important P and D finding from the Birchler-Vincent study indicated that distressed and nondistressed couples selected on the basis of the Locke-Wallace scale, an interview rating (see below), and the W-C scale (described above) were significantly different from one another in both their P and D average rates ($t = 2.84$, $p < .005$, and $t = 4.74$, $p = .001$, 46df, respectively). The distressed couple group produced P and D mean rates which were opposite in magnitude to those for nondistressed couples, the distressed group showing significantly lower P's and significantly higher D's. A derived P/D ratio score was found to be related to the Locke-Wallace score, with $r = .54$ ($p < .02$), indicating a modicum of overlap in the variance of self-report via satisfaction and daily observation of discrete events.

The issue of self-report of marital satisfaction is methodologically complex (cf. Wills, 1972), involving a global, usually retrospective report. Wills, in a methodologically precise fashion, sought to dissect out the ingredients of reported marital satisfaction by attempting to relate to this five likely individual contributors to the global rating of satisfaction: pleasurable and unpleasurable instrumental and affectional events taken separately, and ratings of quality and daily experiences outside of the marriage. Subjects, seven paid volunteer couples, recorded Pleasurable and Displeasurable instrumental events daily on standardized check sheets, while the two classes of affectional events were recorded on wrist counters during a daily fixed time together. On a specially prepared 3 x 5 card, the subjects recorded the degree to which outside (nonspouse related) daily experiences were enjoyable. Finally, at the end of each day the spouses independently rated the pleasantness of the interaction with their spouse for that day. By means of multiple regression (R) the five dimensions of pleasing and displeasing spouse behaviors and outside enjoyment were related to the rating of satisfaction with spouse interaction.

The overall $R = .508$ ($p < .001$) indicated that indeed these five predictors could be combined to account for 25% of the satisfaction-with-spouse rating. Both sexes weighed the occurrence of both affectional and instrumental D's in making their satisfaction-with-spouse rating, but the source of P's differed for the sexes: for males, instrumental P's and for females affectional P's, were the main contributor to the satisfaction ratings. Outside events contributed only slightly to the global rating of pleasantness of spouse interaction.

The finding that Displeasurable events accounted for far greater variance of spouse ratings than did Pleasurable events suggests that in married couples, tracking aversiveness may be better established than tracking positively. (P's, it should be noted, actually occurred at a far greater frequency than D's, so it cannot be argued that because of frequency D's were more easily tracked.) Additional analyses supported this conjecture. The daily P (or D) rate was determined for each spouse over the 14 days of observation. An r was computed for each couple with n = days. Reciprocity of P's or D's would be shown by a significant average r (averaging the R's obtained for each couple). For affectional, but not for instrumental, events the $\bar{r} = .29$ (NS) and .59 ($p = .025$) for P's and D's respectively. On a daily basis spouses reciprocated D's although reciprocity for P's was not evident. Similar findings were also obtained in an earlier pilot study by Wills and Weiss (1971).

Still another form of reciprocity is possible—covariation between spouses over a time span greater than one day. A positive relationship would indicate something analogous to a couple "signature" of P's and D's characteristic of their relationship. In this instance couples are the covariates (N = 7). Rank order correlations (rho) were computed on mean rates per hour for affectional P's and D's; the rhos for P's and D's were 1.00 and .61, respectively. Similar results were obtained when pilot data (Wills and Weiss, 1971) and the Birchler-Vincent data were re-analyzed in this format. Reciprocity as couple signature was obtained for P's but not for D's. Thus over a two-week period husbands and wives exchanged P's at a similar average rate; for some this rate was low and for some this rate was quite high.

One additional feature of the Wills (1972) study bears mentioning. On the 12th day of the study the *E* called the husbands and requested that they double their output of affectional P's. Each was given his prior average rate as a reference point. To be successful this manipulation would result in a 100% increase in the wife's report of affectional P's for these two last days. The results confirmed the expectation in that wives reported a significant increase in mean P rate of 78%. There were no changes for reported D's, and while an increase in P's was also reported by husbands it was not statistically significant. (There may have been a tendency for wives to reciprocate their new found fortunes!)

Numerous other analyses were reported which need not concern us here, except to note that P's and D's were not significantly related to one another, and that only affectional P's were positively related to time together. Recalling that these were nondistressed couples it seems reasonable to conclude that they utilized opportunities (time together) to positively reinforce more than to punish, and that "score keeping" was not in evidence: Many D's did not entail few P's for these couples.

The findings suggest that P's and D's, as conceived within our framework, are sensitive to experimental manipulation, figure into global ratings of satisfaction with spouse interaction, and serve rather different ends for males and females, i.e., affectional P's are important to females, while a good meal is still the way to a man's heart.

Observational Techniques

To date we have employed three types of observational methods: (a) structured interviews, (b) coded samples of ongoing problem solving behaviors (Marital Interaction Coding System), and (c) home observation of family interaction (Patterson and Hops, in press).

Structured interview. For research purposes interviews are structured around topics of courtship, sources of past and current attraction, and problems with marriage. During the session the interviewer, blind as to whether a couple scores as distressed or nondistressed on other indices, makes a continuous recording of ongoing positive and negative exchanges, both verbal and nonverbal. A final seven point rating is then made for degree of couple distress based upon the interview data. Highly significant relationships ($p < .01$) were obtained between these interview ratings and (a) P/D derived scores ($r = .56$), (b) reported conflicts from a daily diary ($r = .43$), and (c) Marital Activities Inventory Percentage of Activities with Spouse ($r = .53$). These findings were based upon the data from the Birchler-Vincent study mentioned above. In each instance the higher the interview rating the less the judged marital distress. Thus couples do display their distress both behaviorally in front of interviewers as well as on various formats of self-report and self-observation devices.

With clinical cases we employ an expanded version of the focused interview by systematically exploring conflict in the major areas of marital living, e.g., finances and management, background differences, sex and affection, etc. The procedures here are to cover each item of the check list with the couple in order to elicit the degree of difficulty related to the item, whether a major or minor marital problem. These are then used for samples of the couple's problem solving behavior.

Marital Interaction Coding System (MICS). It readily becomes apparent when reviewing a video tape of marital conversation that communication occurs at all levels and that the uninitiated outsider (therapist) has enough difficulty keeping track of content without also tracking the nuances of the interaction. Therefore it was necessary to develop a coding system which embodied those aspects of the interaction deemed important within a social learning framework. Roughly, these broke down into Problem Solving behaviors, Problem Description statements, and categories of verbal and nonverbal Positive and Negative Exchanges, such as affectional smiles, supportive statements, gestures of scorn, criticisms, etc. The result, shown in Table 1, was a 29 item[1] behavioral code (Hops, et al., 1972) fashioned largely after the family interaction coding system developed by Patterson, et al. (cf. Patterson and Hops, in press). The ongoing (usually ten-minute) interaction of husband and wife attempting to solve problems preselected from their responses to the inventory of conflicts is video taped and then played back for later coding. Trained coders score the interaction for both husband and wife on separate lines in units of 30 seconds. Scores are reported as frequency of each behavioral code and then either normalized for total output of verbal and nonverbal behaviors or expressed in per minute rate terms. A couple with a high frequency of critical and aversive interchanges, fewer problem solving statements, and many problem descriptions typifies a rather hostile, standoffish, or wheel-spinning approach in their interaction. The usual procedure is to have couples negotiate a solution to each of four problems gleaned from the interview. The problems are identified as either major or minor to provide samples when both difficult and nondifficult material is involved.

Reliability of coding is reported for each session scored by two coders, and a minimum criterion of 70% agreement is set. (Coders go through a training program and then undergo weekly calibration checks to keep reliability at a satisfactory level.) Reliability is expressed as average percentage agreement for a 30-second line, a stringent criterion of agreement.

The first question to be asked of a new assessment device such as the MICS is whether it is sensitive to changes brought about by skills training. In the initial report describing this approach (Patterson and Hops, 1971) and in two subsequent clinical studies designed to replicate the treatment effect on larger samples (Hops, Patterson, and Weiss; Weiss, et al., in preparation) significant changes over baseline were found which could be attributed to the intervention. These data will be considered below in more detail in conjunction with the intervention procedures themselves.

The sensitivity of the MICS to within-session training can also be seen by referring to Figure 1. *Problem Solving* codes (consisting of Problem Solving, Accept Responsibility, and Compromise) are represented collectively as the proportion of all verbal behaviors for husband and wife. Samples one through four show the level of Problem Solving behavior during baseline. Samples 5a, 5b, and 5c, were taken within a single session of intervention and represent negotiations followed by immediate video tape feedback and instructions to the couple to score their own interactions on the preceding tape sample. The systematic increase in Problem Solving behaviors reflects the "on target" training effectiveness, i.e., the couples now focus on moving their deliberations forward toward a solution. In the samples numbered 6 and 7, different problems were being considered on subsequent days, and while there was a slight loss in the Problem Solving codes, they were still above baseline levels. Sessions 8 and 9 were for a one-month follow-up with this couple.

It should be pointed out that our scoring of Problem Solving behaviors is restricted only to those statements which would be instrumental in problem solving, i.e., solution proposals, attempts to take responsibility for action, etc. Whether in fact these are workable

Table 1 Marital Interaction Coding System (MICS)

	Verbal Code Name		Nonverbal Code Name
AG	Agree	AS	Assent
AP	Approval	AT	Attention
AR	Accept Responsibility	CO	Compliance
CM	Command	LA	Laugh
CP	Complaint	NC	Noncompliance
CR	Criticize	NO	Normative
CS	Compromise	NR	No Response
DG	Disagree	NT	Not Tracking
DR	Deny Responsibility	PP	Positive Physical Contact
EX	Excuse	SM	Smile
HM	Humor	TO	Turn Off
IN	Interrupt		
NS	Negative Solution		
PD	Problem Description		
PS	Problem Solving		
PU	Put Down		
QU	Question		
SP	Solution (Past)		
TA	Talk		

Combined Codes for Levels

	Verbal Codes		Nonverbal Codes
I.	Problem Solving (AR, CS, PS)	V.	Positive (AS, LA, PP, SM)
II.	Problem Description (NS, PD, SP)	VI.	Negative (NR, NT, TO)
III.	Negative (CP, CR, DR, EX, PU)		
IV.	Positive (AG, AP, HM)		

solutions is not reflected in the system, nor does it need to be. The first step is to increase the behaviors that could possibly lead to conflict resolution; the question of validity comes later.

Another approach to the sensitivity or range of the MICS itself is to look at changes in individual code categories over baseline sessions. Goldstein, et al. (1966) argue that psychotherapeutic research conducted without a control group reduces the internal validity of the design. To increase confidence in the effectiveness of the therapeutic manipulation, it is absolutely necessary, therefore, to

Figure 1

Sensitivity of MICS to Training in Problem Solving Skills

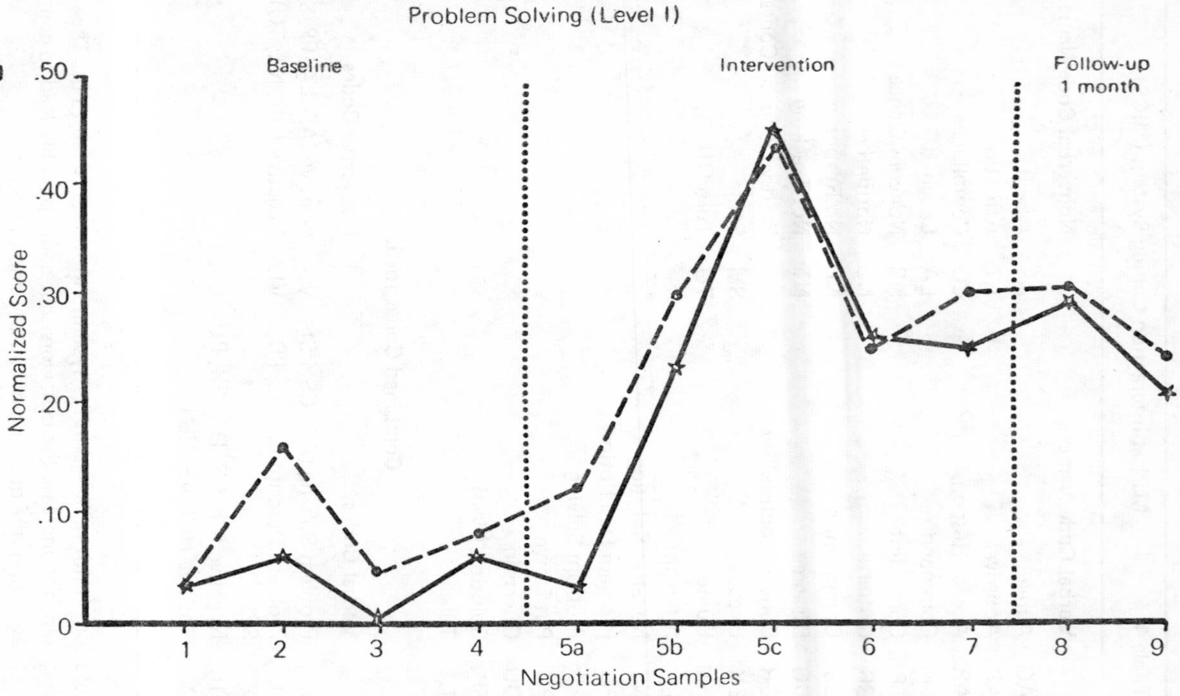

demonstrate the absence of changes in the hypothesized direction during the baseline condition. In the Hops, Patterson, and Weiss study, two sets of laboratory negotiations obtained during the two weeks of baseline were analyzed using the MICS and each category subjected to an analysis of variance for repeated measures.

Four code categories showed significant "trials" effects at p values less than .10, indicating change in the behavior of the spouses. The behavioral categories of Assent (AS) and Attend (AT) were less frequently scored, indicating a decrease in the partners tracking each other by looking at each other and communicating via head nods or brief verbal responses. In addition, there was an increase in the rate of No Response (NR) category demonstrating increased periods of silence and less tendency to respond to one another even when the situation clearly called for a response. The fourth category to show change during baseline was Problem Solution (PS) where both partners increased rates of stating possible solutions to the problems. This effect may have been due to the demands of the negotiation setting since they were specifically asked to work toward the solution of each problem they discussed.

During baseline, then, only one category (PS) showed a change indicating improvement; however, this may have been due to the demands of the task. The other three categories which changed significantly suggested that, if anything, the interaction between the couples was getting worse.

In the more recent study (Weiss, et al., in preparation) an attempt was made to assess the effect of major versus minor problem distinction on codes. Understandably there was a significantly higher level of Problem Description ($p = .025$) for major problems relative to minor problems, more positive verbal statements emitted for minor problems ($p = .05$), and more positive nonverbal exchanges during minor problems ($p = .10$). There was a tendency for wives to emit a greater proportion of negative nonverbal behaviors during the discussion of identified major problems ($p = .10$). Problem solving was not systematically related to problem type (major or minor). Thus it appears that with more difficult emotional content, as in discussions of major problems, the couples tended to talk more about the problem itself, and females tended to be more aversive. Both sexes were more positive in their exchanges when talking about minor problems. It would appear that baseline negotiation samples do reflect differences according to intensity of problem attempted, but the specificity is to problem content, not to practice during baseline.

The answer to the question of sensitivity of the Marital Interaction Coding System is that the system reflects ongoing behavior changes within ten-minute samples both within and between sessions. The question of validity will be addressed below.

Home observations. The last of the three observational techniques to be mentioned is probably better known to those familiar with the child and family intervention strategies developed by Patterson and his colleagues (cf. Reid, 1967; Patterson, et al., in press; Patterson and Hops, in press). As with the MICS there are 29 behavioral code categories utilized by trained observers as they make three successive hourly home observations. Among the behaviors coded are Talk, Whine, Yell, Humiliate, Whine, etc., as actions, and Attend, Ignore, Command, Approve, etc., as consequences. Each family member is observed sequentially, so that the resulting chain of behavior codes reflects the natural history of the interaction during the observational period.

To date data are avilable only on a single case (Patterson and Hops, in press) and indicate that talk duration between spouses increased significantly following marital negotiation training. Change in aversiveness of family members was not significant overall, although individual trends were observed, e.g., the father became less aversive to other family members.

The inclusion of this measure may prove to make excessive demands on the efficacy of our treatment package for marital conflict and discord, since generalization to a family interaction may be more than we can accomplish without direct training in family techniques. This question will be answered from data collected in the Weiss, et al. (in preparation) study.

Intervention Techniques

Having laid the foundation by considering the various techniques developed for assessing treatment effects, we now turn to the more avowedly clinical aspects of the program, the treatment or intervention procedures.

Earlier it was noted that the work of the marital dyad falls into three general categories: (a) affectional exchanges, (b) problem solving and utilitarian behaviors, and (c) behavior change attempts. Our treatment modules are designed to accomplish these ends by providing training in each area of deficiency or excess.

Treatment Modules

The modules are illustrated in Figure 2 in an idealized treatment sequence and flow diagram. The initial intake interview is concerned with systematically covering conflict areas and dissatisfactions. Couples have a "story" to relate which is their subjective reality, and they also test for possible alliances with the new outsiders, the co-therapists. By using the problem area check list and focusing on exchanges of Pleases and Displeases we introduce the behavioral approach, which then moves into a more precise consideration of pleasing exchanges. Since the couple usually complains about "lack of communication" and since they have considerable resentment toward one another, being specific about their daily interactions is not one of their most practiced skills. Specific training in pinpointing functional relationships must be undertaken. It is also likely, depending upon a host of factors, that the partners have well established aversive sequences involving active put-down behaviors, conflict escalating maneuvers, etc. In other words, destructive fighting and other nonproductive behaviors dominate and prevent communication. It then may be necessary to move into a communications training mode which involves explicit training in listening, scheduled talk times, and practice in increasing verbal reinforcements and in decreasing operant "zaps." In some instances it has been necessary to train couples to paraphrase the communications of one another to demonstrate listening behaviors.

Both the pinpointing or discrimination training module and the communication module support, as it were, the skills involved in collecting P and D data. Being specific about mate behaviors which are pleasing is frequently very difficult for couples. In addition to providing a continuous check on the affectional exchanges in the relationship, the P's and D's set the stage for the next important step in treatment, namely, the formulation of *quid pro quo* statements. Since the final point in the intervention package is training negotiation and contracting skills, it is necessary for the couples to be able to group their behaviors in behavioral economic terms. Thus to specify the utility of routine behaviors or the reward value of other behaviors is the goal of this module. With this kind of discrimination applied to one's behavioral environment it is then possible to enter into negotiations about behavior change. In this final module, negotiation and contracting training, the couple learns the format for establishing exchange agreements designed to bring about behavioral changes in one another and in the living situation. It is also important to note, before going into detail about the modules themselves, that each module has a verti-

Figure 2   Flow Chart of Intervention Modules

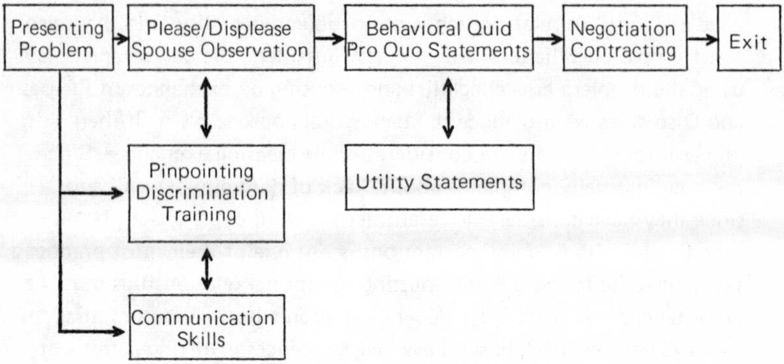

cal dimension as well. We can train in depth, if necessary; if simple labelling by the therapists is not sufficient, we would then utilize video tape feedback, therapist role playing and modelling, or even smaller units involving home use of tape recorders for micro practice sessions. To provide a common language for the sessions the couples are assigned *Families* (Patterson, 1971), and professional contact sessions are made contingent upon having read assigned material and having completed assigned practice or data collecting tasks.

We turn next to a more detailed description of the modules.

Presenting problem. Couples are seen by male and female co-therapists, and, from the start, sessions are video taped with observers present behind an observation screen. As the couple considers each of 26 items on the Potential Problem checklist, the therapists note possibilities for the couple's P and D lists. For example, a D which might come up when considering information about "Care of Children" is that "Husband never spends time with the children." An example of a D pinpoint might be "Husband does not participate in child initiated activity before dinner."

The checklist also serves a disinhibiting function by laying out a wide range of problem areas with the expectation that all couples have something to say in each. The rule of thumb is that either person may declare an area a problem; there need not be couple agreement on what constitutes a problem. The universal list of P's and D's and an extensive listing of affectional P's and D's are coordinated with the checklist. From these lists couples derive their own P and D lists to be used during a two-week baseline period and, with modifications, during intervention. Typically, daily phone calls are made to couples to obtain the P and D data count and to reinforce the importance of these records.

Also during the initial session, and derived from the consideration of problem areas, two problems, one major and one minor, are selected by the couple for attempted solution in the session. Each of the two problems is discussed for ten minutes with the instruction to reach a solution. During a second meeting a week later two additional problems are discussed for solution. These are the baseline negotiation samples which are scored according to the MICS. (See Table 1, above.)

Clearly, then, during baseline the therapists are active only in directing the flow of information and in assisting in the creation of idiosyncratic P and D lists. Active intervention is avoided in the two baseline sessions, and phone conversations are limited largely to the data and problems in that regard.

Pleases and Displeases. These have been discussed before; consequently, only a few additional points need be made. The P's and D's serve a discrimination training function during intervention since by sharing them the spouses each learn what behaviors are valued by the other. Also it is possible to use acknowledgement of a P as a training technique. For example, when Wife engages in a P behavior toward Husband he is instructed to acknowledge this behavior by either thanking her or emitting a positive recognition gesture. This device ties together the two persons and emphasizes their mutual dependency for gratification.

Along these same lines of using P and D exchanges therapeutically, we have employed the device of "love days." A love day is a specified time when a partner has an obligation to the therapists to substantially increase his (her) rate of P's to the spouse. Understandably couples are amazed at the effects this kind of attention has on their relationship. Love days can also be viewed as structured practice sessions for a spouse since spouses commonly have limited performance repertoires for giving pleasures to the other.

Pinpointing and discrimination training. The aim here is to focus communications about couple behaviors into operational statements. As therapists, we will use whatever accomplishes this end. Admittedly there is opposition to such a restriction on communication since people are more inclined to use global, intention ascribing statements, or lapse into vague expectation statements. One technique that has been useful is to start with a listing of expectations held by each partner and then ask the partners, in turn, to operationalize for an observer how that expectation would be met in behavior. Wife states that she expects Husband to be a good father. Husband is asked to operationalize that statement of expectation. Wife is then asked whether the operational statement meets her expectation. This technique rapidly uncovers those expectations which are held only because they are impossible to fulfill.

Pinpointing, when done conjointly, is the first step in contracting and negotiation training. By making operational statements the utility of the behavior becomes clearer ("You expect me to wash the dishes three times a week!"), and by mutual shaping the couple may decide that the heretofore privately held expectation is not important in their day-to-day behavior.

Pinpointing provides still another side benefit in that it now becomes possible to move away from "I know just what you are thinking" controlling statements. It sets the stage for therapists by establishing a norm of reciprocity—"You don't know what is in my head any more than I can know what is in your head." For the reticent partner who is outtalked or outthought by his or her spouse, this provides an obligation to produce overt statements which enable the other person to know what is in his (her) head, and concomitantly elevates the importance of any thoughts he might have.

Finally, pinpointing can be accomplished by replaying segments of a problem solving interaction and asking the partners to score instances of behaviors which otherwise have escaped identification. To be told that one's rate of eye contact is very low is more effectively demonstrated by such video tape replay, and it takes the onus off the observer. It may be necessary, after a pinpoint has been established, to move temporarily into a skill training session for the behavior, such as establishing eye contact, since the partner may have little experience in this regard.

Communication module. In this mode we make a distinction between those activities which specifically train for negotiation and problem solving skills and those activities which serve an en route function, such as laying the basic skill elements to be utilized later. If, for example, one spouse has an output rate which makes it impossible for the other partner to talk, it is clearly necessary to build in stops. On a content level it may be important to teach a partner to be a Rogerian and reflect or paraphrase. The latter is based on the simple assumption that it is reinforcing to be "understood," and that paraphrase statements have a reinforcing effect on the speaker.

Another aspect of this module is creating clear distinctions between problem solving, information gathering, and catharsis modes. Confusion results when one partner starts to problem solve in response to communication from the spouse, when in fact the latter is only "sounding off." We have utilized the device of "Administrative Time" which is a fixed time period during which the couple will generate an agenda (of weekend activity alternatives, for example) which will then be dealt with during a time designated for problem solving. With this kind of stimulus control, feelings about one thing and another cannot be brought up when in the Administrative Time mode.

The kinds of communication skills lacking in couples are best modeled and trained in the sessions with the co-therapists. By modelling adequate information gathering ("I had a difficult day, what was your's like?") the partners can see the necessity for making specific information available to one another before undertaking remediation for the needy spouse. If it has been established immediately upon meeting at the end of the day that both partners are down, i.e., are in need of support from the other, there is a better opportunity to deal with this as an administrative crisis rather than in terms of "why have you failed me again?" The sessions also make possible training in real life playback, just as with the video tape. We frequently ask the couples to start over and replay the action both in the sessions and at home. Frequently it is because of a "bad start" that the chain runs off poorly; this is most often true in sexual invitations to one another. By literally taking the action back to the pre-start point and playing it anew couples can train themselves in more pleasant outcomes.

Behavioral utilities. The success or failure of behavioral contracting depends upon a clearly stated set of contingency options (positive and negative consequences) and pinpointed behaviors to be accelerated or decelerated. Contingency options are those objects, events, or behavior which each spouse values either positively or negatively. Table 2 illustrates a contingency matrix which incorporates the value of the consequence (positive or negative), the originator source of the consequence, and the recipient of the consequence. Each of the items listed can be specified in terms of units of value so that reward and penalty equity is possible, e.g., a backrub and dinner out would not be of equal behavioral utility. Negative consequences controlled by the spouse are included here, but these should be avoided, if possible, in contracting, since the aim is to increase the reinforcingness of the spouse, not his or her

Table 2 Illustrative Contingency Matrix

	Positive Consequences:		Negative Consequences:	
From:	To Husband	To Wife	To Husband	To Wife
Spouse	Backrub Sexual variety	Dinner out Shopping trip	Lose spending money to spouse Specified spouse chore	
Environment	Free time Beer	Hairdresser Art class	Clean garage Clean oven	Lose free time units Wash windows
Therapist	Reduce Rx fee	Movie tickets	Fine or loss of deposit money	

aversiveness. Similarly, spouse-controlled positive consequences should not be aversive for the provider. While sex may be a positive spouse-controlled consequence it would be of questionable therapeutic utility if this behavior was aversive to the provider spouse.

Negotiation training and contracting. Negotiation training refers to the fact that couples are taught to think in terms of behavioral utilities and the resources they are willing to offer in exchange for resources gained. Contracting refers to the use of a systematic procedure for setting forth behavior change agreements. Consider first the logical basis of contracting.

The objective of contracting is to provide an orderly procedure for spouse initiated behavior change based upon the tenet that each person can gain only by holding to the contractual obligations. Typically one thinks in terms of response contingent *quid pro quo* arrangements of the sort "If you do X, I'll do Y." The failure of X entails the failure of Y. With couples in distress, X and Y are too often the chronic aversive behavior sequences which do not readily break into smaller units of approximation. The implicit message of this model is "You go first!" On both accounts, aversiveness of the target behavior and the implied disadvantage for one partner, this is not the best approach when dealing with significant problem behaviors.

An alternative model, one that allows for variations of reinforcing control, is the implicit exchange or "good faith" contract. This is of the form "X and Y; if X then H+, if Y then W+, . . ." Letting X and Y represent Husband and Wife target behaviors, respectively, and H+ and W+ represent a reward to Husband and Wife, the model emphasizes independent change contracts. Target behaviors are those pinpointed behaviors of the spouse that a partner wants changed, usually stated in the accelerated format "Husband *will* spend 10 minutes before dinner with the children," not "Husband *will not* read the paper by himself before dinner." The rule is that whenever X or Y occurs, H+ or W+ occurs. If not X then not H+, but this does not entail negation of Y. In this sense, the independent control of X and Y, the failure of one person to emit target behaviors does not necessarily terminate the contract nor the behavior of the other. There are no benefits, real or imagined, to playing "you go first," since there is no first. The benefits for change are built into the contract, and targeted behaviors are not cross-linked as inevitably as they must be in the various *quid pro quo* models involving the "If X then Y" format.

A frequent pitfall in this contracting procedure is cross-linking the rewards of the contract (H† and W+). As already noted in considering behavioral utilities, one person's contractual reward should not come at high cost to the other; this may be particularly true if the therapist seizes an opportunity to include a deviant Wife behavior as an H+, e.g., H's reward would be W's cleaning the kitchen. Such an arrangement changes the balance of utilities in the reward system.

The structural features of this form of contracting are illustrated in Table 3. The Rewards and Penalties are derived from the contingency matrix in Table 2. The behaviors to be accelerated and/or decelerated derive from problem pinpoints and the P and D lists, i.e., the complaint behaviors that led to therapy now cast in operational behavioral terms.

An important feature in Table 3 is the marshalling of rewards and penalties. Not every contract would necessarily require the entire inventory of reinforcements built into it, but if simple rewards from spouse or environment are insufficient to maintain desired behaviors, one can marshal therapist rewards. If a reward system by itself is deemed to be ineffective, it is advisable to build in a two-value system, viz., rewards *and* penalties. Non-reward should normally exert a controlling effect, but this can be bolstered by introducing contractual penalties. It should now be apparent why penalties from the environment will be better than those coming from the spouse. Sample contracts are presented in Table 4.

An example of a behaviorally poor contract which relies on aversive control is also presented in Table 4. Note that couples can expertly produce these no-gain contracts in the guise of a behavioral model. For both partners their penalties are cross-linked with deviant target behaviors, since sexual avoidance was a problem with this couple, and the contingency "no work on records produces a hot lunch" is highly questionable behavioral engineering.

Table 3 Negotiation Training Form

Husband	Wife
Problem Behavior:	Problem Behavior:
Accelerate: ________	Accelerate: ________
Decelerate: ________	Decelerate: ________
Reward:	Reward:
1. From Wife: ________ (H+)	1. From Husband: ________ (W+)
2. From Environment: ____ (Nonspouse +)	2. From Environment: ____ (Nonspouse +)
3. Therapist: ________ (T+)	3. Therapist: ________ (T+)
Penalty:	Penalty:
1. From Environment: ____ (Nonspouse –)	1. From Environment: ____ (Nonspouse –)
2. From Wife: ________ (H–)	2. From Husband: ________ (W–)
3. From Therapist: ______ (T–)	3. From Therapist: ______ (T–)

Some remaining points about contracting should be noted. With adults it is often very difficult to develop the contingency matrix. Husbands notoriously do not tell us what would be reinforcing for them! Wives generate lengthy lists. Like Stuart (1969a) we utilize tokens in the reward mode to be exchanged for backup reinforcers. However it is essential to insure that tokens are being turned into consumable rewards and not hoarded for side contracts.

The contract is enforced for at least one week without change, and its S^D (cuing or pinpointing) function is insured by having it placed in some prominent place in the kitchen. Couples are reluctant at first to structure their activities in this way, but they soon find that there are advantages in having an objective outside source of control that can be "blamed."

Table 4 Sample Contracts

1. Conversation and Sex

	Dick		Jane
Accelerate:	10 minutes of talk about Dick's day as it concerns studies and future—every day.	Accelerate:	Sleep in nude every night except during periods.
Reward:	1 bottle of beer per 10 minutes.	Reward:	30¢ a day to be spent in *any way* I see fit.
Penalty:	Write two letters, e.g., to friends or relatives.	Penalty:	Heavy housework, e.g., 1) wash windows in 1 room 2) clean oven 3) wax floors 4) shampoo rug

2. Home Time and Child Training

	Dick		Jane
Accelerate:	Dick will be home four evenings per week, explicitly Monday, Wednesday, Friday, and Saturday. Of these, Jane will have one night out, one at her option, and two will be shared family nights.	Accelerate:	Jane will spend involved, meaningful time with the children, reading, art projects, excursions, reading readiness, etc., at the rate of 7 half-hour periods per week.
Reward:	One-half hour sense relaxation exercises with Jane.	Reward:	Late cooking or dinner together with Dick is earned for 3 points (one point per half hour with kids). One point may also be exchanged for 15 minutes help from Dick.
Penalty:	Complete the whole kitchen shebang alone after dinner.	Penalty:	Complete RCAF exercises at her level for failure to spend time with kids on any day.

Table 4, continued

3. Behaviorally Poor Contract:

Church and Business Records

I, Phaedra, agree to spend one-half hour a week working with Romulus on his business records.

Consequences for failure to execute:
If I fail to spend one-half hour a week on Romulus' business records, THEN I will prepare one hot lunch for Romulus to take to work during the following week.

Terms of this contract are non-negotiable for a period of one week.

Signed __________________

Date __________________

I, Romulus, agree to go to any church of Phaedra's choice every Sunday.

Consequences for failure to execute:
If I fail to go with Phaedra to the church of her choice on any Sunday, Phaedra will sleep on the outside of the bed every night for the following week.

Terms of this contract are non-negotiable for a period of one week.

Signed __________________

Date __________________

Form:

X and Y
If not X then H^- (from spouse)
If not Y then W^- (from spouse)

Contracting can be faded from the sessions, and couples may bring in a completed contract for therapist evaluation. The goal is to teach a behavior change procedure which continues without professional aid after intervention.

Treatment Effectiveness

Having briefly summarized the major components of the treatment package, we turn to those data collected as part of an ongoing evaluation of the package. In addition to the initial case study (Patterson and Hops, 1972) there have been two separate therapy studies.

Study I. (Hops, Patterson, and Weiss) Five couples, ranging in age from 21 to 33 years of age and married from 1.5 to 8 years (Md = 3 years) were seen in the first study. Only one of the five had taken steps toward divorce action prior to entering treatment. Their occupations ranged from mill worker to teacher and supervisor. They were seen for periods of 10 to 60 days total, on a weekly basis. Eight therapists were involved, with a therapist-pair consisting of an experienced Ph.D. level clinician and a Master's level student. Clients were usually called by phone three or four times per week for a brief reporting of Please/Displease data. Problems brought up at these times were deferred until the regular session.

As noted above, the baseline data for the MICS indicated a slight improvement in Problem Solving coded behaviors and an increase in behaviors associated with aversiveness. The MICS data obtained from the negotiation sessions during baseline were compared to the negotiation data from the post-intervention sessions. A two-way analysis of variance for repeated measures was carried out on each of the code categories. Significant increases ($p < .10$) in rate per minute were found for both spouses in three behavior categories. Significant interactive effects were found for two codes.

The three accelerated code categories were Compromise (CS), Normative (NO), and Talk (TA). The first, CS, appears to be a direct result of the training program. The rate of CS was very low during baseline, the response being almost nonexistent in most couples. In contrast, it was noted earlier that Problem Solving (PS) showed an increase during baseline. During training, the couples were taught specifically to make compromise statements (the behavioral form of the "*quid pro quo*" principle). The increase in NO appears to be an artifact of the training; couples were trained to record their contracts on paper and the chalkboard during the sessions, and these behaviors were recorded as NO. The acceleration of TA, a wastebasket category, merely indicates greater activity on the part of both partners.

Significant decreases were noted in the behavior categories Accept Responsibility (AR), Assent (AS), Disagree (DG), Problem Description (PD), and Put Down (PU) for both spouses. The AR category was used to count "accepts blame for past behavior." However, the intervention program focused on the couple's planning for the future, thereby decreasing the rate of this response. For similar reasons, there was less tendency for the couple to talk about the problem generally (PD) without stating possible solutions. The training in communication skills appeared to be reflected in a reduced tendency to disagree with each other's statement (DG) and to demean, embarrass, or hurt the other psychologically (PU). The drop in AS, shown earlier to have decreased significantly during pre-intervention, did not drop below the level of the second week of baseline.

Complaint (CP) and Criticize (CR) were the two categories which showed significant interactive effects. The same kind of change was noted for both codes; during baseline negotiation, the husbands, in contrast to wives, produced low rates of these behaviors, but following intervention, the husbands showed a slight increase and their wives a large decrease. Couples were more equal in their rates of responding on the post-intervention measures.

The category PU declined for both spouses, but here, too, the wives' rate during baseline was double that of their husbands, whereas following intervention they were very much alike.

It appears, then, that the wives were distressed initially but that at the end of intervention, when their complaints and criticisms had decreased, the husbands tended to increase slightly in their complaining.

In summary, it appears that the therapeutic manipulation or training had the effect of increasing compromise statements for both spouses and reducing those categories presumed to be counterproductive to successful negotiation, such as PU, DG, and PD. In addition, wives had a tendency to have high rates of complaining and critical behaviors during baseline, but with training they reduced these to levels similar to their husbands'.

Changes in the self-observation data were also consistent with expectations about treatment effectiveness. Whereas there was a significant *decrease* in mean rate of Pleasures reported for the second as compared with the first week of baseline, there was a significant *increase* in mean Pleasures rate for the post-intervention period ($F = 13.75$, $df = 1/6$, $p = .01$). The data for Displeasures were not significantly different from chance expectations, most likely because of the smaller N due to missing data.

These data, combining both laboratory and self-observation sources, indicate that the intervention package was effective in producing the kinds of post-intervention changes one would deem important.

Study II. (Weiss, et al., in preparation) Five couples were seen over a period of from 56 to 91 days on a weekly basis. All couples had children at least two years of age so that home observations could be made using the Patterson coding system. Once again occupations ranged from laborer to professional; the median age was 26 years (range 24 to 37 years), and the couples had been married from 4 to 13 years.

As noted above, the baseline sessions showed differences between major and minor problems in terms of the MICS codes. Specifically, it will be recalled that with major problems, regardless of ordinal position in the four baseline sessions, there was significantly more Problem Description, while for minor problems, regardless of order, there was significantly more Positive Verbal behavior coded. (For these data normalized scores were used.) Since training focused on major problem areas during the course of intervention, the baseline effects, i.e., more Problem Description for major problems, could only operate against demonstrating treatment effectiveness.

Comparisons between baseline mean and termination mean normalized scores were made for each of the six MICS combined code levels (cf. Table 1 above). In each instance, based on analysis of variance for repeated measures between baseline and termination means, there was a highly significant change in the predicted direction. (See Table 5 for mean scores of husband and wife separately.) Problem Solving increased ($p < .001$), Problem Description decreased ($p < .001$), Negative Verbal and Negative Nonverbal Behaviors decreased ($p < .05$ and $p < .005$, respectively), and Positive Verbal and Positive Nonverbal behaviors increased ($p < .005$ and $p < .025$, respectively). Once again the MICS was sensitive to the kinds of changes the intervention modules were designed to bring about.

Table 6 lists the pre- and post-intervention measures for the various assessment devices employed in this study, ranging from self-report of marital satisfaction (Locke-Wallace) to the self-observation of Pleases and Displeases. The post-intervention measures, with the exception of P's and D's, were obtained from three to six months following intervention. The P's and D's, however, were completed during the final week after intervention. From Table 6 it may be seen that four of the five measures yielded significant changes over baseline. (The Home Observation data are not yet available and will be reported in an extended version of this study.) The various self-report and self-observation measures were consistent indicators of reported gain. The Locke-Wallace measure showed very substantial gains in all but one case. The

Table 5 Comparison of Baseline and Termination Mean (Normalized) MICS Level Scores

	Baseline H	Baseline W	Termination H	Termination W	F*	p
Level I: Problem Solving (Accept Responsibility, Compromise, Problem Solving)	.16	.17	.32	.64	26.6	<.001
Level II: Problem Description (Negative Solution, Problem Description, Solution Past)	.37	.41	.22	.23	44.3	<.001
Level III: Negative Verbal (Complaint, Criticism, Deny Responsibility, Excuse, Put Down)	.07	.07	.006	.002	5.3	<.05
Level IV: Positive Verbal (Agree, Approval, Humor)	.08	.07	.16	.13	21.0	<.005
Level V: Positive Nonverbal (Assent, Laugh, Positive Physical Contact, Smile)	.37	.47	.43	.66	8.20	<.025
Level VI: Negative Nonverbal (No Response, Not Tracking, Turn Off)	.31	.28	.19	.08	15.8	<.005

*F values based on within treatment effect for husbands and wives combined.

W-C measure showed the predicted change with all but one couple, indicating overall less stated desire for spouse change of behavior. The MAITAO, inventory of activities, did not change as predicted, yet for seven of the ten respondents an increase in percentage time with spouse was noted.

Whereas the Locke-Wallace and the W-C can be construed as "satisfaction" measures, the P's and D's are more like self-observation tied to an immediate data base. The mean rates for P's and D's changed, significantly, in the predicted directions; self-reported Pleasures from spouse increased over baseline rates, and Displeasures decreased over baseline. Our search for a more behaviorally based self-report device seems to have netted a useful indicator with the P's and D's measure.

Table 6	Pre- and Post-Intervention Scores on Assessment Measures for Five Treated Couples										
		Locke-Wallace		Willingness-Change		MAI:TAO		P's		D's	
Couple:		Pre	Post	Pre	Post	Pre	Post	Pre	Post	Pre	Post
1	H	78	106	7	25	48%	49%	.76	1.43	.07	.05
	W	84	89	27	25	44%	59%	2.40	2.95	.47	.13
2	H	52	125	13	10	57%	56%	2.38	2.97	.46	.37
	W	55	134	38	21	57%	59%	3.91	4.621	.63	1.01
3	H	82	106	27	6	42%	55%	.57	1.08	.04	0.0
	W	46	103	38	5	30%	56%	.31	.62	.22	.05
4	H	58	119	17	13	41%	55%	2.57	2.44	.48	.19
	W	87	123	29	15	35%	25%	3.41	3.73	.19	.11
5	H	85	77	13	10	61%	58%	2.02	2.64	.46	.33
	W	74	106	19	10	40%	49%	2.62	2.42	.51	.62
		T = -2*		T = 8		T = -11.5		T = -3		T = 5	
		p<.01		p = .05		p = NS		p<.01		p<.02	

*Wilcoxon Matched-Pairs Signed-Ranks Test. P values are all two-tailed.

Conclusions and Overview

The foregoing presentation has attempted to follow a model which we predict will become more influential in the production of clinical knowledge. One characteristic of the clinical research effort exemplified by the Oregon group is the continual interplay between case study and technique building. In their recently published evaluation of the field of psychotherapy, Bergin and Strupp (1972) argue for this same model for focusing on behavior problems and developing techniques to handle the problems. The work of the Patterson group at Oregon Research Institute (e.g., Patterson, et al., in press) and that of the clinical faculty at the University of Oregon (e.g., Johnson and Bolstad; LoPiccolo and Lobitz, this volume) preceeds in this stepwise fashion, moving from case study to technique development then to replicated case studies with the new techniques. Clearly this is the approach adopted in the marriage research program outlined here. Our accomplishments must be viewed in the context of this newer approach to the development of clinical knowledge.

The approach has been to focus on specific aspects of marital interaction believed to be central in producing disharmony. The conception has emphasized both the stimulus control of these kinds of adult dyadic behaviors as well as the motivational or reinforcing control. Clients, it is assumed, have developed skills largely in the use of aversive behavior control techniques, i.e., reliance on negative reinforcement as a means of consequating one another's behavior, resulting in escalation of either overt conflict or withdrawal from more constructive problem solving approaches. The existing literature for assessment or profile description of marital dysfunction is not particularly helpful to a behaviorally oriented approach. The first part of this chapter dealt with a description of assessment devices newly developed for this work and the supporting research done to further understand these instruments. This was followed by a more clinically focused discussion of the modules developed as part of the intervention package. The final section dealt with the results of two replicated case studies designed to move us further along in our understanding of assessment and intervention for distressed marital relationships.

To what extent can the technology outlined here be taken over by the practicing clinician? At this stage of development we need continued evaluative data about outcomes for all intervention modules. While aspects of the package, such as negotiation training and use of P's and D's with couples, could probably be used more widely at this time, it remains an obligation of the user to incorporate a method for evaluating the outcome of this usage. There will be little gain to clients or to the field itself if our only success is to propagate a few new techniques in a gimmick-oriented era of social responsibility. Thus, rather than advocating a willy-nilly takeover of specific techniques, we would propose a more carefully thought-out method for obtaining pre- and post-intervention measures when utilizing these procedures. The clinician who wishes only to increase his skill repertoire can do so by perusing Knox's (1971) book on marital satisfaction which provides a good summary of numerous behavioral techniques applicable to marital intervention.

What are some likely next steps deriving from this approach? The real economy will come about when the technology is sufficiently well developed and understood to be made available on a programmed or self-administering basis largely under the direction of persons with substantially less than doctorates in psychology. The all important "ingredient" study is yet to be done, one which isolates the effective ingredients in our modules. In working with married couples one quickly perceives the intensity of their felt discomfort and, to the outside observer at least, the devastating punishing behaviors the spouses enact with one another. But we must remind ourselves that as in any behavioral program, the effective treatment of marital disorders requires understanding of the conditions that maintain the deviant behaviors. If the subjectively felt discomfort of our clients is relevant to the treatment technology, it will have to show itself as a maintainer of deviant behavior. Training in behavior change and the equity of contracting may appear to be far removed from the kinds of hurts brought to us by clients, but the empirical question remains whether with these skills couples can find increased dyadic satisfaction. Taking this point of view the next steps would entail group training procedures wherein separate ingredients are brought into play at predetermined sequence points. Continued use of video tape feedback, programmed materials on recording P's and D's, and training in identification of important problem solving behaviors are all examples of ingredients now being considered.

Finally, something should be said about criterion methodology. Because of the diverse role functions contained in long-term heterosexual dyads we call marriage, it is probably best to set specific outcome criteria rather than adopting a pan-satisfaction outcome approach. In the work reported here the traditional self-report techniques were retained so as to provide at least that much of a starting point. But recalling the case studies and the laboratory analogue studies we have done on self-observation measures, it now seems that we must push ahead in this area. If satisfaction is of interest then specific measures of that sort should be employed. If problem solving, i.e., emphasis on the productive role function of the dyad, is of interest, our measures should be designed to tap that outcome. In a word, we need, but do not yet have, a multidimensional approach to assessment of marital functions. The satisfaction criterion has reigned over functions to which it holds no valid claim. Nor should we automatically intervene in problem solving skills for every couple regardless of their assessment profile. These are the kinds of clinical problems which remain for the flexible, knowledge generating approach that has grown out of the social learning model and which has found demonstrable effectiveness in so many areas of clinical psychology. While social philosophers may warn of the demise of institutionalized marriage, adult dyadic exchanges are likely to persist, and with or without "love" they will remain a legitimate interest of clinicians dealing with social learning.

Footnotes

1. The latest version now includes a Negative Solutions code, for a total of 30 items. This code involves an implicit or explicit request for change but phrased in a negating fashion: "I don't want you to . . . ."

2. The research described in this paper was supported in part by ONR Contract N000014-67-A-0446-0003, G. R. Patterson and R. L. Weiss, project directors. The authors also wish to acknowledge the intellectual contributions of R. C. Ziller during the earlier phases of this work, and the enthusiastic support of students and assistants, most notably M. Forgatch, L. Wampler, and T. A. Wills, whose substantive contributions were numerous. Our clients must remain in the shadows, but our involvement in their lives and their influence upon us was indeed an example of the *quid pro quo* we advocate.

References

Bergin, A. E. and Strupp, H. H. *Changing frontiers in the science of psychotherapy.* Chicago: Aldine-Atherton, Inc., 1972, 426-446.

Birchler, G. R. Differential patterns of instrumental affiliative behavior as a function of degree of marital distress and level of intimacy. Unpublished doctoral dissertation, University of Oregon, 1972.

Goldstein, A. P., Heller, K., and Sechrest, L. B. *Psychotherapy and the psychology of behavior change.* New York: Wiley, 1966. Pp. 10-69.

Hops, H., Patterson, G. R., and Weiss, R. L. A social learning approach to reducing marital conflict. Submitted for publication.

Hops, H., Wills, T. A., Patterson, G. R., and Weiss, R. L. The marital interaction coding system (MICS). Unpublished manuscript, University of Oregon, 1972.

Knox, D. H. *Marriage happiness: A behavioral approach to counseling.* Champaign, Ill.: Research Press, 1971.

Lederer, W. J. and Jackson, D. D. *The mirages of marriage.* New York: Norton, 1969.

Lewinsohn, P. M. and Shaffer, M. The use of home observations as an integral part of the treatment of depression. Preliminary report and case studies. *Journal of Consulting and Clinical Psychology*, 1971, *37*, 87-94.

Liberman, R. Behavioral approaches to family and couples therapy. *American Journal of Orthopsychiatry*, 1970, *40*, 106-118.

Locke, H. J. and Wallace, K. M. Short marital adjustment and prediction tests: Their reliability and validity. *Marriage and Family Living,* 1959, *21*, 251-255.

Mischel, W. Continuity and change in personality. *American Psychologist*, 1969, *24*, 1012-1018.

Olson, D. H. Marital and family therapy: Integrative review and critique. *Journal of Marriage and the Family*, 1970, *32*, 501-538.

Patterson, G. R. *Families: Applications of social learning to family life.* Champaign, Ill.: Research Press, 1971.

Patterson, G. R., Cobb, J. A., and Ray, R. S. A social engineering technology for retraining the families of aggressive boys. In H. Adams and L. Unikel (Eds.), *Georgia symposium in experimental clinical psychology*. Vol. 2. Springfield, Ill.: Charles C. Thomas, in press.

Patterson, G. R. and Hops, H. Coercion, a game for two: Intervention techniques for marital conflict. In R. E. Ulrich and P. Mountjoy (Eds.), *The experimental analysis of social behavior*. New York: Appleton-Century-Crofts, in press.

Reid, J B. Reciprocity and family interaction. Unpublished doctoral dissertation, University of Oregon, 1967.

Strauss, M. A. *Family measurement techniques. Abstracts of published instruments 1935-1965.* Minneapolis: University of Minnesota, 1969.

Stuart, R. B. Token reinforcement in marital treatment. In R. Rubin and C. M. Franks (Eds.), *Advances in behavior therapy*, New York: Academic Press, 1969. Pp. 221-230. (a)

Stuart, R. B. Operant-interpersonal treatment for marital discord. *Journal of Consulting and Clinical Psychology,* 1969, *33*, 675-682. (b)

Vincent, J. P. The relationship of sex, degree of intimacy, and degree of marital distress to problem solving behavior and exchange of social reinforcement. Unpublished doctoral dissertation, University of Oregon, 1972.

Weiss, R. L. Operant conditioning techniques in psychological assessment. In P. W. McReynolds (Ed.), *Advances in psychological assessment.* Vol. 1. Palo Alto, Cal.: Science and Behavior Books, 1969.

Weiss, R. L., Patterson, G. R., and Hops, H. Toward the development of a modular social learning approach to marital discord: Clinical assessment and intervention data. In preparation.

Wills, T. A. The contribution of instrumental and affective events to perceived pleasures and displeasures in marital relationships. Unpublished master's thesis, University of Oregon, 1972.

Wills, T. A. and Weiss, R. L. Measuring pleasurable and displeasurable events in marital relationships. Unpublished manuscript, University of Oregon, 1971.

Wills, T. A. and Weiss, R. L. A behavioral analysis of the determinants of marital satisfaction. Paper presented at the annual meeting of the Western Psychological Association, Portland, Oregon, April 1972.

Behavior Therapy of Sexual Dysfunction

13

Joseph LoPiccolo and W. Charles Lobitz

The University of Oregon Psychology Clinic has been operating a treatment and research program for sexually dysfunctional couples for the last two and one-half years. This paper will describe the program, with emphasis on the clinical treatment programs we are developing.

The therapists in this program are advanced graduate students in our doctoral training program in Clinical Psychology. In the past year 28 client couples have been treated using a total of 16 different male-female co-therapy teams.

At the start of the program, we were concerned about whether or not it would be possible to find enough clients with problems of sexual inadequacy in a town the size of Eugene, which has a population of 75,000. As it turned out, this was definitely not a problem. Despite having as many as ten therapy teams treating clients at one point, and limiting treatment to 15 sessions, there has always been a long waiting list. Currently the waiting list stands at approximately 20 couples, which means approximately a six-month waiting time.

The couples treated have a variety of sexual problems. One such problem is erectile failure, meaning difficulty in getting or maintaining an erection sufficient for intercourse. Another is premature ejaculation, which, in the absence of any sensible statistical criteria, is generally defined as ejaculation which occurs before the husband or wife would like it to. Some limits to this definition are warranted as will be seen later. The great majority (80%) of our client couples, however, involve women who have internalized our society's implicit and explicit norms that "good" women do not enjoy sex, do not have a sex drive, and that sexual needs are something to be ashamed of. These women range from those who have never experienced an orgasm and find all sexual behavior aversive, to those who enjoy sex but simply do not reach orgasm with any regularity.

Clients come to us from a variety of sources, including divorce lawyers, ministers, and mental health professionals. The majority of the clients, however, are referred by local physicians, especially gynecologists and urologists. We require that all clients receive a physical examination before entering treatment; the examination is provided by the referring physician if he is a gynecologist or urologist.

In setting up such a program, it is advisable that medical consultants be chosen with care. As Clark Vincent's research has demonstrated, most medical schools did not until very recently teach anything about sexual behavior (Vincent, 1968). Our clients have received advice from physicians such as "Don't worry about it, just pretend you enjoy sex," "It's normal for women not to enjoy sex; sex isn't important for women," and "Your childhood masturbation is what made you frigid." Greenbank (1961) found that 20% of the medical faculty in five Philadelphia medical schools felt masturbation caused mental illness. Obviously, a physician with this type of attitude can seriously undermine a treatment program.

In taking the type of highly focused, behavioral retraining approach in treatment described here, it is necessary to screen out client applicants whose sexual disorder is embedded in, and a symptom of, a severely disturbed marriage, or where one partner is psychotic. It is unrealistic to expect an anxiety reduction and skill training approach to be effective if the sexual problem is not caused by anxiety and lack of skills, but instead reflects basic hostilities between the couple. We screen for severely disturbed marriages with the Locke-Wallace Short Marital Inventory (Locke and Wallace, 1959) and for psychosis with the MMPI. On the basis of scores on these instruments and a brief evaluation interview with the client, we reject just under 50% of those couples referred to us. It should be clarified that when we reject clients because they have marital problems, the problems are severe ones and are *unrelated* to sexual dysfunction—child rearing or financial problems, for example.

The general behavioral model we use is based on the procedures developed by Hastings (1963), Wolpe and Lazarus (1966), Wolpe (1970), and Masters and Johnson (1970). In the absence of any physical pathology, sexual dysfunction is viewed as a learned phenomenon, maintained internally by performance anxiety and externally by a nonreinforcing environment, principally the partner. In addition, a lack of sexual skill, knowledge, and communication on the part of one or both partners contributes to the dysfunction.

Within this social learning framework, the dysfunction is treated through retraining designed to facilitate direct changes in the couple's sexual behavior. Both partners are involved in the therapy process. Treatment consists of 15 sessions in which a male-female co-therapy team plan behavioral training tasks ("homework") to be carried out at home by the dysfunctioning couple between therapy sessions. Performance anxiety is treated through *in vivo* graded exposure tasks following the systematic desensitization format developed by Wolpe and Lazarus (1966) and refined by Masters and Johnson (1970). Premature ejaculation is treated through a retraining program advocated by Semans (1956), as modified by the use of the "squeeze" technique (Masters and Johnson, 1970). In the case of all dysfunctions, intercourse is temporarily prohibited while the couple's repertoire of sexual behavior is rebuilt.

Following the Masters and Johnson model, all work is done by a male-female co-therapy team. This approach has a number of advantages, including providing each client someone who more nearly experientially knows what sex is like for the client. An additional advantage of the dual sex co-therapy approach is in the reduction of problems of transference and counter-transference, which can be especially intense in dealing with clients with sexual problems. (Masters and Johnson report that some of their clients had been seduced by previous therapists.)

The initial phase of our treatment is devoted to assessment. The co-therapists each interview the male and female client during a two-hour sexual history and assessment session. By the end of two hours we usually have a good idea of the origin and nature of the couple's sexual problem. Following this session, the clients fill out the paper-pencil test of sexual functioning we have developed, which we have named the "Oregon Sex Inventory." One of our research projects is currently gathering data on the reliability and validity of this instrument (Steger, 1972).

In the next section of this paper, we will discuss briefly our treatment of the three major types of dysfunction—premature ejaculation, erectile failure, and orgasmic failure.

As stated above, we consider that in the absence of any physical pathology, sexual dysfunction is a learned phenomenon. We also consider that the original cause of the problem may be quite separate from the environmental reinforcing conditions that now maintain it.

To elaborate, consider the problem of premature ejaculation. There is no objective criterion for what consistutes premature ejaculation. We have seen clients who literally could not remove their underwear before ejaculation occurred. At the other extreme, one couple sought treatment complaining that the husband ejaculated too quickly for his wife to be able to reach orgasm. His ejaculatory latency was found to be over 30 minutes, and the case was redefined as female orgasmic failure.

For our purposes, if a man can tolerate 15 minutes of manual and oral "foreplay" stimulation, and about five minutes of unrestrained, vigorous intercourse, there is by definition no problem of premature ejaculation. This rough criterion is based on Gebhard's (1968) data that increasing duration of foreplay and intercourse over these figures does not lead to a significantly increased probability of the female reaching orgasm. Our premature ejaculation clients typically have directly been trained, or have trained themselves, to ejaculate as quickly as possible and with as minimal an amount of stimulation as possible. This may have occurred during adolescent masturbation, when the boy feared being caught by his parents (*Portnoy's Complaint* syndrome), or during premarital intercourse, again for fear of being caught or the girl changing her mind. One of our clients taught himself to ejaculate with no direct genital stimulation, during necking sessions, so he could obtain orgasmic release from pain caused by pelvic vasocongestion. Another was "trained" in the context of having intercourse in a car during a snowstorm with his adolescent friends shivering outside, urging him to hurry up.

Once a man has an established pattern of premature ejaculation, the original conditioning becomes mostly irrelevant. That is, once a man begins to get feedback from his wife that he is frustrating her sexually, he begins to suffer from performance anxiety. He becomes very concerned about delaying ejaculation, so he attempts to distract himself, contract his muscles, and cut down on the stimulation he receives during foreplay and intercourse. All of this anxiety succeeds in lowering still further his threshold of stimulation needed for ejaculation. Thus a vicious cycle of premature ejaculation—performance anxiety—premature ejaculation is established. There is some reason to speculate that this cycle is based on the fact that anxiety is characterized by sympathetic nervous system excitation, and ejaculation is also a sympathetic nervous response. There are some animal data which support this hypothesis (Gantt, 1944; Beach and Fowler, 1959).

Treatment of premature ejaculation is relatively simple. A procedure developed by James Semans (1956) and modified by Masters and Johnson (1970) is reported 98% effective in curing this dysfunction. This technique raises the threshold for ejaculation by allowing the male to experience massive amounts of stimulation of the penis without allowing ejaculation to occur. The procedure therefore extinguishes the conditioned link between minimal stimulation and ejaculation. The wife manually or orally manipulates the penis until the man is nearing ejaculation. At this point, she stops stimulation and squeezes firmly on the frenulum of the penis, thereby preventing ejaculation. This procedure is then repeated several times on each occasion of sexual activity. Over time, the couple begins to use this squeeze technique during penile insertion without movement, then during full, vigorous intercourse. Rather quickly, the male's anxiety disappears as he becomes confident that he can control his ejaculation. As a result of this massive stimulation, his threshold for ejaculation rises dramatically. Soon he can tolerate massive stimulation without the need for the squeeze technique, and the case is, by definition, cured.

Our group has made one modification of the basic Semans-Masters and Johnson technique. We often have the male begin the squeeze procedure in masturbation, rather than in manipulation by his wife. This offers the advantage of reducing his anxiety by allowing him to gain self-confidence about ejaculatory control before he begins again to interact sexually with his wife. This modification is also useful in cases where the wife finds the manipulation and squeeze procedure repugnant. We have found that good transfer of increased ejaculatory latency from masturbation to manipulation by the wife is usual.

We have treated six cases of premature ejactulation with this procedure, all successfully. Masters and Johnson report treating nearly 200 cases with 98% success.

A similar situation occurs with erectile failure, or inability to obtain or maintain an erection sufficient for intercourse to occur. A man may have his first erectile failure for a variety of reasons—fear of intercourse, fear of being caught, guilt about an extra-marital relationship, excessive consumption of alcohol, or simply being fatigued and distracted for some reason such as job pressures. Once a man has had a failure experience, he is likely to approach subsequent sexual encounters with fear and anxiety rather than with joyous anticipation and arousal. Such lack of arousal, of course, leads to further erectile failure, since if one is not aroused, an erection is unlikely. Treatment for erectile failure involves the reduction of the male's performance anxiety through an *in vivo* desensitization approach. As this approach has been well described elsewhere (Wolpe, 1958; Wolpe and Lazarus, 1963; Masters and Johnson, 1970), it will not be emphasized here. Briefly, the clients are initially forbidden to engage in any sexual activity. They are then given, each week, a "homework" assignment to successively increase their repertoire of sexual behaviors. In the first week only hugging, kissing, and body massage (not including the male's genitals) are allowed. This assignment permits the male to relearn enjoyment of sensual pleasures without any worry about whether or not he will be able to achieve an erection. To his great surprise, he typically has erection continuously during these sensual pleasure sessions. In successive weeks, the behaviors added are breast and genital touching, stimulation of the penis in a "teasing" manner (Masters and Johnson, 1970, p. 206), simultaneous genital masturbation and manipulation by each other, penile insertion with no movement, penile insertion with male pelvic thrusting, mutual genital manipulation and masturbation to orgasm, and finally, mutual pelvic thrusting with ejaculation during intercourse. To eliminate performance anxiety, the timing of introduction of these behaviors is such that they are "allowed" only after the male client has become confident that he can accomplish them. For example, intravaginal ejaculation is not "allowed" until after the client has been unable to restrain himself from ejaculating intravaginally. Thus the male never has to worry about whether he will be able to perform and is free to become aroused.

As noted previously, this procedure has been used extensively by Masters and Johnson, with generally good results. They report, however, that homosexual orientation is an etiological factor which may contribute to unsuccessful treatment (Masters and Johnson, 1970, p. 213). This treatment failure may be explained as follows. In cases of erectile failure where the male has a homosexual orientation, it seems logical to assume that lack of heterosexual arousal in addition to performance anxiety is a factor in the inability to attain and maintain an erection. Thus treatment which focuses only on reducing performance anxiety, and not on reconditioning sexual arousal, would seem likely to be unsuccessful in such cases.

Accordingly, our group has developed a program which adds to the anxiety reducing program a conditioning procedure to establish sexual arousal to heterosexual stimuli. This procedure involves the directed use of fantasy and masturbation. The program can be described most clearly by use of a case example.

The clients in this case were a young couple, married for about a year. The husband had been and was still an overt homosexual. He had no difficulty achieving erection in homosexual relations but was able to achieve erection on only about 25% of the occasions he and his wife attempted to have intercourse. In addition, he was unable to become aroused enough to ejaculate on half the occasions that he did have an erection. He was not aroused by his mate and indeed experienced revulsion and disgust at the sight or touch of her sexual organs.

In attempting to raise the client's heterosexual arousal, use was made of masturbation initially. At intake the male client was masturbating several times weekly to exclusively homosexual fantasies. McGuire, et al. (1965) have suggested that the orgasm experienced during masturbation is the reinforcer which conditions arousal to the fantasy or other stimulus materials accompanying masturbation. Davison (1968) and Marquis (1970) make use of this principle in an "orgasmic reconditioning" procedure designed to eliminate sexual perversions. In a manner similar to the procedure developed by Davison and Marquis, the male client was instructed to use homosexual fantasies to attain erection and approach orgasm in masturbation. At the instant of orgasm, however, the client was instructed to switch to fantasies of sexual relations with his mate. If arousal was lost, the client was instructed to briefly switch back to homosexual fantasies and then return again to fantasies of his partner. Over successive occasions of masturbation, the time of the switch from homosexual to heterosexual fantasies was gradually moved backward from the point of orgasm, until the client was finally using exclusively heterosexual fantasies during the entire masturbation session.

One modification of Marquis' procedure was made for this particular client. As Annon (1971) has suggested is typical of male homosexuals, the male client had difficulty in visualizing or fantasizing heterosexual stimuli during masturbation. To deal with this problem, the therapists provided the clients with a Polaroid camera and had them take pictures of the female for use as heterosexual masturbation stimuli.

This procedure worked quite well, and in the later stages of therapy the male did gain the ability to fantasize arousing heterosexual situations without the aid of these pictures.

Because this fantasy switching program worked well in masturbation, it was also used to facilitate arousal in the *in vivo* performance anxiety desensitization sessions with the female. The male was instructed to use homosexual fantasies as necessary to facilitate arousal in these sessions but to switch back frequently to focusing on the reality of what he and his partner were doing, and in any case to always switch back to heterosexual reality just before orgasm. This program was also successful in that initially the male was fantasizing homosexual activities during much of the time he was engaging in sexual activity with his mate, but eventually came to be highly aroused while focusing *exclusively* on the heterosexual reality.

At the close of treatment, the male was able to obtain and maintain erections 100% of the times he and his mate attempted intercourse, solely through the use of heterosexual fantasies and activities. In addition, he was able to ejaculate intravaginally on virtually every occasion. A follow-up contact initiated by the therapists, six months after termination, revealed that these same results were being maintained. Thus the addition of an arousal conditioning procedure to the basic anxiety reduction procedure seems promising in treating some types of erectile failure.

Orgasmic dysfunction in women is perhaps inevitable in our society, which prohibits premarital sex, does not educate people in effective sexual techniques, and basically makes women ashamed of their sexuality. Many of our inorgasmic clients have been directly trained to have sexual dysfunction. Their parents indoctrinated them with anti-sexual attitudes ("Sex is a woman's burden."), severely punished childhood sex play or masturbation, and modeled poor husband-wife relationships. We have had clients who had their hands tied to the bedposts to prevent nighttime masturbation as children, and one client who was forced to bathe in her underpants as a child so that she would never see or touch her own genitals.

These negative attitudes towards sexuality are only one part of the constellation involved in the case of a woman who has never achieved orgasm. Also of central importance are her husband's lack of sexual skills and her own inhibition about displaying sexual arousal.

One way we try to deal with negative attitudes towards sexuality is, through role-playing training, to teach the husband to be very reinforcing towards sexuality displayed by his wife. In the protective environment of the therapy session, we use modeling and role-playing techniques until we are certain that the husband can convincingly reassure his wife that he values her sexuality and will love and respect her more as she becomes more sexually active and assertive.

Something that we use both for producing attitude change and also for disinhibiting inorgasmic clients about their own sexuality is self-disclosure by the therapists. In advocating self-disclosure, Jourard (1964, p. 71) has emphasized therapist spontaneity during the session but has stated that one need not tell the client about one's life outside the therapy hour. Indeed, psychoanalytic therapists typically refuse to answer any personal questions for fear of creating unmanageable transference (Menninger, 1958). In our program not only do therapists answer client questions, but also they volunteer information about their own sexual behavior. Given that the therapist role is a respected position of authority in our culture, the therapist unashamedly discussing his or her own enjoyment of sexual activity is an effective way of disinhibiting clients about their own sexuality and/or producing attitude change. In particular, self-disclosure by the therapist about masturbation and oral-genital sex has facilitated client attitude change about these behaviors. Such self-disclosure is appropriate only after the clients have developed some regard and respect for the therapists. The shock of premature self-disclosure may alienate clients from their therapists. For self-disclosure to be effective, of course, the therapist must be genuinely comfortable with his or her own sexuality, and candid, specific, and unembarrassed when discussing it.

We feel that one program we have developed is extremely effective in producing orgasm in the woman who has never experienced an orgasm from any source of sexual stimulation in her entire life. This program involves a nine-step process of directed masturbation and training the husband in sexual technique. Briefly, the program is based on data that masturbation is the most probable means for a woman to reach orgasm (Kinsey, et al., 1953), that more women can reach orgasm through masturbation than through any other means (Kinsey, et al., 1953), and that masturbation produces the most intense orgasm (Masters and Johnson, 1966).

The nine steps are as follows:

Step 1: The client is told that she is "out of touch" with her own body, that indeed she has never really known her own body nor learned to appreciate the beauty of her sexual organs. Accordingly, she is given the assignment to increase her self-awareness. She is told to examine her nude body carefully and try to appreciate its beauty. The client is to use a hand mirror to examine her genitals closely, identifying the various areas with the aid of the diagrams in the book *Sexual Expression in Marriage* (Hastings, 1956). Many of our clients express amazement after following this step. Typical statements are "I never really knew what was down there" and "I was amazed at how little I knew about myself." At this time, the client is also started on a program of Kegel's (1952) exercises for increasing the tone and vascularity of the pelvic musculature, which presumably will increase her orgasmic potential.

Step 2: Next the client is instructed to explore her genitals tactually as well as visually. To avoid putting her under any performance anxiety to arouse herself sexually, the client is *not* given any expectation that she should be aroused at this point. In these first two steps, we merely want the client to become desensitized to the sight and feel of her genitals and become used to the idea of masturbation. It is also useful for the therapist to tell the client that we expect her to feel some apprehension or aversion at this point but that these feelings usually disappear once she begins actually following the program.

Step 3: The client is instructed to continue visual and tactual exploration of her genitals, but with an emphasis on locating sensitive areas that produce feelings of pleasure. She is not to focus on any area in particular, rather to thoroughly explore the clitoral shaft and hood, the major and minor labia, the vaginal opening, and the whole perineum, especially that area immediately adjacent to the clitoris.

Step 4: With the pleasure producing areas located, the client is now told to concentrate on manual stimulation of these areas. The female co-therapist at this time discusses techniques of masturbation with the client. As most of our clients locate the clitoris as the most pleasureable area, the discussion is usually about techniques of clitoral manipulation; topics covered include variations of stroking and pressure, and the use of a sterile lubricant jelly to enhance pleasure and prevent soreness.

Step 5: If orgasm does not occur in Step 4, the client is told to increase the intensity and duration of masturbation. She is told to masturbate until "something happens," or until she becomes tired or sore. We also recommend the use of so-called pornographic reading material or pictures to enhance arousal. In addition, we suggest the use of erotic fantasies to further increase arousal.

Step 6: If orgasm is not reached in Step 5, we instruct the client to purchase a vibrator of the type sold in pharmacies for facial massage. These can be purchased for as little as $5.00, and, as the classified ads in any underground newspaper will attest, they are extremely effective in producing sexual arousal. The client is instructed to masturbate, using the vibrator, lubricant jelly, and pornographic materials and erotic fantasy. In our most difficult case to date, three weeks of vibrator masturbation, with daily 45-minute vibrator sessions, was required to produce orgasm.

Step 7: Once a woman has achieved orgasm through masturbation, our focus shifts to enabling her to experience orgasm through stimulation by her husband. As the first step in this process, we instruct the woman to masturbate while her husband observes her. This desensitizes her to visibly displaying arousal and orgasm in his presence and also functions as an excellent learning experience for her husband.

Step 8: The next step simply involves having the husband do for his wife what she has been doing for herself. If she has been using a vibrator, he now uses it on her. If she has been manually manipulating her genitals, he now begins to do this for her.

Step 9: Once orgasm has occurred in Step 8, we instruct the couple to engage in intercourse while the husband stimulates the wife's genitals, either manually or with a vibrator. We recommend the female superior sitting, lateral, or rear entry coital positions for this activity, as all these positions allow the male easy access to the female's genitals during intromission. Once orgasm has occurred at this step, the client should logically be considered "cured," since the clitoris and not the vagina is now known to be the major focus of sexuality and orgasm in the normal woman (Masters and Johnson, 1966; Kinsey, et al., 1953; Lydon, 1970; Weisstein, 1970; Ellis, 1960). Some clients, however, especially those who have been exposed to psychoanalytic theory and its specious distinction between "clitoral" and "vaginal" orgasm, express a wish to achieve orgasm without the necessity for concurrent manual stimulation during coitus. For such clients, we emphasize the importance of achieving adequate clitoral stimulation from some source (e.g., the husband's symphysis) during coitus, and point out that this stimulation is most effectively achieved through direct manual manipulation.

In some cases it is necessary to have the clients *role play* the experience of orgasm before real orgasm can be achieved. Orgasmic role playing has proved useful at two points in this nine-step program. First, it is helpful for the woman who can become highly aroused through masturbation during Steps 1-6 but becomes frightened of the approaching orgasm and loses arousal as sexual stimulation continues. Secondly, it is useful for the woman who can masturbate to orgasm when alone but cannot achieve orgasm if her partner is present (Step 7). In either case we instruct the couple to engage in sexual activity at home. At some point the woman is to role-play not just an orgasm, but a gross exaggeration with violent convulsions and inarticulate screaming. Knowing that this orgasm is not real, the couple is free to make a game, even a parody, of the response. We instruct them to repeat this until they pass from their initial anxiety and embarrassment to amusement and finally boredom with the procedure.

Orgasmic role-playing has been especially useful with intellectual, controlled clients who are ashamed and embarrassed about the muscular contractions and involuntary noises which accompany orgasm, or who fear loss of bladder or bowel control. In three cases where the women had been unable to reach orgasm despite the use of all our other treatment procedures, this technique led to their first orgasm.

Over the past two years 11 previously totally inorgasmic women have been treated with this nine-step program. All 11 currently experience orgasm during manipulation by the husband, and nine are orgasmic during intercourse. Some of these nine women have orgasm in intercourse without the need for concurrent manual stimulation of the external genitalia, while the others continue to require it. In one case, the client is orgasmic 100% of the time provided her husband stimulates her clitoris with the vibrator during intercourse. We felt somewhat dissatisfied with this outcome and designed a stimulus generalization program to gradually fade out the electric vibrator for this woman. She quite correctly resisted this and reminded us of our earlier statements that the clitoris is the major source of female sexual pleasure. She also pointed out that "There is nothing intrinsically evil about electricity," and was thus able to convince us to stay out of her now very satisfying sex life.

The previously described treatment procedures are extremely directive in nature. Occasionally, it is difficult to get clients to follow directions, and all our treatment procedures depend on what the clients can be persuaded to do at home. Therefore, we need to know what the clients are actually doing, and we need some method of keeping them motivated to do what we want them to do. We have two somewhat artificial procedures to accomplish these aims.

A hallmark of behavioral approaches to treatment has been the reliance on observable, quantifiable, client behavior. Most problems which lend themselves to a behavioral approach, e.g., phobic or aggressive responses, are readily observable. Home observations of client behavior have become commonplace in behavioral assessment and intervention (e.g., Lewinsohn and Shaffer, 1971; Patterson, et al., 1968). However, for both ethical and practical reasons neither home nor laboratory observations of client behavior is possible when treating sexual dysfunction. Yet, in the behavioral retraining approach that we use, therapists must know exactly what the clients are doing and must also be certain that the clients are following the treatment procedures at home. Our clients are asked to be their own data collectors. On each day of treatment in which any sexual activity occurs, clients fill out a *daily record form* detailing their sexual behavior. For each activity, the client specifies its duration, numerical ratings of the pleasure and arousal that he obtained, and subjective comments about the activity. In addition, he specifies numerical ratings of the degree of pleasure and arousal which he perceived his partner to have obtained. Throughout treatment these daily records provide therapists with regular feedback; using this data they tailor the program to the clients' progress.

While clients are generally motivated to carry out the treatment program, including filling out daily record forms, at times all clients find it difficult to follow the program's prescriptions. For example, clients may be tired or busy with other activities and thus resist engaging in the prescribed number of "homework" sessions. They may be tempted to break the prohibition on intercourse or to resist trying new sexual activities that the therapists prescribe. A *refundable penalty deposit* provides incentive for following our program. At the beginning of treatment, the clients pay their full 15-session fee plus an equal amount as a penalty deposit. Providing that the clients do not violate any of the treatment rules, their deposit is refunded in full. However, should a violation occur, 1/15th of the deposit is not refunded. On a second violation, another 2/15ths is forfeited. The progression continues arithmetically until on the fifth violation 5/15ths of the deposit is forfeited. Since this uses up the entire deposit, a sixth violation would cause the therapists to terminate treatment. Treatment rules are specified in a "penalty contract" which the clients sign at the beginning of the therapy. Basically, the rules are that the clients must keep appointments, turn in the daily record forms prior to their appointment, and engage in only those sexual behaviors programmed for them by the therapists.

Although this procedure has not been systematically evaluated, the fact that more than one violation rarely occurs attests to its effectiveness in motivating the clients to follow the program rules. Over the last 19 cases treated, 0.7 is the mean number of times couples were fined. Three was the greatest number of times any couple was penalized. For some clients, the penalty deposit is a more effective motivator than for others. Younger couples, especially those in the counterculture for whom money is not a powerful reinforcer, are less apt to be influenced by the threat of losing their deposit. However, for older, middle class couples, the penalty deposit provides a powerful motivation. For example, a successful Certified Public Accountant resisted completing his assigned "homework" sessions with his wife, complaining that he had too much office work to do. Rather than cajole her husband, the wife quietly reminded him of the penalty fee. A quick mental calculation convinced him that it was financially worthwhile to forego his office work in favor of the session with his wife.

Some outcome statistics to document the effectiveness of our program are perhaps called for at this point. Like all psychotherapy outcome researchers, we struggle continually with the issue of what the criteria for "cure" are. As mentioned previously, over the last two years one of our major research efforts has been devoted to the development of the "Oregon Sex Inventory"—an outcome measure for cases of sexual dysfunction (Steger, 1972; LoPiccolo, 1972).

For cases of premature ejaculation, Masters and Johnson (1970) use a "success" criterion of the wife's being orgasmic on 50% of coital opportunities. Such a one-item test has numerous problems, but accepting for a moment their definition, and applying it to all cases, over the past three years we have "succeeded" with all 13 of the cases of primary orgasmic dysfunction we have treated, with all six cases of premature ejaculation, with four of six erectile failure cases, and with only three of nine cases of secondary (situational) orgasmic dysfunction. Obviously, secondary orgasmic dysfunction remains the Achilles heel of the Oregon program. However, we have recently begun to do much better with such cases, as a result of some changes made in our treatment program following an analysis of all our data on secondary orgasmic dysfunction cases (McGovern and Stewart, 1972).

While our generally good results are encouraging to us as therapists, perhaps the major theoretical import of our work lies in its implications for the way mental health experts conceptualize sexuality. That is, the success of our brief and simple behavior modification approach raises serious questions about the traditional view of sexual problems as symptoms of a deep-seated personality disorder.

In closing, we might say that while we enjoy our work and find it very reinforcing, we hope someday to be unable to find any clients who need our services. We hope that eventually our society will have such positive attitudes towards sexuality and will so effectively teach people the elements of effective sexual technique that sex therapists will become extinct.

References

Annon, J. S. The therapeutic use of masturbation in the treatment of sexual disorders. Paper presented at the fifth annual meeting of the Association for the Advancement of Behavior Therapy, Washington, D. C., September 1971.

Beach, F. A. and Fowler, H. Effects of situational anxiety on sexual behavior in male rats. *Journal of Comparative and Physiological Psychology*, 1959, *52*, 245-249.

Davison, G. S. Elimination of a sadistic fantasy by client-controlled counter-conditioning technique. *Journal of Abnormal Psychology*, 1968, *77*, 84-90.

Ellis, A. *The art and science of love*. New York: Lyle Stuart, 1960.

Gantt, W. H. *Experimental basis for neurotic behavior*. New York: Hoeber, 1944.

Gebhard, P. Factors in marital orgasm. *Journal of Social Issues,* 1968, *XXII*, 88-95.

Greenbank, R. K. Are medical students learning psychiatry? *Pennsylvania Medical Journal*, 1961, *64*, 989-992.

Hastings, D. W. *Impotence and frigidity*. Boston: Little, Brown, 1963.

Hastings, D. W. *Sexual expression in marriage*. New York: Bantam, 1956.

Jourard, S. M. *The transparent self.* Princeton, N. J.: D. Van Nostrand, 1964.

Kegel, A. H. Sexual functions of the pubococcygens muscle. *Western Journal of Obstetrics and Gynecology*, 1952, *60,* 521.

Kinsey, A. C., Pomeroy, W. B., Martin, C. E., and Gebhard, P. H. *Sexual behavior in the human female*. Philadelphia: W. B. Saunders, 1953.

Lewinsohn, P. M. and Shaffer, M. Use of home observations as an integral part of the treatment of depression: Preliminary report and case studies. *Journal of Consulting and Clinical Psychology*, 1971, *37*, 87-94.

Locke, H. J. and Wallace, K. M. Short marital adjustment and prediction tests: Their reliability and prediction. *Marriage and Family Living,* 1959, *21*, 251-255.

Lydon, S. The politics of orgasm. In M. Garskof (Ed.), *Roles women play*. Belmont, Cal.: Brooks/Cole, 1970.

Marquis, J. N. Orgasmic reconditioning: Changing sexual object choice through controlling masturbation fantasies. *Journal of Behavior Therapy and Experimental Psychiatry*, 1970, *1*, 263-271.

Masters, W. H. and Johnson, V. E. *Human sexual response*. Boston: Little, Brown, 1966.

Masters, W. H. and Johnson, V. E. *Human sexual inadequacy*. Boston: Little, Brown, 1970.

McGuire, R. T., Carlisle, J. M., and Young, B. G. Sexual deviation as a conditioned behavior: A hypothesis. *Behaviour Research and Therapy*, 1965, *2*, 185-190.

Menninger, C. *Theory of psychoanalytic technique.* New York: Basic Books, 1958.

Patterson, G. R., Ray, R. S., and Shaw, D. A. Direct intervention in the families of deviant children. *Oregon Research Institute Bulletin*, 1968, *8*, No. 9.

Semans, J. Premature ejaculation: A new approach. *Southern Medical Journal*, 1956, *49*, 353-357.

Vincent, C. E. *Human sexuality in medical education and practice.* Springfield, Ill.: Charles C. Thomas, 1968.

Weisstein, N. Psychology constructs the female, or the fantasy life of the male psychologist. In M. Garskos (Ed.), *Roles women play*. Belmont, Cal.: Brooks/Cole, 1971.

Wolpe, J. *The practice of behavior therapy*. New York: Pergamon Press, 1970.

Wolpe, J. and Lazarus, A. A. *Behavior therapy techniques.* New York: Pergamon Press, 1966.